ENCYCLOPEDIA OF
THE NAVY SEALS

ENCYCLOPEDIA OF THE NAVY SEALS

CHARLES W. SASSER

☑® Facts On File, Inc.

Encyclopedia of the Navy SEALs

Copyright © 2002 by Charles W. Sasser

Facts On File, Inc.
132 West 31st Street
New York NY 10001

Library of Congress Cataloging-in-Publication Data

Sasser, Charles W.
Encyclopedia of the Navy Seals / by Charles W. Sasser
p. cm.
Includes bibliographical references and index.
ISBN 0-8160-4569-0
1. United States. Navy. SEALS—Encyclopedias. I. Title.

VG87 .S27 2002
359.9′84′0973—dc21   2001054769

Facts On File books are available at special discounts when purchased in bulk quantities for businesses, associations, institutions, or sales promotions. Please call our Special Sales Department in New York at (212) 967-8800 or (800) 322-8755.

You can find Facts On File on the World Wide Web at
http://www.factsonfile.com

Text design by Joan Toro
Cover design by Cathy Rincon

Printed in the United States of America

VB Hermitage 10 9 8 7 6 5 4 3 2 1

This book is printed on acid-free paper.

For my old friend, the first SEAL, Lt. Cdr. Roy Boehm

AUTHOR'S NOTE

The author must apologize to persons who may have been neglected, overlooked, shorted, slighted, or omitted in the preparation of this encyclopedia—likewise for entries that may also have been excluded. I have attempted through extensive research and interviews to ensure the accuracy of this encyclopedia, but I am sure to have made occasional errors in a work of this scope. Where that occurs, I must take full responsibility. I can only apologize in advance and trust that readers otherwise find the book in its entirety a consummate reference for the U.S. Navy SEALs.

CONTENTS

ACKNOWLEDGMENTS

Although I am not, nor have I ever been, a Navy SEAL, I *was* a member of special operations (U.S. Army Special Forces, the "Green Berets") for 13 years, and I am a retired veteran of 29 years' service in both the U.S. Navy and the U.S. Army. This association provided me a unique insight into the world of SpecWarfare that, along with acquaintances, friendships, and associations with other unconventional men, proved invaluable in compiling this *Encyclopedia of the Navy SEALs.*

I have been honored to participate in portions of SEAL history. I flew with the SEAL parachute demonstration team, the Chuting Stars, in 1962–63 and led SEALs in training and on missions in combined operations. I have written several magazine articles, a novel (*Operations No Man's Land,* as Mike Martell, Avon, 2000), and a definitive autobiography with the man who became the U.S. Navy's first SEAL. (*First SEAL,* with Roy Boehm, Pocket Books, 1997.) I am eternally indebted to all those SEALs, too numerous to mention here, whose association over the past four decades I treasure and who provided me insight into a truly unique band of warriors.

I am particularly indebted to Lt. Cdr. (retired) Roy Boehm, whose place in history is assured not only by his indelible mark on the building of the SEALs but also by the legends built upon his exploits in both the underwater demolition teams (UDTs) and among the Navy SEALs. During months of work with him in the writing of *First SEAL,* I came to appreciate the incredible history associated with the training of American undersea warriors. Roy's guidance, direction, and introduction to others involved in the building and growth of the SEAL community opened the door for much of the history contained in this encyclopedia.

I therefore owe thanks and appreciation to many of the SEAL "plank owners" and "old-timers" I came

to know through Roy: Chief Petty Officer Rudy Boesch; Cdr. John Callahan; Chief Petty Officer James C. "Hoot" Andrews; Bill Bruhmuller; Louis A. "Horse" Kuzcinski; James C. "Tip" Tipton; Harry R. "Lump Lump" Williams; and others. They, individuals and in combination, have contributed immeasurably to the compilation of this book.

I would like to give particular thanks to many involved in preserving and maintaining SEAL histories who have helped me, either in personal interviews or through their works. Some are chroniclers or historians, such as Kevin Dockery (who also provided photographs and encouragement), Edwin B. Hoyt, Bill Fawcett, Mark Bowden, John Carl Roat, and John Weisman. Others are SEALs or former SEALs, whose interviews, memoirs and published recollections added to the flavor of this encyclopedia: Richard Marcinko, Orr Kelly, Capt. Norman H. Olson, Michael J. Walsh, Chief Petty Officer James Watson, and others.

The Navy SEALs have roots that reach deep into Special Operations both past and present. Thanks for this book go to old SpecOps friends like Sgt. Maj. (retired) Galen Kittleson (Alamo Scouts and Army Special Forces); Capt. Jim Morris (Army Special Forces and Vietnam veteran); historian and author Col. Harry G. Summers, who until his death was editor, mentor, and friend; and Delta Force commander Col. Charlie Beckwith, who once attempted to recruit me and who, over the years before his death, provided insight into the largely secret world of counterterrorism.

Particular acknowledgment is also extended broadly to the many people within the U.S. Navy, active and retired, who answered my questions and directed me to various sources. I would like to highlight Mark Werthheimer, head of the Navy Historical Center Small Arms Collection; Cdr. Don

Crawford, Naval Special Warfare Library; Ens. Julie Wiegese and Lt. Katie Licup, Public Affairs Officers at the Naval Special Warfare Center, Coronado, California; and H. T. Aldhizer of the UDT/SEAL Museum in Fort Pierce, Florida.

Final words of thanks go to editor Gary Goldstein, who began this work with me; to editor Owen Lancer, whose encouragement led to its completion; and to my wife Donna Sue, without whose patience and understanding few of my books could have been written.

In expressing my thanks to those mentioned or unmentioned who provided comments, advice, and material, I must add that the conclusions, and such errors as this book may contain, are solely my responsibility.

Charles W. Sasser, Wagoner, Oklahoma

INTRODUCTION

On May 25, 1961, five weeks after the Cuban Bay of Pigs debacle, President John F. Kennedy addressed a joint session of Congress in one of the most important speeches of his presidency. He set a goal for rocketing an American to the Moon before the end of the decade, then called for a major restructuring of the nation's military to limit its sole reliance on nuclear weapons. He announced that he wanted unconventional warriors for unconventional times.

"I am directing the Secretary of Defense to expand rapidly and substantially, in cooperation with our allies, the orientation of existing forces for the conduct of non-nuclear war, paramilitary operations and sub-limited or unconventional war. In addition, our special forces and unconventional warfare units will be increased and reoriented."

Shortly after this announcement, U.S. Navy lieutenant commander William "Bill" Hamilton summoned a rogue 37-year-old former enlisted boatswain's mate named Roy Boehm to his office in Little Creek, Virginia. Lieutenant (junior grade) Boehm, operations officer of Underwater Demolitions Team 21 (UDT-21) and a combat veteran of both World War II and Korea, was known as a brawling, ham-fisted, hard-drinking fleet sailor who for more than 20 years had dreamed of training and leading unconventional "sea warriors." Hamilton placed Boehm in charge of selecting and training men for a new navy commando unit.

On January 7, 1962, backdated to January 1, the U.S. Navy SEALs (Sea-Air-Land) were commissioned into service as the navy's answer to guerrilla warfare and the U.S. Army Special Forces in the cold war.

Although the Battle of Tarawa, which began on November 20, 1943, is looked upon in SEAL legend as the date of the birth of the underwater demolition teams, the direct ancestors of modern SEALs, the genealogy of waterborne commandos actually stretches back much farther than that. Syracuse, in ancient Sicily, under siege by Athens in 414 B.C., constructed palisades to impale enemy craft, and it dispatched swimmers to sabotage ships threatening the city. Athenians in turn sent out their own swimmers to dive down and cut off pilings supporting the defensive works. Tyre, in present-day Lebanon, used swimmers to cut the anchor ropes of enemy ships when Alexander the Great besieged it.

The Italians in the early days of World War II were the first actually to utilize combat swimmers in a modern sense. Using manned torpedoes and swimmers with underwater breathing devices, Italians sank three British ships and made frequent forays against warships at Gibraltar.

Americans had access to a remarkably sophisticated self-contained underwater breathing system before Pearl Harbor, but they failed to utilize it. Christian J. Lambertsen had developed his Lambertsen Amphibious Respiratory Unit (LARU), which permitted men to breath underwater for an hour or so without emitting telltale streams of bubbles. When the U.S. Navy showed no interest in underwater combat swimmers, Lambertsen volunteered for the U.S. Army and was placed in charge of equipping and training "operational swimmers" for the OSS, the Office of Strategic Services, an innovative, fast-moving unit that combined intelligence gathering with guerrilla operations behind enemy lines.

In May 1942, the navy established Scouts and Raiders, while in New Guinea the U.S. Army banded together the Alamo Scouts. Both navy and army commandos operated similarly in island warfare, but neither became as broadly based as the later SEALs or U.S. Army Special Forces.

On June 6, 1943, Adm. Ernest J. King gave the order for the training of naval combat demolition units (NCDUs), whose primary mission would be to scout beach landing areas and clear them of natural or man-made obstructions prior to an amphibious assault. Although the NCDUs were used very effectively at Normandy in June 1944, D-day, they were never utilized in the South Pacific as such. Instead, the concept was expanded upon and enlarged to underwater demolition teams (UDTs).

The Battle of Tarawa is considered the birthplace of UDTs and SEALs not because swimmers were used there but because they *weren't.* Landing ships carrying tanks and follow-on waves of marines ran aground on coral reefs surrounding the island. Murderous fire from the shore cut down troops floundering in the surf. More Americans were killed trying to reach the island than were killed in the fighting on the island.

Vowing not to let this happen again, Adm. Richmond Kelly Turner, the amphibious fleet commander, sent out urgent orders for the creation of special teams of men trained to scout out enemy beaches, remove natural and man-made obstacles, and guide invading forces ashore. The UDTs were formed.

By VJ Day, August 14, 1945, UDTs had developed a distinctive pattern and some of the methods that would later be assimilated into the SEALs. The "frogman" still used no breathing apparatus; his ability to operate underwater was limited by how long he could hold his breath. Nonetheless, the idea of "sea warrior" had been born, and the pattern was beginning to emerge.

During the Korean War, there were few operations of the kind in which the frogmen had built their reputation in World War II. Instead, UDT men were increasingly working both submerged, with underwater breathing apparatus, and ashore, experimenting with commando-type operations.

By the beginning of the 1960s, the navy's frogmen had vastly expanded their horizons. They had learned to operate for long periods of time underwater, were learning to operate ashore, and were taking to the air in parachutes—all of which lent itself to the idea of the U.S. Navy SEALs when they were commissioned in 1962.

The Vietnam War became the testing ground for the U.S. Navy SEALs in combat. Never at any one time were there more than 200 SEALs in Vietnam. However, their reputation and results far exceeded their numbers. In several parts of the Mekong Delta they completely eliminated the Viet Cong as a functional force. They were awarded decorations far out of proportion to their small numbers, including several hundred Purple Hearts, two Navy Crosses, 42 Silver Stars, 402 Bronze Stars, two Legions of Merit, 352 Navy Commendation Medals, 51 Navy Achievement Medals, three Presidential Unit Citations, and three Medals of Honor, the nation's highest award for valor.

Today, the naval Special Warfare community includes a number of relatively small organizations within the U.S. Navy, all dedicated to a common goal of taking conflict to the enemy from a maritime environment by unconventional means. The SEALs are perhaps the toughest, most specialized, and most elite Special Operations force in the world. Operating in units from as small as two men to as large as platoons of 100, these formidable commandos work with deadly efficiency, whether parachuting into the thick of the enemy from the air, swimming in from sea, or tramping across a desert.

They and their forebears—Scouts and Raiders, the OSS, UDTs, perhaps all the way back to Rogers's Rangers or Scyllias the ancient Greek—have always gone where the action is. Usually they arrive first, clandestine and prepared for action.

"Hit the enemy tonight if he expects you tomorrow," was the way one SEAL put it. "If he waits for you to come by sea, go across the mountain or arrive by parachute. If he's looking for a chopper, fly in an airliner. If he comes at you with a knife, shoot him. Throw the rule book away. There are no rules in this kind of war."

From the invasion of Kwajalein Atoll during World War II, SEALs and their immediate predecessors have fought in Korea, Vietnam, Panama, Grenada, Iraq, Bosnia, and Afghanistan, and they have conducted hundreds of missions in dangerous and little-known corners of the world. SEALs, as Lt. Roy Boehm envisioned in 1961, are truly men for all seasons, ready and prepared to conduct *any* mission anywhere in the world.

Until recent years and the publication of a number of widely read and popular books about Navy SEALs (*Brave Men, Dark Waters,* by Orr Kelly; *SEALs in Action,* by Kevin Dockery; *Rogue Warrior,* by Richard Marcinko and John Weisman; *First SEAL,* by Roy Boehm and Charles W. Sasser), the public knew little of what SEALs did, how they did it, or who they were. Although much of what SEALs do is still classified, scores of books are still written and hungrily devoured by a public captivated by warriors who make no apologies for being warriors.

"When you go in the field," said SEAL Hershal Davis, "and you're behind enemy lines and you're outnumbered three hundred or four hundred to one, you better be a bad dude. . . . SEALs are trained to hurt folks and blow things up."

Now, for the first time, *Encyclopedia of the Navy SEALs* brings an informative, interesting, and complete reference work for this unique organization of unconventional American warriors. It provides in one exciting volume a comprehensive study of the Navy SEALs—their origins, organization, history, personnel, equipment, weapons, terms, and training. *Encyclopedia of the Navy SEALs* is intended to be the ultimate guide to an understanding of the U.S. Navy SEALs, their work, and their function, from their deep origins until the present time.

ENTRIES A–Z

Acheson, Bill

The World War II invasion of Tarawa Atoll in the South Pacific was such a disaster that it forced Rear Adm. Richmond Kelly Turner, principal commander of the amphibious assault, to reevaluate tactics for the American "island hopping" campaign toward Japan. The only intelligence he had possessed about the landing area prior to the assault came from briefings of former residents of the atoll and from charts and tide tables provided by the British. As a result, assault elements swept toward the beach without knowing what awaited them.

The invasion boats ran solidly aground on coral offshore. Combat-laden marines had to wade several hundred yards under heavy enemy fire. More marines drowned in unseen sink holes and craters trying to reach Tarawa than were killed by the Japanese in the fighting for the island.

Admiral Turner was determined not to repeat this blunder. U.S. Navy combat demolition units (NCDUs) had already been formed for clearing beaches for an Allied landing on mainland Europe. Turner seized two of these teams of about 100 officers and men each and sent them to Maui, Hawaii, for a crash course in hydrographic reconnaissance,

mapping, and other skills needed for reconnoitering beachheads and removing obstacles. The two teams were redesignated as Underwater Demolition Teams (UDTs) One and Two. From now on, American commanders would have firsthand intelligence prior to beach assaults.

The new UDTs first went into action before the invasion of Kwajalein Atoll, in the Marshall Islands, in February 1944. Air reconnaissance photographs had showed the Japanese on Kwajalein were working on a seawall of rock set in concrete, with hardwood posts sticking seaward to repel Amtraks and assault boats. Admiral Turner sent UDT-1 on two daylight recon missions, one at high tide and one at low, to check out the wall and the reef offshore.

At 10 A.M. on January 31, the battleships *Pennsylvania* and *Mississippi* began a heavy bombardment of the island to cover four ramped landing craft loaded with UDT men and intelligence personnel. The craft reefed in shallow water on a high tide about 500 yards from the beach. Ahead lay the wall behind which the enemy crouched for protection from shelling. Very little hostile fire erupted from the island.

UDT men at this point in their evolution were "walkers," not swimmers. They wore normal combat uniforms, which included an inflatable life belt for each man and a lifeline that tethered him to his boat. Standard operating procedures required them to *wade* to their targets. They wore boots to protect their feet from sharp coral. Because such highly trained men were considered too valuable for direct combat, the only weapons they carried were heavy knives, usually marine Ka-bars or navy Mark II knives.

Stranded on the reef off Kwajalein, too far away to be sure of the condition of the beaches and the state of the seawall, two of the UDTs stripped down to swim trunks worn underneath their uniforms. Against both navy regulations and the warnings of their commander, Seabee Chief Petty Officer Bill Acheson and Ens. Lewis F. Luehrs dived overboard and swam toward shore. They waded along the beach to measure the depth of the water, pinpointed enemy gun emplacements, and studied the seawall and a log barricade laid all the way across the tip of the island. They sketched everything on waterproof slates with grease pencils.

After about 45 minutes in the sea, they returned to the landing craft and were immediately rushed to Admiral Turner's flagship. Using information the two rogue swimmers brought back, Turner changed his tactics for the invasion. Amtraks, with their treads and shallow draft, were used instead of heavy, deep-hulled LCVPs (Landing Craft, Vehicles, Personnel) to roll over coral obstructions. The invasion was successful and resulted in a small percentage of casualties suffered at Tarawa.

With their daring swim to the beach that morning at Kwajalein, Acheson and Luehrs forever changed the shape of naval special warfare. Naval combat swimming had entered the UDTs' mission essential task list.

Nineteen days later, at Eniwetok, UDT men swam in with goggles to mark coral heads with warning buoys and make notes of Japanese positions. When Admiral Turner returned to Pearl Harbor, he reported that the only way to deal with coral and underwater obstacles was to send in swimmers.

UDTs were becoming true "frogmen."

See also KWAJALEIN; TARAWA; TURNER, RICHMOND KELLY; UNDERWATER DEMOLITION TEAMS (UDTS).

Achille Lauro

U.S. Navy SEALs learned that politics stirred up by international terrorism can be both deceitful and treacherous after the Popular Front for the Liberation of Palestine (PFLP) hijacked the Italian luxury liner *Achille Lauro* on the morning of October 7, 1985.

Most of the tourist passengers aboard the 23,629-ton cruise ship had gone ashore for sightseeing in Alexandria, Egypt, that Sunday morning when the four terrorists slunk from cabin 82 armed with Soviet AK-47 rifles, pistols, and hand grenades. The 80 or so tourists remaining aboard and many of the crew of 320 were in the dining room when the gunmen burst in, shouting and wildly discharging their firearms. Two people were wounded. The others, terrified, were quickly subdued and sequestered.

The terrorists' mission was to hijack the ship and hold it and its passengers hostage in order to secure the freedom of 560 Palestinians held by the Israeli government. British and American passengers were singled out and placed on deck in the center of a wall of fuel drums, which the terrorists threatened to ignite. The liner captain was then ordered to set sail for the Syrian port of Tartus, and the hijackers began announcing their demands.

When news of the hijacking reached Washington, D.C., President Ronald Reagan activated units of Army Delta Force and Team Six of the SEALs' special counterterrorism force. Since the action was taking place at sea, the SEALs would be responsible for the main action. They immediately flew to Sicily, where they were to work with Italian commandos.

In the meantime, the U.S. State Department successfully put pressure on Syria to refuse the ship entry at Tartus. The frustrated terrorists decided on a show of force to demonstrate their resolve. They selected from among the passengers the most helpless of them—Leon Klinghoffer, 69, who was partially paralyzed and confined to a wheelchair by two recent strokes. Klinghoffer was also an American Jew, which may have been another reason why he was singled out. The terrorists thrust his wife aside and hauled their victim to the main deck, where he was shot once in the chest and once in the head and hurled overboard, still in his wheelchair. His body washed up on the Syrian coast a few days later.

The hijackers then ordered the ship to steer for Cypress. Again the terrorists were denied entry.

Instead, the liner sailed to Port Said and anchored there on October 9. American E2-C Hawkeye electronic surveillance airplanes shadowed it all the way.

The Italians and Americans agreed upon a plan to take down the liner. SEALs aboard the amphibious assault ship USS *Iwo Jima* waited outside the harbor for the fall of darkness. In order to preserve their anonymity, secrecy being so paramount that even their number was classified, the SEALs would conduct the actual assault but then silently withdraw to let the Italian Commando Raggruppamento Subaquaried Incurso and the Gruppi Interventi Speciali take credit for it.

The plan called for SEALs to approach *Achille Lauro* in the night in small boats with silenced engines, climb aboard, find the terrorists, and eliminate them. It was at this point, however, that international politics tossed a monkey wrench into the operation. Action by the SEALs was placed on hold.

Yasser Arafat, a former terrorist himself and leader of the PLO, sent two emissaries to negotiate a peaceful settlement. The two PLO representatives and ambassadors from Italy and West Germany went aboard the cruise ship bearing a guarantee from Egypt that the hijackers would receive safe passage to a country of their choice if they would release their hostages without harm. Strangely enough, the terrorists had not yet announced their execution of Klinghoffer.

The terrorists took quick advantage of the opportunity: they were off the ship before dark on October 9. The American ambassador to Egypt, Nicholas Veliotes, learned of Klinghoffer's murder that evening and was enraged. He radioed his aides at the American embassy: "You tell the Foreign Ministry [of Egypt] that we demand they prosecute those sons of bitches."

Egypt insisted the terrorists had already left the country, which was a bald lie. They were actually planning to fly out of Cairo to PLO headquarters in Tunisia the next morning. U.S. Marine lieutenant colonel Oliver North, President Reagan's National Security Council representative for counterterrorism, assured the president that in spite of Egypt's perfidy it was not too late to let loose the SEALs. Reagan agreed.

On the morning of October 10, an Egyptian Boeing 737 took off from Cairo carrying the four terrorists, the PLO negotiators, and four men from the Egyptian counterterrorist unit. At the same time, four U.S. Navy F-14 Tomcat fighter jets shot into the sky from the carrier USS *Saratoga,* which was in the Aegean Sea. They pulled into escort formation around the 737.

In response to American demands, both Tunis and Tripoli refused to allow the airliner to land. Unable to contact Egypt, his radio transmissions jammed by U.S. electronic countermeasures, the pilot submitted to commands to land at the NATO air base in Sigonella, Sicily. At first the air controller at Sigonella refused the 737 permission to touch down; the United States had not informed Italy of what was happening. It was only when the liner pilot declared a fuel emergency that he was granted clearance.

SEALs of SEAL Team Six were already at the airport, fully armed, ready to kill. They expected the terrorists to resist.

As the SEALs surrounded the landed airliner, the ugly head of international politics once more heaved into view: armed Italian *carabinieri* surrounded the Americans, who were surrounding the terrorists' airplane. The two heavily armed forces, guns pointed at each other, were in an impasse so tense that at one point a U.S. State Department official eavesdropping on radio communications overheard a conversation that chilled his blood. "It was a crazy situation," he explained later. "At one time we heard one of the SEAL officers discussing whether or not he should order his men to open fire on the Italians. That would have been very embarrassing."

The standoff ended only after Secretary of State George Shultz received assurances from the Italians that the terrorists would be tried for murder. The prisoners, who did not resist being taken into custody, were handed over to the Italians. The Egyptians went home. But the SEALs had twice confronted political duplicity over the affair and did not trust the Italians to keep their word. Therefore, when the Italians flew the prisoners to Rome, the SEAL commander and a small contingent of his men shadowed the terrorists' plane in a U.S. C-141 all the way. Claiming engine trouble, they even landed in Rome, directly behind the *carabinieri* and the hijackers.

Ultimately, the Italians lived up to their word to try the terrorists for murder. Few people, however, were ever to realize to what extent the operation's success depended on action, determination, and pressure from the Navy SEALs of Team Six.

See also SEAL TEAM SIX; TERRORISM.

Advanced Seal Delivery System (ASDS)

Requirements by the naval Special Warfare community for a silent, clandestine method of inserting commandos from the sea onto hostile shores led to experimentation with various underwater transportation systems. The idea traces its lineage back to the Italian human torpedoes of World War II. As early as the late 1950s, underwater demolition team (UDT) members assigned to the Submersible Operation Department (SUBOPS) in the UDT at Norfolk, Virginia, were experimenting with one- and two-man underwater propulsion units, along with mixed-gas diving rigs, underwater communications, hand-held sonar, and other untried equipment and techniques.

The first swimmer delivery vehicle (SDV), later SEAL Delivery Vehicle, was a simple device, little more than a battery-powered motor with handles that could pull one or two divers through the water at speeds of three to four knots. W. T. "Tom" Odum, head of the ocean engineering department of the Naval Coastal Systems Center in Panama City, Florida, recalls a one-man vehicle that used a bicycle-like system that turned a small propeller.

In the mid-1950s, Aerojet General built the Mark 2 SDV. It looked like an airplane on the outside and like a 1956 Ford pickup on the inside. It

A SEAL examines an SDV (seal delivery vehicle) prior to a mission. (U.S. Navy)

was the navy's first effort at building a sophisticated swimmer delivery vehicle. It was powered by silver-zinc batteries.

Unfortunately, Odum described it as "a hydrodynamic nightmare—it just didn't have any stability." It never evolved beyond the experimental stage. UDTs and SEALs continued to use the Sea Horse SDV developed by the Italians.

In the mid-'60s, General Dynamics produced the first U.S.-designed SDV, the Convair Model 14. The Coastal Systems Center further developed it as the Mark VI SDV, intended more for training and experimental purposes than for combat missions. It carried four swimmers arranged in tandem, like the Sea Horse. It proved extremely stable and easy to "fly."

Next came the 19-foot-long Mark VII. Powered by six sixteen-cell cadmium batteries, it could attain a maximum speed of approximately four knots for up to eight hours at depths of 200 feet, with a maximum range of about 40 nautical miles (60 statute miles). It had a cargo capacity of 55 pounds, in addition to the four swimmers. The breathing system consisted of eight 90-cubic-foot aluminum air tanks feeding four Conshelt VI single-hose regulators. An integral air supply meant that commandos could save their personal air tanks for the final insertion. For combat operations, a semiclosed air-supply system that emitted few or no air bubbles provided greater endurance and depth capacity while increasing stealth. One of its major improvements over the Sea Horse was a sliding canopy similar to those on fighter aircraft. It allowed the little boat to be sealed off from the surrounding sea, although it was still a wet, cold ride; it was like an expensive tin can filled with water.

It was an awkward-looking boat but stable and quite dependable. It was the first SDV to move from the experimental stage into use in combat. Two of the little VII models were used, and lost, in Operation Thunderhead during the Vietnam War.

By 1972, two new designs based on the Mark VII had been developed—the Mod (Modification) 2 and the Mod 6. Both had fiberglass hulls with fittings constructed of nonferrous materials to reduce acoustic and magnetic signatures. All instruments and electrical systems were encased in watertight compartments. Sliding canopies covered both cockpits, not simply the pilots' compartment, and the pilots, who had heretofore driven blind, were provided with a view port. Control was provided by a vertical rudder at the stern and two bow planes.

The Mod 2 was 212 inches long with a draft of 57 inches and a beam of 35 inches, not including the bow planes. It weighed 2,200 pounds fully equipped, but without its crew. The Mod 6 was lengthened by 18 inches to allow greater cargo capacity and weapons payload. The view port was eliminated as unnecessary. This allowed lights to be used inside the cockpit without being detected from outside or from the surface. Both models traveled at speeds of four to seven knots and could remain submerged for five hours.

"It's a strange ride," said one SEAL. "You can't see out. You fly on instruments the entire time. You are a diver the entire time you're in it. The SDV provides more speed and range than swimming. . . . Exposure to the cold and ambient sea pressure puts tremendous strain on the human body that becomes a limiting factor for missions with the SDV. . . . It is a complicated thing to support and deliver. But if you plan its use properly, if you get it within range, it is an extremely effective tool because it is almost undetectable. The ability to deliver either SEALs or ordnance is just phenomenal."

As improvements continued, the SDV evolved into today's Mark VIII, a sophisticated machine with an advanced steering system and better buoyancy control. It is equipped with an onboard breathing system with full-face masks that allow talk among crew members, a Doppler computerized navigation system, an obstacle-avoidance system using sonar, and radio that can be used when the craft surfaces. A third sensor system is sometimes installed—a side-scanning sonar for locating and identifying objects like mines and for recording bottom contours. Although still a "wet" submersible, it can travel twice as fast as a diver can swim, with a maximum capacity of six commandos and their gear, and will tolerate depths of 500 feet. Its length is 254 inches, with a beam and draft both 52 inches. Crew and passengers sit side by side rather than in tandem.

In 1985, the navy initiated a program that would allow the SDV to launch torpedoes, much like a regular submarine. A special SDV was designed. The Mark IX, first known as the EX-IX, was unusual—a flattened rectangle rather than the normal whale shape. It was wet, like the other SDVs, and was designed to carry only two combat swimmers and their gear and the torpedoes. Its length is 233 inches, with a beam of 76 inches and a draft of only 32 inches. It weighs about 5,000 pounds.

Out of these original wet SDVs evolved what is now known as the Advanced SEAL Delivery System (ASDS). The detailed design was completed in fiscal year 1994. Three machines were funded right away, and three more were planned to join the SEALs from 1998 to 2003. Much about the ASDS is still classified. What is known is that it is a true mini-isubmarine, with a dry interior. Unlike other SDVs, which expose SEALs to extremely cold water for long off-shore transits, the ASDS will keep them warm and dry until the start of the operation.

Whether a Mark VIII SDV or the ASDS, all swimmer delivery vehicles are designed for a wide range of operational scenarios, ranging from clandestine insertions and beach reconnaissance to underwater mapping, terrain exploration, recovery of lost or downed objects, transportation of ordnance or materiel, or any number of other missions, limited only by the imagination. They can be delivered to the target area by a variety of means—landing craft, ships, submarines, trailers, aircraft, or on a sled towed by a boat. The top of the Mark VIII is a lifting rail that allows it to be raised out of the water by a standard crane. The ASDS is transportable by C-5 aircraft.

As the SDVs became more sophisticated, specialized training had to be given to pilots and navigators. Eventually, specialized SDV teams (SDVTs) were established to support all the SEAL teams within a group. SDVT-1 is on the West Coast with Special Warfare Group One, and SDVT-2 is on the East Coast with SpecWarGru Two.

See also DRY-DECK SHELTER (DDS); USS GRAYBACK; SEAL DELIVERY VEHICLE TEAMS (SDVTS); OPERATION THUNDERHEAD.

aerophore

The aerophore was a primitive SCUBA (self-contained underwater breathing apparatus) developed in 1865 by Frenchmen Benoit Rouquayrol and Auguste Denayrouse. A horizontal steel tank of compressed air was carried on a diver's back. It was connected through a valve arrangement to a mouthpiece that admitted air only when the diver inhaled. It was the first demand regulator for underwater use.

The diver was tethered to the surface by a hose that pumped fresh air into his tank, but he was able to disconnect from the hose for short periods of time and dive with only the air on his back.

The aerophore was a forerunner of modern SCUBA equipment.

See also COUSTEAU, JACQUES-YVES; DIVING, HISTORY OF.

airborne

SEALs have developed various methods for insertion into and extraction from contested areas by and from the sea, air, or land. Perhaps their most spectacular clandestine mode of arrival into a war zone or potential combat area is from the air, by parachute. Today's square-mattress parachutes are a far cry from the early round military parachutes, the T-7s, T-10s, and even the more "steerable" MC-1Ss or MT-1Bs presently used by airborne forces. SEALs cruising in a C-141 at 35,000 feet over England can now jump out, fly across the English Channel at speeds of 25 mph, and easily land 50 miles away in France. They can land silently in the middle of the night, undetected by radar, prepared for any mission.

The concept of using a parachute did not have to wait for the Wright brothers and their flying machine at Kitty Hawk, North Carolina. Leonardo da Vinci designed a parachute in 1495; he called it a "tent roof." The first successful parachute jump was made from a tower in 1783 by the French physicist Sebatien Lenormand. Another Frenchman, Andres Jacques Garnerin, made the first parachute jump from a hot air balloon in 1797.

Although parachute troops did not figure in the U.S. military until near the beginning of World War II, Americans had a history of parachuting for pleasure and profit dating back to 1887, when Tom Baldwin bailed out of the balloon *Eclipse* at Golden Gate Park in San Francisco. Another American, Albert Berry, was the first man in history to make a parachute jump from an aeroplane, on February 28, 1912. Seven years later, the U.S. Army convened a special board of officers to determine the best type of escape parachute to issue to army pilots. That same year, 1919, Leslie T. Irvin designed and used the first parachute that was not automatically opened by a "static line" attached to the aircraft; the jumper opened the chute himself after leaping out into the air. The era of the free-fall parachute had arrived.

The German invasion of Crete in May 1941 provided the greatest single impetus to build an airborne force in the United States. Within two months of the invasion, anticipating American involvement in the war, the War Department called on the U.S. Army Air Forces to develop new cargo aircraft for use by combat airborne troops. The first U.S. airborne unit, the 550th Infantry Airborne Battalion, was activated on July 1, 1941. Before World War II ended, the 82d and 101st Airborne had made themselves legendary.

The parachute, it was found, could be used for a variety of purposes other than emergency escapes from airplanes and delivering troops to a battlefield. Some jet planes use "drogue" 'chutes as brakes for landings. When the U.S. space program began, parachutes were used to return space capsules to earth. Canopies were enlarged from the 24-to-28-foot diameter for human use to 100 feet for dropping cargo onto the battlefield and for emergency-relief purposes.

It was only in the mid-fifties, however, that the navy, through its underwater demolition teams (UDTs), started parachuting and became airborne. The first detachment of UDT frogmen was sent to the Army Airborne school at Fort Benning, Georgia, in 1956. By the time the SEALs were commissioned in 1962, many frogmen had a good deal of experience at jumping, although much of it had been done on their own time and at their own expense.

The problem in the beginning was in obtaining equipment. "We couldn't buy parachutes, we didn't have any money," remembers Henry S. "Bud" Thrift, who served as air operations officer for both UDT-21 and SEAL Team Two in the mid-'60s and early 1970s. "We would go to salvage—the place in Supply where things go that are out of date, or not good, or have done their tour, or were turned in to be sold as scrap or destroyed. We would get parachutes out of salvage, their ten-year life expectancy over, and repair 'em. That's what we were free-falling with. . . . We would get four or five jumps before they started tearing."

Parachutes at the time were the standard, round-canopy, nonsteerable military version. First jumps were made in classic army paratrooper fashion: jumpers lined up in "sticks," shuffled in step to the door, and thrust themselves out. A static line automatically opened each parachute. The format and equipment were intended for dropping troops at low level over a drop zone (DZ); they were hardly suitable for the stealth operations required by commandos. SEALs began making modifications in both parachutes and tactics to meet their special needs.

"We would take these 'chutes and mark 'em with a Magic Marker," recalled William "Bill" Bruhmuller, plank owner of SEAL Team Two, "then take scissors and cut it out, whatever modifications we wanted to make." Such alterations turned the canopies into reasonable copies of the more sophisticated parachutes being used by sports jumpers. Cutting holes in the gores (panels) permitted a forward speed of four or five knots and made the parachutes steerable, converting T-10s into predecessors of the steerable military MC-1s and MC-4s.

Then came the challenge of jumping at night, into water, from both high and low altitudes, and in free-falling groups. A SEAL team was assigned to the Naval Air Test Center at Patuxent River Naval Air Station in Maryland to develop methods for using the parachute in support of the SEALs' special mission. A SEAL and his gear—swim fins, underwater breathing apparatus, weapons, ammo, radios, raft, food, water—may well weigh 400 pounds.

Day after day, night after night, SEAL guinea pigs parachuted into Chesapeake Bay, learning when and how to release their equipment before entering the water, how to jettison 'chutes before becoming entangled in them, how to recover their equipment and get everything into a rubber boat. It was possible, they found, to jump safely into heavy seas, but wind speed could be critical. On essential missions, jumps might be made in winds up to 18 mph.

Eventually, through experimentation and borrowing from both sports jumpers and the army, SEALs refined the three basic combat parachute insertion techniques—static line, HAHO (high altitude, high opening), and HALO (high altitude, low opening.)

Parachuting is only one method SEALs use to insert themselves into hostile territory. (U.S. Navy)

Static-line insertions are utilized most frequently when a team needs to be dropped in quickly, aircraft cannot be landed, secrecy is not essential, and a great deal of gear must accompany the team. All SEALs are airborne qualified, but not all are qualified at HAHO and HALO.

The invention of "square," "wing," and "mattress" parachutes in a variety of a basic configurations made possible the precise jumping required by both HAHO and HALO. The front of the square parachute, called the nose, is honeycombed with cell openings. Since the back is closed, air inflates the cells, creating lift that turns the parachute into a wing and allows it to "fly" through the air. The jumper controls it by two toggles. Pulling down on one toggle curls the inside of the canopy downward at the rear and bends the flow of air, resulting in a braking force, around which the parachute rotates until the toggle is released. Pulling down both toggles produces a "flare," which slows the parachute for landing.

The HALO technique (high-altitude bailout, low-altitude opening) is utilized for clandestine insertions when aircraft can fly directly over the drop zones. Since the jump may begin at 25,000 feet or higher, depending upon mission requirements, the jumper needs insulated clothing and an oxygen supply. In 1963, SEAL Jack Macione jumped from an A-3D heavy attack bomber at 37,900 feet. The temperature was 50 degrees below zero Fahrenheit. He free-fell for almost five minutes before opening his parachute.

SEALs had to overcome a number of challenges when they first began ejecting at extremely high altitudes. Goggles, warmed in the airplane, shattered when they hit the cold air. Eyes teared up, and tears froze. "Relative" work, in which the jumpers guide on each other during free fall in order to land together, is made more difficult by darkness. SEALs initially sprayed themselves with fluorescent paint, but a can of paint in the low air pressure at high altitudes could fill the whole interior of an airplane. They settled for wearing lights on their backs, a different colored one for the leader, upon whom the others would form during the descent. It's a matter of follow-the-leader, with everyone equipped with radios for communicating.

Normally, free-fall reaches speeds of about 120 mph, but in the thinner air of higher altitudes speeds can reach over 300 mph. A jumper "flies" by creating varying pressure at different parts of his body. He stabilizes by symmetric distribution of arms and legs, slightly bent to create wind resistance. Pulling in one arm toward the head and moving the leg on the same side closer to the body's centerline causes a decrease in drag that moves the body in that direction. If the jumper gets into a spin, possibly caused by air turbulence, he can regain control by "snapping to attention," slapping both arms against his sides. Drag from his feet throws him into a headfirst dive, which stops the spin and allows him to regain control.

The higher the altitude, the less control the jumper has in the thinner air, because of lack of air resistance. A jumper can actually feel the air get thicker and his speed decrease as he nears the earth.

From 20,000 feet, a free fall lasts from about a minute and a half to two minutes, depending upon air density, temperature, weight, and other factors. The HALO jumper will pull his rip cord at 2,000 to 2,500 feet, again depending upon the mission, and land upon his preselected target.

HAHO (high-altitude drop, high-altitude opening) is the insertion method of choice when the drop plane cannot fly over the target for some reason. An airplane transporting a team of SEALs can fly past a hostile or target nation over international waters, 20 to 25 miles at sea, 30,000 feet in the air, and still put the team on the target. The free fall lasts only eight to 10 seconds before the SEALs deploy their parachutes to "fly" to target. Settling to earth at the rate of 15 to 25 feet per second, depending again upon conditions, the SEALs may be in the air, gliding cross-country, for over an hour. As they go through the various altitude levels, it may be raining in one cloud, snowing or sleeting in another. Using compass, altimeter, and GPS, the SEALs navigate their way to their target, settling to earth silently to accomplish their mission, whatever it may be.

See also LOLEX; MACIONE, JACK; OLSON, NORMAN H. URGENT FURY; SCOUT DOGS.

Alamo Scouts

Although the "Alamo Scouts" of World War II were U.S. Army soldiers, they came closer in tactics, mission, and combat philosophy to modern SEALs than any other military unit until the underwater demolition teams (UDTs). Trained from the beginning to infiltrate from the sea to operate behind Japanese lines, they contributed significantly to the development of such unconventional warfare units as the U.S. Army Special Forces and the U.S. Navy SEALs.

On January 22, 1943, the Sixth U.S. Army, commanded by Gen. Walter Krueger, operating under the code name "Alamo Force," joined in the campaign to take New Guinea from the Japanese during Gen. Douglas MacArthur's march to fulfill his promise to return to the Philippines. Krueger formed his own intelligence unit within the Sixth Army following a conflict with the navy over intelligence gathering. On November 28, 1943, he issued an order establishing the "Sixth U.S. Army Special Reconnaissance Unit." It was immediately dubbed "Alamo Scouts."

The selection of candidates for the Scouts and their subsequent training were models for the selection and training of later commandos. It took a special blend of courage, drive, skill, intelligence, judgment, and physical prowess to become an Alamo Scout. The candidates had to be physically fit, able to endure the fatigue of long, arduous marches with little or no rest, and be capable of swimming at least a half-mile through rough surf. They had to be emotionally stable, possess a high sense of duty and self-discipline, and be willing to place mission and the welfare of their teams above themselves. Adventurous men were needed who could think on their feet and improvise under challenging situations, without being reckless.

Although the Scouts were created for reconnaissance and intelligence gathering and not for direct combat, their operations behind enemy lines required them to be prepared to fight if necessary. They were trained, as are modern SEALs, to be experts in all sorts of weapons, both conventional and unconventional—the M1 carbine, M1 Garand, .45 caliber Colt pistol, Browning Automatic Rifle (BAR), the Thompson .45 submachine gun, grenades, and others.

"Each trainee had to take a live grenade," recalled former Scout Robert W. Teeples, "pull the pin, place it on the edge of his foxhole and duck into the foxhole until it went off. We were trained in about everything imaginable."

Scouts learned how to assemble and fire Japanese weapons, how to set snares and booby traps, and to use explosives and demolition charges. They were taught sniping skills and the use of silencers. A Scout could kill in close combat with a knife, a garrote, a stick, or even his bare hands.

Although rubber boats would be the primary means by which the Scouts would infiltrate into enemy territory, they were also trained in the use of small motorized utility craft and native dugout canoes. They trained day and night to maneuver and land their rubber boats through dangerous surf. They were wet at least half of their training time, their teeth chattering from chill and fatigue. One trainee complained wryly that he hadn't joined the army to be in the navy.

Scout Andy Smith remembers, "We always went from physical training right to swimming. We would swim out from the beach to a pier or a boat and climb up on it—then we would put on our full combat gear and swim back. Other times they would have a couple of strings out in the water about 50 feet apart. As soon as you came to the first string you would have to swim underwater because they would fire a machine gun into the water in between the strings."

Like the Navy UDT frogmen working in the Pacific farther north, Alamo Scouts had to master the techniques of observation. They spent hours sketching coastlines and beaches and learning how to conduct detailed analysis of beach gradients, tides, reefs, fresh-water sources, vegetation, soil, and sand composition. They practiced silent infiltration methods. Once they attained expertise in scouting and patrolling, training went into its second phase, wherein small teams of six or seven men

The U.S. Army "Alamo Scouts" of World War II came closer in tactics, mission, and combat philosophy to modern SEALs than any other military unit prior to the rise of the underwater demolition teams (UDTs). (National Archives)

were dispatched into lightly occupied enemy territory. If they survived, they were considered ready for real-world missions.

From February 1944 until the Scouts were disbanded in November 1945, the unit performed 106 reconnaissance and intelligence-gathering missions, involving a total of 138 Scouts. They operated normally in six-man teams, deep inside enemy country, often for months at a time. They performed two prison-camp liberations: at Oransbari, New Guinea, on October 4, 1944, where they raided a Japanese camp to liberate a Dutch governor, his family, and eighteen Javanese servants; and at Cabanatuan in the Philippines on January 30, 1945, when Scouts and U.S. Army Rangers freed 516 prisoners of war who had survived the notorious Bataan Death March and nearly four years of brutal captivity.

During that period, the Scouts also killed approximately 500 enemy soldiers and captured over 60 prisoners—all without losing a single man, a record still unmatched in U.S. military history.

After the war, the Defense Department interviewed numerous Alamo Scouts to incorporate their experiences into textbook lessons on amphibious warfare, scouting and patrolling, intelligence collecting, raiding, and guerrilla operations. In 1988, the Alamo Scouts were finally awarded the Special Forces tab and recognized by the John F. Kennedy Special Warfare Center at Fort Bragg, North Carolina, as one of the forerunners of the U.S. Military Special Forces.

See also MACARTHUR, DOUGLAS; UNDERWATER DEMOLITION TEAMS (UDTS).

Alexander the Great (356–323 B.C.)

The concept of using combat swimmers was not unique to the twentieth century. Alexander the Great, king of Macedonia and one of the greatest generals in military history, best known as the conqueror of much of what was then the civilized world before his death of malaria at age 33, was undoubtedly aware of the use of swimmers in battle. He was very much interested in the Greek civilization and had likely heard the story of how Athenians had thwarted the defensive efforts of Syracuse during Athens' siege of that city in 414 B.C. by using swimmers to inflict damage on ships threatening the city.

In 333 B.C., Alexander himself confronted combat swimmers when he laid siege to Tyre. After routing the Greek and Persian heavy infantry with his phalanx formation and capturing the king of Persia, he marched his army south into Phoenicia to lay siege to Tyre. The city on an island held out against Alexander for seven months before it fell. During that time, Alexander's ships faced the constant threat of swimmers sabotaging his ships and cutting anchor ropes to allow them to be smashed against shoals and rocky shores.

Although there is no record of Alexander's using divers himself in his conquests, there is no question but that his armies faced enemy swimmers and that he was intrigued by the idea. Legend has it that, foreshadowing the appearance of SCUBA (self-contained underwater breathing apparatus), he himself went to the bottom of the ocean in a type of crude diving bell and remained there for a full day. A Hindustani painting from the late 1500s depicts him descending into the Mediterranean in a kind of barrel.

Centuries were to pass, however, before man actually learned to live, breathe, and move about underwater to the point of becoming undersea warriors.

See also DIVING, HISTORY OF; SCYLLIAS.

ALICE

The primary load-bearing system for the special forces soldier is called ALICE, the acronym for *all-purpose lightweight individual carrying equipment*. It is composed of a large pack, an aluminum frame with kidney pads and cargo shelf, and shoulder straps. It is designed to carry large loads and can be customized to accommodate a wide variety of roles. For airborne operations, the ALICE pack is attached to a lowering line and carried below the reserve parachute in front until after the parachute opens. The pack is then released to hang on its 16-foot lowering strap to reduce the weight of the jumper when he lands.

The ALICE system may soon be replaced with a new rucksack rig already in service with the U.S. Marine Corps. It is known as the Modular Lightweight Load-Carrying Equipment (MOLLE) system. Improvement in the MOLLE system starts with a load-bearing vest to spread the load out over the entire body, to permit the bearer to carry greater weight with more comfort and agility.

ambush

An ambush is a surprise attack from a concealed position on a moving or temporarily halted target. It enables a small unit to harass or destroy large, better-armed units. Since SEALs frequently operate in small elements behind enemy lines, where they are both outnumbered and outgunned, the ambush is a favorite tactic. It was used extensively by SEALs and other Special Forces during the Vietnam War.

There are two categories of ambushes—the hasty and the deliberate. The "hasty" ambush occurs when one enemy element spots the other first, shifts quickly into some sort of firing line, and grabs the opportunity to bushwhack him.

A "deliberate" ambush requires more time and planning; it directs specific action against a specific target. Of the two types of deliberate ambushes, the "point ambush" deploys to attack a single killing zone, or KZ. For example, a supply convoy might be attacked at a bend in a trail. The "area ambush" may include a number of point ambushes and is rarely launched by elements smaller than a platoon. It requires a central primary ambush, supported by smaller ambushes set to hit and destroy other enemy units attempting to enter or leave the KZ.

The two most common ambush formations are the "line" (in which the ambushers line up on one side of a trail or road to attack a target) and the L-shape. The shorter leg of the L forms a blocking force across the direction of travel, while the longer side forms a line parallel to the enemy column to deliver the main fire onto the KZ at the ambush site.

The secrets to success are surprise, coordinated fire, control, and planning. There are three elements of an ambush, which must quietly move onto the site from an ORP (organizational, or operational, rally point) and set up in advance of any expected enemy target or target of opportunity. The assault element is the main body, supported by a security element that sets up ahead to give advance warning of an enemy approach and to provide security so that the ambushers are not themselves surprised by an ambush. The support element, depending upon the numbers and makeup of the attackers, will include the patrol leader, RTO (radiotelephone operator), and perhaps special elements for capturing prisoners, searching bodies for intelligence, and the like. The

An ambush is a surprise attack from a concealed position. Here, Special Operations troops move through the aftermath of an ambush to take prisoners and search for intelligence. (Charles W. Sasser)

various elements move stealthily into position, where they may remain, unmoving, for as long as 24 to 48 hours.

SEALs in Vietnam were noted for their ability to blend completely into their background. Said one SEAL, "It's incredible to explain what you can become, the illusion that you can present to people. You can become a bush, a log, if you just concentrated hard enough on being that. They told us in our training that you could become a master of illusion if you believe enough in the illusion."

An ambush can be triggered by a number of different means: arm or hand signals, radio, field phone, or some prearranged signal, such as the explosion of a Claymore mine. One of the most common methods of signaling is by the use of a long cord laid out from man to man. It can be silently tugged to alert everyone in the net that something is about to happen.

An ambush must be sudden and extremely violent. The enemy must not be permitted an opportunity to regroup, escape, or counterattack. The "mad minute" of an ambush commonly begins with the explosion of Claymore mines arranged to send hundreds of steel balls fanning into the target, supplemented by machine guns positioned to rake up and down the body of the target.

Lt. Cdr. Roy Boehm, the man who organized and trained the first Navy SEAL team, recalls an ambush he set in Vietnam.

"One of the *Biet Hai* [Vietnamese military river patrols] on leave visiting his family's village returned with news that a VC [Viet Cong] tax collector confiscating one-third of the village's rice crop had ordered the hamlet to prepare to feed seven or eight travelers on a specific date. Undoubtedly, they were high-ranking NLF [National Liberation Front] members. I couldn't let a target like that pass.

"[My] raiding party was dropped off in three sampans at the mouth of the canal that flowed past our *Biet Hai*'s father's village. . . . We paddled the dugouts through the inky night to where the canal narrowed at a bend near the ville. . .

"The ambush set itself in thick grass alongside the canal. For several hours there was nothing but the swarming buzz of mosquitoes and an occasional animal call or cry. Then, just before dawn, I heard the soft dip of paddles in black water.

"Shortly, two sampans loaded with men shadowed into view.

"I gave the order.

"A withering hail of fire chewed the canal surface into a froth stained pink by the blood of the dead and the dying. The night's take included five enemy KIA [killed in action], two WIA [wounded in action] prisoners, two sampans, and two AK-47 rifles that were dropped inside the sampans rather than into the canal."

See also VIETNAM WAR.

Amphibious Ready Group

The Amphibious Ready Group is that SEAL unit placed on "ready" status, immediately available to the fleet for action or missions.

See also COMMANDER, AMPHIBIOUS TASK FORCE (CATF).

Amphibious Roger

During World War II, the United States and China formed a joint guerilla operation to operate in China against the Japanese. It was assigned the code name Amphibious Roger.

See also AMPHIBIOUS SCOUTS AND RAIDERS; KING, ERNEST J.

Amphibious Scouts

The development of naval special operations forces may be traced back to a number of units created to confront the challenges of World War II—Alamo Scouts, Amphibious Scouts and Raiders (as distinct from Amphibious Scouts), the Office of Strategic Services (OSS), naval combat demolition units (NCDUs), underwater demolition teams (UDTs). In fact, the tactics and philosophy of naval special warfare may go even farther back than that—to Alexander the Great, for example, and to Rogers's Rangers of the American Revolution. Abraham Lincoln foresaw the advantage of the unconventional use of the navy when he remarked in 1863, during the Civil War, "Nor must Uncle Sam's web feet be forgotten. At all the watery margins they have been present. Not all on the deep sea, the braced bay, and the rapid rivers, but also up the narrow muddy lagoon and wherever the ground was a little damp, they have been and made their tracks."

Tracks made by a little-known unit, formally known as the Seventh Amphibious Force Special Service Unit One, more commonly referred to as the Amphibious Scouts, have at least a small place in the SEALs' lineage. The outfit, seldom more than company-sized, was formed in the Pacific on July 7, 1943 and was placed under the command of Navy lieutenant commander William B. Coultas. A year before Pearl Harbor, Coultas had been dispatched to the Pacific posing as a birdwatcher for *National Geographic*. In reality, he was collecting intelligence for the Allies. War with Japan was anticipated.

Originally, it was intended that the Amphibious Scouts replace the Australian coastwatchers, positioning themselves on islands to keep tabs on enemy shipping and movements. The ranks of the coastwatchers had been severely decimated by their perilous work on Japanese-occupied soil. However, once the Allies began planning an offensive, the unit assumed more value as a mobile force that could "sneak and peek" in enemy country.

It was made up of volunteers from both the Australian and U.S. armed forces, navy, marines, and army. Candidates attended a rigorous six-week training course at Cairns, Australia, where they were trained in pidgin English, scouting and patrolling, hand-to-hand combat, jungle survival, and rubber boat handling. Small operational teams were led by Australian officers.

Although the Amphibious Scouts were to be used for two years, until they were disbanded at the end of the war, their utilization was limited, largely due to an incident that occurred in the fall of 1943, when the Allies were planning the seizure of western New Britain Island, in New Guinea. The island's western tip overlooked the waterway through which American troops would have to pass on their way to the Philippines. Gen. Douglas MacArthur placed Gen. Walter Krueger's Sixth Army at the spearhead of the attack against the Japanese. Krueger lacked reliable estimates of the strength of the enemy near Gasmata on New Britain Island. It was decided that the Amphibious Scouts were better suited for a sea/land reconnaissance mission than were the naval combat demolition units (NCDUs). A small scout patrol was scheduled to be put ashore on Gasmata on October 6 and retrieved on October 16. General Krueger personally briefed Lt. Milton Beckworth, an army member of the party, on the specific intelligence he required.

Murphy's Law, which states that anything that can go wrong *will,* soon reared its head. Communications between the landing party and the captain of the PT (patrol torpedo) boat that was supposed to make the extraction became confused. The Scouts were forced to remain on the island for an additional eleven days, during which time they barely avoided starvation and capture.

The SNAFU did little to ingratiate the navy to General Krueger. To make matters even worse, interservice rivalry prompted the U.S. Navy to detain Lieutenant Beckworth after the mission. He was hustled off to Milne Bay for debriefing by naval intelligence, after which he was secreted onto a small naval craft, the skipper of which was instructed to take him anywhere he wanted to go except to Australia. Exactly why he was restrained

from reporting to General Krueger has never been determined. It was not the navy's finest hour.

Beckworth jumped ship, however, after four days and made his way to Sixth Army headquarters. Furious at and disgusted by what General Krueger considered the navy's lack of cooperation, to put the matter delicately, Krueger formed his own "Sixth U.S. Army Special Reconnaissance Unit"—the Alamo Scouts.

Sixth Army no longer used the Amphibious Scouts. All non-navy personnel were reassigned. The unit, renamed Seventh Amphibious Scouts, received a new mission—to go ashore with assault boats, lay buoys in channels, erect markers for incoming craft, handle casualties, take offshore soundings, blow up beach obstacles, and maintain voice communications linking troops ashore, incoming boats, and nearby ships. Although the Seventh Amphibious Scouts conducted operations in the Pacific for the duration of the conflict, participating in more than 40 landings, they became a minor, dead-end offshoot of the navy's journey to special warfare and the U.S. Navy SEALs.

See also ALAMO SCOUTS; AMPHIBIOUS SCOUTS AND RAIDERS; COULTAS, WILLIAM B.

Amphibious Scouts and Raiders

Of the several units formed during World War II whose important influences contributed to the development of naval special warfare, the navy considers the Amphibious Scouts and Raiders, also known as Navy Scouts and Raiders, to be the earliest forerunners of today's SEALs and therefore in the direct lineage of both the underwater demolition teams (UDTs) and Navy SEALs. This unit was distinct from the Seventh Amphibious Force Special Service Unit One, the Amphibious Scouts, with which it is often confused, and which began operations in the South Pacific over a year *after* the Amphibious Scouts and Raiders were formed.

By the time the United States entered the war, after Pearl Harbor, the Germans had occupied almost the entire European continent and threatened to take over Egypt and the Suez Canal. The Japanese controlled large sections of China and had swept into the Pacific to capture the Philippines, Indochina, Singapore, and most of the islands north of Australia. It was obvious that the Allies would have to land troops on many beaches against fierce opposition.

Navy lieutenant Philip H. Bucklew, who was to become known as "the Father of Naval Special Warfare," was at the time a physical instructor in the Navy's Physical Training (PT) Program, commanded by ex-heavyweight prize fighter Gene Tunney. When Bucklew learned of plans to form a team of what were originally referred to as amphibious commandos, he immediately volunteered, along with nine other men from Tunney's PT cadre. The ten of them made up the first Scouts and Raiders class to begin training at the Amphibious Training Base, Little Creek, Virginia, in May 1942. In January 1943, the Scouts and Raiders moved to Fort Pierce, Florida, about sixty miles north of West Palm Beach. Subsequent training classes included a few army candidates, although the unit remained for its lifetime almost exclusively navy.

Scouts and Raiders were never intended to become broad-based commandos like the SEALs. Brave men were needed to reconnoiter landing beaches, mark the locations of obstacles and defensive works, and guide assault waves ashore. For this mission, volunteers were trained in handling small boats (which would be their primary mode of travel), running, swimming, obstacle courses, log PT (during which heavy logs were lifted and carried as part of a conditioning program), hand-to-hand combat, signaling, radios, demolitions, and gunnery.

The Scouts and Raiders first saw combat in November 1942 during Operation Torch, the Allied landing on the north coast of Africa. The Americans planned to place 100,000 troops ashore in two separate forces. One would approach through the Mediterranean and strike near Algiers, while the second attacked the coast of what was then known as French Morocco.

Prior to the Mediterranean landing, 17 hurriedly trained Scouts and Raiders set out after dark in a small, wooden-hulled boat from a transport offshore. Their mission was to penetrate a river, the Wadi Sebou, and cut cables anchoring a boom and antishipping nets stretched across the steam. This would allow American warships to fight their way up into the harbor and into the river's entrance to cover soldiers moving in to seize the Port Lyautey military airfield. The Scouts had to pass directly underneath the machine guns and cannon of a Vichy French fort overlooking the river and harbor.

Even before the little Higgins boat entered the harbor, it was buffeted by a rain squall that cut the visibility to nearly zero. A groundswell rose up from the winds and tide, picked up the frail wooden craft, and sent it careening upriver, almost out of control. Suddenly, a red flare arced across the inked sky. Searchlights from the fort probed the rainswept night. Heavy 75 mm guns roared and cracked, their rounds geysering around the defenseless boat. The Scouts turned tail and made it back to sea in spite of the battering they took from ocean waves.

Undaunted, the Scouts made a second attempt the following night. This time, they slipped into the river without detection. They clamped explosives to the one-and-a-half-inch cable that held the antishipping net in place, neatly shearing it and setting adrift a chain of small boats that supported the net.

As soon as this cable and a smaller reinforcing cable were cut, clearing the river for navigation, machine guns from the fort opened up with a deadly hail of fire. Zigzagging frantically to avoid being hit, the Higgins boat, full of Scout sailors, cut for the mouth of the river. Again, it fought past a wall of monstrous waves before scooting out into the open sea. There were 13 bullet holes in the boat by the time it reached the waiting transport, but the mission had been accomplished, and not a man had been wounded. Scouts were awarded seven Navy Crosses for valor.

Plans for a massive cross-Channel invasion of mainland Europe began more than a year in advance of the scheduled D-day. In January 1943, Cdr. Draper L. Kauffman was selected to organize and train demolition units to cope with the obstacles Hitler and Tojo would undoubtedly erect to hinder landings in Europe and the Pacific. Training of the naval combat demolition units (NCDUs) began in June 1943, next door to the Scouts and Raiders (S&R) School at Fort Pierce, Florida. The NCDUs and the Scouts and Raiders would eventually merge into the underwater demolition teams (UDTs).

In November 1943, six men of NCDU-11, along with Lieutenant Bucklew and four of his Scouts and Raiders, were sent to England to prepare for the Normandy invasion. In what could be construed as a breach of security, Bucklew was shown the operations order and plans for the Operation Overlord landing on the French coast. He and his Scouts were sent to a special school to teach them how to resist interrogation should they be captured. Then they were assigned to reconnoiter the landing beaches.

Operating from small rubber boats at night, the Scouts took soundings offshore. Bucklew, who might be considered the first invader of German-occupied Europe, even crawled ashore one night and brought back buckets full of sand for army experts to test for its ability to support tanks and heavy vehicles. He and his men also spent weeks on surveillance missions up and down the French coast, sketching it and studying its silhouette so they could guide the invading force.

On D-day, June 6, 1944, under heavy fire, NCDUs and S&R teams blew eight complete gaps and two partial gaps in the German defenses at Omaha Beach. These defenses included steel posts driven into the sand and topped with explosives, along with three-ton steel barricades called "Belgian Gates." At the same time, demolitions teams cleared 700 yards of Utah Beach for the landing. Heavy tides pushed many of the demolitions crews well ahead of the first invading waves; they found themselves spearheading the assault. Of the 175 NCDU and S&R men participating in the assault on Omaha Beach, 31 were killed, and 60 were wounded. Four were killed and eleven wounded on Utah Beach.

In the meantime, an offshoot of the Scouts and Raiders was deployed to fight with the Sino-American Cooperation Organization, or SACO. Adm. Ernest J. King had ordered that 120 officers and 900 men be trained for "Amphibious Roger" at the S&R School to form the core of what was conceived to be a "guerrilla amphibious organization of Americans and Chinese operating from coastal waters, lakes and rivers employing small steamers and sampans."

Three small groups of Amphibious Roger actually saw service, conducting a survey of the upper Yangtze River in the spring of 1945. Disguised as coolies, they also conducted a second three-month survey of the Chinese coast from Shanghai to Kitchioh Wan, near Hong Kong. Phil Bucklew and a handful of his Scouts prowled mainland China for a short time, disrupting enemy lines of communications and gathering intelligence. Other S&Rs helped train Nationalist Chinese guerrillas for operations against Japanese forces.

By the time the war ended in September 1945, Scouts and Raiders had participated in landings in Sicily, Salerno, Anzio, the Adriatic, Normandy, and southern France. Some of the bolder ones had even continued inland with the army after D-day to fight for the liberation of France. Over 1,200 men were ultimately to be trained to serve in the Scouts and Raider teams.

Members of the S&Rs were sparingly used in the South Pacific, generally being merged into NCDU and UDT teams. The unit was disbanded at the end of the war. Some of the men joined UDT. A few, like Master Chief Boatswain's Mate Rudy Boesch, a member of Amphibious Roger Five, the last Scouts and Raiders training class, went on to become SEALs in the evolution of naval special warfare.

See also ALAMO SCOUTS; AMPHIBIOUS SCOUTS; BOESCH, RUDOLPH E.; BUCKLEW, PHILIP H.; KAUFFMAN, DRAPER L.; NAVY COMBAT DEMOLITION UNITS (NCDU); UNDERWATER DEMOLITION TEAMS (UDTS).

antiterrorism

The term "antiterrorism" refers to policies and actions designed to prevent and deter international terrorism and to reduce the vulnerability of individuals and property to terrorism, as opposed to active measures to combat terrorists themselves. SEALs, especially the Naval Special Warfare Development Group (DEVGRU), have been trained in both antiterrorist and counterterrorist measures.

SEALs have been trained in both antiterrorism and counterterrorism operations. This is a TV image of a terrorist threatening a TWA pilot in a standoff at a Beirut airport in 1985.

See also NAVAL SPECIAL WARFARE DEVELOPMENT GROUP (DEVGRU); SEAL TEAM SIX; TERRORISM.

Apex boat

Apex boats, a version of the "Stingrays," whose attempted use created chaos in the South Pacific, were first used at Salerno, on the Italian coast. The unmanned drone craft, filled with explosives, were intended to take the place of swimmers in breaching the formidable beach obstacles erected by the Germans on the coasts of occupied France. The project to build the boats and train operators was so secret that even the frogmen of the naval combat demolition units (NCDUs) who were training for the mission, and who would control the drones, knew nothing about where they would be used or about the waters or beaches of the intended targets.

Apex boats came in two sizes. The smaller boats were called "males," the larger, "females." Males would each carry one ton of high explosives and be guided in ahead of an amphibious operation to blow small gaps in the static obstacle defenses. Females, each packed with four tons of explosives, would follow to widen the gaps.

At the same time that demolitions men were training with the boats at Salerno, they prepared to blow the obstacles themselves if the drones failed. This turned out to be a wise precaution. Apex boats proved to be every bit as unreliable as Stingrays.

Apexes were not used at Normandy. They were, however, utilized two months later, on August 15, 1944, at the Allied landing in southern France. At 3 A.M. on that date, as naval and aerial bombardment began against the beach, Apex drones were sent toward the shore in waves.

At Cavalaire Bay, the first wave of six males appeared to detonate as planned. Fifteen of the 18 females also appeared to function properly. Of the three that malfunctioned, two simply did not explode. The third ran out of control and chased an American subchaser, exploding near enough to it to put it out of commission for the rest of the invasion.

NCDU men who went in to check the obstacles after the drones had their chance at them discovered that the Apexes had not done their jobs. Frogmen completed the task the normal way—by swimming in and personally setting charges.

There were no further amphibious beach landings during the war in Europe.

See also STINGRAY.

Aqua Ho Motor

The key to water operations for "sea warriors" like the SEALs, and the underwater demolition teams (UDTs) before them, is secrecy and stealth. After World War II ended, UDT men of foresight and vision, like Cdr. Francis Douglas "Red Dog" Fane and Lt. Cdr. Francis Riley "Frank" Kaine, began experimenting with ways to make swimmers more deadly, more silent—and faster.

Under ideal conditions, which means without waves and currents, a strong swimmer can move at about one nautical mile an hour. Quite obviously, he will not go anywhere if he is bucking a one-knot current. Fane, Kaine, and a number of other individuals, some of whom worked out of the Submersible Operations Department (SUBOPS) at Norfolk, Virginia, tested various devices for pushing, pulling, or carrying swimmers underneath the sea. One of the first of these was called an "Aqua Ho Motor."

The Aqua Ho looked like a three-tank Aqua-Lung. The tanks on either side in the backpack held air, but the middle tank contained batteries that powered a shrouded propeller at the bottom of the tank. A swimmer strapped on the pack, submerged, turned on his motor, and was powered through the ocean at speeds up to four knots as long as the batteries lasted, which was about 40 minutes.

"You don't need a lot of speed to improve yourself thousands of percent underwater," explained Lieutenant Commander Kaine. "A piece of equipment that can move three knots for forty minutes is a tremendous improvement underwater."

The Aqua Ho failed to catch on. It soon disappeared, evolving into new generations of submersibles. "It was a beauty," Kaine recalled. "It was just a great, great thing. But whoever was in the power seat for buying equipment for the UDTs just didn't want it. I haven't any idea what happened to the thing. Most of the equipment that was developed in those times was pretty good, but you have a hard time, when you're an operator, selling to non-operators. It was very hard to convince them that a thing was a necessity, especially if it looked like a toy. And most of the things you operate with underwater look like toys, they look like fun. The Aqua Ho Motor looked like fun. They don't see the practicality in things."

See also ADVANCED SEAL DELIVERY SYSTEM (ASDS); SWIMMER PROPULSION UNIT (SPU).

Aqua-Lung

Men over the centuries have been fascinated by the prospect of swimming with the fish and exploring that vast area of the earth covered by water. Although many inventors and adventurers have experimented with diving apparatus, using everything from barrels and pumps to long diver-to-surface air hoses, contemporary sports divers as well as military divers like the SEALs owe modern SCUBA (self-contained underwater breathing apparatus) diving to the work of one man. That man is Jacques-Yves Cousteau, a Frenchman.

Prior to Cousteau, SCUBA offered no way to regulate the flow of air from tanks to the diver. The diver merely breathed by opening a tap that allowed the air to flow continuously. Exhaled and unused air escaped into the water from around the edges of the diver's mask. Cousteau complained that this arrangement, the continuous discharge of air, allowed only short submersions.

In 1942 and 1943, in the midst of World War II, Cousteau, then a French naval lieutenant, and engineer Emile Gagnan redesigned a car regulator to provide compressed air automatically to a diver on his demand. A valve opened at the diver's intake of breath to furnish air, then closed at his exhaling. The expelled air was released into the water through an escape valve. The two Frenchmen attached their demand-valve regulator to hoses, a mouthpiece, and a pair of compressed air tanks, thus inventing the first workable, "open-circuit," demand-type SCUBA. They patented it in 1943 as the Aqua-Lung.

This simple device fundamentally altered diving and revolutionized man's perception of the planet by offering the opportunity for extensive underwater investigation. Although the Aqua-Lung was an open circuit arrangement, meaning that bubbles were emitted into the water, leaving a telltale trail on the surface, it was soon adapted to military purposes,

both in its original form and "closed circuit," to make the approach of underwater swimmers virtually undetectable.

Without their ability to travel like fish underneath the surface of the sea, U.S. Navy SEALs would simply not be SEALs.

See also COUSTEAU, JACQUES-YVES; DIVING, HISTORY OF.

area of operations (AO)

A specific zone or sector in which a SEAL unit is assigned to operate within a theater of war or region of conflict is called an area of operations, or an AO. AOs are more commonly assigned during periods of actual war or hostilities, rarely during limited missions against pinpoint targets. SEALs serving in the Vietnam War, for example, were assigned by teams, platoons, or squads to work in particular tracts of territory within the war zone, generally in the swamp-studded and river-laced Mekong Delta.

The size of an AO depends upon the nature of the terrain, the size of the operating force, the types of missions involved, enemy strength, and other factors. It can be hundreds of square miles in size, or it can be restricted to square yards and include a time limit. Often, several friendly forces will be working the same AO, requiring methods of command and control. The U.S. Army's Ninth Infantry Division, for example, worked an AO in the Mekong Delta that included the U-Minh Forest and the My Tho River. Also working the same AO were SEALs, riverine forces, and Army Special Forces.

An AO can be compared to a patrolling district for an urban police department. District squad cars are responsible for crime fighting within those boundaries.

The U.S. Naval Special Warfare Command (SPECWARCOM), the parent headquarters for all Naval Special Operations, has divided the globe into areas of interest for its lower echelons, which include SEALs, special boat teams (SBTs), and SEAL delivery vehicle teams (SDVTs). In effect, potential AOs have already been carved out on a global scale.

SPECWARCOM has control of two special warfare groups, Groups One and Two. Each of these groups include three SEAL teams, a special boat squadron, and an SDVT. Special Warfare Group One, based in Coronado, California, is responsible for deploying forces to the Pacific, the Persian Gulf, and around the globe to Africa's east coast. Group Two, headquartered at Little Creek, Virginia, on the East Coast, is responsible for operations in and around the Atlantic, Europe, and Latin America, from the Baltics to Cape Horn.

In addition, each group has developed forward bases closer to potential hot spots and has assigned elements to them, called naval special warfare units (NSWUs). They are scattered over the world ready to reorganize into a naval special warfare task group and its units. Two SWUs serve the European Command, from bases in Spain and Scotland. One operates out of Guam for the Pacific Command; a fourth serves the Southern Command out of Rodman Naval Station in Panama.

When a hot spot develops, such as the Gulf or Kosovo, SEALs from the appropriate NSWUs may be assigned AOs within the hostile zone to carry out operations.

See also NAVAL SPECIAL WARFARE; NAVAL SPECIAL WARFARE GROUPS; ORGANIZATIONAL STRUCTURE, SPECIAL OPERATIONS; U.S. NAVY SPECIAL WARFARE COMMAND.

arm and hand signals

Due to the necessity for maintaining noise and light discipline during a combat mission, SEALs and other combat forces develop SOPs (standard operating procedures) for the use of arm and hand signals for communication. For example, a clenched fist suddenly raised denotes *Danger.* Fingers pointed at the eyes means *Enemy in sight.* A hand descending with palm down warns the rest of the unit to *Take cover.*

Army of the Republic of Vietnam (ARVN)

Although SEALs during the Vietnam War avoided working with South Vietnamese forces as much as possible, they were inevitably assigned to operate with indigenous troops from time to time. Some of these warriors were very good, especially the Vietnamese SEALs and PRUs (provincial reconnaissance units), with whom SEALs had most

association. These, however, were the exception rather than the rule. In general, American forces, including the SEALs, had a very low opinion of their Vietnamese allies. They felt that if the ARVN had been doing its job, there would have been no need to call in Uncle Sam.

"Our men would go out into the field and do the ARVN's fighting for them," recalls SEAL Rudy Boesch. "They were more than happy to let us go out and get shot at rather than them. A lot of friction developed between our forces and theirs because of these things."

In 1965, the South's armed forces—which included the army, marines, air force, navy, regional and provincial forces, police and civilian irregular defence groups (CIDG), commonly lumped together as the Army of the Republic of Vietnam (ARVN)—totaled nearly 675,000 men. That was over 30 percent of South Vietnam's adult and almost-adult male population. It was expected that this massive armed force, which outnumbered enemy Viet Cong and NVA (North Vietnamese army) in the South by nearly a three-to-one margin, would triumph handily. That was not quite how it occurred. Time after time, much smaller enemy units soundly defeated the ARVN.

The battle at Ap Bac in January 1963 helped establish the pattern. An entire ARVN division, some 10,000 soldiers, was hammered by just three VC companies, 350 men, less than 65 kilometers from Saigon. The ARVN lost 61 dead, 100 wounded, to three confirmed enemy kills.

Vietnamese soldiers, most of whom were illiterate or semiliterate peasant farmers, were drafted into the military for three-year hitches. Three years didn't mean *three years;* it meant for the *duration,* until the war ended. An ARVN soldier received about eight dollars a month in pay, existed on a poor fare of rice, dried fish, and vegetable soup, and rarely received furloughs or R&R (rest and recuperation) leave. He spent most of his time in the field in two to three-month stretches.

Leadership was not only poor but corrupt. In the officer corps, promotion depended upon whom you knew or could bribe, not upon combat performance. Middle-ranking officers sold drugs and prostitutes to American GIs, while local warlords stole rice that should have gone to feed troops.

The average ARVN, understandably, simply did not invest his heart and soul in the war. As in any

SEALs had mixed feelings about the fighting ability of the ARVN. Here, a platoon of ARVN prepare for an operation. (Charles W. Sasser)

civil war, families were torn apart geographically and ideologically. An ARVN officer might be fighting against a VC cadre who was his uncle, cousin, or brother. Opposing sides often leaked word of their operations to each other.

"What happens," explains Drew Dix, who was a civilian senior adviser for the Civil Operations and Revolutionary Development Support Pacification Program, "is that Charlie [the enemy] stages an op. Marvin [ARVN soldier] goes out to hit him, and a lot of shots get fired, but no one is hit. Then they both withdraw and go home for the night."

While the South Vietnamese soldiers might have been grateful to the Americans for doing their fighting for them, they were also envious and resentful. Marvin's wife might have turned "hooch girl" for an American colonel, his sister might have started working as a good-time bar girl, and his children begging or peddling "Coke-Cola, GI?" Traitors and turncoats were common on both sides of the Vietnamese lines. Desertion rates in the ARVN were appallingly high. There were over 115,000 ARVN

desertions in 1966, more than one in every five men then serving in the armed forces.

Some elite ARVN units, like the Rangers, Airborne, and the Lien Doc Nguoi Nhai (LDNN, equivalent to the U.S. Navy SEALs), were different, being better paid, better housed, and possessing a macho mentality, but they made up less than 5 percent of the South's forces. It was with these select troops that U.S. SEALs operated when they were required to work with the Vietnamese.

SEALs "advised" both PRUs and LDNN. PRU units in particular were made up of tough mercenaries ranging from VC *chieu hois* (turncoats) to convicted robbers and even killers. However, they provided excellent translation services, were frequently exceptionally loyal to their American SEALs, and often exhibited a high degree of combat discipline. The only Vietnamese to be awarded a U.S. Navy Cross during the war was a PRU interpreter, Nguyen Van Kiet, who accompanied SEAL Tom Norris deep behind enemy lines to rescue a downed pilot in Quang Tri Province.

Some of the missions that SEALs and their Vietnamese counterparts conducted were locating and destroying arms dumps and food caches, reconnaissance and rescue forays, ambushes, raids on enemy weak points, prisoner snatches, and assassinations of VC tax collectors. SEALs helped select and train both PRU and LDNN units.

See also LIEN DOC NGUOI NHAI (LDNN); NORRIS, THOMAS R.; PROVINCIAL RECONNAISSANCE UNITS (PRUS).

attack board

Also called a "Compass Board," the attack board is a simple board, often constructed of plastic, to which is attached a compass, depth gauge, and watch. It is used as a basic navigational tool for SEALs during subsurface combat swims.

B

Bailey, Larry W. (b.1939)

Reared on a little farm in east Texas between Marshall and Longview, Larry W. Bailey enlisted in the U.S. Navy in 1962, completed Officer Candidate School, and served a hitch on destroyers before volunteering for UDT/SEAL training in 1963. Four years later, he was second officer of SEAL Team Two, Second Platoon, when it became the first American combat unit of any kind assigned to operate in the Mekong Delta of South Vietnam. SEAL Team One, from the West Coast, was already working in the Rung Sat Special Zone, but the Rung Sat Forest was not properly in the delta.

"My experience is," says Bailey, who later commanded the BUD/S (Basic Underwater Demolition/ SEAL) training center at Coronado, California, and retired with the rank of captain, "every time somebody dies [killed in the SEALs], somebody has screwed up. We don't charge enemy trenches. People get killed because that's their job. Ten percent of your troops going over the berm, across the barbed wire, are going to get killed, actually, demonstrably. We don't play that kind of game. Take this with a grain of salt, but every SEAL that got killed, that I

know of, got killed unnecessarily because somebody screwed up. That doesn't say anything bad about SEALs. It says we are so damn good we are the only ones who can get ourselves killed, in a perverse sort of way."

Bailey was an officer with a strong interest in engineering. Shortly after his arrival in Vietnam, he and two other SEALs, Lt. Jack "Blackjack" Macione and Petty Officer Bob Gallagher began tinkering with the trihulled fiberglass patrol boats sent over to run the rivers, swamps, and marshes of the delta. Team Two had four of the boats, each powered by twin 100 hp Mercury outboards. They were fast, light boats, but not adequate for combat.

The three SEALs armored the boats to withstand .30-caliber fire. They built 10 weapons stations into the hull to allow the mounting of .50-caliber and M60 machine guns and 40 mm Honeywell grenade launchers. The twin Mercurys pushed the armored trihull at 30 knots, even carrying a six-man fire team and a load of ammunition. This was the first specialized SEAL combat boat, dubbed STAB (SEAL team assault boat). After Vietnam, it was replaced with other specialized boats.

While in Vietnam, Bailey was also involved in one of the more controversial events in the history of the SEALs. It occurred during a routine ambush on the night of March 13, 1967. Ens. Richard Marcinko, later made famous by his *Rogue Warrior* books, written with John Weisman, commanded Squad Two-Bravo, which was placed ashore to set up an ambush of a known VC transit point on the Bassac River. Bailey and the other SEALs in an armored LCM-8 (known as a "Mike boat") and a STAB continued downriver for a mile or so to provide backup and await the outcome of the ambush. This was to be Team Two's first land combat operation.

While waiting, Bailey was attracted to a blip on the Mike boat's radar screen, indicating a craft of some size churning upriver. Bailey, along with Bill Bruhmuller and coxswain Ron Fox, jumped into the STAB and gave chase. The unidentified boat turned out to be friendly, a little Vietnamese mini-destroyer left over from the French.

In the meantime, Marcinko's ambush was triggered by what he later described in *Rogue Warrior* as "One Vietnamese in black pajamas, no hat, no visible gun; an Asian gondolier." The ambush killed the gondolier, then, according to Marcinko, took fire from another source. "We moved down the bank, shouting for covering fire as we slithered, ducked and rolled our way through the jungle underbrush, as VC bullets sliced the leaves just over our heads or dug divots too close for comfort as we scrambled toward the STAB."

The STAB, Marcinko later charged, wasn't where it was supposed to be. Marcinko accused Bailey of failing to support his squad when it got in trouble, of chasing sampans instead of minding business. In effect, he accused Bailey of being a coward, an unforgivable offense in the SEALs.

On the other side of the story, none of the other SEALs recalls the furious firefight described by Marcinko. Bailey admits that he indeed chased the minidestroyer, but he points out that it was going upriver and therefore brought him nearer to Marcinko's position than he had been at the original anchor point.

Bailey, Bruhmuller, and Fox in the STAB heard the rattle of small-arms fire as Marcinko's squad killed the sampan driver. Bailey waited for the emergency-extraction signal, the shooting of a little blue-green pencil flare. None came. He attempted

repeatedly to raise Marcinko on the radio; the ambush RTO (radiotelephone operator) later noticed that he had turned off his radio.

Finally, Bailey nosed toward shore in the darkness, not knowing what to expect, and beached the STAB. Everything was quiet. There was no firefight. Bailey and Bruhmuller jumped ashore and went into the jungle about twenty meters, where they ran into one of the ambush SEALs. The ambush team, unscathed, climbed into the STAB.

Although other SEALs present during this incident support Bailey's account of events, Marcinko's accusation has continued to cause controversy.

See also SEAL TEAM ASSAULT BOAT (STAB).

banana clip

The "banana clip" is more correctly termed a banana *magazine,* and even more precisely an extension of the weapon's own intrinsic magazine. A *clip* is a spring steel frame holding a number of cartridges, always the number required to fill the weapon; it is used for loading cartridges directly into the weapon's magazine. The U.S. M-I Garand rifle uses a clip. A magazine, on the other hand, is a thin-walled aluminum box that serves as a reservoir for weapons, like the M16, which do not have their own magazines.

A spring inside the magazine pushes the cartridges into the weapon's chamber as each is fired and the casings are discarded through the ejection port. The term "banana clip" came into common use with the introduction of the M16 rifle during the Vietnam War. The original magazine contained 20 5.56 mm cartridges and was in the shape of a rectangular flattened box. The 30-round magazine was introduced late in the war to increase firepower. Because of the shape of the cartridges, the diameter of the cases being greater than that of the bullets, the increased-capacity magazine was slightly curved toward the bullet, in order to contain the extra cartridges and feed them properly. The shape is rather like that of a banana.

SEALs on mission often tape banana clips together in opposing directions. Once the magazine in the weapon is expended, it can be released and the other magazine immediately reversed and inserted into the weapon, greatly speeding up reloading. The process takes less than one second, thus effectively doubling firepower from 30 rounds to 60 rounds.

See also M16 RIFLE.

"barndance cards"

The first SEAL platoons to arrive in-country for the Vietnam War were from the West Coast's SEAL Team One. They operated in the Rung Sat Special Zone of IV Corps, in the area around Saigon. Lt. James Barnes, who commanded a Team One detachment in Vietnam in 1966, made a lasting contribution to the wartime SEAL structure when he initiated what became known as "barndance cards."

A barndance card was a brief report, like an after-action report, written at the conclusion of each combat mission. It summarized where the mission had occurred, who had participated, what if anything had happened, any intelligence garnered, such as enemy strength, tactics, location, or anything else that might prove helpful to subsequent SEAL missions into the same area. It often included such practical tips as "Remove leeches with mosquito repellant."

The cards served as guides to other SEALs, preserved valuable intelligence information, recorded and preserved SEAL combat history, and were even studied back at the Coronado training center in California.

basic load

Unlike conventional military forces, which are required to equip themselves uniformly, from the clothing they wear to the weapons they carry, the special operations community has a great deal of leeway in selecting both clothing and equipment. In Vietnam, the well-dressed SEAL sometimes wore blue jeans, sneakers, and a "go-rag" around his head. Flight suits are treasured, especially where clothing must be worn over wetsuits. Occasionally, civilian attire is required, as when Lt. Cdr. Roy Boehm was sent undercover to the Dominican Republic on an assassination mission. The mere appearance of a squad of combat SEALs may give conventional officers coronaries.

The same discretion applies to SEAL weapons. Whereas the regular military is issued either the M9 Beretta 9 mm pistol—or, more rarely now, the Colt .45 M1911—as sidearms, SEALs can be seen with Sig-Sauers, Browning HPs, or even a Mark 22 "Hush Puppy."

Even with such latitude in equipment, however, SEALs have developed through experience a fairly standard collection of gear to serve all sorts of needs—a "basic load." A SEAL preparing for a mission thinks of his equipment in three separate groups, each group designed to help him survive and continue to fight, independently of the other two.

The *first line* of his basic load is formed with rudimentary survival in mind, in the event he loses everything else. This includes his personal weapon, one magazine of ammunition, and his clothing—uniform, hat, boots, socks, scarf, gloves, articles he will wear during the entire operation. Other critical first-line items, either worn or stuffed into his pockets, are a map, compass, watch, money (both U.S. and local currency), aircraft-signaling panel and mirror, pocket knife, condoms for waterproofing weapons and documents, parachute suspension line, a small emergency medical kit, a few Power Bars or candy bars, flashlight, matches, nylon line, and whatever else he considers necessary or useful. The idea is that with these fundamental provisions, coupled with his training, he should be able to survive while following his escape and evasion (E&E) plan.

His *second line* goes either into his combat vest or LBE (load-bearing equipment), whichever he prefers to wear. His LBE or combat vest contains extra ammunition and magazines, grenades, at least a day's food rations, insect repellant if needed, strobe light with suitable filters, canteen of water and water purification tablets, a battle dressing, a knife, a snap link, plastic tie-wraps for handcuffing prisoners or chance contacts, a hand radio, GPS receiver, and whatever else he considers useful.

The *third line* of his basic load contains specialty and comfort items in his combat rucksack. If he's a radioman, he will carry his radio, batteries, antenna, and mikes. If a medic, his ruck may bulge with a complete field medical kit, to include IVs, airways, suture kit, chest drains, and perhaps a minor surgery pack. In the ruck will also be carried such mission-essential materials as explosives,

Claymore mines, detonating cord, wire cutters, binoculars, entrenching tool, rescue radio, night-vision goggles, and whatever else may be required to complete the mission.

If there is room left over, he may use it for comfort items such as extra food, water, poncho and liner, a ground sheet, and spare socks and clothing. Too often, however, SEALs live by the old phrase, "Travel light and freeze at night," although "light" may not appropriately describe a basic load. A SEAL team may be inserted into an area with each man carrying a hundred pounds or more.

The basic load method and organization make sense. If the SEAL must ditch his ruck or even his LBE, he can still escape and evade with only his first-line equipment.

Basic Underwater Demolition/SEAL (BUD/S) training

Above the door of the training quadrangle at the Naval Special Warfare Center on the Naval Amphibious Base at Coronado, California, hangs a wooden plaque embellished with two carved SEALs. One is diving, the other is standing. The legend states, *The More You Sweat in Peace, The Less You Bleed in War.* Elsewhere on the base, where Basic Underwater Demolition/SEAL (BUD/S) training is conducted, fronting U.S. 75 near San Diego and backed by the Pacific Ocean, another sign hangs on the Philip H. Bucklew Building, headquarters for Special Warfare: *The Only Easy Day Was Yesterday.*

Together, they state the philosophy of SEAL training, unquestionably the most demanding, challenging, and brutal learning experience any military man can have. It is here that machinists, boatswain's mates, and men of other navy ratings are forged into elite underwater warriors. SEAL successes in combat and combat-related missions since the unit was formed in 1962 are no accident. The training is designed to test a man physically and mentally, to weed out those who don't belong, who can't "hang in there." The survivors are men who can be counted on when the going gets tough and dangerous. Above all, a SEAL never quits. SEALs passionately hate quitters.

"The business we are in is inherently dangerous, combat or not," says Cdr. Gary Stubblefield, a

SEAL. "If you take away the risk that goes with the training, you take away the mental stress that you put people under to know how they'll respond in the real world, in actual combat. . . . You have to be sure that they will stick with you when the going gets tough."

SEAL training programs were adapted largely from the experience and training of World War II underwater demolition teams (UDTs) and were extensively modified through unabashed borrowing from training courses developed by the U.S. Army Special Forces (the Green Berets). One of the ideas retained in BUD/S from early UDT days was that of Draper Kauffman, who believed a man could put forth 10 times as much physical effort as he thinks he can if he has the proper spirit, training, and indoctrination. Since combat is the toughest experience there is, training has to be tough.

Originally, SEAL Team One and Two each conducted its own training. UDT was a separate unit. In 1983, UDT and SEAL missions were unified under one concept, and UDT merged into the SEALs. Training is now conducted at the single training center in Coronado.

The training center is built around a courtyard known as "the Grinder." At one corner of the Grinder stands a post upon which is mounted a brass "quitting bell," an idea that originated with the West Coast team. A trainee could quit—or DOR (drop on request), as it is now called—at any time, simply by ringing the bell, no questions asked. A trainee on the East Coast had only to remove his helmet to end his training. Now, in order to quit, the trainee stands on green-painted frog's footprints, rings the bell three times, says "I quit"—and he's out of there. His helmet liner is placed in formation next to the bell with those of all the others who have quit that particular class before him. Week by week, the line of helmets grows longer. It literally blossoms during "Hell Week."

In the old days, a man who flunked any portion of the course was dropped and sent back to the fleet. Today, he can be "rolled over," dropped for injury or an area of unsatisfactory performance and take up with the following class. As few as 5 percent of those who start a particular class finish with it.

The average dropout rate, those who start to become SEALs but never make it, is about 60 percent. Six out of 10 change their minds, lose heart in

The BUD/S training course is the toughest training in the U.S. military, as these recruit UDT "tadpoles" are discovering while explosives go off around them. (U.S. Navy)

the face of the challenges and DOR, or simply fail. Not a single man completed Class 78; they *all* failed or quit.

"Throughout training I kept having the thought—Well, all they can do is kill me. It seemed to help," says SEAL Forrest Dearborn Hedden, Class 29.

The Naval Special Warfare Center runs around eight BUD/S a year, in addition to teaching 24 other scheduled classes in special operations, such as "Special Warfare Craft Crewman" and "Closed-Circuit Diving Procedures." Because the navy spends in excess of $80,000 to make a single SEAL, the weeding-out process begins well before BUD/S. Prospective SEALs, all volunteers, must first confront and face a rigorous screening process, which includes physical, intelligence, and attitude challenges.

Part of the modern screening process is a BUD/S indoctrination course, a five-day pre-BUD/S program to give the applicants a taste of what to expect. Of the 1,510 sailors who took the screening test for

Class 44, only 34 passed it and actually showed up later for training.

In order to qualify to attempt BUD/S, a sailor must: be male and no more than 28 years of age; be in good enough physical condition to pass the fitness test, including a swimming test; score high on the military written exam; possess vision correctable to 20/20 without color blindness; come from specified occupational ratings; obtain the endorsement of his commander; and have plenty of time remaining on his enlistment.

The entire focus of the training is on teamwork. From the beginning, the "tadpoles," as trainees are called (among other things), are taught that life in the teams depends upon your mates. At the same time, each SEAL is expected to be an innovator, a man capable of thinking and operating on his own if necessary. As Lt. Roy Boehm, who formed and led the first SEAL team and selected the first candidates, explains it:

"They had to be more than killers, all muscle and neck and attack-dog mentality. I wanted—*demanded*—creative men who could operate with their brains as well as with their muscles. The UW [unconventional warfare] brand of warfare required men of courage, dedication to duty, sacrifice, personal dexterity, and intelligence. Team and mission must come first. At the same time, they must be individuals, near rogues in fact. Rough men, tough men, who could kick ass and operate outside protocol. *Desirable* undesirables."

There is a sign on the wall of SEAL Team Two headquarters: *Defeat is worse than death. . . . You have to live with defeat.*

Each volunteer for BUD/S is given in advance a "BUD/S Warning Order" informing him of what it takes to complete the course. The course is six months long, divided into three phases, plus an additional three weeks of basic parachute training at the Army Airborne School in Fort Benning, Georgia. Some ratings may also require specialty post-BUD/S training on top of everything else. Navy corpsmen who become SEALs, for example, attend two weeks of Special Operations Technician Training and a 30-week intensive course of instruction in diving medicine and medical skills called 18D (Special Operations Medical Course). Part of that training is at the Fort Bragg school for army Special Forces medics. Only after successfully completing all this will the tadpole, in the phrase of the teams, be "good to go."

Officers and enlisted attend the same BUD/S.

The first phase of BUD/S is basic conditioning, eight weeks of running, swimming, and calisthenics, all administered and received with the SEAL rallying cry of "Hoo-ya!" During this phase, tadpoles run long distances along the beach, which extends far to the south of the training center. They learn to swim distances in the Pacific Ocean, which remains a constant 55 degrees Fahrenheit all year round.

Piled on the beach is a group of wooden telephone poles, each of which weighs several hundred pounds. The logs are part of conditioning and teamwork training, collective exercises intended to build strength and cooperative spirit. "Boat crews" of seven men each must do sit-ups while lying with a log across all their chests, do bench presses with it, and do pushups with their toes on top of the log.

They compete in running races with the logs on their shoulders, at distances up to 14 miles. One drill requires the boat teams to race across the sand dunes, drop the log into the surf, flop down in the water themselves, get up, pick up the log, and race back across the dunes to the finishing line. A shirker, complainer, or poor performer may earn his whole crew a session with Old Misery—a 300-pound monster log emblazoned with the taunt *Misery Loves Company*. All are punished for the failings of one. The lesson to be learned is that everything a member of the team does or does not do affects everyone.

The same exercises are carried out with an IBS (Inflatable Boat, Small) or with a combat rubber raiding craft (CRRC). It weighs 289 pounds, is 12 feet long and six feet wide, and is designed to carry seven men with 1,000 pounds of gear. The team must carry it everywhere, keeping it inflated and in good condition. One man of the boat team, day or night, must guard the boat, to protect it against sneaky instructors. Sometimes during boat drills, a boat is filled with water, and the crew must carry it on their heads. An instructor may jump into the boat for added avoirdupois.

The obstacle course at Coronado is one of the most demanding of its kind. It includes a 50-foot stand with climbing ropes, a 60-foot net climb, pole stumps, walls, water swings, barbed wire, and other obstacles. Tadpoles go through the course again and again to build up strength, endurance, and confidence.

Trainees in phase one also attend classes in everything from hydrographics to first aid and are required to pass written tests. Inattentiveness or falling asleep in class may earn a special treat—"sandblasting." The sinner must sit at the edge of the ocean prior to a run and hold open his trousers legs to let the surf blast sand all the way up to his crotch. Then he gets up to make the run.

The first month of phase one leads to "Hell Week," or "Motivation Week," the most dreaded, demanded, celebrated, despised, and revered period of the entire course. It begins one minute after midnight and lasts for six days. It begins with shouting instructors turning on the barracks lights, to the accompaniment of grenade explosions and machine-gun fire.

During that single week, in which trainees will receive a maximum of four to six hours of sleep in all, they are driven past exhaustion into a state of pure animal survival, forced to make physical and mental exertions they never believed possible. The purpose is to instill in the candidates a memory of the incidents and a strong feeling of association with the system. They might hate all of it, but those who survive draw strength and confidence from having conquered it. During this period, the brass bell accompanies the tadpoles everywhere, reminding them that all they have to do to return to clean sheets and hot-and-cold running water is to step up and ring the bell. Many at this point find they do not possess the "right stuff."

Hell Week is based on combat experiences. A CRRC race may be planned to coincide with a tide change, so that when the teams come paddling in they find the tide pushing them back out. It may take hours to negotiate the last few hundred yards and reach the beach, after which they may have to run miles with the boats on top of their helmets or perform some impossible task, such as the caterpillar race. In this maneuver the entire team sits in a line, links arms and legs, and then is ordered to move backward as a unit.

Sleep-deprivation symptoms, such as hallucinations, are common. "While paddling late at night, we all saw weird things," recalled one SEAL. "I saw a train cutting across our path, and it was a pretty pink train, too." Hell Week culminates with maneuvers in the mud pits, followed by an actual beach landing with barbed-wire obstacles, gunfire, and half-pound blocks of TNT exploding, re-creating as nearly as possible the noise and confusion of battle.

Three more weeks of basic training confront the ragged survivors of the U.S. military's most demanding week. After that, the much-decimated class moves into the second phase of training.

The second phase of BUD/S, seven weeks in length, is diving. During this phase, physical training and classwork continue. Times for completing the various evolutions are cut: a two-mile ocean swim, down from 90 minutes to 75 minutes; a four-mile run reduced from 32 minutes to 31; the obstacle course must be run in 12 minutes instead of 15. Times will be cut yet again during the third phase.

This third phase is devoted almost exclusively to combat SCUBA and basic combat-swimmer skills, starting with "drownproofing." Prospective SEALs are tossed into a pool wearing full uniforms and boots. They must float face down for an hour.

Days and nights are filled with long-distance underwater compass swims, practice attacks on ships, submarine operations, and hydrographic reconnaissance. A real gut buster of a swim occurs when the tadpoles are tossed into Wilson Cove, in the San Clemente Islands, shortly after breakfast one morning. They are required to swim to Northwest Harbor, a distance of only five miles; however, the swimmers must fight the current all the way. The only rules are not to lose your buddy and to arrive before dark.

San Clemente Island, primarily a naval gunnery range, populated by wild goats and hogs, lies roughly 75 miles off the coast of California. It is here that the remaining members of the class end 10 weeks of the third and final phase of BUD/S training by learning and practicing land warfare, with a three-week final battery of practical exercises in everything they've learned. The attrition rate by now may be as high as 80 percent.

All techniques previously learned are applied, along with new skills in land navigation, small-unit tactics, patrolling, raids and ambushes, military land and underwater explosives, and weapons training. Students are taught how to move surreptitiously behind enemy lines, perhaps for days, carrying everything they need to sustain themselves and to fight effectively; how to insert and extract from an operation; how to make "kitchen table explosives" from readily available materials, such as guano and diesel oil; and any number of other techniques they may someday have to use in fighting an unconventional war.

Firing live ammo on the range, they cement the trust they have built up in each other over the past weeks and months. One three-man group lies on the ground behind a downed telephone pole pouring fire onto an "enemy" downrange. A second unit positions itself behind and to one side of the first group. On command, the lead SEALs jump up and fold back to the rear, in a "shoot and maneuver" movement, while the supporting element lays down covering fire. Bullets zing past only feet away. This is the way it would really happen in combat, except that the enemy would also be shooting.

This phase marks the end of BUD/S.

"Survival instincts carried us all through, and I relied on mine 100 percent," explains SEAL Michael J. Walsh. "Some men got through BUD/S out of pure determination, as in my case. Others by hatred, and some. . . . Well, I still haven't figured out how they made it, but they did. The process is extreme, and some consider it cruel, but no man would make it any less than it is." Say what you will about the BUD/S training, the program works. It turns out what are undoubtedly the best commandos and special operations specialists the world has ever seen.

After graduation, the remaining members of the class are sent off to parachute school at Fort Benning, then to their specialized post-BUD/S training. They are then assigned to SEAL teams for a six-month probationary period. If they survive probation, they go before a board that evaluates their qualifications. Only after they are "boarded" successfully will they be able to wear the Naval Special Warfare Command insignia, the trident, and belong to the most exclusive society in the world's military.

See also AIRBORNE; BOEHM, ROY; KAUFFMAN, DRAPER L; UNDERWATER DEMOLITION TEAMS (UDTS).

battle dress uniform (BDU)

The standard military work, utility, and battle uniform issued to U.S. and NATO (North Atlantic Treaty Organization) troops began appearing during the Vietnam War to phase out the traditional green GI fatigues. Army, marines, air force, and navy have all adopted the battle dress uniform (BDU) for combat. Most sailors continue to wear dungarees, but SEALs have gone almost exclusively with BDUs.

Although BDUs are manufactured in several different patterns and colors, the issue for U.S. troops comes in two basic patterns—four-color "woodland camouflage," predominately green, brown, and black; and "desert camouflage," of either three or six varying hues of brown, loam, and sand. The uniforms are designed to be loose fitting, even baggy, as a tight fit reduces air flow needed for ventilation and cooling.

The uniform comes in four basic items, not including underwear, belt, socks, and boots. These items are the BDU cap, shirt, trousers, and cold-weather coat. All are made of wind-resistant, ripstop nylon and cotton. The shirt is a single-breasted "bush type" design with a back yoke, collar, and four-patch bellows-type pockets with flaps, two on the breast and two below them. The trousers contain four standard pockets, two leg bellows-type pockets, adjustable straps at the waist, and leg hem draw cords for "blousing." Reinforcement patches have been added to the elbows, seat, and knees. The cold-weather coat in matching pattern is lined, hip-length with a bi-swing back, convertible stand-up collar with a concealed hood, and slide-fastened front closure, with two breast and two lower pockets.

Other items of apparel, such as the black raincoat, parka, poncho, and the like may be added to this basic uniform as the need arises.

All insignia are subdued, including name tags, unit patches, and either collar pin-on rank or sew-on rank tabs. When SEALs go on missions, they usually wear no insignia. Clandestine operations may require "plausible deniability," which means that the United States would disavow all knowledge of the unit should its members be captured or killed. Nothing the SEALs wear or carry, therefore, must identify their nationality.

See also BASIC LOAD.

Bay of Pigs

If any single historical event thrust America into accepting the concept of limited unconventional warfare, it was Fidel Castro's takeover of Cuba. The so-called cold war had blossomed fully, along with its companion "domino theory." According to this theory, one country after another would fall to communism until the United States stood alone and isolated in a hostile world. In expanding the U.S. Army Special Forces, the Pentagon at least acknowledged the value of covert and overt guerrilla-type operations in stopping the Third World dominos from falling. Cuba provided a test of wills between communism and the free world.

Plots to invade Cuba began almost as soon as Castro swept out of the Sierra Maestra to take over Havana and admitted that he was a communist. Cuban exile organizations vowing to topple the island's bearded *jefe* sprouted like mushrooms in Florida, only 90 miles from the Cuban coast. Vice President Richard M. Nixon and the CIA fanned the invasion conspiracy. When John F. Kennedy assumed office in 1961, the government's top-secret "5412 Committee" had already conceived a plot for invading the island nation. The plan called for exile forces to establish a beachhead on Cuban soil; behind them a Cuban government-in-exile would broadcast to the world as a government-in-arms. Under international law, the United States would then have an excuse to supply and reinforce the invaders.

News broke in American and Mexican newspapers shortly after New Year's Day 1961 that a U.S.-sponsored attack force known as Brigade 2506 was training on a coffee plantation and refurbished airstrip near Retalhuleu in the mountains of southern Guatemala. Word also leaked out that American underwater demolition teams (UDTs) and Army Special Forces would be involved in the invasion of Cuba.

In March 1961, Lt. (j.g.) Roy Boehm, then operations officer for UDT-21, was assigned as senior instructor in training and infiltrating a band of 14 Cuban revolutionaries into their home island. He linked up with the Cubans in Panama Beach, Florida, and flew with them in a CIA-chartered DC-3 to a secret training camp in Virginia. There training commenced immediately in escape and evasion, survival, communications, and demolitions. That no underwater procedures were taught showed how deeply frogmen had ventured into land-based warfare even then.

The Cubans were ready to go by the first week of April. CIA agents briefed the infiltrators on their missions. They would be blowing up roads, bridges, and railroads in support of the invasion.

An ex-UDT frogman turned CIA spook, "Smarty Marty" Martinez, flew with Boehm and the guerrillas to the U.S. base at Guantanamo Bay, on Cuba's southeastern coast. A couple of days later they were guided to an APD assault transport that sailed them under cover of darkness into the Caribbean off the island's long southern coast. Each of the 14 Cubans was armed with an M14 rifle and carried a backpack containing dynamite, C-4 plastique explosives, radio, and survival gear. They were divided into teams and sent ashore in rubber boats at various points along the coast, including one team at an inlet known as the Bay of Pigs.

Castro's Cuban forces take prisoners during the failed Bay of Pigs invasion by anti-Castro forces in 1961. (AP)

Boehm and Martinez did not accompany them. "Keep your sorry ass off Cuban soil," UDT-21 skipper Lt. Cdr. Bill Hamilton warned Boehm. "I don't give a damn what happens down there. All Khrushchev needs to start an international incident is to capture a U.S. personnel inside Cuba."

At dawn on Saturday, April 15, 1961, six American-built B-26 bombers flown by Cuban exiles struck each of three Cuban airfields of Castro's small air force. Fidel, however, had anticipated an attack and dispersed his planes. He still possessed a formidable force to use against invaders. President Kennedy scrubbed further air attacks that would have crippled Castro's defensive capabilities, but he gave his approval for the invasion.

The invasion brigade of 1,453 soldiers had been trained and equipped with four-deuce (4.2-inch) mortars, 75 mm recoilless rifles, bazookas, surplus M1 rifles from World War II, machine guns, pistols, and five M-45 Sherman tanks. To transport the assault troops with this vast weapons stockpile to Cuban soil, the CIA leased a rundown six-ship freighter fleet, to which were added nine landing craft obtained through the Pentagon.

Invasion plans had called for bombers to knock out the enemy's air force, which had not been done, after which a rebel paratrooper battalion would drop onto Santa Clara to secure the airfield there and cut the island in half. Maritime feints would then distract Castro while the main seaborne thrust was made against Trinidad, on the southern coast. The brigade would march east and west off the beachhead toward Havana and Santiago, picking up local strength as it went. Castro's 200,000-man army would be caught by surprise and conquered.

During the final days, however, the CIA changed the landing site from the sandy beaches of Trinidad to the Bay of Pigs, more than 100 miles farther east along the southern coast. CIA intelligence showed the area to be a sparsely populated stretch of territory isolated by the treacherous Zapata Swamps. It was determined that since there was no rapid communications between the Bay of Pigs and Havana, the invaders could land, capture the airfield at Giron, and begin landing and flying in supplies before Castro realized what was happening.

The rebels were still under the impression that American fighter planes would cover the invasion while a U.S. naval task force stood ready to help the government-in-exile. Instead, JFK had not only withheld follow-up strikes against Castro's airfields but reneged on the CIA promise that an "umbrella" of U.S. planes would protect the landing. The navy would perform only picket duty off the coast. JFK was keeping his word to the Alliance for Progress that the United States would not openly involve itself in an invasion, while at the same time breaking his world to the invasion force. The rebels, however, did not know this.

The brigade landing began shortly before dawn on April 17. By six A.M., even while the invasion fleet was still off-loading infantry and equipment, Castro's troops and aircraft were in full counterattack against Brigade 2506. JFK's ill-advised decision not to provide U.S. air cover, coupled with his not permitting follow-up strikes on enemy airfields, exposed the invasion to disaster. By midnight, Fidel and 20,000 soldiers had the invaders trapped on the beaches and were squeezing them into tighter and tighter perimeters. Tanks and infantry battered the brigade with artillery fire for 48 straight hours. Russian-made Stalin tanks rumbled against the dug-in rebels.

Abandoned by the United States, surrounded by a force ten times larger, pounded by artillery and fighter bombers, pushed back to the beaches and swamps, out of ammunition, the command broke into smaller groups, which tried to escape however they could. "Am destroying all equipment and communications," the invasion com-mander, Pepe San Roman, radioed in a final message. "I have nothing left to fight with. Am taking to the woods."

Brigade 2506 lost 120 men killed in combat. Castro eventually captured 1,180 survivors. Out of the defeat and the U.S. refusal to aid the rebels grew a communist perception that the United States might no longer possess the moral courage to honor its commitments. Out of this presumption grew the Berlin Wall, the communist intervention in the Dominican Republic, guerrilla warfare in Latin America, the Cuban missile crisis of 1962, and, arguably, the Vietnam War.

Out of the Bay of Pigs too, arising from the memory of those bloody beaches, sprang a special unit to wage combat cold war–style with a ferocity, deadly intent, and skill that had rarely been seen. Cuba and the Bay of Pigs changed the course of American military history.

On May 25, 1961, five weeks after the Bay of Pigs fiasco, President Kennedy addressed a joint session of Congress. He called for a major restructuring of the nation's military to pull it back from sole reliance on nuclear weapons.

"I am directing the secretary of defense to expand rapidly and substantially, in cooperation with our allies," he said, "the orientation of existing forces for the conduct of non-nuclear war, paramilitary operations and sub-limited or unconventional war. In addition, our special forces and unconventional warfare units will be increased and reoriented."

Lt. Cdr. Bill Hamilton immediately fired off a letter to the Chief of Naval Operations in which he proposed creating a naval commando force capable of operations on land and in the air as well as on and underneath the sea.

See also BOEHM, ROY; HAMILTON, WILLIAM H.; SEALS.

beach clearance

The first men ashore on D-day, June 6, 1944, were from the naval combat demolition units (NCDUs), whose nasty chore it was to destroy the obstacles implanted by the Nazis along the Normandy coast of France and thus clear the beach for an amphibious landing. These early "frogmen" had been created specifically to reconnoiter beach landing sites

SEAL George Walsh dives in a Hagensen Pack of demolitions to clear beach obstacles during a clearing exercise. Beginning during World War II with the underwater demolition teams (UDTs), this attire became standard for "frogmen"—swim trunks, flippers, mask, and sheath knife. (U.S. Navy)

and clear them for assault by removing natural or man-made obstacles. Beach-clearing routines developed by the NCDUs and the underwater demolition teams (UDTs) in the Pacific became standard operating procedure and are still taught today, because they work. Today's SEALs still have the beach-clearing mission.

The clearance process normally begins with the CATF (Commander, Amphibious Task Force,) the admiral who will bring the assault elements to the beach. He designates several beaches for study as possible landing sites and directs his staff to begin planning. The most readily available SEAL unit, usually the ARG (amphibious ready group) platoon is tasked with reconnoitering the beach and providing hydrographic survey information.

Depending upon the situation, the recon and survey may be conducted either at night or by day, and either surreptitiously or under the cover of naval guns and close air support. The insertion will normally be from a boat that skims along the water 600 to 1,000 meters off the beach in a high-speed "splash run." One after the other, the swimmers roll out of the boat and into the water. Spreading out, they swim in line abreast. At such distances, especially at night, a man's head bobbing in the waves is essentially invisible.

As the SEAL swimmers move in for the beach reconnaissance, they chart the varying depths of the water with a lead line, recording the results on a plastic slate. This method is still used, although high-tech gear has now simplified the process. They also record reefs, rocks, or other obstacles, whether natural or emplaced by man, all the way to the beach. They note likely lanes for landing and develop a hydrographic survey chart of the offshore, then crawl out of the water to chart the nearshore, foreshore, backshore, and near hinterland. Fortifications such as bunkers, weapons positions, structures, roads, and terrain features, like sea walls, are also noted.

Beach surveys prior to the beginning of the war in the Persian Gulf identified several suitable beaches for landing an invasion force, but SEALs doing the recons discovered they were very well defended by Iraqi units. Other plans therefore had to be made based on this information.

When the recon and survey are completed, the SEALs swim back out to sea, where boats extract them from the water. Again, it is a high-speed operation. The boat, or boats, zoom along the line of waiting SEALs with a rubber sling extended. By forming a crook with his arm and kicking hard just before the boat reaches him, a swimmer snags the sling in his elbow and is plucked into the boat in a slingshot fashion.

After the CATF digests the hydrographic survey results brought back by his SEALs, he selects a landing site. SEALs may then be sent back in to the selected beach to clear it for the passage of boats and landing craft. Normandy, for instance, had been spiked with a formidable array of concrete blocks, "Belgian Gates," steel spears, mines, and barbed wire.

Once again, swimmers insert by boat, but this time they go in with satchel charges of explosives. Each swimmer or team is assigned a particular obstacle, to which is attached a charge. Flank swimmers at either end of the line carry long rolls of detonating cord, which they string from one end of the obstacle line to the other. Shorter lengths of det cord are then run from each obstacle charge to the longer line and attached to it. Once everything is ready, the long line is then double-primed at each end with blasting caps and time fuzes. Each time fuze is touched off with a waterproof fuze lighter. The team forms up quickly and is picked up before the "powder train" is initiated. This arrangement permits all charges to detonate within a fraction of a second of each other.

Once the beach is cleared, the success of the landing depends upon the amphibious force. The SEALs have done their job.

See also BELGIAN GATES; EXPLOSIVES; INSERTION/EXTRACTION; NAVY COMBAT DEMOLITION UNITS (NCDUS); NORMANDY LANDING; UNDERWATER DEMOLITION TEAMS (UDTS).

Beach Jumpers

Organized during World War II, Beach Jumpers were U.S. Navy tactical cover-and-deception units that persist to the modern era. When they were first commissioned in 1943, they trained along with underwater demolition teams (UDTs) for tactical cover, diversionary, and deception missions in support of amphibious landings. Although not in the direct ancestry of Navy SEALs, the Beach Jumpers were part of a broad spectrum of amphibian forces that contributed to the birth of SEALs and navy unconventional warfare.

The concept grew from the experiences of Lt. Douglas Fairbanks, Jr., Hollywood actor turned naval officer. As part of an officer-exchange program with England, he was assigned to work with British admiral Lord Louis Mountbatten's Combined Operations, a commando force. He acquainted himself with training, planning and execution of raiding parties, diversions, and deception operations, and even participated in several cross-Channel harassment raids.

He was subsequently transferred to Virginia Beach, Virginia, where he came under the command of Adm. H. Kent Hewitt, Commander, Amphibious Forces, who was supervising the training of U.S. naval forces in preparation for deployment to North Africa and the Mediterranean. Fairbanks pitched the idea for a similar unit in the U.S. Navy to create diversions for amphibious actions. Hewitt pushed the idea up to Ernest J. King, commander in chief, U.S. Fleet, and Chief of Naval Operations. King issued a secret letter on March 5, 1943 tasking the Vice Chief of Naval Operations with the recruitment of 180 officers and 300 enlisted men for the Beach Jumper program.

The best theory on how the "Beach Jumpers" attained their name comes from the Stevens Institution of Technology, which was working on a navy contract to study the physiological and psychological effects of sound on men in warfare. When a Mr. Harold Burris-Meyer was asked about the purpose of his work, he responded, "To scare the be-Jesus out of the enemy." "Be-Jesus" was abbreviated to "BJ" and is said to have led to the cover name of *Beach Jumpers*.

On March 16, 1943, volunteers reported to the amphibious training base at Camp Bradford, Virginia, and Beach Jumper Unit One was commissioned. Its mission statement read simply, "To assist and support the operating forces in the conduct of Tactical Cover and Deception in Naval Warfare."

The training program was very similar to that offered the naval combat demolition units (NCDUs) and underwater demolition teams (UDTs). Courses included seamanship, small-boat handling, ordnance, demolitions, gunnery, and pyrotechnics. After graduation, BJU-1 was issued 10 63-foot-long air-sea rescue boats (ASRs). They were double-hulled plyboard craft, each powered with twin 750 hp Hall-Scott or Packard engines, crewed by seven men armed with twin .50-caliber machine guns and carrying the team's deception gear.

Window (chatt) rockets, smoke generators, time-delay explosive packs, amplified sound systems, balloons to which radar reflective strips could be attached, and other similar equipment permitted a few boats offshore to simulate an amphibious landing as a diversion while the actual invasion took place somewhere else.

BJU-1's first mission was with Operation Husky, the Allied assault on Sicily. On two nights prior to the landing, on July 10, 1943, and again on July 12, Beach Jumpers conducted a diversion off Cape San Marcos, 100 miles west of the real Husky landing area. Their boats lay a smokescreen, sound-amplified the noise of ship engines, fired guns and rockets, and detonated explosive packs. German shore batteries responded with salvos; the Germans were convinced this was where the invasion would take place and were ill prepared and caught by surprise when the Americans actually landed elsewhere.

Beach Jumper Units One, Three, and Five supported naval operations in Europe with their deception interventions into the summer of 1944. In the Pacific, BJU Six and Seven supported a number of island landings. They were working on deception schemes to support the scheduled British landings on Singapore when the war ended. All Beach Jumpers were deactivated shortly thereafter.

However, on June 18, 1951, BJU One and Two were reactivated as a top secret outfit under the command of Philip H. Bucklew. Throughout the late 1950s and early 1960s, Beach Jumper expertise was employed in revolutionary new ways in the area of manipulative and imitative deception and electronic warfare. Beach Jumpers were also given a secondary mission, "to plan and execute Psychological Operations in support of commands to which it has been assigned."

During the Vietnam War, the Beach Jumpers operated in propaganda leaflet drops and aerial loudspeaker broadcasts. They also conducted monitoring, Soviet signal intelligence (SIGINT), and radio jamming.

On August 1, 1972, the Beach Jumpers were redesignated as Fleet Composite Operational Readiness Group One to emphasize their importance in all areas of naval warfare. Twelve years later, in 1986, the unit was again redesignated into a Pacific unit and an Atlantic unit—Fleet Tactical Deception Group Pacific and Fleet Tactical Deception Group Atlantic, with a new mission statement: "Assisting commanders in planning and conduct of tactical military deception operations."

The Beach Jumper lineage lives on in the planning and execution of the art and science of seaborne deception.

See also BUCKLEW, PHILIP H., II; KING, ERNEST J; OPERATION HUSKY.

beach landing site (BLS)

A BLS is a location selected by SEALs for an across-the-beach operation involving infiltration, exfiltration, or resupply.

Belgian Gates

Navy combat demolition units (NCDUs) dispatched to England to prepare to clear the beaches for the D-day landings on the coast of France received ominous intelligence: Field Marshal Erwin Rommel had himself visited the potential invasion sites and helped plan formidable defenses. These included steel posts driven deep into the sand, connected with barbed wire and covered by machine-gun emplacements, mortars, and big guns.

But of even more concern were the huge metal structures hidden in the water and along the beaches of the entire French coast. These "Belgian Gates" were steel latticework barriers, 10 feet square, and weighing three tons each. They were designed to be propped up by heavy steel braces at low tide on the sand to block access to the beaches.

Fortunately, the NCDUs learned of the Belgian Gates in time to build exact replicas and experiment with blowing them up. They had to be destroyed without littering the beaches with tangles of steel that would form barriers as troublesome as the original obstacles. A young naval lieutenant, Carl P. Hagensen, designed a waterproof bag filled with plastic explosives. A cord at one end of the bag and a hook at the other provided quick attachment to any obstacle.

Using 20-pound charges in the packs, the NCDUs discovered they could blow the braces away from the gates and drop the big frontal latticework pieces flat on the sand. Ten thousand Hagensen Packs were ready for use by the time of the invasion. The NCDUs organized themselves into 13-man gap-assault teams, one team for each of the 16 50-foot-wide gaps to be torn through to the two American beaches, Omaha and Utah.

By noon on D-day, only five of the gaps had been opened. But by evening, 13 had been cleared and marked. The Americans gained a firm foothold on Hitler's "Fortress Europa," but at a high price for the NCDUs. Of the 175 navy men involved in the assault on Omaha Beach, 31 died and 60 were wounded, a casualty rate of 52 percent. Four more were killed and 11 wounded on Utah Beach.

See also BEACH CLEARANCE; GAP ASSAULT TEAMS; HAGENSEN PACK; NAVAL COMBAT DEMOLITION UNITS (NCDUS); NORMANDY LANDING.

bends

Decompression sickness, otherwise known as caisson disease.

See also CAISSON DISEASE.

Beretta M9 9 mm pistol

To a man facing the enemy, the comfort of a sidearm readily available for defense is a solid comfort. Although the issuance of pistols is ordinarily restricted in the military, especially in the navy, they are readily available to SEALs, in a variety of makes and calibers. The Beretta 9 mm M92S has been a standard SEAL issue since 1985.

The antiterrorist SEAL Team Six first picked up the new pistol and had it available for issue in 1982. The adoption of the pistol SEAL-wide was delayed due to a lawsuit by Smith & Wesson declaring unfairness in testing by the Joint Service Small Arms Program (JSSAP). Another test was conducted. Again, the results favored Beretta. In January 1985, it was declared to be the new M9 service sidearm. The rest of the SEAL teams received it for issue.

The Beretta semiautomatic M9 fires a 9 mm Para-bellum (9 × 19 mm) ball M882 190-grain cartridge, fed from a 15-round removable box magazine. Empty, the weapon weighs 1.91 pounds, loaded 2.57 pounds. It is 8.54 inches overall, with a barrel length of 4.94 inches. It fires double action at the rate of 45 rounds per minute, with a muzzle velocity of 1,280 feet per second and a muzzle energy of 445 foot/pounds. The sights are fixed, with an open square-notch rear sight and a front blade.

The Beretta is currently being replaced in the SEAL teams by the Sig-Sauer P226, which also fires 9 mm Parabellum ammunition.

See also SIG-SAUER P226.

Black Berets

Lt. Roy Boehm, who formed, trained, and led the first SEAL team in 1962, unofficially started the custom of SEALs' wearing jaunty black berets as their own distinctive headgear, much as the Army Special Forces had adopted the green beret. At the time, Adm. Horacio Rivero, Chief of Naval Operations (CNO), came out adamantly against SEALs wearing anything other than navy-issue items already in stock.

"We call [sailors] white hats in the navy," he said. "I don't know any black berets and I want that term wiped out."

Although SEALs unofficially wore black berets from their conception, the headgear was not authorized by the navy until later in the 1960s. Black berets were made standard headgear for the U.S. Army in 2000.

"Blackbird"

"Blackbird" was the nickname given to a C-130 Hercules Tactical Aircraft Command aircraft that played a prominent role in special warfare.

See also C-130 HERCULES.

blasting cap

Also called detonators, blasting caps are devices that initiate the detonation of a charge of high explosives by subjecting it to a shock wave.

See also EXPLOSIVES.

USS *Blessman*

The blast and resulting fire from a 500-pound Japanese bomb dropped on the USS *Blessman* (APD 48), destroyer transport for Underwater Demolition Team 15, was the worst disaster suffered by the UDTs in the South Pacific during World War II.

On February 16, 1945, UDTs-12, 13, 14, 15, roughly 500 men, arrived off Iwo Jima to conduct beach surveys for the impending marine assault. The Japanese had turned the tiny rocky island into an almost impregnable fortress. Notwithstanding the bloody reputation Iwo Jima earned among the marines who fought there, the UDTs suffered few casualties.

UDT-15's beach survey assignment was the east shore of the island. On the afternoon of February 18, the team and its boats came to within 100 yards of the island's defenses. The swimmers were strafed by enemy fighter planes, but they took no casualties. After performing their mission, they were picked up by boats, given stiff shots of brandy, dry long underwear, and brought safely back to the USS *Blessman*.

The invasion was to be launched the next morning. That evening before, most of the UDT-15 men gathered in the mess decks of the *Blessman,* where they wrote letters home, played cards, read, or passed scuttlebutt. It had been a tough day of peril, rain, and a cold fog that gnawed through to the bone.

One of the other destroyers in the screen came down with engine trouble. At about 2120 hours (9:20 P.M.), the *Blessman* steamed out to take the disabled warship's place on the outer screen. It was moving at flank speed across the sea at 22 knots, leaving a wide wake turned iridescent under a pale moon. The wake made a glowing highway that could be seen in the air from miles away. It led directly to the destroyer's fantail.

A twin-engined Japanese Betty bomber intercepted the ship's wake at low attitude, followed it to the ship, passed over, made a 180-degree turn, then came screaming back on the destroyer's beam. It dropped two 500-pound bombs. One ricocheted off boat davits on the main deck and exploded in the water, causing little damage. The other struck the port side, punctured the deck, and detonated in the starboard mess decks, filled with frogmen. It opened up the ship like a matchbox, engulfing the midships section of the *Blessman* in roaring flames.

The next day, 18 "Naked Warriors" from UDT-15 were buried at sea; 23 more were either wounded or burned. Nearly half the team was out of action. The *Blessman* was towed to Saipan, while the survivors of UDT-15 made their way to Maui before returning to the United States for reorganization at Fort Pierce, Florida.

UDT losses from that one bomb were second only to the 31 killed and 60 wounded on Omaha Beach at Normandy on June 6, 1944, D-day.

Blue Hawks

The helicopter group supporting West Coast SEAL operations is called the Blue Hawks.

See also HELICOPTERS; REDWOLVES; SEAWOLVES.

Boehm, Roy (b. 1924)

"Growing up next to the sea, I had always been intrigued by it," retired lieutenant commander Roy Boehm writes in his autobiography, *First SEAL* (with Charles W. Sasser). "*Underneath* the sea—now that seemed a real challenge."

Born and reared in Long Island, New York, Boehm, at 17, enlisted in the U.S. Navy nine months before Pearl Harbor. His fascination with the sea, *underneath* the sea, led him immediately into hard-hat diving. That was before the SCUBA era. He devoured all the information and material he could find about the use of divers in combat, from Alexander the Great and Augustus Siebe to military divers who had experimented with closed-circuit breathing apparatus as early as World War I.

"The seed was planted," he recalls. "The ideas grew in my mind—*undersea warriors.* That could be used in a variety of ways to revolutionize warfare, *if* they could be freed from the air lines that tethered them to the surface. I envisioned battalions of troops rising out of dark waters in surprise attacks against an enemy. Swimmers invisible from enemy guns until they suddenly surfaced with weapons blazing."

Rather than killing the seed planted in the young sailor, World War II nourished it. Assigned as a boatswain's mate to the destroyer USS *Duncan* in the Pacific, he dived on the USS *Arizona* in the aftermath of Pearl Harbor to help recover the bodies of those killed in the surprise Japanese attack. He used

In 1961, Lt. Roy Boehm was picked to select, train, and become the first commander (acting) of the first U.S. Navy SEAL team. The SEALs were commissioned on January 1, 1962. (Roy Boehm)

a "Jack Brown" outfit, which consisted of a full face mask with an air-adjustment valve, a leather belt with lead weights, and about 300 feet of two-inch oxygen hose. Throughout the war, he continued to hard-hat dive when required to repair a ship or recover bodies or gear.

On the night of October 11, 1942, the *Duncan* was sunk at the Battle of Cape Esperance, off the western shore of Guadalcanal. The battle claimed the lives of 107 Americans. More than 200 seamen from the *Duncan* took to the water to escape the flaming inferno. For the rest of that night and into the next morning, Boehm swam through the sea, towing a semiconscious shipmate—until the sharks came and a particularly large one actually snatched the wounded man from Boehm's grasp.

Somehow, the encounter fed Boehm's dream of undersea warriors. The thought of commandos rising out of the depths like sharks to strike terror into the hearts of the enemy fascinated him.

Even as early in the war as late 1942, he had heard about and made inquiries into a special swimmer unit training in Florida and Hawaii. From what information he collected, he knew that the unit, whose members would soon become known as "frogmen," was going to be used in secret water operations against the Japanese during America's island-hopping campaign. Its members were "combat divers" who blew up coral reefs and other obstructions in order to open passages for troop landings.

He first encountered them during the invasion of Saipan. His new ship, the destroyer USS *Bennett,* had taken aboard some of the swimmers when their APD collided with the USS *Pennsylvania* and took on water. They were members, he learned, of a special unit called a UDT—underwater demolition team. It was said a man had to be "half fish and half nuts" in order to sign up.

"There was no comparison between my diving and theirs," Boehm observed. "I might as well have been diving in a swimming pool. Chiseled, hard-muscled young specimens, they carried themselves with a reckless, *special* air. Each man was flagged with blue-green paint as camouflage and then marked with black stripes from toes to chin and down each arm in order to use his body to measure the depth of water near the shore.

"Their gear consisted of: helmets, dive masks, cork gloves to protect their hands from coral; swim fins, which they obviously knew how to use; swim trunks; knee pads; knives and life belts; first aid packets; pencils that wrote underwater; and small Plexiglas slate tablets."

"Look at them, Boats," one of Boehm's gunners chided. "Ain't that what you been talking about—commandos in the sea? Why don't you go with them? Get your ass shot off."

It was not until some time after the war ended, however, that Boehm volunteered for UDT. In the meantime, throughout the late 1940s and early 1950s, he continued as a navy diver. He attended the U.S. Navy Mine Countermeasures School, the First Class Diving School, and the Underwater Swim School at Key West, Florida, where he helped in experiments with submersibles, mixed-gas diving

apparatus, SCUBA, and other diving gear. He also went to another war, in Korea, as a boatswain's mate aboard the light cruiser USS *Worcester.*

At 31 years of age, he signed up for UDT and became the oldest member to graduate in UDT Class 13, which began training in July 1954. For the next several years, he knocked around the teams. He was an instructor at the UDT school for a while. He also continued his diving experiments with the Submersible Operations Department and at SUBOPS's Testing and Evaluation. Through the Limited Duty Officer program, he commissioned as an officer, becoming the oldest ensign in the U.S. Navy.

In 1961, he trained Cuban guerrillas for the Bay of Pigs invasion and inserted them on the island prior to the attack. He returned to the UDT base at Little Creek, Virginia, where, now a lieutenant (junior grade), he was made operations officer of UDT-21. Cdr. Bill Hamilton, skipper of UDT-21, summoned him to his office.

"Lieutenant," Hamilton began, "you and I share a vision. Can you make commandos out of our people?"

"We've already been training them. They're the perfect people out of which to make commandos."

"Do it, then. Start selecting the men you want from UDT. . . . This is classified Top Secret. I'm not only commanding officer of UDT-21, I'm also Commodore, Underwater Demolitions Unit, Atlantic Fleet. You report directly to me. . . . I want you to select and train men as a nucleus for a Special Operations force to be incorporated into the Underwater Demolition Unit. . . .

"Roy, do you know what this means? We've somehow been granted *carte blanche* to create the finest band of unconventional warriors in the world."

"JFK wanted sea warriors," Boehm recalled. "I wanted sea warriors. The commies were already spreading like lice throughout Latin America and you could smell Vietnam over the horizon. What the country used my sea warriors for was up to the commander-in-chief and the Pentagon. What they could use them for was up to me. I started the project determined that we could be used for *any damned thing.*"

He had studied unconventional tactics and trained in them for years with the lingering hope that he could one day use them. The vision he had for the unit was clear—swift, deadly, like the shark; capable of infiltrating or striking from the air by parachute or airplane, from over land, from the surface of the sea, or from underneath the sea. He envisioned competent strong, *thinking* men, able to operate alone or in small groups behind enemy lines, but proficient enough to perform direct-action missions against enemy targets in combat—men for all seasons, who could and would do literally anything required of them.

They had to be more than killers, all muscles, neck, and attack-dog mentalities. He wanted creative men who could operate with their brains as well as with their muscles. The unconventional warfare brand of warfare required men of courage, dedication to duty, sacrifice, personal dexterity, and intelligence; team and mission had to come first. At the same time, they had to be individuals—rough men, tough men, who could operate outside protocol if necessary. The name of the UW game was *win*.

In selecting the first complement of men, 10 officers and 50 enlisted men, Boehm set high standards that would define navy men who would become U.S. Navy SEALs then and later.

Boehm foresaw UDT training as *minimum* basic training, a foundation upon which to build all other training. He started stripping choice men from the East Coast UDT teams and sending them to schools and training courses all over the navy and the army, with a few civilian classes thrown in. He had the green light to go anywhere, do anything.

He laid on Ranger training, jungle warfare, martial arts. One group went to Annapolis to learn how to sail boats. Others went to prisons to learn safecracking from experts. He ordered people to become auto hotwire artists and lock pickers. Frogmen learned trick shooting, photography, and intelligence gathering.

Everyone would be parachute qualified—not merely conventional hop-and-pop, but also HAHO (high altitude, high opening) and HALO (high altitude, low opening). They learned water-entry procedures from low-flying aircraft, improvised demolitions, foreign weapons, combat tactics, survival, and escape and evasion. He exchanged training with U.S. Army Special Forces (the Green Berets).

Only Lieutenant Commander Hamilton and Boehm knew the true purpose of the training. Selection of men and training continued throughout

1961. In December, Bill Hamilton received orders transferring him out of UDT. Boehm feared the project had been put on hold. During the Christmas holidays, an old friend at BUPERS (Bureau of Personnel) telephoned Boehm.

"What in hell is a SEAL?" he asked.

"Furry little creature lives in the ocean?"

"You'd damned well better find out for sure, ol' buddy. 'Cause you *are* one now, with a license to steal."

On January 7, 1962, the navy made the decision. It's unclear exactly who came up with the acronym SEAL (Sea-Air-Land), but as of January 1, 1962, the U.S. Navy SEALs were commissioned into service as the navy's answer to guerrilla warfare and the Army Special Forces in the cold war. Boehm's sea warriors had become reality.

He received orders as acting commanding officer of SEAL Team Two on the East Coast. SEAL Team One, under the command of Lt. Dave Del Guidice, would be established on the West Coast. Boehm, now promoted to full lieutenant, received the first SEAL orders. Roy Boehm, salty old seadog, World War II and Korea veteran, former boatswain's mate, was now *acting commander* of the very first SEAL team to be commissioned in the U.S. Navy—the *first* SEAL.

See also AMBUSH; BAY OF PIGS; CALLAHAN, JOHN F.; CENTRAL INTELLIGENCE AGENCY (CIA); CUBAN MISSILE CRISIS; DEL GUIDICE, DAVID; HAMILTON, WILLIAM H.; KENNEDY, JOHN F.; NAVAL COMBAT DEMOLITION UNIT (NCDU); PLANKOWNERS; SEALS; UNDERWATER DEMOLITION TEAMS (UDTS).

Boesch, Rudolph E. (Rudy) (b. 1928)

Shortly after graduating from U.S. Navy basic training in 1945, Rudy Boesch was lined up in formation when his company commander asked if anyone wanted to volunteer for duty with a special outfit. Boesch's was the only hand raised. He had just volunteered for the Amphibious Scouts and Raiders, a predecessor of modern SEALs. Thus began his long association with naval special warfare. Before he retired from the navy in 1990, he would become known as "the Bullfrog," the senior man in terms of length of service in special warfare. He would also be a SEAL "plankowner," one of the original SEALs selected by Lt. Roy Boehm for the very first SEAL team.

At the age of 16, Boesh had dropped out of high school in Rochester, New York, to join the merchant marine. A year later, in 1945, he enlisted in the navy. He saw little action in World War II with the Amphibious Scouts and Raiders, however, as the war was already winding down. He returned to the "regular fleet" when the Scouts were disbanded in 1945 and spent the next six years at various assignments.

In 1951 he went back into special warfare, volunteering for underwater demolition team (UDT) training. He stayed with UDT-21 for 11 years, attending numerous specialized schools and regularly deploying to the Mediterranean and Caribbean with the naval amphibious forces. He became a proficient combat swimmer and an expert in small-boat operations.

In 1961, after President John Kennedy announced his new emphasis on unconventional warfare, and Lieutenant Boehm, also of UDT-21, was charged with forming a SEAL team, Boesch was one of the first enlisted men selected. He was known to be "regulation" and commanded the respect of both men and officers. He was then a chief petty officer. Boehm appointed him master-at-arms, the senior enlisted person for SEAL Team Two, around whom the rest of the enlisted members would be molded.

"Mr. Boehm, what in hell is a SEAL?" was Boesch's first question.

Boesch remained with SEAL Team Two until he retired on August 1, 1990. During that long period of service, he served two combat tours in Vietnam, where among his other awards he received a Bronze Star for valor and ran more than 45 combat operations. He advanced to the rank of master chief and became command master chief for the SEAL teams.

In the late 1980s he became "the Bullfrog," the senior member of the special warfare community in terms of length of service and the last plankowner of SEAL Team Two still on active duty. He served as the senior enlisted adviser to USSOCOM (U.S. Special Operations Command) and was awarded the Defense Superior Service Medal, an award not often given to an enlisted man.

His retirement ended 45 years of active duty with the U.S. Navy, 39 years of which had been spent in special warfare, either with Scouts and Raiders, UDTs, or SEALs.

"Being a SEAL is one of the best things in the navy," he is quoted as saying. "I obviously like what I am doing or I wouldn't have stayed so long. . . . When you get up in the morning, you don't know whether you'll soon be finding yourself 30 feet underwater or 10,000 feet in the air."

See also AMPHIBIOUS SCOUTS & RAIDERS; "BULLFROG"; PLANKOWNERS.

booby traps

Booby traps, defined in the dictionary as "a concealed bomb, mine, etc., placed so as to be detonated by casual or careless movements of the unwary victims," were not an innovation of the Vietnam War. Booby traps have been a part of warfare since Neanderthals slung rocks at each other. However, it was during the Vietnam War that U.S. Navy SEALs first encountered a variety of the nefarious devices intended to kill or maim, and that the SEALs themselves developed the art and science of utilizing booby traps. Vietnam was a nasty war; booby traps were one of its nastier aspects. Every inch of terrain in Vietnam could kill or maim.

It has long been acknowledged that it is better tactically to wound or maim an enemy soldier than to kill him. Kill him and you eliminate one soldier; wound him, and you disable not only him but also those who have to care for him and transport him off the battlefield. A wounded soldier places a greater strain on an enemy's resources than does a dead soldier. That is a harsh but practical fact.

Fear is the primary purpose and result of booby traps. They exert a terrible psychological effect on troops, making them cautious, hesitant, fearful, sapping their morale, and eroding their will to fight. Seeing the bloody stump of your buddy's foot after it has been blown off by a trip-wire grenade, or seeing his torso punctured by the steel spikes of a Malayan gate, are enough to give anyone second thoughts about how badly he really wants to fight. The fear of booby traps was so rife among American troops in Vietnam, including SEALs, that rumors circulated about how Saigon hookers booby-trapped their sexual parts with broken glass and razor blades and deliberately infected themselves with a deadly "black syphilis" in order to pass it on to their American paramours. Guerrilla warfare plays by no rules.

Although the Viet Cong (VC) were not as creative at booby traps as had been the Germans and the Japanese of World War II, they nonetheless introduced a whole range of deadly tricks and devices into the Mekong Delta, where most SEALs operated. The most widespread of these was simply a grenade and a trip wire. It was commonly set up by placing inside a can a grenade with the pin pulled but the safety handle still in place. The can was then attached to a tree with a trip wire stretched from the grenade's handle across a trail. It took little contact with the wire to pull the grenade from the can, thus releasing the safety handle and detonating the little bomb.

This device was used in a variety of configurations. It could be daisy-chained along a trail and set off by either a trip wire or a hidden VC. It could be set low to blow off legs, or in bamboo arched above a trail to cause messy face and head wounds. A grenade buried shallow with a short trip wire attached to the bottom of a gate proved particularly effective.

These booby traps seemed to be everywhere, all connected to little silver-colored fragmentation grenades that the VC cast themselves in jungle workshops. VC would come into an area and order farmers to set up the devices around their villages and farms. If a farmer didn't do what he was told, the VC would kill him and string up his corpse somewhere as a warning against disobedience.

The VC also set up other vicious contraptions, such as the punji-stake trap. Punji stakes were sharpened bamboo sticks, barbed wood, or metal spikes concealed in foot traps. The stakes were smeared with human excrement in order to cause infection and blood poisoning in any hapless victim who blundered into one of the traps. They were placed on trails or in the grass on the banks of gullies and streams. "Monkey bridges" over streams or rice paddies might be sawn through the middle so that they could collapse under weight and drop pedestrians onto punji stakes under the water.

The "punji bear trap," sometimes called a man trap, and the "bamboo whip" were two particularly diabolical traps. The bear trap consisted of two boards with steel spikes driven through them. It was designed to pivot up out of concealment when stepped on and impale its victim's legs, chest, or face. The bamboo whip used a piece of green bamboo bent into tension and then wedged in place. A trip wire released the bamboo, which was studded with spikes, and it would whip viciously across a trail.

Giant punji stakes were also used to booby-trap landing zones. They were hidden in six or eight-foot-tall elephant grass and designed to transfix landing helicopters.

The use of booby traps was limited only by the user's imagination, with which the VC seemed to be vividly endowed. A "mace," for example, was a boulder studded with spikes suspended on a camouflaged rope. Released by a trip wire, it swung down a trail with devastating results. Mines were made from coconut shells filled with gunpowder. A cartridge trap could be made by burying a cartridge in the ground inside a bamboo sleeve, with its tip barely protruding and its primer resting on a nail or firing pin. A heavy footfall would set it off, firing the bullet through the victim's foot. The VC routinely booby-trapped "souvenirs" that Americans might be tempted to pick up. Sometimes they rigged the corpses of their own dead to explode if GIs attempted to search them for intelligence.

As inventive and creative as the VC were with booby traps, however, American SEALs proved their equal. As soon as SEAL teams began arriving in Vietnam, they adapted to this strange and cruel war and quickly learned how to "out-G" (out guerrilla) the guerrillas. Not only did they become adept at the guerrillas' own booby traps, they conceived ingenious designs of their own.

One of the most successful of these depended upon the enemy's own ammunition supplies. Whenever SEALs found one of these caches, they often left it undisturbed—except for a few small details. They took the bullets out of a number of 7.62 rounds, replaced the powder with C-4 explosives, reseated the bullets, and then left them to be fired by the VC.

For a while, there was actually a program in the United States to manufacture enemy ordnance modified to explode whenever it was used. B-40 rockets, mortar rounds, grenades, and even small-arms ammo were all filled with explosives instead of propellant powder. Cased in regular Chinese and Soviet packaging, they were salted in enemy caches. Not all the ammo would explode, of course—just enough of it so that VC using the supplies began noticing a certain portion of it blowing up in their faces. It was a good psychological operation.

SEALs also made good use of the fact that VC scrounged through U.S. supplies whenever they found them lost or discarded. SEALs frequently created bivouac sites where they left C-rations rigged to claymore mines. Also, since the enemy sometimes booby-trapped their own dead, SEALs did it right back to them, re-booby-trapping dead VC and NVA soldiers.

Although psychologically effective, booby traps have a downside. SEAL Gene Fraley who, with Mike Boynton, was in charge of ordnance at My Tho, loved to make weird booby traps. He was constructing a booby-trapped flashlight with a special fuse when the charge went off and killed him.

See also VIETNAM WAR.

Bosnia

Although U.S. Navy SEAL operations in Bosnia are still classified Secret, it is known that SEALs participated with other U.S. special operations forces in at least two deployments following the signing in December 1995 of the Dayton Peace accords that ended the civil war.

In December 1995, 10 naval commandos braved the Sava River's 40-degree water to scout the best places to erect a bridge that would carry most of America's peace keeping troops into Bosnia. Dressed in black flak jackets and helmets, and carrying CAR-15 assault rifles because of the heavy hostile activity around the area over the previous four years, the SEALs checked the river's bottom composition and current to help U.S. Army engineers plan a pontoon bridge across the swift-flowing stream.

Two years later, in December 1997, an unusual shipment arrived at the U.S. base in Tuzla, Bosnia—several eight-foot-high metal containers secretly housing a total of 65 commandos from the counterterrorist SEAL Team Six—modern-day Trojan horses. Once unpacked under heavy security, the SEALs dispersed undercover into various safe houses in the surrounding countryside. Their mission was to detect and apprehend five PIFWCs (persons indicted for war crimes) in northern Bosnia.

Because of poor intelligence, this first SEAL mission ended in abject failure, without a single capture. The SEALs flew home. SEALs returned to Bosnia a few weeks later, however, this time securing better results on more accurate intelligence.

Western officials reported that three of the originally targeted PIFWCs "surrendered" to SEALs in two separate events. A source disputed the "surrender," claiming, "Those were apprehensions pure and simple." One suspect, named Miroslav Tadic was physically tackled by SEALs. Two of the high-priority subjects remained at large but were eventually captured. So far, dozens of PIFWCs have "surrendered" or been captured and taken to trial by U.S. special operations forces in Bosnia.

SEALs were also used extensively in Bosnia for various other missions. They were tasked as bodyguards for visiting diplomats and utilized for searching for the locations of mass graves.

See also SEAL TEAM SIX.

Boston Whaler

In spite of all the training SEALs receive in exotic insertion and extraction techniques with SDVs (SEAL delivery vehicles) and submarines, perhaps 90 percent of all actual operations depend upon boat rides. SEALs have any number of boats, ranging from patrol coastal ships and Mark V Special Operations Craft to combat rubber raiding craft and rigid-hull inflatable boats. The Boston Whaler is the oldest in the SpecOps fleet, having served in the army, air force, coast guard, and the navy, including the underwater demolition teams and SEALs, since it was first introduced at the 1958 Boston Boat Show. It was used in Vietnam as a gun, patrol, or support boat in the brown waters of the Mekong Delta. It is still in use today.

Unibond™ foam-filled construction gives the fiberglass Whaler the reputation of being unsinkable. There are stories asserting that it can support 10 people when filled with water, take 1,000 rounds of automatic weapons fire and stay afloat, and run when cut in half (that is, the half with the engine).

The first Whaler was only 13 feet long. That original design has evolved into everything from dinghies to big-muscled offshore fishing boats, all called Whalers. More than 70,000 of them have been manufactured, many going into the armed forces as well as into police departments, the Drug Enforcement Agency, NASA, rescue squads, and fire departments.

Within the Navy SEALs, the Whaler is better known as a PBL (Patrol Boat, Light), a heavily armed craft constructed of unarmored fiberglass with a reinforced transom and a weapons-mount area that can accommodate 50-caliber heavy machine guns or 7.62 mm machine guns. The 25-foot craft is powered by dual 155 hp low-profile outboards that provide eight hours of continuous operations at a cruising speed of 25 knots or more. It is useful in interdicting a lightly armed adversary but should not be used to engage a heavily armed or well-organized enemy. Its unique hull design allows it to operate in virtually any water depth. It functions effectively in policing actions, harbor control, diving and surveillance operations, riverine warfare, drug interdiction, and other offensive or defensive purposes. It weighs 6,500 pounds fully loaded and is transportable via trailer, helicopter sling, or aircraft. Normal crew size is three people.

In 1983, during the Grenada operation, one group of SEALs parachuted into the sea near the Point Salines airfield with a mission to go ashore to prepare for a landing by Army Rangers. Two Boston Whalers loaded with gear were dropped with them by cargo parachute.

See also LIGHT PATROL BOAT; OPERATION URGENT FURY.

Boyle's law

Robert Boyle (1627–1691) was a 17th-century Irish chemist and physicist who studied the compression and expansion of air and other gases. In his experiments, he observed a gas bubble in a snake's eye that had been compressed and decompressed, the first recorded observation about decompression sickness (caisson disease, or "the bends").

"I have seen," he wrote, "a very apparent bubble moving from side to side in the aqueous humus of the eye of a viper at the time when this animal seemed violently distressed in the receiver from which the air had been exhausted."

"Boyle's Law," which he formulated in 1667 is one of the most important factors in diving. It states simply that the volume of a gas at constant temperature varies inversely with its pressure. Air is composed roughly of 78 percent N_2 (nitrogen) and 20.94 O_2 (oxygen). The remaining 1.06 percent is rare gases—carbon dioxide, hydrogen, neon, helium, krypton, and xenon. Nitrogen is the dangerous gas. Not only does it make a diver "drunk" at great depths, a condition known as "rapture of the deep," or "nitrogen narcosis," but it penetrates blood vessels under pressure and lodges in fatty tissues and bone joints. A slow ascent from a deep dive allows gases to escape from tissues properly, but surfacing too rapidly, causes the gases to expand inside the tissues (and in the lungs), producing painful and possibly lethal decompression sickness.

Instructor "Snake" Dennison of the Navy's First Class Diving School explains the process this way: "An inverted coffee cup on the surface is full of air. Submerge the cup to a depth of one atmosphere—33 $^1/_3$ feet—and approximately one-third of the cup would be full of water due to water pressure against the air. The deeper you dive, the smaller grows the bubble of air until eventually it would be so small you could hardly see it—small enough to seep through your blood vessels into tissue and bone joints.

"Reverse the process now. Place the almost-invisible bubble of air into a small balloon and start to the surface with it. The bubble expands to fill the balloon. By the time you reach the surface, you have a cupful of air again. But say you are at depth and fill the balloon with a cupful of *compressed* air and start to the surface. The balloon would pop. That's the same thing that happens to your lungs if you fill them at depth and start up too quick. They'd rupture and give you an air embolism. It could kill you unless you recompress immediately."

See also CAISSON DISEASE; NITROGEN NARCOSIS.

briefback

During mission planning, SEALs are required to prepare an operations plan and to brief higher command on it. This is called a "briefback."

See also MISSION PLANNING.

"Bright Light"

On June 24, 1964, a highly classified intelligence and commando unit, MACV-SOG (Military Assistance Command, Vietnam—Studies and Observation Group) was established under authorization of President Lyndon Johnson to disrupt clandestinely the enemy's sanctuaries in Laos. The Joint Personnel

Recovery Center (JPRC), also highly classified—so secret that its existence became public only after the end of the war—was created under SOG auspices in September 1966. Also known as the Recovery Studies Division, or OP-80, JPRC and with the DIA (Defense Intelligence Agency) were tasked with maintaining intelligence data on missing prisoners of war (POWs), and with efforts to rescue them. JPRC also developed various escape and evasion programs, briefed air crews on survival techniques, recovered the remains of American servicemen missing in action, and coordinated the rescue of downed airmen.

Its unclassified code name was "Bright Light," a generic term for a program that collected and acted upon intelligence on all friendly military and civilian prisoners as well as data about Americans. The unit was actually only a small staff office with headquarters in MACV. It was never assigned reaction forces or assets, such as troops, helicopters, and air support. As a result, it had to go begging for field forces in order to launch rescue attempts. This, along with a number of other factors, kept Bright Light from becoming more than minimally successful. Among the other factors were difficult terrain and dense foliage, the secret war in Laos, the political ramifications of sending troops into North Vietnam, inability to generate definitive intelligence, cultural differences, and micromanagement from higher echelons.

The U.S. Navy SEALs, especially in the Mekong Delta, offered the perfect rescue-force combination. They were a highly trained quick-reaction unit, intimately familiar with the waterways of the delta. SEALs liberated a significant percentage of the prisoners freed during the war.

The first SEAL POW operation occurred shortly after JPRC was formed. Chief Petty Officer James Watson, SEAL Team Two, Sixth Platoon, led a force consisting of 10 helicopters, 12 SEALs, and about 100 Vietnamese soldiers against a suspected camp where about 20 Vietnamese and possibly three Americans were being contained. Watson's lead helicopter was shot down when it attempted to land on the wrong landing zone. Although no American POWs were recovered, about 25 Vietnamese prisoners managed to escape from the prison on their own in the confusion. None of the rescuing SEALs was lost or wounded.

It was not until mid-June 1970, however, that SEALs were used with any regularity in POW res-

cue efforts. A Vietnamese Soldier who escaped from a camp near the town of Sa Dec provided intelligence that two U.S. prisoners were being held there. On June 14, SEALs attacked the campsite and destroyed several huts. The source of the intelligence accompanied the raid. "After entering the alleged campsite," a SEAL report stated, "[the source] determined it was not the location at which he had been held prisoner."

Two separate loss incidents in 1969 set off a series of raids and operations in the delta that lasted until 1972. In the first incident, Lt. Richard Bowers and Staff Sgt. Gerasimo Arroyo-Baez were captured on March 24, 1969, by the North Vietnamese after their outfit was overrun. In the second incident, naval aviators Cap. Robert White and Lt. John Graff were shot down on November 15, 1969. The search for these four men became the longest manhunt since the search for Amy Special Forces captain Nick Rowe.

In July 1970, SEALs guided by a *hoi chanh* (former VC who had "come over") raided a VC prison camp, but it had been evacuated immediately before the arrival of the assault force. "A small campfire was still burning with fish and rice ready to eat in large bowls," one SEAL noted in his barndance card. "The spot where the two Americans had been restrained was quickly located: bamboo racks off the ground that had larger ropes for the Americans' hands and feet."

SEALs again came agonizingly close to a rescue a couple of weeks later at another camp about 30 kilometers away. A SEAL team and one platoon from the army's First Air Cavalry Regiment were inserted, but the POWs had left the area two days previously.

On August 21, 1970, a Vietnamese soldier fled a POW camp near Vi Thanh and brought word that Americans, possibly one or more of those who had been captured the previous year, might be imprisoned there. Knowing speed was essential, Lt. Louis H. Boink III organized one of the fastest Bright Light raids in the program's short history: he received the intelligence at 1800 (6 P.M.) and led the raid, code-named "Story Book," the next morning at 0918.

He landed his SEAL team and a Vietnamese Regional Forces platoon on a beach line six kilometers east of the reported POW camp. He assaulted one side of the compound while supporting fire from navy ships, Australian bombers, and U.S. Army helicopters placed pressure on the other three sides. The plan was to strike with such lightning speed that the Vietnamese guards would abandon their posts.

It almost worked. The escaped Vietnamese led Boink's men directly to the camp, while the destroyer USS *Sutherland* fired cover to the south, B-57s from the Royal Australian Air Force pounded a nearby canal, and army gunships strafed with rockets and miniguns to the north and east. Boink found the camp abandoned. VC camp personnel had fled south with all their prisoners through fire from the navy. "For two hours," a SEAL historian later wrote, "the SEALs remained in hot pursuit through the swamp, following a trail of clothing and abandoned equipment. At 1245 hours, they discovered 28 Vietnamese prisoners whose guards had fled for their lives. No Americans were discovered in the camp."

While the raid was successful in terms of recovering ARVN prisoners, again no Americans were found. So far, no Americans had been recovered by Bright Light since its inception in 1966.

SEALs made several other raids before the year ended, only one of which produced any results. That raid, the last major one of 1970, occurred the day after the famous Son Tay raid. SEAL lieutenant Dick Couch, acting on information from two captured VC, led a force against a prison camp on the Ca Mau Peninsula, on the southern tip of South Vietnam. The camp was surrounded by thick jungle and treacherous swamps. Couch's platoon broke into the camp just before dawn and exchanged fire with 18 guards. The SEALs rescued 19 Vietnamese prisoners—but again, no Americans. One of the POWs reported that some 20 men had died in the camp of malnutrition during the year, while another 60 had been executed for various "crimes."

Bad luck also plagued the last efforts of the SEALs to find and rescue U.S. captives. On June 23, 1971, the senior adviser for An Xuyen Province reported that an agent knew the location of a POW camp that contained 270 prisoners, of which five were American. The only way to get to the main camp of the three in the complex was by sampan through a mangrove swamp.

A Bright Light report of the operation stated that "enroute from the naval surface vessel the sampans experienced buoyancy problems and sank. It was decided that the noise created rescuing survivors compromised the operation, so it was terminated. It is felt the compromise resulted in the POWs being removed. . . . [I]f credible intelligence is received, a future operation will be mounted."

Of the four men lost in the delta in 1969, only White returned, and that was not due to rescue—he was released near the end of the war. The other three men died in captivity.

Reports that American prisoners had been spotted continued to tantalize Bright Light planners. JPRC continued to receive reports of large men, presumably Americans, being moved. SEALs even saw footprints that could have been made by Americans. But American prisoners, if they were there, remained always just beyond reach of rescuers.

Lieutenant Boink, who led the Story Book raid, submitted the idea of devoting the complete attention of special SEAL teams to Bright Light efforts. His plan was rejected by JPRC and the Central Intelligence Agency. JPRC continued to work piecemeal, begging and borrowing assets for rescue attempts. JPRC's failure to allow the SEALs free rein in the delta to coordinate recovery efforts may have been its most serious policy mistake.

Operation "Thunderhead," the most highly classified Bright Light effort of the war, was a last-ditch, desperate attempt to rescue captives of the heavily guarded prison called Hoa Lo (the "Hanoi Hilton") in North Vietnam. Americans held there had worked up an escape plan by which they would get to the Red River and drift out into Haiphong Harbor to rendezvous with SEALs on the far side of a small island, "Point Delta."

On the night of June 4, 1972, the SEAL submarine USS *Grayback* launched a SEAL team in a motorized SDV (SEAL delivery vehicle) off the coast of North Vietnam. However, the current sweeping out of the mouth of the Red River and across Haiphong Harbor was so strong that the SDV made little headway. The vehicle's batteries died, and the SEALs were left stranded at sea.

A second SDV attempt with a fresh SEAL team was made the next night, with the same results. Then disaster struck. The first team, which had been rescued by helicopter, wanted to be dropped back into the sea to rejoin the *Grayback*. It was a dark night with wind, not ideal flying conditions. Instead of dropping the team at 10 feet as requested, the pilot mistakenly hovered at 30 feet. Lt. Melvin S. Dry slammed into the water, hitting a bit of flotsam that crushed his throat. He died instantly. A second SEAL suffered a broken rib. The helicopter, its crew not knowing what had occurred, departed.

In the meantime, the *Grayback* had also departed the rendezvous site, having been warned away because of a patrolling enemy boat in the area. Its captain assumed the SEALs would not be dropped. The seven surviving SEALs linked up and stayed afloat the remainder of the night, until they were rescued by helicopter the following morning.

In spite of repeated surveillance flights around the islands and the river mouth, no POWs were ever found. The mission was called off on June 15.

The Joint Personnel Recovery Center was disbanded on January 23, 1973. More than 125 rescue operations had been launched during its six years of existence. Almost 500 Vietnamese prisoners had been rescued, and 110 American MIA bodies found, but Bright Light had succeeded in freeing not a single American POW.

See also "BARNDANCE CARDS"; DRY, MELVIN S.; USS *GRAYBACK*; MACV-SOG; NORRIS, THOMAS R.; OPERATION THUNDERHEAD.

brown-water navy

"Brown-water navy" was a slang term applied to riverine forces during the Vietnam War.

See also RIVERINE WARFARE.

"Brown-water navy" was a slang term applied to riverine forces during the Vietnam War. Here, a patrol of SEALs, arms bristling, prepares to disembark on a mission from a PBR (patrol boat, river). (U.S. Navy)

Bruhmuller, William N., II (b. 1935)

Boatswain's Mate Bill Bruhmuller, known as "Panda Bear" among team members, was a "plankowner" of SEAL Team Two, the first SEAL team commissioned in the U.S. Navy. He was among a small unit of SEALs sent to the Dominican Republic during the uprising there in 1965, then went two years later to Vietnam, where he pioneered the use of SEAL scout dogs.

During a subsequent Vietnam tour in 1971, he scored one of the most amazing intelligence coups of the entire war by recruiting as an agent a top Viet Cong official. Bruhmuller was serving with SEAL Team Two in early 1971 when a Vietnamese he had groomed as an intelligence source informed him of a high-level enemy official who, for money, would be willing to turn informant for the Americans. Bruhmuller demanded proof that the official could produce. His contact brought him a number of documents.

"I purposely contacted the Defense Intelligence Agency [DIA] rather than the army because I knew what would happen," Bruhmuller said. "They [the army] would compromise him or not take it as seriously as I thought. The initial documents checked out, and they told me, 'You've got somebody very important.'"

A contact was set up. The unknown Vietnamese turncoat insisted that Bruhmuller meet him alone out in the middle of the jungle, in "no-man's land." It was a big risk, but the SEAL took it. He arranged to be transported to the meeting in a closed Vietnamese police van driven by another trusted Vietnamese. When the van approached the contact point, it slowed but did not stop, in order to fool anyone who might be watching; the SEAL rolled out of the back of the vehicle, alone. He wore jeans, a green shirt, and a bandana over his head to help disguise his appearance. Notwithstanding the agreement to arrive unarmed, he carried a knife and a 9 mm pistol.

He hiked into the jungle for nearly a kilometer before a smallish Vietnamese man, in his thirties or early forties and with a military bearing, stepped from hiding.

"You call me 'John,'" Bruhmuller said during introductions. "I'll call you 'Mister.'" Bruhmuller figured he could never expose the official, even inadvertently, if he didn't know who he was.

Together, they strode back to the road, where they were picked up by the van. They traveled by air to Saigon, where a DIA agent conducted the actual interrogation. That set the pattern for six future contacts. Bruhmuller would meet "Mister" in the forest, clandestinely accompany him to Saigon, and remain until it was time to transport Mister back to VC country. The SEAL understood so little Vietnamese that he was never fully aware of what was being said, but the intelligence passed on was undoubtedly of great importance. The DIA interrogator was extremely excited about it.

"I stayed [with Mister] primarily as a confidence builder," Bruhmuller explains. "We became almost friends. We trusted each other. I didn't want him messed over. I was there to protect him as well as to get information."

During one of the meetings, the two men were walking back to the road to catch the van when Mister suddenly stiffened. "Mister pushed me down into a hole. Within a couple of seconds, a VC patrol went by. I saw 11 guys. I don't know why they didn't hear my heart going. If he was ever going to turn me in, this was it. The man saved my life."

Bruhmuller gradually learned the mysterious informant's history. During the war between the French and the Viet Minh, he had fought with the French, had been captured, and had been sent to Hanoi for schooling and "reeducation." He was then returned to South Vietnam to set up his own Viet Minh organization in the Mekong Delta. The French lost, and the Americans came. Mister continued to fight with the Viet Cong.

After the Tet offensive in 1968, during which the VC suffered a crushing defeat, life turned bitter for the guerrillas. They were forced to grow their own food and fend for themselves. Mister's wife contacted tuberculosis. One of his children turned seriously ill. Disillusioned by the unkept promises of the National Liberation Front (or NLF, the political arm of the Viet Cong), desperate for his family, Mister sought relief by selling what he knew about the VC and its operations to the Americans.

The results of Mister's interrogations were flashed back to Washington by the DIA. There analysts came to the surprising realization that Mister was not only a top NLF official but the commander in charge of all Viet Cong operations in the Mekong Delta. The information he provided exposed the entire VC superstructure and strategy, as well as giving warning of pending attacks and operations. The citation Bruhmuller later received for his intelligence coup stated in part that it "was responsible for saving thousands of American and South Vietnamese lives."

See also AIRBORNE; BAILEY, LARRY W.; DOMINICAN REPUBLIC INTERVENTION; SCOUT DOGS; PLANKOWNERS; VIET CONG.

Bucklew, Philip H., II (1915–1993)

Although Philip H. Bucklew was never actually a member of an underwater demolition team or SEAL team, he was involved in so many aspects of naval special warfare, from the Amphibious Scouts and Raiders of World War II to service as Commander, Special Warfare Pacific, that he became known as the "Father of Naval Special Warfare." It was for him that the Naval Special Warfare Center in Coronado, California, training site for Navy SEALs, was named. His biography reads like an adventure novel. In fact, he served as the model for the character Big Stoop in the immensely popular comic strip *Terry and the Pirates*.

Before 1942, underwater capabilities for the United States were limited to the helmeted navy diver and were restricted primarily to salvage and repair. That changed, however, almost immediately after Pearl Harbor. The first and the most famous of the underwater men was Phil Bucklew.

He had already earned some fame as a standout football fullback at Columbus North High School in Ohio, at Xavier University in Cincinnati, and as a professional with the Cleveland Rams in 1937 and 1938. World War II was only a few weeks old when navy recruiter Gene Tunney, the former heavyweight boxing champion, enlisted Bucklew as one of his first recruits. Bucklew signed up as a navy physical training instructor, the beginning of a career that was to see the tall athlete assume a crucial role in the development of naval special warfare.

Restless at what he perceived to be his exclusion from real action, Bucklew quickly volunteered when he heard of plans to set up a team of what were then referred to as "amphibious commandos." In May 1942, he became one of the first 10 men of the Amphibious Scouts and Raiders, considered by navy historians to be the earliest forerunner of the SEALs.

The Scouts never became broad-based commandos like the SEALs, however. In most operations, they found themselves limited to direct support of the amphibious force, much in the manner of navy combat demolition units (NCDUs) and UDTs, which were being formed at about the same time. The Scouts' mission primarily entailed scouting prospective beach landing sites, checking them for obstacles, marking them, and guiding marines and army forces ashore during the invasions.

Bucklew first saw action in November 1942 during Operation Torch, the Allied landings on North Africa, but not quite in the way he might have envisioned. The young lieutenant was aboard the USS *Leedstown* off the coast of Algiers while another Scouts and Raiders team reconned the river Wadi Sebou to cut antishipping nets stretched across it. A prowling German submarine torpedoed the *Leedstown* and sank it.

Bucklew survived. In the spring of 1942, he and some of his men worked with a British secret unit called COPP (combined operations pilotage parties) in preparing for Allied landings on Sicily. COPP used two-man kayaks instead of boats to reconnoitre the proposed landing beaches. Four small British submarines surfaced at different points and disgorged scouts to do the beach surveys. The little boats leaked badly in choppy seas. The British lost five sailors in the scouting operations; no Americans were lost.

During the Sicily invasion, Bucklew and his team were assigned to guide ashore the soldiers of Gen. George Patton's Seventh Army. Under a quarter-moon at 0100, using a powerboat, Bucklew planted a soldier at either end of the landing beach with a shielded flashlight. He then centered himself on the water between the two ends to use signals from the flank men to guide in the invasion.

An alarming incident occurred during the landing. Enemy machine-gun fire chattered away from exactly the spot from which one of Bucklew's flanking guides was signaling.

"I was getting the flank signal with machine-gun fire coming right over it, and [the signal] was steady," Bucklew explained. "I found my sergeant on the beach the next morning and said, 'What in the hell were you doing?' He said, 'Well, the pillbox was occupied. I felt the safest thing to do was to get my back right against it.' They were firing over his head.

And he was sitting there safe with a shielded light. He was right under the fire."

Two months later, Bucklew also led ashore the landing invasion at Salerno. He and Ray King, his boatswain's mate, set out in a two-man kayak instead of a motorboat. They paddled in from about three miles offshore to set up their guide markers. British destroyers behind them began a bombardment that skipped shells across the water like flat stones, right over the heads of the two men in the tiny kayak. "A shell coming at you in that salvo looks like a big ball of fire, and it looks like it's going to hit you right on the nose. It either goes over or it doesn't."

For his exploits during these two landings, Bucklew received the Navy Cross and a Silver Star.

By this time, plans for a massive cross-channel invasion of Europe had begun. Bucklew was now a veteran of amphibious landings. In early 1944, he and four other Scouts and Raiders arrived in England to begin reconnaissance operations along the Normandy coast.

Operating from small rubber boats on dark nights, Bucklew and his men took depth soundings of all planned invasion beaches. The lieutenant even swam and crawled ashore one night to bring back a bucketful of sand so it could be analyzed for its ability to support tanks and other heavy vehicles. On another of his forays ashore, German soldiers surrounded him. He fled into a swamp and hid until the Nazis gave up and went away.

Before dawn on D-day, June 6, 1944, Bucklew and his Scouts set out in a small boat to lead troops onto Omaha Beach—once more into the breach. He was still some 12 miles from shore when a battle broke out almost 10 miles down the coast to this right. Alarmed at first that he was off course, he remembered that U.S. Army Rangers were scheduled to scale a cliff and create a diversion in that direction. Besides, he spotted the steeple in the French town of Vierville, silhouetted against the slightly lighter sky, and knew he was on track.

Salvos from the battleships flared across the sky. Waves of bombers swept over Nazi defenses. The entire Earth seemed to have gone up in flames. Gap assault teams cleared lanes for the invasion approach. The Allies obtained a toehold on the main European continent and began their march to Berlin.

While the landings on France were the last amphibious attacks of the European war, Bucklew's odyssey was not yet completed. During the Christmas holidays of 1944, he was called to Washington and briefed on secret guerrilla operations being conducted behind Japanese lines in China under the direction of a U.S. Navy officer, Capt. Milton E. "Mary" Miles. Bucklew's new assignment was to join up with the guerrillas, make his way to the Chinese coast, and personally reconnoiter beaches on which Allied troops might be able to land in preparation for an assault on the Japanese home islands.

Posing as a courier, he flew to Calcutta and over "the Hump" to Burma, and then landed in southern China. Captain Miles had been in-country for over two years, during which time he had formed a working alliance with a Chinese warlord to harass the Japanese enemy. Bucklew found some 80 American sailors, soldiers, and marines, part of SACO (Sino-American Cooperation Organization), at a thriving training camp at "Happy Valley" near K'un-ming. The Americans had "gone native," in order to make themselves as inconspicuous as possible within Miles's network of raiding groups, scattered widely across central and southern China.

Bucklew was particularly interested in the intelligence net Mary Miles had established along 800 miles of coastline from near Shanghai to Hong Kong, then up the Pearl River to Canton. Coastal watchers kept tabs on Japanese shipping in and out of Chinese ports and provided weather reports, which were passed along to American commanders in the Pacific.

From K'un-ming, Bucklew, dressed as a Chinese coolie, set out on foot with a band of guerrillas led by a tough Chinese who wore black coolie pajamas, a derby hat, and a pistol on each hip. The American carried two grenades and a .45-caliber pistol concealed underneath his baggy coolie's suit. He was so much taller than any Chinese that he drew double-takes. "We would be walking along and would pass coolies coming head on, with their minds a hundred miles away," he later recalled. "As we would pass one another, I would be looking back at them from under my big straw hat to see if they detected me, and they would be looking back at me, saying, 'What was that?' because I was so out of proportion to their size."

Twice he had narrow escapes. Guides smuggled him from village to village when the Japanese learned of the presence of an American in the area and searched for him. On another occasion, he hurriedly burrowed into a haystack as a Japanese patrol approached.

When he finally reached the coast and inspected it as an amphibious site, he found it unsuitable, even hazardous. "Within three to five miles of the hoped-for landing beaches was a very rugged, mountainous terrain with no roadways whatsoever. It would have been a case of landing and being bogged down on a limited sand strip." He recommended against a landing. His recommendation was accepted, and a decision was made to advance directly toward Japan rather than launch from the Chinese mainland.

Bucklew was given one final assignment in China—to prepare for a daring commando raid against a Japanese base near the port of Amoy, in an attempt to acquire a book containing one of the few Japanese codes the Americans had not already broken. A marine working for "Mary" Miles was already under cover in Amoy, where he had rented a house, hired a cook, and settled down in a village across the harbor from the city. The operation was scuttled at the last moment. Bucklew was relieved of further duties in the Orient when the war ended.

He returned to civilian life for two years, then came back into the navy in 1948. There he continued his efforts in behalf of naval special warfare. In 1951, he set up shop in an old brig on the amphibious base in Little Creek, Virginia. As commander of a top-secret outfit known as Beach Jumper Unit II, a continuation of the World War II Beach Jumpers, he built up a squadron of a dozen boats, 30 officers, and 220 enlisted men. The boats bulged with high-tech electronics for their mission of intercepting, monitoring, and jamming hostile communications.

Eventually, the boats evolved into a fleet of slow-moving converted merchant ships meant to cruise waters off the coasts of potential foes, listening to their communications and plotting the locations and frequencies of radar installations. Beach Jumper II continued operating until 1968, when the North Koreans seized one of its ships, the USS *Pueblo*, and her 83-man crew and held them captive for almost a year. A proposed rescue attempt by the SEALs was rejected as too risky.

During the Vietnam War, Bucklew played several roles. As early as January 1964, he was sent by the

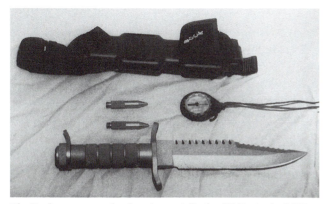

The Buckmaster was developed especially for SEALs in the 1980s but was never well received. (Kevin Dockery)

navy on a survey trip to Vietnam to determine how the enemy in the South was receiving resupply. Either war materiel was being carried down from North Vietnam along the Ho Chi Minh Trail network, or it was being infiltrated from the sea. Bucklew concluded that most supplies came down the Ho Chi Minh Trail.

As commander of the Pacific Fleet's Naval Operations Support Group One (now Naval Special Warfare Group One), and thus in command of naval special operations, he was an ardent supporter of both use of unconventional tactics in Vietnam and of a role for the SEALs in them. When SEAL lieutenant James Barnes, who began what are known as the "barndance cards," protested in a memo to Bucklew that the Vietnam War was "not for us," the captain fired back a reply, "This is the only war in town. If the SEALs want to stick around, they damn well better be involved."

Air assets, ships, and even submarines were already in the navy's inventory and available to the SEALs. What was lacking was a high-speed, shallow-draft boat that could operate in a hostile coastal environment and insert, support, and extract SEAL platoons. Captain Bucklew was influential in the development of both the PTF (fast patrol boat) and riverine programs to give the navy a "brown water" capability in the rivers and streams of Vietnam in support of SEAL and other operations.

To many in naval special warfare, Phil Bucklew was the epitome of the unconventional naval hero, a model for all such sea warriors to come. To others, the fact that he had never completed UDT or SEAL training but ended his career in command of West Coast SEALs was a bone of contention.

In 1987, the Naval Special Warfare Command was established at the amphibious base in Coronado and was dedicated to him. His influence in special warfare still hovers over the various training schools headquartered there.

He died in 1993 and was buried at the Arlington National Cemetery.

See also AMPHIBIOUS SCOUTS AND RAIDERS; BEACH JUMPERS; MILES, MILTON E.; NAVAL COMBAT DEMOLITION UNITS (NCDUS); NAVAL SPECIAL WARFARE; NORMANDY LANDING; OPERATION TORCH; PTF (PATROL TORDO, FAST) BOAT; RIVERINE FORCES; UNDERWATER DEMOLITION TEAMS (UDTS); VIETNAM WAR.

Buckmaster knife

The blade design for the SEAL Buckmaster knife was developed in the mid-1980s by Phrobis International, Ltd., to meet the specifications of the U.S. Special Operations Command. The design was modified for production by Buck Knives, which manufactured it as the Model 184 BuckMaster. A large quantity was purchased by the U.S. Navy to be supplied to SEALs.

Made of stainless steel to minimize corrosion, the Buckmaster was a hollow-grip, long-bladed Bowie weighing 1.39 pounds, with a blade length of 7.63 inches, 12.56 inches overall. The blade had a single edge with a serrated edge, sharp clip, and a saw back.

Removable guard horns could be screwed into sockets at either end of the grip guard, spreading out slightly from it. By fixing a line to a removable metal lug at the end of the pommel, the entire knife could be made to serve as a grappling hook, or even a small-boat anchor. Survival gear could be stowed in the hollow handle.

The scabbard had special features of its own, including a plastic squeeze-type buckle on the belt loop to permit it to be unsnapped from a combat harness without the wearer's having to remove his belt or combat harness.

For some reason, probably because of its weight and complicated design, the knife was not well received. It languished on the supply shelves. Operators preferred the Mark 3 Mod 0.

See also MARK 3 COMBAT KNIFE.

"Budweiser"

The Special Warfare insignia, or trident, is commonly referred to as a "Budweiser" among SEALs. The origin of the nickname is unknown.

See also SPECIAL WARFARE INSIGNIA.

"Bullfrog"

During World War II in the Pacific, UDT men came to be known as "frogmen," partly because they were amphibious, and partly because before they went on missions they sometimes painted their near-naked bodies in colors resembling frogs. The term *Bullfrog* came to mean the same as "stud" or "dominant." It stuck. Today, it is applied to the SEAL who has served longest on active duty in special warfare.

See also BOESCH, RUDOLPH E.; UNDERWATER DEMOLITION TEAMS (UDTS).

buoyancy control device (BCD)

An integral part of a SEAL's diving equipment is his buoyancy control device (BCD), sometimes called a buoyancy compensator (BC). The most common BCD is worn like a vest, to the back of which is attached the diver's air tanks. The BCD can be inflated by a hose attached to the air tank, or by mouth, and deflated through a valve, the object being to regulate the air in the vest to attain homeostasis in the water—in other words, to maintain "neutral buoyancy," like a fish. If there is too much air in the BCD, the diver rises to the surface; too little, and he sinks.

When Jacques Cousteau and others were pioneering SCUBA diving in the 1940s and 1950s, they discovered that the weight of their equipment had a tendency to drag them to the bottom. They compensated for this by wearing ordinary life vests, which could be inflated or deflated to maintain neutral buoyancy. The first BCDs were nothing but flimsy boat jackets with an air valve for inflation by mouth. It is little more than that today, in spite of features for balance, and pockets, valves, and attachments.

See also DIVING, HISTORY OF.

USS *Burrfish*

One of the most daring missions of World War II was the odyssey of the U.S. submarine *Burrfish* and its cargo of underwater demolition team (UDT) frogmen and OSS (Office of Strategic Services) men. It left Pearl Harbor on July 9, 1944, to obtain intelligence about the islands of the Palaus in the South Pacific. Five members of UDT-10 led by Chief Petty Officer Howard Reeder were joined by five OSS specialists from the Amphibious Operations Base at Waipio, Hawaii.

The submarine traveled on the surface in safe waters for three days and nights before submerging on the morning of the fourth in Japanese-controlled seas. For the rest of the journey, it traveled under water by day and surfaced only at night to recharge its batteries.

Early in August, it reached its operating area around the Palaus and Yap. For two days it was pursued by a Japanese subchaser, which repeatedly dropped depth charges.

After escaping the subchaser, the *Burrfish* and its commandos played tag with other Japanese forces around the islands of Angaur and Peleliu for the next two weeks. UDT men went ashore in rubber boats to conduct beach surveys of assigned areas. The *Burrfish* took periscope pictures of shorelines. It discovered that the Palau Islands and the nearby island of Yap were all heavily fortified, garrisoned by Japanese forces, and that the beaches and surf were studded with obstacles.

On August 18, Chief Reeder, along with UDT members Robert Black and John McMahan, failed to return from a mission to the submarine. They were never heard from again. Postwar records indicate they were captured, but they apparently never reached a prisoner of war camp.

The *Burrfish* returned to Pearl Harbor with its intelligence in time for the September 1944 amphibious invasion of Peleliu.

Butcher, Kenneth John (d. 1983)

Machinist's Mate First Class Kenneth Butcher disappeared with three other SEALs after parachuting into high seas during the Grenada action, Operation Urgent Fury, in 1983.

See also OPERATION URGENT FURY.

C-130 Hercules

If any one aircraft may be associated with Navy SEALs, Green Berets, and other special warfare forces, that airplane is the multipurpose C-130 Hercules, manufactured by Lockheed Martin. Designed as a medium-range tactical airlift aircraft for transporting personnel and cargo, it has served many other purposes in its various configurations: close air support, air interdiction and armed reconnaissance, intratheater air drops, airborne battlefield command and control, psychological warfare through radio and TV transmissions, jamming and electronic warfare, search and rescue, arctic and antarctic support, air refueling, weather reconnaissance, and global day, night, and adverse weather special operations.

The C-130 was originally flown in 1954 and has been in continuous production ever since. SEALs served with this military workhorse in Vietnam and saw action with it in several other hot spots, such as Grenada, Panama, and Bosnia. There are currently about 700 C-130s on duty in the U.S. Air Force.

"The Herk" is capable of operating from rough, dirt strips, and it is the prime transport for airdropping troops and equipment into hostile areas. It can haul 92 combat troops or 64 fully equipped paratroopers on side-facing seats. Paratroops can exit the plane through two doors on either side of the aircraft behind the landing gear, or off the rear loading ramp.

It is a big, tough plane powered by four Allison T56-A-15 turboprops, each of which generates 4,300 horsepower. It is 97 feet nine inches long (41 feet of which is cargo space) and 38 feet three inches high; it has a wingspan of 132 feet seven inches. It can reach speeds in excess of 374 mph, with a ceiling of 33,000 feet, and a range of 2,356 miles with a maximum payload of 45,000 pounds, or 5,200 miles with no cargo. Each airplane costs $14.1 million to build, in 1996 dollars.

The Hercules acquired a special warfare mission in the summer of 1964, when the Tactical Air Command ordered the creation of the 779th Troop Carrier Squadron, which would support long-range special operations teams deep inside hostile territory. For this mission the plane wore sinister-looking black camouflage, earning it the nickname "Blackbird." A beetle nose contained "Skyhook" (Fulton Recovery System) capabilities for extracting ground troops. High-speed airdrop and electronics warfare capabilities were later added.

If any one aircraft may be associated with Navy SEALs and other special warfare types, it is the C-130 Hercules. It was originally flown in 1954 and has been in continuous production ever since. Here, a C-130 lands at a forward base in Vietnam. (Charles W. Sasser)

The 779th began rotations to Nha Trang, Vietnam, in 1966. In Vietnam and elsewhere since then, Blackbirds have participated in numerous covert and overt operations involving SEALs and other special operations groups. They were involved in the Son Tay raid in 1973 and in the ill-fated Iranian rescue effort in 1979. Combat Talon Mc-130s led the invasion of Grenada, during which four SEALs were killed, and dropped Rangers into Panama.

One of the C-130's more interesting configurations is that of AH-130H Spectre, which delivered devastating air support to conventional and nonconventional troops in Vietnam, Grenada, and Panama.

The Spectre concept began in the early 1960s when U.S. Air Force technicians at Bien Hoa Air Base in Vietnam installed miniguns on a World War II–vintage C-47 transport and called it Spooky, its radio call sign. It was so effective in providing fire support against enemy troops that the Air Force went to a much-larger transport, the AC-130 ("A" indicated "Attack") and called it Spectre. It became a hunter, patrolling Vietnam's night skies.

All of Spectre's target-detection gear and armament is arranged on the plane's left side. Below the cockpit is an RDF (radio direction finder) that can hone in on the radio beacons of friendly troops or on the electronic noise produced by enemy vehicles' ignition systems. In a door aft of the nose wheel is a sensor mount for a low-light-level television camera that displays on a TV screen images that are virtually indistinguishable from an ordinary black-and-white television, even on pitch-dark nights. In the same location is a laser attached to a computer that assists in aiming the flying battleship's weapons so accurately that projectiles strike within five feet of a target when fired from 5,000 feet in the air.

Armament consists of two six-barrel 20 mm Vulcan cannon mounted ahead of the wing for use against troops and light vehicles; a 40 mm Bofors automatic cannon aft of the main landing gear, for trucks and light armor; farthest aft is a 105 mm howitzer firing a 32-pound shell that can annihilate tanks and buildings.

The average age of the active duty C-130 fleet is now over 25 years, but it is still a major part of the U.S. Air Force Special Warfare forces. In the late 1990s, the Air Force began buying a new 'J' model C-130 from Lockheed; it climbs higher and faster, flies at higher cruise speeds, and takes off and lands in shorter distances. The Herk is expected to remain an integral part of special warfare into the foreseeable future.

See also FULTON SURFACE-TO-AIR RECOVERY (STAR); (STAR); OPERATION URGENT FURY.

caisson disease

Caisson disease, also known as decompression sickness, or simply "bends," is the most potentially dangerous condition a SEAL—indeed, *any* diver—may suffer as a result of breathing compressed air at depths. The sickness occurs as a result of the presence of nitrogen in the air we breathe.

The pressure of the air around us at sea level is considered to be "one atmosphere." That pressure increases when diving, each 33 feet underwater adding an additional atmosphere of pressure. The pressure at 33 feet is two atmospheres, at 66 feet is three atmospheres, and so on. This means the air a diver breathes and the air inside his body can be greatly condensed, according to his depth under water.

Nitrogen, which constitutes about 78 percent of the air, penetrates blood vessels under pressure and lodges in fatty tissues and bone joints. If the diver surfaces too rapidly to allow the nitrogen to dissipate properly, it expands inside joints and tissue to cause excruciating pain, damage to the body, and even death. The lungs may even explode or produce an air embolism. The cure is to redive to previous levels or to recompress in a decompression chamber, which reproduces atmospheric pressure at different depths.

Several men were instrumental in discovering the cause of this phenomena, its symptoms, and its remedies. Robert Boyle, an English physicist, was the first to observe it, in the eyes of serpents. From that observation he formulated Boyle's law, which states that the volume of a gas at constant temperature varies inversely with its pressure. That was in 1667.

Two centuries later, in 1873, Dr. Andrew H. Smith, surgeon to the New York Bridge Company, noticed an ailment commonly suffered by workers who emerged from pressurized caissons after surfacing from working on the Brooklyn Bridge under water—bends. Although Smith's report made no mention of the true cause of decompression sickness, nitrogen bubbles, he did recommend chamber recompression for future bridge projects. It was from this incident of caisson workers that the condition took its name—caisson disease.

Five years later, in 1878, Frenchman Paul Bert published *La Pression Barometrique* about his physiological studies of pressure changes. It was he who demonstrated that decompression sickness is due to the formation of nitrogen gas bubbles. He suggested gradual ascent as one way to prevent the problem.

In 1906, the British government asked John Scott Haldane to do research in the prevention of decompression sickness. With two coauthors, he published a paper that laid the groundwork for staged decompression and for the formulation of tables based on gradual ascent. These "decompression tables" were soon adopted by the Royal Navy, later by the U.S. Navy, and they are still in use today.

See also BOYLE'S LAW; DECOMPRESSION CHAMBER; NAVY DIVE TABLES.

Callahan, John F.

The creation of the U.S. Navy SEALs was formally authorized in December 1961, and the first unit was commissioned in January 1962. Lt. (j.g.) Roy Boehm received the first SEAL orders, making him not only the *first* SEAL but also acting commanding officer of SEAL Team Two at Little Creek, Virginia. Lt. John Callahan was named as the actual commanding officer, but due to delays traveling from the West Coast and meetings he had to attend in Washington, D.C., on how to use the new unit, he didn't actually arrive at Team Two for several months. Boehm then reverted from acting CO to executive officer.

"I've been looking forward to your arrival," Boehm greeted his skipper. "I'm damned happy the ball is finally in your court. What are your plans and what do you want me to do?"

"Roy, keep doing what you're doing. I'm going to Washington."

According to Boehm, he only saw Callahan one or two times the entire year. "Hamilton [William H., CO of UDT-21] and Callahan were both good men and good leaders," said Boehm. "They realized I was the man best equipped to make the SEALs go. They simply turned me loose."

Most of the new SEALs of Team Two recall Lieutenant Hamilton making a speech to them upon his introduction to the team. SEAL plankowner James Watson remembers it well: "Men, you are very lucky to have been selected to form such a unit," he said. "I advise you to set your aims high, because with every year, and every new commanding officer, a little bit of what we create here today will be lost. The day will come where the only difference between the SEAL Team and being aboard ship will be that the building won't rock and roll."

As it turned out, he was wrong. Most SEAL old-timers feel that the U.S. Navy SEALs have only gotten better with the passage of time.

See also BOEHM, ROY; HAMILTON, WILLIAM H.; PLANKOWNERS; SEALS.

camouflage

The Trojan horse—Greek troops camouflaged themselves inside a giant wooden horse—may have been the most successful example of military troops concealing or misrepresenting their identities. Because SEALs and other modern special warfare soldiers must often operate behind hostile lines and in small units, they have become masters of misrepresenting, concealing, or disguising themselves. Camouflage entails more than wearing uniforms that blend in with terrain and face paint to cut down skin sheen and regularity of features. Successfully done, camouflage considers sight, sound, and scent.

In Vietnam, SEALs were figures of fear to the enemy in the Mekong Delta. Viet Cong spoke of them with respect, even awe, as "men with green faces." When SEALs went into the field, they took all precautions to blend into their surroundings. That included using face camouflage paint in irregular patterns to cover all exposed skin—face, neck, and hands. They also wore face veils or nets and disguised their outlines with foliage or "ghilly suits," sniper clothing constructed of strips of burlap.

All weapons and equipment used by SEALs are constructed of nonreflective materials in green, brown, flat black, or similar hues to blend into any battlefield terrain. For example, desert BDUs (battle dress uniforms) such as those used during Desert Storm are of a light-colored clay, sand, and loam pattern; forest BDUs are patterned in dark shades of green and shadow. Face-camouflage paint likewise comes in different colors.

By an extension of the definition, certain actions, such as parachuting onto an objective or clandestinely arriving ashore from beneath the sea, may be considered camouflage, since the idea is to conceal your presence from the enemy. The techniques of sight camouflage are limited only by the imagination. The goal is to fool the enemy into not seeing you—or if he does see you, not to recognize what you are.

The camouflage of sound is equally important. SEAL boats are powered by carefully mufflered engines, often exhausting into the water to cut down noise. A HAHO (high altitude, high opening) parachute insertion may be made so the foe will not see or hear the high-flying airplane or hear the paratroopers when they land silently in the darkness. All loose equipment that may clank or rattle is padded and taped. Arm and hand signals are employed rather than spoken communications. SEALs have learned through experience a number of little tricks to cut down sound, from how to walk stealthily in the woods to how to fill canteens. When on a mission, for example, the entire team will drink water from the same canteen, to empty one at a time. This prevents water from sloshing around inside partly depleted canteens.

No SEAL would dare go into a combat situation wearing aftershave or following a bath with scented soap. People can actually smell each other in the woods, sometimes over great distances. Koreans often smell of kimchi, a pickled cabbage that forms a mainstay of their diets. Vietnamese smell of fish and fish sauce. Americans exude an odor of meat. The idea is to disguise these odors as much as possible and not to replace them with something else equally distinctive, such as filthy body odor or chemicals.

Lives have been lost or saved through camouflage. All militaries use it, ranging from the colors ships are painted (Atlantic and Pacific ships require different-colored camouflage) to the individual soldier smearing his face with greasepaint, sticking twigs in his helmet, and bathing in plain water. New techniques are constantly being discovered and tested. SEALs and U.S. Army Green Berets are perhaps the world's most talented chameleons.

See also ARM AND HAND SIGNALS.

Cannon, William T.

The first SEAL teams had barely formed and were still in the process of organizing themselves when they were thrown into action during the Cuban missile crisis. Lt. William T. "Red" Cannon led a team of seven men from SEAL Team Two and Underwater Demolition Team 22 on a covert reconnaissance of Cuba's San Mariel Harbor in 1962 to determine if frogmen could swim in and knock out enemy patrol boats in the event of open hostilities between the United States and Cuba.

See also CUBAN MISSILE CRISIS.

Carley, Norman J.

The Naval Special Warfare Development Group (DevGru) at Dam Neck, Virginia, is responsible for U.S. counterterrorism efforts in the maritime environment. The creation of the command can be traced back through SEAL Team Six to the aftermath of Operation Eagle Claw, the failed 1980 attempt to rescue American hostages held at the American embassy in Iran, and before that to MOB Six (Mobility Six).

MOB Six was the brainchild of Lt. Norman J. "Norm" Carley, operations officer of SEAL Team Two on the East Coast. Although SEAL teams on both coasts had already begun counterterrorism training in response to rising incidents of international terrorism against Americans and American interests, Carley took the training another step forward. In 1978, he formed what turned out to be a new kind of SEAL team—an element of about 20 senior enlisted men and himself within SEAL Team Two that devoted about half its time to planning and training for counterterrorist operations. He called the unit Mobility Six, or simply "MOB Six."

Later that same year, MOB Six received the opportunity to practice some of its theories when a major NATO symposium, Sealink 78, was held at Annapolis, Maryland. Some of the NATO commanders had received terrorist threats. Carley and MOB Six were tapped to form a platoon to provide waterfront security during the conference.

Whether because of MOB Six or not, there were no incidents. Top navy officials were so impressed by the concept of a SEAL counterterrorism force that two years after the Iranian rescue debacle, SEAL Team Six was created. The new unit's sole mission was anti- and counterterrorism. Since only one such force was needed, MOB Six was disbanded in October 1980. Carley and many of his men were asked to join the new group. Carley became SEAL Team Six's executive officer, under the command of Lt. Cdr. Richard Marcinko.

Carley went on to command SEAL Team Two. In 1989, he was involved in the planning and execution of Operation Just Cause, the U.S. invasion of Panama.

See also MARCINKO, RICHARD; NAVAL SPECIAL WARFARE DEVELOPMENT GROUP (DEVGRU); OPERATION JUST CAUSE; "RED CELL"; SEAL TEAM SIX.

Casey, Thomas W.

Lt. (j.g.) Thomas J. Casey was squad commander of "Golf One" at the fight at the Paitilla Airfield in Panama during Operation Just Cause in 1989. Four SEALs were killed in the action.

See also OPERATION JUST CAUSE.

cast and recovery

The "cast and recovery" method of deploying and retrieving SEALs from the water was developed by the underwater demolition teams (UDTs) during World War II and is still used by modern SEALs.

A rubber boat is attached to a powerboat that speeds along offshore. SEALs in rapid succession "cast" themselves by rolling from the boat into the inflatable craft and thence, holding their face masks in place, into the water.

The "recovery" occurs in reverse. Each SEAL prepares for pickup by raising one arm and kicking hard with his flippers to lift himself high in the water. The recovery boat, towing the inflatable boat alongside, passes by at speeds up to 15 knots. Aboard the inflatable is a SEAL who snares the

SEALs are deployed and recovered from a rubber boat during "cast and recovery." This is the "cast" phase. (U.S. Navy)

upraised arm with a rubber hoop and hauls the swimmer aboard.

See also INSERTION/EXTRACTION.

Central Intelligence Agency (CIA)

The nature of the SEAL mission in both covert and overt operations requires SEALs to work closely with the Central Intelligence Agency (CIA). President Harry Truman created the CIA in 1947 with the signing of the National Security Act. That act charged the CIA with "coordinating the nation's intelligence activities and correlating, evaluating and disseminating intelligence which affects national security." The CIA was also to conduct "counterintelligence activities, special activities, and other functions related to foreign intelligence and national security, as directed by the President." It is within this area of "special activities and other functions"

that the CIA found American special warfare forces to be invaluable assets.

The CIA utilized special warfare units from as early as the Korean War, when underwater demolition teams (UDTs) began experimenting with commando-type operations. Sometimes on their own, sometimes working with the CIA, UDTs inserted themselves and South Korean guerrilla units far behind enemy lines to disrupt supply lines and lines of communications. Francis Douglas Fane recalls, "We landed North Koreans, who had been trained in the South as guerrillas, on the east coast of Korea up within sixty miles of the Soviet port of Vladivostok, using the techniques of the UDT. We landed upwards of fifty a night for a couple of nights, from rubber boats, at two or three in the morning. We'd lie in the rocks while the Chinese passed by twenty or thirty feet away and wait until the coast was clear."

SEALs and the CIA have worked closely together since the commissioning of the SEALs in 1962. A few

Even today, many aspects of operations carried out during the SEALs' early beginnings remain highly classified and inaccessible to the public. Spying and intelligence networking, electronic eavesdropping, and other practices of the CIA were engaged in by SEALs, to varying degrees. Low-intensity conflicts (LIC)—limited, unconventional warfare—is the perfect battleground for CIA activities, as well as for special warfare. While details of most covert actions remain classified Secret, SEALs tell stories of their CIA affiliations. These stories provide some insight into SEAL-CIA associations.

SEAL lieutenant Jack "Blackjack" Macione recalls a mission his team was assigned during the Dominican Republic rebellion in 1961. The team was to blow up a radio station in Santo Domingo. The CIA was running the show and wanted to make sure the team was "nonattributable" should any of its members be killed or captured. That meant they must not be identifiable as Americans.

Lieutenant Macione pointed out that Mike Boynton had a tattoo on his arm—*God Bless America.* The team was drawing sanitized clothing (that is with no marks to link it to the U.S.) from tents in the middle of the jungle when an Army Special Forces medic showed up. "Roll up your sleeve," he said to Boynton. Boynton rolled up his sleeve. The medic whipped out a can of ether, sprayed the tattoo, took out his scalpel and scraped the tattoo right off. Boynton became immediately "nonattributable."

Assassinations of foreign dignitaries by U.S. forces and agencies were outlawed during the Reagan administration. Before then, however, several attempts were made to assassinate Fidel Castro in Cuba. None of these, as far as is known, directly involved SEALs. However, Roy Boehm, in his autobiography *First SEAL* (with Charles W. Sasser), describes an assassination he conducted for the CIA in 1962.

President Rafael Trujillo of the Dominican Republic had been assassinated more than a year previously; Rafael Bonnelly had assumed control of the provisional government. Trujillo had housed and trained a group of international assassins, and these assassins were still at work. CIA spies uncovered a plot by these assassins to kill a Cuban in Havana who happened to be working with the CIA to overthrow Castro.

Boehm was assigned to kill the would-be assassin before he could carry out his task. He was provided

SEALs are deployed and recovered from a rubber boat during "cast and recovery." This is the "recovery" phase. (U.S. Navy)

of their cooperative missions included the effort to rescue Americans from Iran, the recovery of the hijacked cruise ship *Achille Lauro,* and military actions in the Dominican Republic, Cuba, Grenada, Panama, Bosnia, Serbia, Iraq, and, of course, Vietnam and Afghanistan.

SEALs were closely involved with the CIA from the very beginning of the Vietnam War, and they were involved at the very end. In fact, the first SEAL detachment of two officers and 10 enlisted men sent to Vietnam in early 1963 became part of a small group of military men assigned to work under the CIA. The CIA mission at the time was to infiltrate agents into the North to stir up resistance movements against the government in Hanoi. The SEALs' job was to set up a system to land agents from the sea.

a photograph of his target—a pudgy Latino of about 40 with dark hair, balding on top, a sharp nose, and a knife-slash of a mouth. "He must be stopped before he can kill our man in Havana," CIA agents said in briefing the SEAL. "He must be neutralized within the next fifteen days."

"Political assassinations—call them *murder*—were still legitimate covert actions in the early and mid-1960s," Boehm writes. "I realized that spying, dirty tricks, and political killing were all part of the unconventional warfare scenario into which I had bought stock once I committed to training the SEALs. Still, the hard reality of it took a little getting used to. Like most SEALs this early in the unit's existence, I had never killed a man face-to-face."

The plan was a simple one. Boehm flew to Santo Domingo, using as cover an assignment as adviser to the Dominican underwater demolition teams. Once there, a CIA undercover he knew only as "Raul" pointed out to him his target, a man called Manuel. A third man, Renaldo, who also worked with the CIA undercover in Cuba, had set up Manuel for the kill.

"You have a meeting scheduled with [Manuel]," Raul informed the SEAL. "It's arranged that he thinks you are an American friend of Renaldo's. You will meet at Renaldo's residence. . . . He will think he is meeting both you and Renaldo. It is very clever. Castro will think Renaldo is also in danger. He will never suspect him." Boehm was provided a 9 mm German Luger, equipped with a makeshift silencer as long as the pistol itself.

> Everything was so *ordinary*, so *normal*. Some guy gives me a pistol. *Now go kill this other guy.* This was all there was to it?
>
> A Dominican military Beechcraft flew me from Santo Domingo to the little airstrip in Las Calderas. A driver in a Land Rover met me. The afternoon was still full of sunshine when he dropped me off in front of one of the most expensive houses in the valley between the hills above the bay. It was a neat, open house painted a shimmering gray. . . .
>
> I got out of the vehicle. I had dressed casual for the occasion in slacks and a loose tropical shirt. Inside my valise were a manila envelope containing my notes and reports on the Dominican navy and UDT, a clean shirt, and the silenced Luger.

> "I'll be here when you are done," the driver said, and drove off. . . .
>
> Manuel rushed outside like the attentive host to greet me. . . . He was smiling and gracious as he escorted me into a breezy, tile-floored room whose curtains over wide windows breathed with breezes coming from the sea. I repressed a pang of guilt as I noted how Manuel was no warrior, not even an armed opponent sworn to cause me personal harm. He was merely a pudgy middle-aged Cuban with skin like dark walnut, dressed in a loose shirt, baggy shorts, sandals, and a modified fedora to keep the tropical sun from burning his bald spot.
>
> "Where's Renaldo?" I asked to make conversation.
>
> "He will return very shortly, senor. That's why we are waiting."
>
> That *wasn't* why we were waiting.
>
> "Would you like a drink? A rum or a beer?"
>
> I could have gone for a beer, but I declined. I took a chair across from Manuel. I placed the valise next to my foot. It was already unsnapped. We made small talk for a while as I improvised a plan, such as it was, and we ostensibly waited for Renaldo to make his appearance. I had already looked Manuel over and decided he was unarmed.
>
> Manuel removed his hat. I picked out a spot behind his ear as he lounged in his chair across from me, swirling ice cubes in a glass. A bullet behind the ear was quick, clean, and painless.
>
> "My people have given me some money for you," I announced presently to fill in a silence.
>
> Manuel looked puzzled, but said nothing. Trying to appear casual, I reached into my valise and extracted the manila envelope. I deliberately dropped it on the floor as I reached to hand it to him. He bent to retrieve it.
>
> My hand darted for the Luger. The goddamned thing with its outlandish silencer hung on the inside of the valise. The valise came off the floor with the weapon.
>
> Sloppy. This whole . . . thing was sloppy.
>
> Still reaching for the envelope, Manuel peered up at me through thick brows. He looked surprised, then startled, starting to frown as I shook the Luger free.
>
> His eyes focused with terror then on the last thing he was to see on this earth—the rough-looking silencer and the little hole at its very end. He started to rise from his chair.

I sprang up in a half-crouch and thrust the pistol toward the little spot behind his ear. He twisted his head. I squeezed the trigger.

The Luger spat with a noise not much louder than that of a Daisy air rifle. The bullet splashed into his forehead. He lunged facedown to the floor, losing all control of his muscles and nerves. His body did the chicken, jerking and flailing weakly about.

The action had turned me cold and emotionless. Mission always came first, ahead of men, ahead of self, ahead of God. I calmly shot Manuel again. This time I did not miss the spot behind his ear. He went still. Blood poured thick and rich and copper smelling from the two holes in his skull.

I wiped prints from the Luger and placed it at the entrance to the room where the police would hopefully see it first and pick it up. . . . I had been careful to touch nothing else while I was inside the house. I took a last look around, like a criminal at a crime scene, to make sure I had overlooked nothing. Then I mock-saluted the dead man and went out the back door and around to the front. The Land Rover appeared immediately.

See also ACHILLE LAURO; BAY OF PIGS; CHINA BEACH; DOMINICAN REPUBLIC, INTERVENTION; GRENADA; OPERATION JUST CAUSE; PHOENIX PROGRAM.

Chariots

The development of Chariots—British manned torpedoes—was an important step toward the evolution of SEAL submersibles and SDVs (SEAL delivery vehicles).

On the night of December 18–19, 1941, six Italians mounted three torpedoes, two men on each, and guided them under water into the harbor at Alexandria, Egypt, where they blew up two English battleships and a tanker. At the time, the Brits were not in the lead in developing manned torpedoes, but they were definitely in the race. They soon produced their own manned torpedoes, which they called "Chariots."

A Chariot was essentially a torpedo upon which had been mounted seats of sorts and a guidance mechanism. The crew wore LARU (Lambertsen Amphibious Respiratory Unit) underwater breathing devices and "drove" the torpedo to its target. While the torpedo could act as the explosive itself when so armed, it was primarily designed as a platform with which swimmers could rapidly approach a moored ship and plant explosives onto its keel. It was a primitive submersible able to carry swimmers.

English "frogmen" planned their first combat swim using Chariots for the night of October 31, 1942. The target was the German battleship *Tirpitz,* then hidden in the inner harbor at Trondheim, far up the Trondheimfjord from the North Sea. The plan called for two Chariots and crews to be transported aboard a merchant ship disguised as a small peat-carrying freighter, which would steam up the fjord until it was close to the anchorage at Trondheim. The two men assigned to each Chariot would then dress in cumbersome gear, climb aboard their underwater steed, approach the battleship under water, and place explosive charges to break its keel.

In order to evade German patrols, the merchant ship lowered the Chariots over the side and towed them beneath the water. Just as the ship approached Trondheim, however, it hit a large wave that caused the ship's propeller to cut the Chariots' tow lines. They sank to the bottom, thwarting the mission.

The next attempt, three months later, in January 1943, met with more success. Eight two-man Chariots attacked ships of the Italian navy berthed in the harbor at Palermo. They sank a cruiser, three submarine chasers, and two merchant ships.

Although the Chariots had proved their worth, the British were already developing much more sophisticated undersea craft, a true minisubmarine that they called the "X-Craft." The Chariots were soon retired from action. Americans never used manned torpedoes.

See also ADVANCED SEAL DELIVERY SYSTEM (ASDS); MAIALE; X-CRAFT.

Chief of Naval Operations (CNO)

The Department of the Navy is one of three military departments within the Department of Defense of the U.S. government, the other two being the Departments of the Army and the Air Force. The secretary of the navy, a civilian headquartered in Washington, D.C., heads the Navy Department, under the direction of the secretary of defense. The Chief of Naval Operations (CNO), an admiral and the Navy's highest-ranking officer, serves as the secretary's principal naval adviser and represents the navy on the Joint Chiefs of Staff.

See also ORGANIZATIONAL STRUCTURE, SPECIAL OPERATIONS.

China Beach

When the first SEAL detachment of two officers and 10 enlisted men arrived in Da Nang, South Vietnam, in 1963, it was assigned to work with the Central Intelligence Agency (CIA) infiltrating agents into North Vietnam to stir up trouble for Hanoi. The SEALs were assigned to a special top secret program under the CIA-run MACV-SOG (Military Assistance Command Vietnam—Studies and Observations Group). Operation Plan 34A (OP-34A) was a year-long campaign to increase intensity against North Vietnam. SEALs under the command of Lt. (j.g.) Cathal "Irish" Flynn went to work training guerrilla fighters to carry out harassing raids against the North. In the beginning the commandoes were all ethnic Vietnamese; later, they included Chinese, Thais, Nungs, Montagnards and Cambodians.

OP-34A training bases were hidden in secret little camps along a 10-mile stretch of beach between Monkey Mountain on the north and Marble Mountain on the south, near Da Nang. At various times, up to seven groups of 40 or 50 guerrillas each occupied these camps. Their boats were docked in a little cove at the base of Monkey Mountain, where the SEALs had established a base they called "China Beach."

A number of raids were made out of China Beach; some of them were failures, others were more successful. During the spring and summer of 1964, China Beach operations were a constant irritant to the North Vietnamese. Commandos captured a junk, destroyed a storage facility, blew up a bridge, and shelled a lighthouse.

SEALs, who were strictly prohibited from accompanying their charges north of the 17th parallel, which separated the two Vietnams, were in little danger at this early juncture of the war. Duty was relaxed and unstressful. They had a lovely beach all to themselves. Lt. Maynard Weyers, who relieved Lieutenant Flynn and commanded the SEAL Team One platoon at China Beach in the fall of 1964, recalls running alone for miles along the beach without a weapon, and without feeling threatened.

Since the SEALs did not bother the local Viet Cong, the VC did not bother them.

When the U.S. Marines arrived in Vietnam in 1965, a marine general commandeered a little hideaway near China Beach, prompting one SEAL to remark that "generals and SEALs know how to get through the war."

Pinpricks through they were, the OP 34A missions played a significant role in the changing of the United States role from one of covert support to open involvement of American forces.

See also CENTRAL INTELLIGENCE AGENCY (CIA); FLYNN, CATHAL L.; GULF OF TONKIN RESOLUTION; MACV-SOG; OPERATION PLAN 34A. (OP-34A).

Chuting Stars

During the early 1960s, as SEALs acquired more and more skills as parachutists, they formed their own informal parachute demonstration teams—the Leap Frogs on the West Coast and the Chuting Stars on the East Coast. Both teams put on demonstrations at air shows and other military and social functions for a number of years before they were officially commissioned on April 16, 1974.

Colored smoke trailing behind SEAL jumpers as they fell failed to impress spectators. Jumpers therefore began to stress "relative work," in which they performed maneuvers so close that parachutes actually touched. In one of these maneuvers, called "stacking," one parachutist sat on top of another man's canopy. That was often followed by the "biplane," in which the top jumper swung into the lower man's lines and stood on his shoulders.

Pierre Ponson, a veteran of the Chuting Stars, asserts that the two maneuvers were quite safe, except for the transition from one to the other. That had to be done very carefully. On September 16, 1980, during a demonstration at Lakehurst, New Jersey, two Chuting Stars attempted a transition from a stack to a biplane when the upper man inadvertently cut loose from his parachute. He instinctively grabbed for the lower man's parachute, collapsing it. Petty Officers Third Class Paul P. Kelly and Richard Doheny plummeted 4,300 feet to their deaths.

The Chuting Stars were disbanded in 1984. The Leap Frogs remain the official U.S. Navy SEAL parachute demonstration team.

See also AIRBORNE; OLSON, NORMAN H.

The Chuting Stars were commissioned as one of two U.S. Navy SEAL parachute demonstration teams in 1974, although they had been conducting demonstrations since the early 1960s. They were decommissioned in 1984, leaving the Leap Frog as the only U.S. Navy official parachute demonstration team. Here, Chuting Stars prepare to exit an aircraft. (Charles W. Sasser)

clandestine operations

A clandestine operation is one conducted in such a manner as to ensure concealment of the operation, as compared to a covert operation, which is executed in such a manner as to conceal the identity of the sponsor.

See also COVERT OPERATIONS.

Claymore antipersonnel mine

The Claymore M18A1, which replaced the M18 and became standard in 1960, is described as an antiper-

sonnel mine, although its uses are limited only by the imagination. It is a fixed, directional-fragmentation mine designed primarily for use against massed infantry attacks. SEALs commonly used it in ambushes in Vietnam. It can be particularly devastating when it explodes into an enemy approaching along a trail or road.

The weapon weighs three and one-half pounds and comes in a curved, rectangular, olive-drab, molded case of fiberglass-filled polystyrene. It is eight and a half inches long, one and three-eighths inches thick, and three and one-fourth inches high.

In the front portion of the case is a "fragmentation face" containing steel spheres embedded in a plastic matrix. The portion of the case behind the matrix contains a one-and-one-half-pound layer of C-4 explosive. Two pairs of scissors-type folding legs located on the bottom of the mine enable it to be emplaced on the ground. It can also be tied to posts, trees, or other objects.

Two detonator wells on the top of the mine allow for single or dual priming. It may be electrically fired on command, using wire and an M57 electrical firing device, (a "clacker"), or it may be fired using a nonelectric blasting cap and detonating cord or fuse. This latter method may be employed using the claymore as a "booby trap," which the victim sets off by unknowingly pulling or cutting a trip wire.

When detonated, the mine delivers a deadly hail of steel fragments over a sixty-degree fan-shaped "killing zone" two meters high, 50 meters wide, and 50 meters out. Fragments are moderately effective up to a range of 100 meters, the length of a football field.

closed-circuit breathing apparatus

SEALs do not normally use SCUBA (self-contained underwater breathing apparatus) of the type used by sports divers. Ordinary divers use a system of compressed air in an "open circuit" design, which emits bubbles and noise readily detectable by an alert enemy.

Instead, SEALs on real-world missions use a closed-circuit breathing apparatus, a concept that diving pioneers like Hans Haas and Jacques Cousteau began experimenting with in the late 1930s and 1940s. One SEAL rig, called a Draeger Mark V, has been in use since 1975. An Austrian design, the Draeger replaced a system of a similar American manufacture, the Emerson. These devices use a supply of oxygen, a system of bags and hoses, and a canister of baralyme. The air is circulated and recirculated; no bubbles are emitted.

Because of the hazards of oxygen poisoning associated with breathing pure oxygen at great depths, the SEALs soon turned to "mixed gas" diving. The commonly used Draeger Mark V mixed-gas closed-circuit breathing apparatus is similar in function to the original oxygen-breathing Draeger.

Both the oxygen and the mixed-gas systems work like this. The centerpiece is a cylinder that holds air/mixed gases compressed at 2,000 psi. The first thing a SEAL does upon donning his gear is open the bottle to carefully purge his equipment. Oxygen or mixed gases flow from the bottle and through a hose to the swimmer's mouthpiece. The diver breathes in oxygen/mixed gases and exhales. The mixture is recycled through the canister of baralyme, where the CO_2 is absorbed; the purified oxygen/mixed gases pass back to the mouthpiece. Only what is actually consumed by the diver needs to be replaced from the tank.

"You can usually get up to four hours' use with one, under ideal conditions," explained one SEAL. "But the biggest lesson we learned . . . is that when you put people under stress on a real-world situation, gas consumption doubles over what you see in tests and hard training."

Although the Draeger, which weighs about 35 pounds ashore, becomes neutral-weighted in the water, it is bulky and laborious to swim with on long insertions.

During Operation Just Cause, the invasion of Panama, SEALs used Draegers to swim under water into Balboa Harbor on a classic ship-attack mission to blow up Gen. Manuel Noriega's yacht to prevent his using it to escape.

See also COUSTEAU, JACQUES-YVES; DAVIS SUBMARINE ESCAPE APPARATUS; LAMBERTSEN, CHRISTIAN J.; MIXED-GAS BREATHING; OXYGEN POISONING.

Colby, William Egan (1920–1996)

During World War II, William Colby served in the Office of Strategic Services (OSS). He was dropped by parachute behind enemy liens in German-occupied France, where he commanded a squad of saboteurs. After the war, he obtained a law degree from Columbia University and in 1950 joined the fledgling CIA. In 1963, he was promoted to bureau chief of the Far Eastern Division, where he was in charge of two controversial CIA projects in Vietnam that involved covert operations by Navy SEALs.

Operation Plan 34A (OP-34A) was a top-secret plan to infiltrate agents into North Vietnam to disrupt communications and supply lines. From 1963 to late 1964, SEALs trained indigenous guerrillas for missions into enemy territory. The successes of OP-34A were minimal. Colby was one of the first to become disillusioned with the whole effort.

"Our experience demonstrated, quite frankly, that there was not much hope of generating any substantial resistance in North Vietnam," he later noted. "And having made a college try at it and having come to zero results in positive terms[,] . . . I came to the conclusion—and I was in charge of them—that he operations should be called off. They really were not contributing what they had hoped to, and they were suffering losses, and there was no point in it." OP-34A ceased operations after slightly more than a year.

The so-called Phoenix Program was then conceived by the CIA in 1967. Under this program, run by Colby, the CIA, U.S. Army Special Forces, and U.S. Navy SEALs were supposed to infiltrate the South Vietnamese peasantry to gather information and to arrest or kill communist cadres. By 1969, according to statistics released by the American mission in Saigon, 19,534 Viet Cong organizers, propagandists, tax collectors, and other VC personnel had been neutralized, 6, 187 of them assassinated. Colby later claimed that the Phoenix Program was responsible for eliminating some 60,000 authentic VC agents during its tenure.

Colby was promoted to Director of Central Intelligence in 1973, serving until President Gerald Ford replaced him with George Bush in 1976. He returned to the business world, serving as a consultant to businesses with international interests (specializing in the Far East) and giving speeches on national security, the role of intelligence in a democracy, and current world affairs. He died on April 27, 1996, in a canoeing accident.

See also CHINA BEACH; CENTRAL INTELLIGENCE AGENCY (CIA); MACV-SOG; OFFICE OF STRATEGIC SERVICES (OSS); OPERATION PLAN 3YA (OP-3YA); PHOENIX PROGRAM; PROVINCIAL RECONNAISSANCE UNITS (PRUS).

Colt AR-15 rifle

The immediate predecessor to the M16, the U.S. main battle rifle, was the Colt AR-15. Manufactured by Colt (after Colt Firearms Corporation purchased the license to produce it from the Fairchild Stratos Corporation in 1959), the AR-15 rifle became commercially available shortly thereafter. At first, the U.S. military was not interested in a new rifle; the 7.62 M14 had just replaced the World War II and Korea–era M1 as the new service rifle in May 1957. It would not be until 1965 that the AR-15 was adopted by the U.S. military, as the M-16.

Prior to its general acceptance by the U.S. military, however, the AR-15 was enthusiastically received by the SEALs. It was lightweight and highly lethal, with full selective fire. Because of the light weight of its ammunition, a great deal of it could be carried. The weapon itself weighed only slightly over seven pounds with a full 30-round magazine.

Lt. Roy Boehm and his SEAL Team Two tested the weapon on their own, following poor reports from other sources. The SEAL program was only months old at the time. Boehm and his men shot the AR-15 and fully tested it. They tossed it into the surf, covered it with sand, silt, and salt water—and it continued operating. Boehm purchased 136 of the rifles directly from the company for his fledgling SEALs.

"The best package of firepower and weight we had were the new AR-15 rifles," says one SEAL. "Half of the weapons went to the West Coast and SEAL Team One with the remainder staying with us. Those were the first rifles of their kind in the Navy and were later adopted by the military as the M-16. We had them first because we needed them."

The AR-15 fired a .223 (5.56 mm) Remington cartridge, 56 grain, at a practical rate of fire of 45 to 65 rounds per minute, and a cyclic rate of 700 to 950 rounds per minute. It came equipped with either a 20 or 30-round magazine. Loaded, the weapon weighed 7.46 pounds and was 38.6 inches long. The carbine model was five inches shorter.

See also COLT AUTOMATIC RIFLE, CARBINE (CAR-15); M16 RIFLE.

Colt automatic rifle, carbine (CAR-15)

The Colt AR-15 rifle began making its appearance in the U.S. armed forces in the early 1960s to replace the M14 7.62 mm main battle rifle. By 1965, the AR-15, modified somewhat and redesignated as the M16, was being phased in as the primary infantry weapon. Lt. Roy Boehm obtained a number of the newer AR-15s when he organized the first SEAL team in 1962. He also obtained at least one of the very rare AR-15 carbines (CAR-15), the Model 605.

The CAR-15 was exactly the same as the AR-15 except the barrel had been cut back to just in front of the front sights and a flash suppressor installed. This reduced the overall length by five inches, from 38.6 inches for the AR-15 to 33.6 inches for the carbine. The carbine was offered by Colt for situations "where stowage is a problem," which certainly applied to the SEALs.

The CAR-15 was little used, however, and saw little field service during the Vietnam War, although it became more popular afterward with counterterrorist units.

See also COLT AR-15 RIFLE.

combat rubber raiding craft (CRRC)
SEAL inflatable craft.

See also INFLATABLE BOATS.

combat survivor evader locator system (CSEL)
Special operations personnel are now being equipped with the new PRQ-7 combat survivor evader locator (CSEL) system that combines a Global Position System (GPS) receiver and a remote tracking beacon to allow combat search-and-rescue units to remotely track an individual or team with GPS precision. It eliminates the need for risky voice transmissions.

See also GLOBAL POSITION SYSTEM (GPS).

combat tactics
Tactics is defined as the science and art of handling troops in the presence of the enemy or for immediate objectives. Strategy, on the other hand, is defined as the science and art of conducting a military campaign on a broad international or global level.

SEALs are rarely involved in strategic operations, because the average size of a SEAL combat element is at the platoon or squad level. Combat tactics for

SEALs in training launch a CRRC in rough seas. (U.S. Navy)

SEALs focus on those suitable for small units operating in unconventional warfare. That means SEALs must develop tactics for functioning behind enemy lines against larger, conventional forces as well as against other unconventional troops. SEALs have therefore perfected the arts of the raid, the ambush, the "snatch," stealthy movement, and the patrol.

Tactical operations must consider the effects of enemy forces, air power, nuclear and chemical weapons, enemy mobility, electronic warfare operations, the morale and capability of soldiers, and all the other tangibles and intangibles that go into making up an enemy's strength. Most important are the nonquantifiable elements of combat power: courageous, well trained soldiers and skillful, effective leaders. In this area especially, Navy SEALs have always excelled.

Combined Operations Pilotage Parties (COPP)

During World War II, while Americans were experimenting with and forming combat swimmer units like the Amphibious Scouts and Raiders, Naval Combat Demolition Units (NCDUs), and Underwater Demolition Teams (UDTs), the British were also looking into using swimmers to help prepare the way for the amphibious landings that lay ahead in Europe. In 1942, the British formed a secret unit called the Combined Operations Pilotage Parties (COPP).

Whereas Americans developed procedures using powerboats to drop-off swimmers to make their way toward shore to conduct beach surveys, British COPPs utilized low-profile kayaks. Small British submarines quietly dropped off the scouts and their kayaks at sea, close to shore. The scouts then paddled toward land, where they checked the gradient of the beach, compared the terrain to the latest charts, and looked for shoals, reefs, and other underwater obstructions; then they paddled back to the submarine. All this was conducted under cover of darkness

Philip H. Bucklew, the "father of naval special warfare," operated with the COPPs during both the Sicily and Salerno invasions. He actually used a kayak to lead ashore the invasion of Salerno. Whatever influence the COPPs, through Bucklew, may have had on the American development of naval special warfare was minuscule. The kayaks were leaky, unstable, and dangerous at sea. Five British COPPs drowned during the Salerno landing, four were captured, and two, unable to retrace their way back to their submarine, had to paddle over 80 miles to reach the nearest island of Malta. The British soon abandoned kayaks in favor of boats.

See also BUCKLEW, PHILIP H., II; NAVAL COMBAT DEMOLITION UNITS (NCDUS); OPERATION HUSKY.

Commander, Amphibious Task Force (CATF)

The admiral in charge of a particular action and responsible for assembling assault elements, including SEALs, for an amphibious operation is referred to as Commander, Amphibious Task Force (CATF).

Commander in Chief, Atlantic Fleet (CINCLANTFLT)

The U.S. Atlantic Fleet under its commander in chief, Atlantic Fleet (CINCLANTFLT), a four-star admiral, provides fully trained, combat-ready forces to support U.S. and NATO commanders in regions of conflict throughout the world. The Atlantic Fleet consists of more than 118,000 sailors and marines, 186 ships, 1,300 aircraft, and 18 major shore stations. Its area of responsibility encompasses a massive geographic area that includes the Atlantic Ocean from the North Pole to the South Pole, the Caribbean Sea, the Gulf of Mexico, and the Pacific Ocean waters from Central and South America to the Galápagos Islands. Its area also includes the Norwegian, Greenland, and Barents Seas and the waters around Africa extending to the Cape of Good Hope.

See also ORGANIZATIONAL STRUCTURE, SPECIAL OPERATIONS.

Commander in Chief, Pacific Fleet (CINCPACFLT)

The U.S. Pacific Fleet under its commander in chief, Pacific Fleet (CINCPACFLT), a four-star admiral, supports the U.S. Pacific Commands theater strategy and provides interoperable, trained, and combat-ready naval forces to the commander in chief, U.S. Pacific Command (USCOMPAC) and other U.S. unified commanders. Its area of responsibility encompasses more than 50 percent of the Earth's surface, just over 100 million square miles.

The Pacific Fleet consists of approximately 200 ships, 2,000 aircraft, and 250,000 sailors and marines.

See also ORGANIZATIONAL STRUCTURE, SPECIAL OPERATIONS.

commandos

When Lt. Roy Boehm was assigned the task of organizing the U.S. Navy SEALs in 1961, it was his intent that they be commandos, sea warriors who, as he put it, "could be used for *any damned thing.*" It was this image of commandos rising out of the depths like sharks to strike terror into the heart of an enemy that set the pattern and direction for what the SEALs are today.

"Commando" is the British term for a soldier trained to take part in specialized operations, but it was originally a Portuguese word used in South Africa during the Boer Wars (1899–1902) to describe surprise attacks by Dutch and Portuguese settlers against hostile African tribesmen. Prime Minister Winston Churchill later suggested the name be used for the British "combined operations unit," which staged hit-and-run raids during World War II. Commandos destroyed war factories and materiels, rescued Allied agents, carried out raids, and conducted ambushes.

The term has come to apply to all special fighting forces trained for quick, destructive raids into enemy territory. U.S. Army Special Forces and Rangers, U.S. Air Force Special Operations, and Navy SEALs are all examples of American commandos, who today operate conjointly under the U.S. Special Operations Command. SEALs have been utilized commando-style in operations in Cuba, Vietnam, the Dominican Republic, Grenada, Panama, Iraq, Bosnia, Serbia, Colombia, and other places around the world.

See also BOEHM, ROY; ORGANIZATIONAL STRUCTURE, SPECIAL OPERATIONS; SEALS; U.S. SPECIAL OPERATIONS COMMAND (USSOCOM).

compact laser designator (CLD)

The compact laser designator (CLD) is a man-portable target-marking device that can be used by a ground operator to mark a target electronically for laser-guided ordnance or laser tracker–equipped aircraft. It weighs 16 pounds, operates on a lithium battery, and has a range of up to a thousand meters. The device is useful to SEALs and other commandos working behind enemy lines who need to pinpoint for destruction a target that is beyond their own capability to handle. SEAL detachments used CLDs in Iraq and Kuwait during the 1991 war against Iraq (Operation Desert Storm) and in Afghanistan in 2001–2002. They set up hidden observation posts overlooking carefully selected targets, which they marked with the CLDs for attack by American air power.

See also TERMINAL GUIDANCE.

compass board

A compass board is utilized by SEALs for underwater navigation. It is more commonly called an "attack board."

See also ATTACK BOARD.

composition-4 (C-4)

A malleable plastic explosive—a military mainstay.

See also EXPLOSIVES.

Connors, John Patrick (1964–1989)

SEAL lieutenant John Connors was shot and killed during the Punta Paitilla airfield raid in Panama during Operation Just Cause, in 1989.

See also OPERATION JUST CAUSE.

Coronado

The Naval Special Warfare Command, which encompasses the Naval Special Warfare Center, where SEALs are trained, is located on 900 acres of beach front at Coronado, California, across the bay from San Diego. The command is responsible for the administration, training, maintenance, support, and readiness of all United States–based active and reserve Naval Special Warfare forces. It is part of Naval Air Station, North Island, complex.

The naval air station was commissioned in 1917. The amphibious training base became a part of the command in 1943, was renamed in 1946 as a naval amphibious base, with one prime duty—the training of West Coast underwater demolition teams (UDTs).

When the SEALs were commissioned in 1962, one team of 50 enlisted men and 10 officers was assigned to each coast—one at Little Creek, Virginia, part of the Norfolk Naval Base complex, the other at Coronado, California. Each team would conduct its own training.

That changed, however, with the commissioning of the Naval Special Warfare Command on April 16, 1987. All SEAL training is now conducted at Coronado, but the course is basically the same as those developed separately by the two original teams. Today, Special Warfare Group One is located at Coronado, and Group Two is headquartered at Little Creek. Each group is made up of three SEAL teams (Teams One, Three, and Five at Coronado), one special boat squadron, and a SEAL delivery vehicle (SDV) team. Group One generally deploys its forces to the Pacific and Persian Gulf.

When asked where he is stationed, a SEAL will generally say either "Coronado" or "Little Creek," not bothering to provide further information.

See also BASIC UNDERWATER DEMOLITION/SEAL (BUD/S) TRAINING; LITTLE CREEK, VIRGINIA; NAVAL SPECIAL WARFARE COMMAND; ORGANIZATIONAL STRUCTURE; SPECIAL OPERATIONS.

Coultas, William B.

In July 1943, a special unit was created in the South Pacific, the Amphibious Scouts, to be used as a patrolling and reconnaissance unit for Gen. Douglas MacArthur's sweep toward Japan. It is considered one of the several forerunners of underwater demolition teams (UDTs) and modern SEALs. Coultas was its commander.

See also AMPHIBIOUS SCOUTS.

counterinsurgency

SEALs do not conduct counterinsurgency as much as constitute a tool by which counterinsurgency is conducted. Counterinsurgency is defined in the dictionary as "measures, usually of a military nature, designed to combat guerrilla warfare or to suppress revolutionary activities," and by the U.S. Joint Chiefs of Staff as "those activities that are concerned with identifying and counteracting the threat to security posed by hostile intelligence services or organizations or by individuals engaged in espionage, sabotage, or subversion."

SEALs and their supporting special boats, craft, and ships offer a unique combination of clandestine and covert operations for counterinsurgency activity, including intense attacks and surgical applications of force. They are the fleet's eyes and ears. They go first into hostile areas to conduct intelligence collection, raids, and ambushes, perform combat search and rescue, and train foreign military forces.

Vietnam, at least in the early stages of the war, was a classic example of counterinsurgent activities initiated and maintained by Americans. It may shed some light on how future operations will be conducted. The plan from the beginning was to "win hearts and minds," to attract the populace away from the communists and thus isolate the Vietnamese guerrillas from their support base. The effort involved a two-pronged attack, persuasion on the one hand, coercion on the other. It prompted special warfare troops to give the phrase "winning hearts and minds" a unique twist: *Once you got 'em by the balls, their hearts and minds will follow.*

"Just remember this: communist guerrillas hide among the people," preached U.S. Army colonel Edward G. Lansdale, who devised a counterinsurgency training course for Americans bound for Vietnam. "If you win the people over to your side, the communist guerrillas have no place to hide. With no place to hide, you can find them. Then, as military men, [you can] fix them . . . finish them."

In April 1961, President John Kennedy created a task force to prepare comprehensive economic, social, political, and military programs aimed at defeating insurgents in South Vietnam and preventing communist domination of the country. Counterinsurgency programs on the positive side of winning hearts and minds included strengthening the South Vietnamese army and providing American Special Forces and SEAL advisers to train it. Other special warfare soldiers were distributed among the provinces to teach Vietnamese peasants how to do everything from breeding pigs and constructing radio stations to digging wells and building houses. American doctors, schoolteachers, accountants, mechanics, even disc jockeys were recruited in this effort. Medicines, milk, gasoline, fertilizers, and other products were imported to generate cash to help pay for the Saigon government and its armed forces.

On the "got 'em by the balls" side, counterinsurgent forces—SEALs and Green Berets—were charged with denying the enemy food and supplies through raids, ambushes, and other overt military actions. American operations involved such programs as Operation Phoenix, to eliminate North Vietnamese cadres, and OP-34A, to infiltrate agents into North Vietnam. Secret intelligence networks were established, with "black bags" full of "dirty tricks" and psychological-warfare options. Rumors, supported by counterfeit VC documents, were spread of Viet Cong (VC) and North Vietnamese atrocities. Agents laced oil destined for Hanoi's trains with acid and concealed explosives in piles of coal intended to fuel the enemy's power plants. Imagination, the more devious the better, continued to direct counterinsurgency efforts throughout the war.

SEALs operating in the Mekong Delta were given tremendous freedom to conduct operations as they saw fit and to use their imagination in counterinsurgency efforts. Platoons developed their own intelligence, plans, and procedures, executing missions largely without outside interference, support, or direction. SEALs today are fond of commenting, "We were winning our part of the war."

See also CHINA BEACH; MACV-SOG; OPERATION PLAN 34A (OP-34A); PHOENIX PROGRAM; PROVINCIAL RECONNAISSANCE UNITS (PRUS).

counternarcotics operations

Special operations forces (SOF), including U.S. Navy SEALs, have been very active in counternarcotics operations in Latin America and the Caribbean. The Goldwater-Nichols Act of 1986 authorized special operations forces to "train host nation counterdrug forces to detect, monitor and counter the production, trafficking and use of illegal drugs." Counterdrug missions account for much of the SOF activity in Latin American and the

Caribbean. U.S. special operations forces, according to a Southern Command publication, are well represented in "an interconnecting network of military teams . . . [providing] intelligence, planning and training to countries actively engaged in countering cocaine cartels."

The exact extent of Special Forces training activity in Latin America and the Caribbean remains unknown. However, on the first of April each year, the secretary of defense must submit a report to Congress discussing the extent of SOF activities with foreign forces. Within the most recent three-year period, SpecOps forces, including Navy SEALs, participated in at least 80 counterdrug training missions in Latin America and may have been active in as many as 291 operations.

counterterrorism

The term "counterterrorism" refers to direct action to prevent, deter, and respond to international terrorists. SEALs have been trained in both antiterrorist and counterterrorist measures.

See also *ACHILLE LAURO*; DEVGRU (DEVGROUP, DEVELOPMENT GROUP); "RED CELL"; SEAL TEAM SIX; TERRORISM.

Cousteau, Jacques-Yves (1910–1997)

With his invention of the Aqua-Lung, which automatically provided compressed air to a diver on demand, Frenchman Jacques Cousteau fundamentally altered diving. Although modern SEALs primarily use a closed-circuit breathing apparatus on actual missions, it was the development of SCUBA (self-contained underwater breathing apparatus), especially the regulator valve, that freed divers from breathing hoses and opened up the potential for commando swimmers.

Ideas about how to free divers to explore the underwater world had been tried for many centuries. It is said Alexander the Great went down into the sea in a crude diving bell. As early as 1865, Frenchmen Benoît Rouquayrol and Auguste Denayrouse patented an apparatus for underwater breathing. The device consisted of a horizontal steel tank of compressed air on the diver's back. Called an "Aerophore," it delivered air to a mouthpiece via a membrane sensitive to outside water pressure. It was the first demand regulator for underwater use. There was one catch—the diver was still tethered to the surface by a hose that pumped fresh air into his low-pressure tank. He was able to disconnect for only a few minutes at a time.

In 1933, French navy captain Yves Le Prieur modified the Rouquayrol-Denayrouse apparatus by using a specially designed valve with a high-pressure air tank to free the diver from all hoses and lines. However, there was no regulator. Once the tap was open, air flowed continuously, the excess escaping around the edges of the diver's mask.

Prior to Cousteau, in spite of all the experimentation, the only practical options for underwater exploration were the diving bell and the helmeted diving suit. Cousteau became fascinated with the possibilities of diving after being injured in an automobile accident in 1933. He began swimming daily in the Mediterranean to strengthen his arms, both of which had been broken. He first experimented with watertight goggles, then tinkered with homemade snorkel hoses, insulated body suits, and portable breathing devices based on the recently invented compressed-air cylinder.

His search for a self-contained underwater breathing apparatus that would transform a swimmer into a "manfish" led him to the Paris office of an engineer named Emile Gagnan. Gagnan had constructed an ingenious valve that allowed automobiles during World War II to run on bottled cooking gas instead of gasoline. The two men redesigned the valve to feed compressed air automatically to a diver on demand and at the pressure of the surrounding water. On Cousteau's first dive, in January 1943, he went down 60 feet in the cold Marne River outside Paris, wearing the bulky 50-pound contraption. "I experimented with all possible maneuvers—loops, somersaults and barrel rolls," he recorded in his journal. "I stood upside down on one finger and burst out laughing, a shrill, distorted laugh. Nothing I did altered the automatic rhythm of the air. Delivered from gravity and buoyancy, I flew around in space."

He and Gagnan patented the SCUBA as the "Aqua-Lung." Cousteau went on to become a household name in many parts of the world through his popular books, films, and television programs documenting his 40-plus years of undersea exploration.

See also AEROPHORE; AQUA-LUNG; DIVING, HISTORY OF; SCUBA.

covert operations

The terms "clandestine" and "covert" are often used interchangeably, but that is technically incorrect. A clandestine operation is executed in such a manner as to ensure *concealment of the operation;* a covert operation is one intended to ensure *concealment of the identity of the sponsor.* A SEAL mission may be clandestine, covert, or both.

SEALs assigned to infiltrate Libya and blow up a chemical weapons plant that the Libyan government says does not exist—that would be a *covert* operation. Raiders would wear "sterile" (unmarked) uniforms and carry nothing that might link them to the U.S. government and thereby prevent "plausible deniability" by the United States. It is the old story—"If you get caught, we will deny all knowledge."

During Desert Storm action against Iraq, SEALs were assigned to land on hostile shores to make Saddam Hussein think that the Americans were going to attack from the sea rather than from Saudia Arabia across the sands. That was a clandestine mission. The true purpose of the mission, to create a diversion, was concealed; there was no effort or need to conceal the identity of the sponsor.

At the beginning of the Vietnam War, before the marines landed in 1965, SEALs were engaged in Operation Pan 34A at China Beach, by which Vietnamese agents were trained for insertion into North Vietnam. SEAL involvement in the training of these agents was covert, in that the United States could not be implicated. The operations themselves were clandestine.

Crabb, Lionel Kenneth Philip (1910–1956)

The exploits of Lionel "Buster" Crabb, recounted in a number of books and articles, made him one of history's legendary frogmen. Although he was British and had no direct connection with the evolution of the U.S. Navy SEALs, he contributed to the tactics and the development of all underwater commandos by his efforts in World War II and afterward.

Early in 1942, after Italian frogmen riding torpedoes sank several ships in Gibraltar Harbor, Crabb was appointed mine and disposal officer, with orders to stop the raids. He devised a two-fold defense. First, sailors dropped explosive charges at intervals into the water at the harbor's entrance, hoping to kill any divers present or force them to the surface. Second, Crabb formed a small group of hastily trained swimmers to search constantly the hulls of ships in the harbor to keep them free of mines. The strategy worked, and no more ships were sunk.

After the war, he headed an underwater bomb disposal team until he was demobilized in 1947. It was then he entered the mysterious world of underwater espionage, either employed by the Admiralty or doing other secret diving work. Several times during the cold war period he conducted missions for or under the direction of America's Central Intelligence Agency (CIA). On the evening of April 17, 1956, under CIA auspices, he was engaged to check out the Soviet cruiser *Ordzhonikidze,* which had brought Premier Nikita Khrushchev to England and was moored in Portsmouth, England. While searching the ship's hull for special antisonar gear or minelaying hatches, he mysteriously disappeared.

His death was listed as due to drowning, but theories persist as to what might actually have happened to him. One of these maintain that he was captured and murdered by the Russians. Others are more bizarre, such as one suggesting that he had been sent on a secret mission that called for him to be captured in order to penetrate the Soviet combat-swimmer teams.

Cuban Missile Crisis

The SEALs' first missions after being commissioned in 1962 were against Cuba, only 90 miles from Key West. In fact, the two teams, one on the East Coast and the other on the West, barely had time to organize before they were thrown into action. Had the United States gone to war during the Cuban missile crisis of October 1962, SEALs would have played a small but important part in the invasion.

After the defeat of anti-Castro rebels at the Bay of Pigs in April 1961, the CIA continued the idea of fomenting revolution among patriot Cubans in Florida. That the United States was still planning an invasion of the communist island was made quite apparent at the end of April 1962, one year after the Bay of Pigs and five months before the missile crisis, when a six-man SEAL team was sent on a highly secret mission to reconnoiter the Havana shoreline for a possible amphibious assault.

Lt. Roy Boehm, executive officer of SEAL Team Two and the man responsible for forming the first SEAL teams, was picked to lead the reconnaissance. Because he believed that SEALs and underwater demolition teams (UDTs) should merge into a single unit, which would not occur until 1983, he formed his team of equal numbers of SEALs and UDT frogmen. Boehm, Harry "Lump-Lump" Williams, and J. C. Tipton made up the SEAL side; Gene Tinnan, George Walsh, and Chief Schmidt represented the UDTs.

Mission planning originally called for a two-man recon unit—Boehm and Tipton—to use swimmer propulsion units (SPUs) and an electronic depth finder to measure and calculate the depth of the water and chart the underwater terrain off the Cuban shore. The four remaining swimmers would stay aboard the insertion submarine as a backup. However, a logistical foul-up resulted in failure to obtain SPUs and the Draeger closed-circuit underwater breathing apparatus Boehm had requested. The Scott apparatus, which Boehm considered inferior, would have to be used instead. The outcome was that the entire six-man team locked out of the submarine USS *Treadfin* and began swimming on the surface to the coast, under cover of darkness.

Soviet-made Komar patrol boats sped directly over the swimmers, who dove to avoid detection. While his men conducted the hydrographic survey—the old World War II way, using plumbing lines and slates—Boehm scouted a military outpost on the beach, actually entering the barracks while six or seven Cuban soldiers were sleeping. A mounted sentry rode directly past the beach where the team was conducting its survey but failed to detect anything extraordinary. The team returned to the *Treadfin.* Boehm's report made its way into the Pentagon planning for a Cuban action.

By autumn of 1962, it was apparent that the Soviets were moving intercontinental ballistic missiles into Cuba. That led to one of the most daring missions in SEAL history. Up to now, SEALs had been involved in mapping possible invasion sites, training resistance forces, and conducting spy and assassination missions against Castro. They were now committed to proving the existence of Soviet missiles on the island.

Boehm was ordered to pick one other SEAL to accompany him on a top secret hazardous mission. He chose Harry "Lump-Lump" Williams. The two commandos were in the dark about what the mission entailed until they boarded the submarine USS *Sea Lion* in Florida. There they were introduced to a CIA "spook" who called himself John. John provided high-altitude U-2 photos of Bahía del Mariel, a deep-water harbor a few kilometers west of Havana. Pictured were Soviet ships tied up to docks, and large, flatbed trailer trucks that seemed to be hauling away long cylindrical objects covered with tarps. "We must obtain irrefutable proof that they're missiles," John explained.

He was a photographer. The SEALs' job was to infiltrate him safely into Cuba, where they would meet a contact, then get him out again after he finished photographing the missiles. There was one problem—John couldn't swim very well, and he wasn't qualified as a diver. As a result, the three men locked out of the sub outside Bahia del Mariel, code-named "Pinlon" for the mission, and surface-swam to shore. The two SEALs pushed John and his equipment on an inflatable raft.

They landed near midnight on Punto Barlovento, the harbor's outer tip. An in-country contact met them and directed them through a rundown warehouse area on the waterfront toward where the freighters were docked, about a thousands yards ahead around the harbor. Boehm and Williams hid in and underneath a fisherman's shack the rest of that night and the following day, while John and the contact guide left to go about their business.

On the second night, the guide returned. He directed the SEALs to an abandoned warehouse where John was waiting; the photographer needed them for security. For the rest of that night, the two SEALs, the CIA agent, and the guide lay concealed on the roof of the warehouse overlooking the harbor while John photographed the remarkable scene below.

An operation was under way on the docks. Armed Komars, their running lights extinguished, made slow, vigilant rounds at the harbor's entrance. The only illumination came from lights thrown over the sides of the freighters to discourage frogmen. Stevedores rigged lines and cables around a long, canvas-covered cylinder aboard one of the ships. A long tractor-trailer truck was having trouble maneuvering around a sharp corner on the way to the piers; a crane arrived to pick up the end of the truck and move it around.

The trailer was specially designed with chocks and blocks as if to receive a missile. Using a light-collecting telephoto lens, John shot several rolls of film as workers transferred what seemed to be a missile from the Soviet ship to the Cuban truck. Although he could not photograph it, little imagination was required to know that the canvas covering concealed an intercontinental ballistic missile (ICBM). It was an awesome piece of ordnance. It harnessed more destructive power than the entire U.S. fleet had expended against the Japanese during World War II, including the atomic bombs dropped on Hiroshima and Nagasaki.

"Not good enough," John fretted. He had to get closer. Leaving his companions on the roof, he slipped down and actually mingled with the stevedores on the docks to obtain close-ups. Boehm thought it one of the most gutsy things he had ever seen.

Photographs John took added to the mountain of evidence accumulating against the communists. Examinations of both air and ground photos by the American intelligence community revealed several missile installations under construction in Cuba to accommodate at least 16 and possibly 32 ICBMs, each with a range of over 1,000 miles. Military experts advised that the missiles could be operational within a week. If released against the United States, it was estimated that they could destroy 80 million Americans, roughly half the population.

On October 16, 1962, shortly after nine o'clock, President John Kennedy called his brother, Attorney General Robert Kennedy, to the White House. On October 20, the nation's military went on full alert. On October 22, Kennedy made his famous and frightening announcement to the United States. The U.S. Navy would establish an embargo against Cuba to prevent any further Soviet missiles being delivered and to force Khrushchev to remove those already within the country. America was forcing a possible nuclear showdown with the Soviet Union, one that could conceivably end with the destruction of all civilization. The world waited with bated breath for the next week as a fleet of Soviet ships steamed toward Cuba.

"Let no one doubt that this is a difficult and dangerous effort on which we have set out," the president said in his speech. "No one can foresee what course it will take or what costs and casualties will be incurred. Many months of sacrifice and self-discipline lie ahead, months in which both our patience and our will will be tested, months in which many threats and denunciations will keep us aware of our dangers. But the greatest danger of all would be to do nothing."

Planes, men, and ammunition were deployed, ready to deliver bombardments and assaults. Ballistic missile crews were placed on maximum alert. Troops moved into Florida and elsewhere in the southeastern part of the United States. The First Armored Division began to thunder out of Texas toward Georgia. Five more divisions were placed on full alert. The navy deployed 180 ships into the Caribbean. SAC, the Strategic Air Command, dispersed to civilian landing fields around the country. B-52 bombers were ordered into the air loaded with nuclear weapons.

Lt. John Callahan, commanding officer of SEAL Team Two, was assigned to the staff of CINCLANT-FLT (Commander in Chief, Atlantic Fleet) for the duration, which left Lt. Roy Boehm in command of the team. Secret orders placed him in charge of both Team Two, at Little Creek, and Team One, from the West Coast, roughly 120 men, to capture the harbor at Bahía del Mariel and keep it open in advance of the anticipated invasion of Cuba.

Part of the SEAL force, along with Army Special Forces, would parachute onto the heights above the seaport, near the Cuban military academy, to secure the terrain around the harbor. It would also seize any ships at the piers to prevent their being sunk in the mouth of the harbor to block it. The rest of the SEALs would embark at sea in sixteen-foot gunboats armed with machine guns and 3.5 inch rocket launchers, with which to take out the Komars and any security forces.

Lt. William T. "Red" Cannon led a covert reconnaissance of San Mariel Harbor to determine if frogmen could swim in and destroy the enemy patrol boats in the event of open hostilities. He concluded it could be done.

For days the SEALs waited at Little Creek for orders committing them to Cuba. But then the approaching Soviet fleet stopped dead in the water, short of an actual confrontation. Khrushchev had blinked first in the stare-down with Kennedy. He sent a letter to the United States stating that the missile launch sites in Cuba were going to be dismantled and the missiles returned to the Soviet Union.

The crisis was over.

See also BAY OF PIGS; BOEHM, ROY; CALLAHAN, JOHN F.; CANNON, WILLIAM T., CENTRAL INTELLIGENCE AGENCY (CIA); KENNEDY, JOHN F.

D

da Vinci, Leonardo (1452–1519)

Although Leonardo da Vinci, one of the greatest painters of the Italian Renaissance, is best known for his portrait *Mona Lisa* and his oil *The Last Supper,* he was also one of the most versatile geniuses in history. He studied anatomy, astronomy, botany, and geology. He designed machines and drew plans for hundreds of inventions. His ideas and designs were far ahead of his time. For example, he drew plans for a flying machine, a parachute, and a diving bell.

One of his most remarkable sketches was of a self-contained underwater breathing apparatus, which could have been a prototype of SCUBA systems invented over three centuries after his death. Da Vinci must be considered one of the earliest visionaries to consider in a practical and workable way the possibility of men actually swimming with the fishes.

See also DIVING, HISTORY OF; SCUBA.

Davis, Bill

Lt. Bill Davis, SEAL Team Six, was the center of one of the most persistent myths about the U.S. invasion of Grenada, Operation Urgent Fury, in 1983—that he had used a credit card to make a telephone call back to the United States to request combat assistance.

See also OPERATION URGENT FURY.

Davis submarine escape apparatus

The Davis submarine escape apparatus (DSEA) was designed prior to World War II to help a sunken submarine's crew members breathe under water long enough to escape and reach the surface. The DSEA was a self-contained oxygen breathing apparatus that used oxygen and a carbon dioxide canister to cleanse exhaled air for rebreathing. It was a primitive forerunner of modern "closed-circuit" SCUBA.

Although designed in the late 1930s by Sir Robert Davis of Siebe, Gorman, and Company of England, it owed much of its development to innovators as far back as 1680, when Giovanni Borelli had the idea that a closed breathing circuit could be achieved by recirculating air through a copper tube cooled by sea water, which would presumably condense all impurities on the inside of the tube.

In 1878, Henry Fleuss, a Royal Marine officer, began to develop an oxygen rebreather using a watertight rubber face mask and a breathing bag connected to a copper oxygen tank. Robert Davis improved on this concept to design and build his own apparatus to be used for escaping disabled submarines. Four of the systems were utilized in 1939 when the British submarine *Thetis* sank by accident. The four sailors who used the DSEA escaped to the surface and survived; the other 99 perished.

See also CLOSED-CIRCUIT BREATHING APPARATUS; SCUBA.

D-day

Preparation for the World War II invasion of German-occupied France began early in 1943, under the code name Overlord. Since it would be an amphibious landing, Gen. Dwight Eisenhower, supreme commander of the Allied Expeditionary Forces, required all the advance intelligence he could gather on suitable beach sites along the Normandy coast. Fledgling U.S. sea commandos—Amphibious Scouts and Raiders and navy combat demolition units (NCDUs)—were used to scout the beaches, perform hydrographic surveys, clear obstacles with gap-assault teams, and guide assault elements ashore once the invasion began.

The British, Canadians, and Americans assembled almost three million soldiers, 16 million short tons of supplies, 5,000 large ships, 4,000 landing craft, and more than 11,000 aircraft for the invasion. At 6:30 A.M. on D-day June 6, 1944, troops started wading ashore along a 50-mile front.

Prior to the actual attack, Amphibious Scouts and Raiders commanded by Philip H. Bucklew had conducted a number of recon operations to map the beaches and the underwater terrain leading up to them. The first men ashore on D-day were from navy combat demolition units (NCDUs), whose dangerous task it was to destroy obstacles implanted by the Nazis so the landing craft could get through. Proportionately, the NCDUs suffered the greatest casualties of the invasion—35 men killed and 71 wounded, out of 175.

The Allies obtained a toehold on the European continent. They were on their way to Berlin.

See also AMPHIBIOUS SCOUTS AND RAIDERS; BEACH CLEARANCE; BELGIAN GATES; BUCKLEW, PHILIP H.; NAVAL COMBAT DEMOLITION UNITS (NCDUS); NORMANDY LANDING.

decompression chamber

Developed during World War II by Christian J. Lambertsen, inventor of the Lambertsen Amphibious Respiratory Unit (LARU), the decompression chamber was an answer to the problem in diving of adjusting to changes in atmospheric pressure. An additional "atmosphere" of pressure is exerted on a diver's body with each 33 feet of descent. The decompression chamber is a compartment in which atmospheric pressure can be gradually raised or lowered; it is used especially in readjusting divers or underwater workers to normal pressures.

When being treated for "bends," or caisson disease, a diver may be "recompressed" to condense the nitrogen bubbles collected in his system, then be returned to normal gradually enough to dissipate the bubbles in his system. The chamber is often called a "recompression chamber."

See also BOYLE'S LAW; CAISSON DISEASE; LAMBERTSEN, CHRISTIAN J.

decompression sickness

Decompression sickness is an affliction of divers arising from pressure changes; also known as "bends" or "caisson disease."

See also CAISSON DISEASE.

Defense Intelligence Agency (DIA)

During the period following 1947, the Army and Navy Departments separately collected, produced, and disseminated intelligence for their individual use. The system proved duplicative, costly, and ineffective. The Defense Reorganization Act of 1958 sought to correct these shortcomings. In February 1961, Secretary of Defense Robert S. McNamara advised the Joint Chiefs of Staff of his decision to establish the Defense Intelligence Agency. The DIA became operational on October 1, 1961, as the nation's primary producer of foreign military intelligence. Among its objectives included more efficient allocation of scarce intelligence resources, more effective management of Department of Defense intelligence activities, and elimination of redundancies in facilities, organizations, and tasks.

Cold war tensions over the Berlin Wall immediately tested the new agency; it was followed by the Vietnam War. The war particularly increased defense intelligence involvement in efforts to account for American service members missing or captured (Operation Bright Light). SEALs proved to be valuable both as an intelligence resource and as an asset for use in gathering intelligence and conducting missions. SEALs have worked closely with DIA on secret and top secret projects from Vietnam through Desert Storm and Bosnia, to present-day counterterrorist activities.

See also "BRIGHT LIGHT"; BRUHMULLER, WILLIAM N., II; OPERATION DESERT STORM.

Deitz, Tom

The only combat beach landing made during the Desert Storm in 1991 was made by U.S. Navy SEALs—six of them, led by SEAL lieutenant Tom Deitz.

Late in 1990, Deitz, an Annapolis graduate, was detached from SEAL Team Five, where he was a platoon leader, and sent to command a SEAL platoon headquartered at the Saudia Arabian coastal base of Ras Al-Mishab. An armada of American ships loaded with an invasion force of 17,000 Marines waited off the Kuwaiti coast, presumably preparing for an amphibious assault landing. Deitz's 16-man SEAL platoon was tasked with scouting the beaches for a suitable landing site.

After the air war kicked off in mid-January 1991, the platoon began an aggressive recon program along the Kuwaiti shoreline. It had no idea when an invasion would occur or how it would be conducted. Its job was to conduct hydrographic surveys and scout the beaches, as underwater demolition teams (UDTs) had done during World War II.

"We didn't know if there was going to be an amphibious invasion or not," Deitz says. "We were told to look for a beach where one could be conducted—or where a deception operation could be conducted. . . . The difficult thing about the mission was the cold. We were wet the whole time, from

dusk until around dawn. That's why we go through BUD/S and why we go through Hell Week—so we can be wet and tired and still think."

A beach was finally selected, just north of a point called Mkina Sa'ud.

On 23 January, Deitz was let in on top secret invasion plans. The attack would be across the desert, from Saudi Arabia. However, Deitz's SEALs were to create a diversion to make the Iraqis think the Americans were coming by sea. It was hoped that the deception would tie down large Iraqi forces.

It was a simple enough plan. Although Deitz had never heard of the Beach Jumpers—the navy men who specialized in deception operations during and after World War II—the scheme could have been torn from that unit's play book. The full coalition invasion, by land, was scheduled to begin at 0400 on January 24. The SEALs were to plant charges along the selected beach and set them to begin exploding at 0100, followed by a mock invasion, with weapons blazing. It was considered the most important SEAL mission of the war.

All 16 SEALs in the platoon were committed to the task. HSBs (high-speed boats) dropped off the SEALs in three Zodiac "rubber ducks" about seven miles off shore. The rubber ducks then approached to within 500 meters of the beach. Six swimmers, including Deitz, made the actual foray to the sand.

It was a moonless night, shortly before 11 P.M., and the water was a cold 50 degrees Fahrenheit. Although the SEALs wore black wetsuits, they carried no SCUBA gear, other than small "bail out" bottles that would provide about three minutes of underwater air in the event they were spotted and had to escape. Three SEALs carried compact CAR-15s with attached M203 grenade launchers. The other three carried Heckler and Koch MP5 submachine guns with noise suppressors.

"The idea," Deitz explained, "was that if a couple of sentries showed up on the beach, and we thought we were compromised, we could take them out with the suppressed weapons without giving away our positions. But if something heavy opened up on us—a machine gun, for example, at longer range—we could lay some grenades on it."

Each swimmer pushed ahead of him in the water a 20-pound Mark 138 satchel charge of C-4 explosives made buoyant. The six SEALs reached shore undetected. They crawled into the surf and lay their charges approximately 50 meters apart. Each satchel was double primed with timers set to begin going off at set intervals, starting at 0100. They also lay out marker buoys, as if to establish lanes to be used for guiding in landing ships.

"We swam into the beach," Deitz explains, "and placed our charges in about one foot of water, since the tide was now receding, pulled the pins on the timers and swam back out to regroup."

Phase one was accomplished. Phase two began. As the explosions shot white water into the air at 0100, the entire SEAL platoon, riding high and fast in two HSBs, sped back and forth about 500 meters out, opening up with all the weapons they had aboard—miniguns, grenade launchers, heavy machine guns. "We ripped the beach apart," exclaimed one SEAL. During a final pass up the beach, the commandos chunked more C-4 charges overboard, primed to go off at irregular intervals to keep the Iraqis watchful and on edge, then zipped back to base.

"The operation went according to plan," Deitz said later. "We were happy but not really excited about it. What we were really excited about was that the ground war now kicked off. It wasn't until later, after we'd gotten cleaned up and had something to eat, that we got a message from Captain [Ray] Smith, the Task Group Commander, reporting that the elements of two Iraqi divisions remained on the coastline even as the ground forces were going up behind them. They remained in position to defend against the amphibious invasion. That's what really pleased us—that the Iraqis paid attention to us, reacted to us, and hopefully we saved some lives."

The U.S. Department of Defense later stated that four Iraqi divisions were set to defend the coast of Kuwait. Other estimates said as many as 10 of the Iraqi divisions in the area were preparing to counter the anticipated amphibious landing. Certainly, half a dozen Navy SEALs had saved 17,000 Marines from having to conduct amphibious ops that would undoubtedly have cost many of them their lives.

See also OPERATION DESERT STORM; SMITH, RAYMOND C., JR.

Del Guidice, David

When the first two SEAL teams were commissioned, effective January 1, 1962, Lt. David Del Guidice was placed in command of SEAL Team One, stationed at the Coronado Naval Amphibious Base, near San Diego, California. Lt. John F. Callahan was assigned as commanding officer of SEAL Team Two, at the Little Creek Naval Amphibious Base, near Norfolk, Virginia, although Lt. Roy Boehm had been placed in temporary command previously. Each team was composed of 50 enlisted men and 10 officers.

Del Guidice, former executive officer of Underwater Demolition Team 12, was a veteran frogman who in the summer of 1960 had led 10 men of his UDT on an epic voyage up the Mekong River from South Vietnam to deliver LCVPs (landing craft, vehicle and personnel) to Laotian forces who were having problems with communist guerrillas. Almost immediately after the SEALs were commissioned, they began a high-priority training program to prepare them for Southeast Asia.

Del Guidice, another SEAL lieutenant, and a U.S. Marine colonel, spent parts of January and February 1962 in Vietnam "to get the lay of the land and see what the SEALs might do." In March, two instructors from Team One arrived in Saigon for a six-month tour of duty teaching the South Vietnamese how to conduct clandestine maritime operations. While Team Two was busy in Europe and Latin America, Team One was preparing for deployment to Vietnam. The first SEAL detachment of two officers and 10 enlisted men from Team One debarked in Da Nang, South Vietnam, in 1963. The SEALs had officially gone to war, for the first time.

See also BOEHM, ROY; CALLAHAN, JOHN F.; CUBAN MISSILE CRISIS; SEALS; VIETNAM WAR.

desert patrol/light strike vehicle (DPV)

The DPV, more commonly referred to as a fast attack vehicle (FAV), is an all-terrain "dune buggy" used by SEALs.

See also FAST-ATTACK VEHICLE (FAV).

Detachment Bravo (Det Bravo)

Late in 1967, a special SEAL unit was formed to work with counterguerrilla South Vietnamese forces known as provincial reconnaissance units (PRUs).

Detachment Bravo, "DET Bravo," was made up of one platoon from SEAL Team One and a partial platoon from Team Two. MACV (Military Assistance Command, Vietnam) assumed operational control. Lt. (j.g.) John S. Wilbur, Jr., was placed in charge of the unit.

The SEALs of Team One came up with the original concept of combining SEALs with the special PRU units. It turned out to be a good and productive marriage. The Vietnamese knew the language, the terrain, and the people. SEALs contributed the technology of modern warfare. SEALs and PRUs working together informally had found their operations were increasingly successful.

A chief petty officer from Team One explains what operations were like before the union of SEALs and PRUs. "We would often stumble around, try to collide with a contact target, have a firefight, try to kill a bunch of people, and then get out well before dawn," he explained. "We were without any Seeing Eye dog at all. We didn't know what the sounds were. We didn't know which parts of the hamlets were trouble and which were not trouble. We didn't know which barking dog was going to alert who. The idea of working with knowledgeable, relatively well-trained counter guerrilla–type personnel was of tremendous benefit to us."

Although Wilbur commanded a reinforced platoon, his men were spread out all over the Mekong Delta, with one SEAL generally assigned as an adviser to each PRU outfit in each of the 16 provinces. PRU outfits ranged in size and competence from a rag-bag collection of 25 or 30 to "really impressive, disciplined and capable companies of maybe 60 to 120 men . . . as good at fighting as any that existed in Vietnam during the war."

Wilbur was wounded in January 1968 during the Tet offensive and was replaced by Lt. (later rear admiral) Chuck LeMoyne, who monitored the program until September 1968. After Tet, PRUs assumed the job of destroying the Viet Cong infrastructure by identifying, locating, and capturing Viet Cong leaders. One of LeMoyne's first policy actions was to encourage capturing VC rather than killing them. Dead VC were counterproductive; live VC could provide valuable intelligence.

Rewards had been offered for captured weapons, making it easier to kill an enemy soldier and bring in his weapon for the bounty than to capture him along with it. LeMoyne offered larger rewards for prisoners than for guns. "Capture rates went way up," he said. "It was remarkable. We were capturing, in the Delta, a thousand to twelve hundred VCI [Viet Cong infrastructure personnel] monthly."

The DET Bravo program with the PRUs proved its worth. It was eventually absorbed into the Phoenix Program.

See also LEMOYNE, IRVE C. "CHUCK"; MACV-SOG; PHOENIX PROGRAM; PROVINCIAL RECONNAISSANCE UNITS (PRUS).

detonating cord (det cord)
An explosive fuse.
See also EXPLOSIVES.

DEVGRU (DEVGROUP, Development Group)
DEVGRU (Naval Special Warfare Development Group) within the U.S. Navy SEALs is responsible for conducting counterterrorist activities.

See also NAVAL SPECIAL WARFARE DEVELOPMENT GROUP (DEVGRU); "RED CELL"; SEAL TEAM SIX.

Devil's Brigade
The First Special Service Force, which became known to German soldiers during World War II as "the Devil's Brigade," is looked upon as part of the lineage of U.S. special operations forces, including the U.S. Navy SEALs. In late 1942 and 1943, the First Canadian Special Service Battalion merged with elite American units to form a spearhead of 1,600 men who possessed an assortment of specialized skills. Trained in Montana as mountain/ski troops, the force had been originally intended to be a parachute unit that would land behind enemy lines to conduct sabotage operations. It became instead a versatile assault group, with a reputation for specialized reconnaissance and raiding.

direct-action mission
Although direct-action (DA) missions are more suitable to such units as Army Rangers, whose primary mission is to operate as a DA force, SEALs and other special operations units may employ the technique, on a more limited scale.

A DA operation is a short-duration strike or other small-scale offensive action designed to seize, destroy, or inflict damage on a specific target or to destroy, capture, or recover designated personnel or materiel. It is normally limited in its objective, of short duration, and intended to achieve specific, well-defined, and often time-sensitive results of strategic or operational significance.

The SEAL attack on the Paitilla airfield in Panama during Operation Just Cause is an example of a direct-action mission.

See also PAITILLA AIRFIELD.

dive mask

Diving bells have been in use since the first one was invented in 1530; hardhat diving has been conducted since at least 1823. It was not until the early 1930s, however, that an American pilot living in southern France, Guy Gilpatric, pioneered the use of rubber goggles with glass lenses for skin diving. Face masks, swimming fins, and snorkels were in common use by the mid-1930s.

The underwater demolition team (UDT) swimmers of World War II at first refused to use dive masks, claiming that reflections from the face plates would give them away to the enemy. Gradually, however, the prospect of better underwater visibility won them over. Masks became standard UDT issue at the end of the war.

Until fairly recently, SEALs were issued the same black rubber "Mark 1 Mod O" design used during the Korean War. One size fit everyone. In the 1970s, SEALs began appropriating and using equipment that had been designed for the sport diver market. Masks became available in 10 or so sizes and in about every "day-glo" color imaginable. For awhile, basic black disappeared as an option. Some SEALs used the bright masks but painted or taped camouflage over the fluorescent colors. Black masks designed for the sports diver market eventually made a comeback and are now also being issued.

See also DIVING, HISTORY OF.

diving, history of

As a profession, diving can be traced back from the U.S. Navy SEALs more than 5,000 years. Evidence of this comes from ancient undersea artifacts found on land, such as mother-of-pearl jewelry and drawings of early divers. Almost from the beginning, divers were active in military exploits. The Greek Scyllias became one of the first, or at least now the best known, when he used a hollow reed as a snorkel in order to cut the moorings of a Persian fleet in about 500 B.C.

Breathing through a hollow reed allowed the body to be submerged, but it is virtually impossible to suck air through a reed more than two feet long. Over the centuries, enterprising "frogmen" experimented with various methods, such as air-filled "breathing bags," that would allow them to work and live beneath the surface of the sea.

Between A.D. 1500 and 1800, diving bells enabled divers to remain under water for hours instead of minutes. The first mention of an actual practical diving bell appears in 1531. Later in the 1680s, a Massachusetts adventurer named William Phipps used a series of weighted, inverted buckets, each containing air, to support divers seeking treasure.

In 1690, Englishman Edmund Halley replenished air in a diving bell by sending down weighted buckets of it from the surface. Twenty-five years later, in 1715, a fellow Englishman named John Lethbridge developed a crude, one-man, completely enclosed diving outfit. Over a century passed before German-born Augustus Siebe, the "father of diving," improved upon the concept in 1837 and received credit for developing the first practical diving dress, the direct ancestor of modern deep-sea "hardhat" diving suits.

Although the first practicable SCUBA (Self Contained Underwater Breathing Apparatus) was invented in 1825 by British inventor William James, it is unclear whether or not the equipment was ever actually used for diving. Others continued to experiment with the idea of SCUBA for the rest of the century.

Benoît Rouquayrol designed and patented a regulator in 1866 to adjust the flow of air from a tank to the diver, a necessary prerequisite for SCUBA diving. This experimentation with open-circuit self-contained-air diving was not picked up again until the late 1930s. Two Frenchmen, Jacques-Yves Cousteau and Emile Gagnan, combined an improved demand regulator with high-pressure tanks to crate the first efficient and safe open-circuit SCUBA, known as the Aqua-Lung. The Gagnan-Cousteau regulator fundamentally altered diving. The Aqua-Lung was marketed commercially in France beginning in 1946 and reached the United States in 1952.

Diving in the U.S. Navy paralleled that in the world's other navies. For the most part, early navy divers were swimmers, skin divers, and eventually "hardhat" divers, with techniques and missions not that much changed from the days of Scyllias. Until 1912, U.S. Navy "hardhat" divers rarely went below 60 fsw (feet of seawater). Starting in that year, Chief Gunner's Mate George Stillson began a three-year test period during which navy divers went progressively deeper, eventually reaching 274 fsw.

Although Cousteau's Aqua-Lung had been invented at the start of World War II, it was not extensively used by underwater demolition teams (UDTs). It was not until 1947 that the navy's acquisition of Aqua-Lung equipment gave impetus to diving as an aspect of UDT operations.

Open-circuit SCUBA soon led to closed-circuit SCUBA, the apparatus of choice for all undersea commandos, including SEALs.

See also ALEXANDER THE GREAT; AQUA-LUNG; CLOSED-CIRCUIT BREATHING APPARATUS; COUSTEAU, JACQUES-YVES; DAVIS SUBMARINE ESCAPE APPARATUS; DIVE MASK; OPEN-CIRCUIT BREATHING APPARATUS; SCUBA; SCYLLIAS; SIEBE, AUGUSTUS.

Dominican Republic, intervention

In April 1965, President Lyndon Johnson sent a brigade of marines and part of the 82d Airborne Division to the Dominican Republic, a Caribbean nation sharing the island of Hispaniola with Haiti, to protect American citizens and to halt a civil war pitting leftist rebels against the government. Both SEALs and underwater demolition team (UDT) frogmen were involved in the action. More than 2,500 Dominican civilians were killed. Five U.S. Marines were killed in action, and 14 were wounded.

Six weeks after the Bay of Pigs disaster, Generalissimo Rafael Trujillo, who had ruled the Dominican Republic as a dictator for 31 years, was assassinated. His popularly elected successor, President Juan Bosh, was overthrown by the military in September 1963. The military junta that took his place became increasingly unpopular, until pro-Bosh supporters revolted on April 24, 1965. They captured the National Palace and arrested Donald Reid Cabral, who dominated the junta government. Fierce fighting broke out in the capital.

The U.S. Navy's six-ship Caribbean Ready Group began moving from Puerto Rico toward the Dominican Republic, in case it became necessary to evacuate U.S. citizens. The USS *Boxer* (LPH 4) airlifted 400 marines into the city of Santo Domingo in a driving rainstorm to protect U.S. citizens. That number increased by another 130 the following morning, and by another 1,000 that afternoon. By May 8, U.S. forces in the island republic would number 14,000 men, including paratrooper units from the 82d Airborne.

Marines sealed off a safety zone between the U.S. embassy and the Embajador Hotel, where refugees gathered for evacuation. Helicopters ferried civilians to the *Boxer* for further transfer to other navy ships, while a UDT team maneuvered an LCPL (landing craft personnel, large) into the port of Haina to rescue U.S. citizens and other nationals. This was the only action the UDTs saw, other than a couple of uneventful hydrographic beach surveys.

Although all American citizens were evacuated unharmed off the island, U.S. forces remained to make sure the island did not go communist with the pro-Bosh factions. President Johnson harbored a fear that Fidel Castro was behind the revolt and that the nation might turn into "another Cuba." The rebellion soon solidified into two opposing factions stalemated across a two-block-wide corridor held by U.S. troops. The rebels held one half of the city, government held the other.

Men from SEAL Team Two ran several missions during the intervention, none of which was significant to the overall strategy but nonetheless provided combat experience and honed SEAL improvisational skills.

After one proposal to destroy a rebel radio station in downtown Santo Domingo was dismissed as unfeasible, Lt. Jack "Blackjack" Macione blew it up using two Dominican National Guard armored personnel carriers (APCs) and 600 pounds of high explosive. He and another SEAL drove the "hot" vehicle, followed by a squad in the second. At three o'clock in the morning, he drove up to the radio building and smashed his APC through the plate-glass windows into the lobby. He pulled 40-second time fuses on the charges, abandoned the APC, jumped into the second, and streaked out of town. The charge went off and blew out the bottom floor of the station, collapsing the upper floors into it.

Prior to being deployed to the Caribbean, Macione had borrowed a starlight scope, a night-vision device, from the Army's Aberdeen Proving Ground, north of Baltimore. Rebels on their side of the "corridor" were sandbagging emplacements during the day, then coming out at night and popping rounds at GIs on the other side. Several marines had been wounded. The area commander asked the SEALs if they could do anything about it. "Funny you should mention it," Macione responded. "But we've got a brand-new thing that might do it."

Every evening, almost at midnight, a rebel sniper appeared in a building cupola to fire random shots. Macione acted as spotter with the scope, while Bill Bruhmuller, a senior enlisted man on the team, took up a sniper position on a nearby rooftop. Sure enough, almost at midnight, shutters opened, and the rebel prepared to get down to business. Macione saw him; Bruhmuller drilled him through the head. After that, the SEALs rigged a manikin on a set of pulleys and "walked" it across rooftops at night as a decoy. They drilled several other snipers before the rebels got wise to the trick.

One of the SEALs' last missions, other than searching sewers for rebel snipers, was against a Cuban ship that docked to unload arms for the rebels. An 82d Airborne artillery battery fired a couple of howitzer rounds through the ship's bridge. The ship caught fire, broke loose, and drifted out into the bay.

Macione and AO2 (Aviation Ordnanceman Second Class) Charles Bump swam out to search the ship. They took automatic fire from the rebel sector ashore as soon as they climbed aboard. Using the vessel's bulkheads as cover, they made their way to the bridge, to discover nothing but bones. The howitzer rounds had burned the crew to a crisp.

This was about eleven in the morning. The two SEALs took more fire as they swam back to shore through a layer of oil leaking from the ship. A squad of SEALs acting as cover at the breakwater returned fire. The exchange was brief. The SEALs suffered no casualties, other than loss of skin when Macione and Bump had to scrub the thick oil off their bodies with gasoline.

U.S. forces remained in Santo Domingo for over six months, until the situation stabilized.

See also BRAHMULLER, WILLIAM H.; MACIONE, JACK; STARLIGHT SCOPE.

Donovan, William J. ("Wild Bill")
(1883–1959)

"Wild Bill" Donovan was founder and director of the Office of Strategic Services (OSS) during World War II. The OSS is considered a forerunner of the Central Intelligence Agency and is looked upon as part of the lineage of special operations forces, including the Navy SEALs.

Donovan, who retired as a major general, is the only American to have received all four of the Nation's highest military awards: the Medal of Honor, the Distinguished Service Cross, the Distinguished Service Medal, and the National Security Medal.

See also CENTRAL INTELLIGENCE AGENCY (CIA); OFFICE OF STRATEGIC SERVICES (OSS).

Draeger Mark V

The Mark V is a closed-circuit oxygen underwater breathing apparatus used by SEAL divers.

See also CLOSED-CIRCUIT BREATHING APPARATUS.

Draeger Mark XV

The MK 15 is a closed-circuit mixed-gas underwater breathing apparatus used by SEAL divers.

SEAL Roy Boehm prepares to dive a German Draeger closed-circuit oxygen rebreather. (Roy Boehm)

See also CLOSED-CIRCUIT BREATHING APPARATUS; MIXED-GAS BREATHING.

driver

The SEAL who memorizes the course and uses the compass or attack board on a two-man swimmer team is called the "driver."

drop on request (DOR)

Tradition in the SEAL BUD/S (Basic Underwater Demolition/SEAL) course has developed a procedure by which a trainee can drop out on his own volition. On "the Grinder" at the training center in Coronado, California, stands a post upon which is mounted a brass "quitting bell." The idea originated with the West Coast team, where a trainee could quit at any point—or DOR, as it is called—by simply ringing the bell, no questions asked. On the East Coast, all a trainee had to do to end his training was remove his helmet and place it on the ground.

Today, in order to DOR, the trainee must stand on green-painted frog footprints in front of the bell, ring it three times, and say, "I quit." His helmet liner is then placed in formation next to the bell along with those of all the others who did not have what it takes to complete the training to become SEALs.

See also BASIC UNDERWATER DEMOLITION/SEAL (BUD/S) TRAINING.

drop zone (DZ)

A drop zone is a designated landing site for parachutists. A DZ may be a pasture, a clearing in the jungle, a sandy river bank, the ocean itself, or any other location suitable for a paratrooper to land. The pinpoint accuracy that can be attained from modern parachutes has reduced the size of a DZ from the large clearings required by jumpers of World War II to areas much smaller. A qualified HAHO or HALO SEAL can bail out of an airplane at 20,000 feet or more and guide himself to a landing in a suburban backyard.

See also AIRBORNE.

Dry, Melvin S. (1946–1972)

Lt. Melvin S. "Spence" Dry was the last U.S. Navy SEAL killed during the Vietnam conflict. He died on June 6, 1972, jumping into the water from a helicopter during Operation Thunderhead, an attempt to rescue American prisoners of war held in North Vietnam.

See also "BRIGHT LIGHT"; OPERATION THUNDERHEAD.

dry-deck shelter (DDS)

SEALs once dropped an SDV (SEAL delivery vehicle) by parachute and broke it while experimenting with ways to deliver them to within range of a war. It became fairly obvious that the best way to transport an SDV and its crew was by submarine. That led to the development of what is called a dry-deck shelter (DDS), which can be attached to the outer hull of a submarine in order to move an SDV and crew.

The submarine USS *Grayback* proved to be an almost perfect match for the SDV when it was assigned to work full-time with the frogmen in the 1960s. It contained a large hangar, which was modified to handle an SDV. The original plan called for the use of two submarines, the *Grayback* on the West Coast and the USS *Growler* on the East. However, money ran out before the second sub could be converted and put to service in the Atlantic.

Since submarines have limited lifetimes, the navy was forced to consider a successor to the *Grayback*. None of the newer submarines came equipped with large hangars. The solution was the creation of the DDS. It is essentially a huge metal watertight cylinder that can be bolted to the upper deck of a submarine and connected to its interior by a watertight hatch.

It is approximately nine feet wide and divided into three pressurized sections—a hangar area, in which the SDV and other systems equipment can be stored; a transfer chamber to allow passage between the module and the host ship; and a hyperbaric, or decompression, chamber, for decompressing and recompressing divers. The DDS is large enough to accommodate an entire SEAL platoon, along with diver gear, rubber boats, radios, and demolition equipment.

A host sub can carry two DDSs mounted side by side. They are installed immediately before an SDV mission and removed afterward. The installation

The dry deck shelter is attached to the outer hull of a submarine in order to move a SEAL delivery vehicle (SDV) and its SEAL crew. (U.S. Navy)

does not appreciably affect the performance of the host submarine, nor do the few permanent modifications made degrade the submarine's performance when it is no longer acting as host. What the DDS does is permit a dry environment for the transportation of SEALs and their equipment; the hangar compartment is flooded only to launch the little delivery vehicle while submerged. The insertion technique is essentially the same as in a submarine lock-out chamber, except it is much faster and less crowded. The DDS can also be used to launch surface SEAL craft and their crews.

Petty officer Philip Martin, SEAL Team One, recalls that the SEALs were often bored on long missions when they were confined to a submarine. "When we were close to a ship [with the submarine]," he said, "we were real quiet. You can't use any of the machinery. You can't flush the toilet. . . . We were just passengers. We'd take all the movies up in the dry deck shelter and watch movies all day. Then they would come in and say, you guys turn the projector off because we have to go on silence."

The first two submarines redesigned to carry a DDS were Polaris-type strategic subs that had been utilized for intercontinental ballistic missiles. They were the USS *John Marshall,* homeported at Norfolk, Virginia, near SEAL Team Two's base at Little Creek; and the USS *Sam Houston,* based at Pearl Harbor, in the Pacific. They were big boats, each 410 feet long and submerged displacements of 7,880 tons. When they had carried missiles, they had been known as "boomers." Sailors dubbed them "spook boats"

when they were switched over to carry SEALs and their SDVs.

As these boats are now at the end of their effective service, plans are under way to adapt SDVs in more innovative ways. The ASDV (Advanced SEAL Delivery Vehicle) system may, with relatively minor modifications, piggyback directly onto a submarine, eliminating the need for a DDS. However, since the SEALs will continue to use the older-model "wet" SDVs for the foreseeable future, there remains a need for shelters from which to operate.

See also ADVANCED SEAL DELIVERY SYSTEM (ASDV); USS *GRAYBACK.*

dry suit

SEALs utilize both "wet suits" and "dry suits" in diving. A wet suit is a skintight body suit made of a foam-rubber material that absorbs a layer of water, which is warmed by body heat and acts as insulation

A diver's dry suit, often made of vulcanized rubber, is sealed to prevent exposure of the body to water. It may also be insulated as further protection against cold water. (U.S. Navy)

against the colder surrounding water. A dry suit, on the other hand, is looser fitting, often made of a vulcanized rubber, and is sealed to prevent any exposure of the body to water. It is often insulated as well. Insulated underwear may also be worn underneath it.

A dry suit is used for deeper dives where the water is colder, for frigid water conditions, or for long exposure to even water of moderate temperatures.

See also WET SUIT.

dynamite

An explosive.

See also EXPLOSIVES.

Dynamiting and Demolition School

The Dynamiting and Demolition School at Fort Perry, Virginia, was where a special emergency team of demolition men was created, trained, and shipped to the Mediterranean in time for the July 10, 1943, invasion of Sicily during World War II. The Naval Demolition Unit (NDU), as it was called, was the stopgap forerunner of the Naval Combat Demolition Unit (NCDU), which would lead to the underwater demolition teams (UDTs) and modern Navy SEALs.

See also NAVAL COMBAT DEMOLITION UNITS (NCDUS); NAVAL DEMOLITION UNIT (NDU); UNDERWATER DEMOLITION TEAMS (UDTS).

E

ELINT (electronic intelligence)

Because of the often clandestine and sensitive nature of their missions, SEALs must have up-to-date intelligence about their current operations as well as about activities within their area of operations. The capability to locate the enemy, interrupt his messages, and hamper his operations at critical periods contributes both directly and indirectly to the effectiveness of SEAL operations.

ELINT (electronic intelligence) is often associated with electronic warfare. It uses the electronic spectrum to deceive the enemy, locate his units and facilities, intercept his communications, and disrupt his command, control, and target-acquisition systems at critical moments. Combat electronic warfare intelligence (CEWI) units use electronics ranging from simple telephone "bugs" to space satellites, from high-tech shipboard gear to ground RDF (radio directional finding), from spy planes to secret "black-bag ops" to identify and isolate radars, eavesdrop, and keep tabs on enemy units and communications systems and their movements. Such intelligence allows commands to cover sensitive operations by disrupting key enemy command and control nets, denying the enemy the ability to react to changes, reducing the effectiveness of enemy fire support and air control nets, denying the enemy his use of air defense fire control nets, and disrupting the enemy's flow of critical supplies, such as fuel and ammunition.

Emerson

The "Emerson" was the closed circuit breathing apparatus used by SEAL divers until 1975, when it was replaced by the Draeger Mark V and Mark 15.

See also CLOSED-CIRCUIT BREATHING APPARATUS; DRAEGER MARK V; DRAEGER MARK 15.

escape and evasion (E&E)

Escape and evasion (E&E) is an activity that assists military personnel and other selected persons to move from an enemy-held, hostile, or sensitive area to zones under friendly control. U.S. Special Operations Command (USSOCOM) plans and directs all E&E activities within a theater. SEALs include a complete E&E "boogie out" or "bug out" plan in all their mission scenarios. Being prepared beforehand, should things go wrong during the mission, may mean the difference between escape and ending up before a firing squad or in a prisoner of war camp.

Not only is each individual combatant in a theater prepared to E&E, but USSOCOM develops plans to assist in his recovery. For example, the Joint Personnel Recovery Center (JPRC), which operated in Vietnam under the code name "Bright Light," maintained intelligence data on the places where POWs were kept, kept track of the POWs' status, and developed E&E plans.

Rally areas, markers for signaling, escape corridors, covert assets behind lines, and reward programs for civilians who offer help are some of the elements of a well-run theater E&E program. Knowing such procedures are in place significantly helps the morale of aviators, SEALs and other special operations people who work over enemy territory or behind enemy lines.

SEALs operate their own E&E training courses; each branch of the military also runs them in conjunction with POW and survival courses. These are held in different terrains—jungle, arctic, temperate—and under different conditions. Most are classified Secret to prevent "hostiles" from knowing what procedures are taught. Such courses are part of regular SEAL training.

See also "BRIGHT LIGHT;" SERE SCHOOL.

explosive ordnance disposal (EOD)

Because of both units' involvement with explosives, the U.S. Navy SEALs and the navy's explosive ordnance disposal (EOD) assets have formed a close working relationship. In practically every conflict since the early months of World War II, navy EOD technicians have been engaged in clearing coastal areas for amphibious landings, clearing minefields, assisting in special warfare operations, and providing intelligence about new terrorist threats, all areas in which SEALs are also committed. SEALs are often cross-trained in EOD.

The U.S. Navy's EOD community evolved from the military and civilian bomb-disposal units organized in Britain at the beginning of World War II to cope with unexploded German bombs and sea mines. In 1940, U.S. Navy lieutenants O. D. Waters, J. P. Roach, and S. M. Archer worked with the British in mine countermeasures, then returned to the United States to establish the Advanced Mine School at the Washington Navy Yard.

At about the same time, Draper Kaufman, later instrumental in developing underwater demolition teams, became a Royal Navy bomb disposal officer. He brought what he learned back to the United States, where he was commissioned by the U.S. Navy. He established the navy's Bomb Disposal School in Florida. Today, while there are EOD people in all branches of the U.S. armed forces, only the U.S. Navy EOD force of 1,000 men and women has the equipment, mobility, and flexibility to tackle a global spectrum of threats ranging from conventional ordnance to nuclear, chemical, and biological weapons.

Technicians are trained not only in unexploded ordnance (UXO) disposal but also as demolition experts, divers, and in some instances, parachutists, in order to work in special operations whenever necessary. Their main focus is eliminating ordnance hazards that jeopardize U.S. national security and military interests. Navy EOD was the critical element in eliminating UXO hazards when the USS *Stark* was hit by two Iraqi antiship cruise missiles in 1987. They worked at clearing some 1,300 mines in the northern Persian Gulf that delayed U.S. Preparations for an amphibious assault to liberate Kuwait during Operation Desert Storm in 1991.

During the Vietnam War, Navy EOD operations were not limited to mine countermeasures. It was not unusual for Navy EOD people to sweep the banks of rivers and canals for land mines and booby traps in support of SEALs and other special operations forces.

EOD techs now receive special small-unit tactics training to enable them to integrate with combat and security forces to provide support in UXO, booby traps, and IEDs (improvised explosive devices), in either a combat theater or under terrorist threat. Basic EOD training comprises two phases. The first phase is conducted at the Naval School EOD facilities at Eglin Air Force Base, Florida. Advanced training is at Indian Head, Maryland; it includes training in diving and underwater ordnance. Many EOD techs have become parachute qualified since 1971.

The navy's operation EOD force is divided into two groups, much the way SEALs are divided into two special warfare groups. EODGRU ONE is headquartered at Naval Amphibious Base, Coronado, California, home of SEAL Team One. EODGRU TWO is at Naval Amphibious Base, Little Creek, Virginia, along with SEAL Team Two.

See also EXPLOSIVES; KAUFFMAN, DRAPER L.; NAVY BOMB DISPOSAL SCHOOL.

explosives

The use of explosives has been an important part of the evolution of the modern U.S. SEALs and their predecessors, dating back to World War II, when early frogmen cleared the water adjacent to invasion beaches of natural and man-made obstructions. Since then, underwater demolition teams and SEALs have used incredible quantities of dynamite, TNT, and C-4 to destroy beach obstacles, bridges, ships, boats, and trains. In Phase Three of the BUD/S course, the demolitions/reconnaissance/land warfare phase, "tadpoles" learn how to blow up things. Some SEALs go on to advanced demolitions training.

It may never be known with certainty who invented black powder, the first explosive. China, the Arabs, the Germans, and the English all lay claim to the honor. The English medieval scholar Roger Bacon wrote explicit instructions for its preparation in 1242. Firearms are frequently mentioned in fourteenth-century manuscripts. There is a record of guns and powder being shipped from Ghent to England in 1314.

Explosives are usually classified in two ways—combustion (or burning) and detonation. Gunpowder is a combustion type; dynamite, TNT, and plastique C-4 are all detonation types. Further, there are three basic types of explosives—mechanical, chemical, and nuclear. Most explosive applications in wartime are from chemical reactions. SEALs are familiar with all types of explosives.

While dynamite is useful for deliberate engineering application, such as construction projects, SEALs rarely if ever use it on strike missions. It primarily consists of a mixture of liquid nitroglycerin, with an absorbent substance to give it solid form. Nitroglycerin, the most powerful explosive in common use, was discovered in 1846 by the Italian scientist Ascanio Sobrero. Dynamite came along afterward, invented in 1866 by Alfred Nobel of Sweden. Ordinary dynamite today uses no nitro and is quite stable. It comes in sticks one or two inches in diameter and about eight inches long, wrapped in brown paper coated with paraffin to keep out moisture. It is ordinarily set off with a detonator or blasting cap.

TNT, also invented by Alfred Nobel three years before dynamite, revolutionized military engineering when it came into widespread use over 50 years ago. It is quite powerful, easily handled, and is somewhat water resistant. TNT was the explosive of choice for UDTs that cleared the way for amphibious assaults across the Pacific and up and down the Normandy beaches. It comes in blocks of cast material the color of rancid butter. It is detonated ordinarily with either a detonator or blasting cap.

Within the SEALs, as within the military in general, the explosive Compound-4, known as C-4, or plastique, is the modern blasting material of choice. It is malleable, like window putty or children's Play-Doh, and is so stable and insensitive that SEALs and Green Berets in Vietnam burned it to heat their coffee and C-rations. A few who lost their toes, however, learned the hard way that you never stomp on it to put out the fire: heat and concussion together set it off. It is easy to mold into whatever shape necessary to do the job, whether ringing the structure braces of a bridge or dropped into Viet Cong tunnels. It can be set off with either electrical or mechanical blasting caps.

There are several other explosives, such as PETN (explosive Pentolite), RDX (the most powerful nonnuclear explosive known) HBX-1 (a combination of RDX and TNT), A-3 (RDX with a wax binder for waterproofing), and of course, SADM (Special Atomic Demolition Munition), but C-4 remains the most common "bang for the buck."

Lacking any of these blasting substances, SEALs have been known to rely on "kitchen table demos"—improvised explosive devices—which may be constructed from a variety of materials. For example, a simple mixture of ammonia nitrate fertilizer mixed with diesel fuel and initiated with a booster charge and a blasting cap can make an impressive bang.

The sequence that leads to the main explosive charge is known as a "firing train." There are two types of firing trains, chemical and electric. Each has three separate components. The initiator is the first component; it starts the sequence. The initiator is connected to a conductor, either something that burns or a wire that conducts an electrical impulse. The conductor in turn leads to a blasting cap, the third component, which is imbedded in the main charge to set it off.

The chemical firing train may be initiated with either a kitchen match or an M-60 fuse lighter. The M-60 consists of a small plastic housing containing a spring-loaded firing point and a shotgun-type primer. The end of the fuse is inserted into one end, the collar is tightened around it, and the device is ready to fire. Pull the plunger back and let it go; it lights the fuse. It can also be rigged with a trip wire and detonation cord to build an effective booby trap.

There are two primary types of fuse, the conductor part of the chemical train. A time fuse is practical for operations when the team needs to be somewhere else when the charges detonate. The time fuse, a pencil-lead core of black powder encased in a reinforced green plastic with yellow bands about every six feet or so, has been around for many years. It burns at about 40 seconds per foot once it has been initiated, with either fire or the M-60. Time fuse is good only for setting off standard nonelectrical blasting caps.

Detonating cord, or "det cord," looks exactly like time fuse without the yellow bands. Instead of burning at 40 seconds per foot, however, it burns at an explosive rate of *five miles per second*. It contains a core of very-high-explosive PETN, powerful enough to cut down small trees by itself. It is issued in 500 or 1,000-foot spools and used primarily to link together a number of different charges that must go off almost simultaneously. Ordinarily, it is initiated by attaching a piece of time fuse to its "bitter end." The time fuse is ignited, and the user has a chance to clear the area before the det cord and the explosives to which it is attached go off.

Primadet, or primacord, is a relatively new development. It is orange in color and is actually only a smaller, safer version of det cord. It can be fired with the M-60. A couple of wraps of primadet or det cord around a block of TNT or C-4 will reliably detonate the charge, skipping the final sequence in the firing train.

The nonelectric blasting cap, when used, concludes the chemical firing train. It is a small metal tube about a half-inch long, closed on one end and open on the other to accept the end of a time fuse. It contains an initiating charge sufficient to boost the main charge into exploding.

The electrical firing train is almost identical to the chemical firing train, except that the initiation is accomplished by a surge of electrical energy rather than fire. The sequence starts with a "hell box," or plunger-type generator, which sends an electrical impulse along a wire (the conductor) to the electric blasting cap contained in the explosive. The wire can be eliminated by using a radio whose receiver, attached to the charge, uses a coded radio pulse to detonate the electrical blasting cap. Only an electric blasting cap responds to this firing train, as only a nonelectric blasting cap can be used for the chemical sequence.

The military has developed a number of imaginative ways to use explosives in combat. SEALs in Vietnam, for example, hid lengths of det cord in roadside ditches alongside an ambush kill zone. When survivors dived for the protection of the ditches, they found themselves landing on secondary explosives.

The limpet mine, named for a mollusk that clings tenaciously to undersea rocks, was designed during World War II to be carried by underwater swimmers and attached to the hulls of ships. The current model is not much different from its predecessor. Attached to the round metal mine is a harness for the convenience of the carrier. Either a metal magnet or an adhesive strap attaches it to the ship's hull. One limpet alone will probably not sink a modern warship, but it will certainly produce a substantial hole in even the biggest aircraft carrier. Several, strategically placed, can break a ship's keel.

The M-138 Hagensen Pack satchel charge is another veteran from World War II. It proved to be a simple, foolproof system for eliminating all kinds of problems in the surf zone, on the beach, or inland. It consisted then, and does now, of a simple shoulder bag containing up to 40 pounds of explosives, primed with a nonelectrical blasting cap at the end of a section of time fuse. Fittings on the bottom of the haversack permit multiple charges to be quickly hooked together. An M-60 waterproof fuse lighter makes it easy to get things started. Limitations are imposed only by the user's imagination.

A ribbon charge can be very effective in cutting door locks, hinges, or other similar applications. It is simply a quarter-inch sheet of C-4 on a strip of self-adhesive.

A snakelike line charge, the Mark 8 Flexible Linear Demolition Charge, comes in 25-foot lengths of two-inch-diameter rubber hose, each containing 50 pounds of explosives. The sections can be connected to increase length. It is particularly effective for blowing paths through natural barriers like reefs and sand bars.

A premolded shaped charge, the M2A3, is formed like a funnel, 17 inches long, eight inches across, and is filled with C-4. It weighs about nine pounds and is used for directing the force of a charge onto a particular point.

While many targets, such as airplanes in hangars, demand little skill in explosives, tougher targets, such as bridges or trains, require special training in the selection and placement of charges. C-4 is particularly adaptable to almost any job, because of its stability and malleability.

The nature of an explosion can be altered by contouring and shaping the charge material. A V-shaped channel cut into one side of a block of C-4, for example, directs explosive force from the center of the groove, creating an explosive knife. Two shaped charges placed on either side of a structure, such as a bridge support, makes an "ear muff" charge that can snap the object apart. Tamping—covering the opposite side with sandbags, rocks, soil, or other materials—strengthens the blast in the direction away from the tamping.

"There are very few of life's problems," goes an old special ops saying, "that cannot be solved with high explosives."

See also BASIC UNDERWATER DEMOLITION/SEAL TRAINING (BUD/S); HAGENSEN PACK; UNDERWATER DEMOLITION TEAMS (UDTS).

F

Fane, Francis Douglas (b. 1909)

The end of World War II looked like the end for American frogmen. In 1945, there were 34 underwater demolition teams (UDTs), consisting of about 3,500 men. By 1946, most of the UDTs had been disbanded and their equipment sold as surplus. In 1948, all that remained was a skeleton crew of seven officers and 45 enlisted men.

Officers were particularly hard hit. Those few who remained were an independent sort, less concerned than their contemporaries with fitness reports and promotions. One officer who stood out in those days, a leader among those unknowingly setting the stage for the transition from UDTs to SEALs, was Francis Douglas Fane, known as "Red" until his hair turned nearly white. If Draper Kauffman's foresight created the underwater demolition teams, it was the insight of "Red" Fane that prevented their extinction.

Born in Scotland, Fane went to sea in the mid-1920s as a merchant crewman. Although he could not swim when World War II began—in fact, he was afraid of the water—he volunteered for the secret UDTs after a tour on a navy ammunition supply ship. All he knew about UDTs was that the duty was especially hazardous and involved the use of explosives. While on leave in Chicago, he took a crash course in swimming that prepared him well enough to qualify for UDT training in Fort Pierce, Florida. He became commanding officer of UDT-13.

He saw a great advantage in UDT swimmers being able to remain underwater for as long as possible. He began experimenting with breath-holding and hyperventilating. Soon, all his men could remain underwater for three, four, even five minutes. One of his "frogs" could hold his breath and swim the length of a swimming pool three times without surfacing. Fane, who became a strong swimmer himself, could hold his breath long enough to dive 100 feet and swim underneath a submerged submarine from one side to the other.

Toward the end of the war, Fane and six other frogmen engaged in an operation that led UDTs closer to the concept of guerrilla warfare. They swam to the Japanese island of Kyushu, where they accepted the surrender of a huge Japanese ammunition depot. The nearby mountains were sprigged heavily with gun revetments, which would have made a landing very bloody had the Japanese chosen to resist.

After the war, Fane struggled to retain UDTs within the navy and to expand their capabilities. "I realized," he explained to higher commanders, "that if we were going to come in, in future wars, we would have to be better prepared than just swimming on the surface as we did. So I thought of the idea of working underwater all the way. Working with submersibles out of submarines. Coming in surreptitiously at night. Of being dropped by helicopter into the water. I envisioned this whole system."

He more than envisioned the system; he researched, designed, and implemented it. In spite of the drawdowns in the size of UDTs during those years following World War II, the period became one of rapid technological developments in undersea breathing. Fane worked with scientists and innovators around the world, including Robert E. Fulton, Jr., and Christian J. Lambertsen, in designing open-circuit and closed-circuit underwater breathing apparatuses and in revolutionary methods of underwater swimming. He experimented with "skim boats" for use by UDTs and with the Aqua Ho Motor for pulling a swimmer through the water. He himself went into convulsions, passed out, and nearly drowned while testing closed-circuit oxygen.

He developed new missions for his sea warriors. As early as 1949, he brought in an army combat infantryman to drill his sailors in infiltration techniques and the use of weapons. He thought of ways in which UDTs could go beyond surveying and clearing beaches for amphibious assaults to actually carrying out commando raids ashore. With the help of an underwater photographer named Eldridge Fennimore Johnson, he documented his work with swimmers and submersibles. He showed the film to Adm. Gerald Wright, Chief of Naval Operations.

"My God!" the CNO exclaimed. "How long has this been going on?"

"About two years, sir."

"If you have any problems," Admiral Wright declared, impressed, "come and see me."

By the time the Korean War began, UDT training had been modified to include land operations, small-unit tactics, and weapons. UDTs were utilized in guerrilla operations in Korea, although on a limited scale. Fane recalled one series of operations in which he was involved in early 1952.

We landed North Koreans, who had been trained in the south as guerrillas, on the east coast of Korea up within 60 miles of Vladivostok [a Soviet port], using the techniques of UDTs. We landed upwards of fifty a night for a couple of nights, from rubber boats, at two or three in the morning. We'd lie in the rocks while the Chinese passed by twenty or thirty feet away and wait until the coast was clear. They [guerrillas] advanced some thirty or forty miles into the mountains, and I went over in a C-47 and dropped rice and explosives to them.

By the end of the 1950s, UDT had gone a long way toward becoming the undersea unconventional warriors Fane had envisioned and worked to create for nearly 20 years. UDTs had learned to operate for long periods of time underwater, to function as competent commandos on land, and to take to the air in helicopters and parachutes. Although the navy would still require specialized men to conduct beach reconnaissance and obstacle removal for amphibious forces, it was clear that something new was rapidly approaching—the SEALs.

See also AQUA HO MOTOR; BUCKLEW, PHILIP H., II; FULTON SEA SLED; KOREAN WAR; LAMBERTSEN, CHRISTIAN J., SKIM BOAT; UNDERWATER DEMOLITION TEAMS (UDTS).

fast-attack vehicle (FAV)

Operation Desert Storm, the war against Iraq in 1991, gave SEALs a chance to try out one of their newest pieces of equipment—the fast-attack vehicle (FAV), also referred to as a DPV (Desert Patrol/Light Strike Vehicle). It is a main mode of land travel for SEALs by virtue of its speed, maneuverability, and versatility. SEALs used it in Desert Storm for reconnaissance deep into Iraqi-held territory, on border patrols, and for pilot rescue. It helped SEALs in liberating the U.S. embassy in Kuwait City and in patrolling the streets around the embassy afterward.

The FAV, a sturdier military version of the off-road "dune buggies" used by thrill seekers in the western deserts of the United States, was originally developed in the 1980s by the army as a weapon for light infantry. The version modified and used by SEALs is made by Chenowith Racing Products of California. It is an off-road, two-by-four racing vehicle with an additional seat added for a gunner and additional mounts for weapons to enhance its wartime survivability. It is designed to operate any-where a four-wheel drive vehicle can, with additional maneuverability and speed up to 100 mph. Besides acting as a weapons platform, it can perform numerous combat roles: special operations delivery, command and control, rear-area combat operations, reconnaissance, forward observation, Military Police Work, and artillery forward observation.

For the SEALs, it carries a three-man crew. The driver and navigator-gunner sit side by side in two bucket seats. Mounted above the engine on the right side is an M-60 machine gun. A third man, the machine gunner, rides in a swivel seat above and behind the driver's compartment. He operates both an M-60 machine gun aimed toward the rear and a .50-caliber machine gun on a swivel covering to the front and sides of the vehicle. FAVs in the Iraqi desert also mounted Mark 19 40 mm grenade launchers and carried AT-4 antitank rockets.

Next to the navigator-gunner is a large meshwork bucket mounted on the outer frame, designed to cradle an injured pilot or carry equipment. The vehicle has no armor protection, relying instead upon its weapons, high speed, and maneuverability. The powerful Volkswagen engine and large shock absorbers permit it to sweep across the trackless Saudi and Iraqi deserts at night at speeds up to 60 mph.

Also see OPERATION DESERT STORM.

fast roping

Fast roping is a process of descending from a hovering helicopter by using gloves to slide down a thick rope of woven wool, much like firemen slide down a pole. It is different from rappelling, in which the infiltrator wears a harness and snaps into the climbing rope to make his descent to the ground.

On a "go" signal, SEALs are out on the rope like monkeys. An entire squad can slide the 50 to 75 feet to the ground in a matter of three to five seconds. The operation is so fast that a SEAL who does not clear the rope the instant his feet hits the ground risks having the feet of the next strike his head.

Father Hoa (Wa)

Father Hoa (pronounced "Wa") is a legend among the SEALs who fought in Vietnam. Part of the leg-end asserts that Father Hoa, a Chinese Catholic priest, left China with Chiang Kai-shek. Whereas Chiang went to Taiwan, Father Hoa came to South Vietnam, where he was given jurisdiction over the village of Hai Yen, near Ca Mau. An ardent anticommunist, he built up the town over the years and taught its occupants to resist communism.

According to one story, he waited on the outskirts of the town with an M3 submachine gun hidden underneath his robes when Viet Cong infiltrators who worked in the town came to be paid for their weekly labors. He lifted up his black robes, produced his submachine gun, and killed all the VC.

Hai Yen was a secure hamlet ringed in wire, observation posts, Claymores, and defensive bunkers when U.S. SEALs began arriving in Vietnam. The priest had also formed his own small army of indigenous fighters, who operated virtually independent of government control. Walking around with a Remington 12-gauge shotgun under his arm, Father Hoa had a greater knowledge of unconventional warfare in Southeast Asia than any military unit in Vietnam. He had also established an extensive intelligence network, all of which he willingly shared with the SEALs, in particular with those of the Sixth Platoon.

Most of Father Hoa's fighters were ex–Viet Cong or former soldiers of the North Vietnamese army (NVA) whom the priest had converted from communists to fighters of communism. No VC who came to Hai Yen with weapons slung would be accosted. He was given a meal, extra rations, medical attention if needed, and occasionally even a little money. Then Father Hoa would take the man aside. "If you come back again," he advised, "it is obvious that the people you work for cannot pay or take care of you. If you return, then you work for me. The job is here if you want to stay now, or come back later. If you come back again, there is no choice—you will work for me."

He was one tough priest, says Bud Thrift, a SEAL who operated with him. Thrift recalls how Father Hoa persuaded a former NVA company commander to work with the SEALs. "This is a new guy who knows the area very well," the priest told the SEALs. "He's taking you to a target. If he moves wrong or even blinks and you don't like it, if you have any hesitation about his loyalty at all, don't bring him back."

SEAL Platoon Six and Father Hoa's irregulars were among the most effective combat units in the Vietnam War. Father Wa was still alive when the war ended.

Fay, Robert J. (d. 1965)

Underwater demolition team (UDT) commander Robert J. Fay was the first UDT/SEAL member killed in action during the Vietnam War. He was chief of security of the Da Nang base when he was killed on October 28, 1965, during a mortar attack while making inspection rounds in a jeep.

firing train

The firing train is the sequence that leads to the detonating of a main explosive charge.

See also EXPLOSIVES.

Flatus I

The Flatus I was a semi–closed-circuit SCUBA invented by Christian J. Lambertsen.

See also LAMBERTSEN, CHRISTIAN J.

Flynn, Cathal L. (Irish)

Cathal L. "Irish" Flynn, born in Ireland but partly educated in a French military school, was the first SEAL officer promoted to admiral's rank. He served over 30 years in the U.S. Navy before retiring in 1990 to become assistant administrator for civil aviation security. Much of his service was in Underwater Demolition Teams (UDTs) and SEALs.

In 1964, as a young lieutenant (junior grade) with SEAL Team One, he was in charge of a detachment of 16 SEALs and four marines at China Beach. Their assignment was to train guerrilla fighters to carry out harassing raids against targets along the North Vietnamese coast. He served two tours in Vietnam and later served as commander of Naval Special Warfare Group One in Coronado. He was the leading advocate of converting all UDT teams into SEAL teams.

The positions in which he served during his career included Deputy Assistant Secretary of Defense for Special Operations (including measures to combat terrorism); Commander, Naval Security and Investigative Command; Assistant Director of Naval Intelligence for Counterintelligence and Anti-Terrorism; Assistant to the Vice Chief of Naval Operations for physical security; Director of Plans, U.S. Special Operations Command.

See also CHINA BEACH; COLBY, WILLIAM EGAN; MARCINKO, RICHARD; NAVAL SPECIAL WARFARE GROUPS; OPERATION PLAN 34-A (OP-34A); UNDERWATER DEMOLITION TEAMS (UDTS).

foreign internal defense (FID)

U.S. special operations forces, including SEALs, all have the same basic list of missions. Among these missions is that of foreign internal defense (FID), defined as training, advising, and teaching the military, paramilitary, and law enforcement personnel of allied nations.

To accomplish this professional development of allies, normally in a noncombat environment, SEALs participate in the following types of operations: training assistance, advisory assistance of intelligence operations, psychological operations, civil-military operations, populace and resources control, and tactical operations. SEAL teams may develop, establish, and operate centralized training programs in support of FID. They may also conduct individual, leader, and collective training programs for specialized units. Subjects may range from basic combat training and leader development to specialized collective training.

This traditional Naval Special Warfare (NSW) role in coalition building through exercises and FID has received increased emphasis in recent years, especially in counterterrorist operations. Many SEALs receive training in foreign languages and regional customs. SEALs having direct interaction with foreign allied counterparts have significant impact upon country-to-country relationships and serve as grassroots ambassadors representing U.S. values.

See also COUNTERNARCOTICS OPERATIONS; MISSIONS.

Fort Pierce, Florida

Fort Pierce, Florida, was the training site for both the Amphibious Scouts and Raiders and the naval combat demolition units (NCDUs) of World War II, both considered to be forerunners of modern SEALs. It is today the site of the UDT/SEAL museum.

The 10 volunteers for the first Amphibious Scouts and Raiders class, including naval lieutenant Philip H. Bucklew, attended training at Little Creek, Virginia, in May 1942. In January 1943, the school moved to an old casino at Fort Pierce, Florida. Four months later, in May, Draper L. Kauffman was called back from his honeymoon and was showed pictures of obstacles being built on the beaches of France. He was ordered to "put a stop to that," by setting up a school to train the first naval combat demolition units. On June 6, 1943, he set up shop and training facilities a short distance away from the Scouts and Raiders casino.

Training began with a one-week ordeal known as "Hell Week," which is still a mainstay of SEAL training. When the first SEAL teams were formed in 1962, much of their training was adapted directly from the curriculums of the NCDUs, Scouts and Raiders, and underwater demolition teams (UDTs).

See also AMPHIBIOUS SCOUTS AND RAIDERS; BUCKLEW, PHILIP H.; KAUFFMAN, DRAPER L.; NAVAL COMBAT DEMOLITION UNITS (NCDU); UNDERWATER DEMOLITION TEAMS (UDTS); UDT/SEAL MUSEUM.

forward bases

Naval special warfare "forward bases" are established near potential hot spots around the world. Naval Special Warfare Units (NSWUs), each with people, facilities, and equipment, are established at these forward bases to speed up the process of planning and launching missions.

See also ORGANIZATIONAL STRUCTURE, SPECIAL OPERATIONS.

Fox, James Earl (d. 1964)

James Fox, a SEAL, was the only man ever to die in experimentation with the Fulton STAR system.

See also FULTON SURFACE-TO-AIR RECOVERY (STAR).

free dive

"Free dive" describes diving without the use of an air supply other than that in the diver's lungs. Early UDTs could "free dive" to depths of 100 feet, holding their breath up to five minutes.

See also DIVING, HISTORY OF.

freefall

"Freefall" describes that period of time between when a parachutist exits an aircraft and when he pulls his ripcord to release his parachute canopy.

See also AIRBORNE.

frogmen

Military divers in nations around the globe refer to themselves as "frogmen," by virtue of their amphibious qualities. It is unclear exactly when and where the term originated; it may have been coined by the Italians, who were referring to themselves as "frogmen" several years before World War II. In the United States, the naval combat demolition units and underwater demolition teams, which were formed in 1942 and 1943, began calling themselves by that name. It may have been partly because of the froglike swimming flippers they wore and the green camouflage paint smeared on their bodies during missions.

SEALs today often refer to themselves generically as "frogmen," a term that to them denotes excellence. As SEAL master chief Hershel Davis remarked, "I fancy myself as a frogman. I prefer the title 'frogman.' There are a lot of SEALs in the navy, but damn few frogmen."

full mission profile

A "full mission profile" refers to a SEAL operational drill or training exercise conducted in "real time." The SEAL units selected for the drill generally do not know that it is not a "real world" mission. They are simply alerted and ordered to prepare for a mission, then conduct it.

For example, SEAL Team Six received word from Joint Special Operations Command that Puerto Rican terrorists had blown up an airplane in San Juan and stolen a nuclear device. The team received orders to take out the terrorists and recover the device. All the elements of the "real world" were present: good intelligence from the National Security Administration, a team scramble and loadout, mass HAHO night jump onto the target, and firefight on target. None of the men realized it was simply a drill until it was almost over. It is a good test to determine how men will react under 'real' conditions.

Fulton sea sled

During the 1950s, Francis Douglas Fane, who had been instrumental in forming underwater demolition teams (UDTs), was busy stretching the limitations of his remaining UDTs. One of his most serious challenges centered on the quickest and most effective way of recovering a group of swimmers once it had finished a beach surveillance mission. He was still using the "cast and recovery" system, whereby a swimmer thrust his arm through a loop held out to him as the recovery boat sped by. The system was slow and permitted the recovery of only one man at a time.

Fane, stationed at Coronado, then met Robert E. Fulton, Jr., an inventor in El Centro, California, who was working on a surface-to-air recovery system known as "sky hook." Fulton came up with a maritime version of his sky hook.

It worked this way. Swimmers following a mission would clump into two groups. The recovery boat would run by and drop a rubber floating sled to each group. A line connected the two sleds. Swimmers would pile onto the sleds, the boat would make a fast turn, and come back between them. A snare on the front of the boat snatched the line and directed it into a bow winch, which reeled in the sleds and swimmers even as the recovery boat continued at full speed.

The navy went so far as to build special recovery boats for the system, after Fulton and the UDTs had tested the "sea sleds" in the Virgin Islands. But then internecine warfare took over, and high-ranking officers jealous of special teams and their special equipment scuttled the project just before it was ready to deploy. The boats were divided up among other navy units, and UDT teams were told to keep using the "cast and recovery" method, which is still used today.

See also CAST AND RECOVERY; FANE, FRANCIS DOUGLAS; FULTON SURFACE TO AIR RECOVERY (STAR).

Fulton Surface-to-Air Recovery (STAR)

In the late 1950s, inventor Robert E. Fulton, Jr., was flying his private airplane over the Rocky Mountains when the thought occurred to him that it would be impossible to rescue him if he crashed in that rugged wilderness. He promptly began work on a system that would permit a low-flying airplane to snatch a man or other "package" off the ground as it flew by and reel him or it into the aircraft like a hooked fish. The system he devised, the Fulton Surface-to-Air Recovery (STAR), which became known as "sky hook," was utilized by the military, primarily by special operations and the Central Intelligence Agency, for the next 35 years.

It worked this way. First, a paradrop was made that included a custom-made uniform, 500 feet of special nylon rope, a deflated balloon 23 feet long and shaped like a dirigible, and helium tanks with which to fill the balloon.

The man to be picked up donned the coverall-type uniform, which had a parachute harness sewed into it. One end of the 500-foot rope was attached to the parachute harness, while the other end was secured to the balloon. The balloon was inflated and rose into the air. Battery-powered lights could be attached to the rope for night pickup.

While all this was going on, the pickup plane circled, then lined up its approach on the rope stretched into the sky by the balloon. A special V-shaped attachment on the nose of the airplane

Inventor Robert Fulton's STAR system enabled a low-flying aircraft to snatch a man off the ground without landing. This photo shows SEAL James Earl Fox being reeled into an aircraft after a pickup. Moments later, the line broke, and he plunged to his death. (U.S. Navy)

scooped the line into a clamp while releasing the balloon. That jerked the man into the sky. Stretch in the nylon rope caused the man to rise vertically and almost instantly to 100 feet altitude, thereby missing nearby trees or other obstacles.

The speed of the aircraft, about 120 mph, and the weight of the man on the other end of the line caused the rope to trail near the belly of the aircraft. Cables stretched from the wing tips to the nose fuselage prevented the rope from becoming entangled in propellers. Crews inside the recovery craft snagged the rope with a long hook and attached it to a winch, which reeled in the recovered man through a belly hatch or into an open tail ramp.

The first planes used were mostly B-17s and Caribous, until the C-130 Hercules became the primary STAR provider. More than 100 pickups were made by the "sky hook" system in the first few years of the 1960s, the majority of which were of underwater demolition team frogmen, SEALs, and army Green Berets. Two attempts were made to use sky hook to pick up downed pilots during the Vietnam War, both of which failed for reasons other than the system itself. Whether it was ever used in an actual operation and if so under what circumstances remains a closely guarded secret. It is no secret, however, that the air force dedicated a fleet of C-130s to the system.

SEALs Norman Olson and Peter Slimpa were early guinea pigs used in developing the system. "It happens so fast," Olson recalled of the pickup. "It's like somebody grabbed you by the top of the head and, whup! You're up there!"

SEALs Jack Macione and R. F. Adams were two other experimental subjects. They were pigtailed to each other on the same line and jerked off a ball field in Coronado. Fulton had made an alteration to the pickup harness in an attempt to improve the way men were dragged through the air. It turned out to be a mistake. "We made the usual few gyrations, the spins, the turns, and then I stabilized out," Macione explained.

All of a sudden I made three whipping rotations to the left, in a second. I no sooner look down

than it happens to me again. Now I can feel Adams above me doing the same thing. And then the thing starts cracking the whip. It's not only spinning, it's cracking. The lift uniform you put on, the legs have gotten torn off, my arms have gotten torn off. My wristwatch is gone. My ears are lacerated. I'm bleeding in the groin. And I'm doing this violent, violent rotation. . . .

And then the plane started flying at five thousand feet and that's a sign they're going to put a parachute on the lift line and cut you loose. But they kept pulling us up. . . . I said to myself, "When I get underneath this airplane, it's going to beat me to death. I'm going to be hamburger." . . .

As luck would have it, the air flow [below the plane] stabilized us. I felt the line stop as they put Adams into the plane. And then it was my turn. They got me into the airplane. . . . I was done for. . . . If someone said they'd give me a million dollars to sit up, I could not have done it. . . . Fulton was there. I remember saying, "Mr. Fulton, there's something wrong with the system."

On June 29, 1964, the navy scheduled a sky-hook demonstration near the SEAL base at Little Creek, Virginia. A SEAL, Photographer's Mate Third Class James Earl Fox, was plucked out of a rubber boat in Chesapeake Bay. The plane roared overhead. Fox leapt into the sky. Suddenly, there was a loud pop, and Fox fell 700 feet to his death. It was discovered that the winch had not been turned off as Fox was being brought into the airplane. It continued to turn until it snapped the nylon line. Fulton recommended inserting a device in the winch to prevent a recurrence.

Fox was the only fatality during 17 years of live pickups before the navy decided there was little to be gained by having SEALs practice being sky hooked. It took no skill to be picked up; the air crews could maintain their proficiency by snatching dummies off the ground. The STAR system remained a part of the military until September 14, 1996, when the last air force Fulton unit was disbanded in a final demonstration and ceremony at Hurlburt Field, Florida.

G

Gallipoli Peninsula

The Battle of Gallipoli early in World War I was one of the worst military disasters in modern history. It offered a perfect lesson in pitfalls to be avoided in planning amphibious operations and pointed out the need for units to conduct scouting and hydrographic missions prior to a beach landing. It stimulated the forming of naval combat demolition units (NCDUs) and underwater demolition teams by the Americans during World War II.

The World War I allies planned to gain control of the Dardanelles, the channel that forms the boundary between Europe and Asia, through a series of coordinated amphibious landings. Troops would land both in Turkey (which was an ally of Germany) on the Gallipoli Peninsula, the European side of the channel, and on the Asian side. The two forces would knock out the Turkish forts and thereby open the Dardanelles for shipping.

In the predawn of April 25, 1915, 4,000 Australian and New Zealand forces rowed small boats ashore on the northwestern side of the peninsula and into a nightmare. One unit, landing in the wrong place, was confronted with a steep hillside off the beach. A second was trapped on the beach

itself by sheer cliffs. The third element faced such heavy machine-gun fire that it could not land at all.

For the next seven months, Australian, New Zealander, British, and French troops fought bitterly to take the forts overlooking the Dardanelles. The allies suffered 265,000 casualties, including 46,000 dead. Turkish casualties totaled about 300,000, 100,000 of these killed in action. Finally, the politicians called it quits, and the allies withdrew.

Lessons were learned. It is absolutely essential: to find out as much as possible about the physical characteristics of a potential landing beach site beforehand; to scout the enemy's defenses; and to direct the assault force ashore to the right place at the right time. Maps and aerial photos can answer some of these questions, but others can be answered only one way—by sending men ashore to survey the beach and water obstacles and to scout a foe's fortifications and forces.

gap assault teams

Naval combat demolition unit teams, which normally comprised six men, were enlarged to thirteen-man "gap assault teams" for the Normandy invasion of France on June 6, 1944.

See also BEACH CLEARANCE; BELGIAN GATES; NAVAL COMBAT DEMOLITION UNITS (NCDUS); NORMANDY LANDING.

"Garcia's Outpost"

As part of the discipline and conditioning of Basic Underwater Demolition/SEAL (BUD/S) training, tadpoles may be ordered to deliver a "message to Garcia"—another instructor whose location is about a mile or so away. The trainee "flies" to "Garcia's Outpost" with a heavy pallet across his shoulders, double-timing and pretending to be an airplane. When he arrives, he may be put in a holding pattern until granted permission to land and deliver his message. The name recalls a once-famous story published in 1899 about a heroic episode of the Spanish-American War.

See also BASIC UNDERWATER DEMOLITION/SEAL (BUD/S) TRAINING.

Global Position System (GPS)

The Global Position System (GPS) is a constellation of 24 satellites in Earth orbit that uses triangulation to yield amazingly accurate position fixes. The first practical use of GPS came during the 1991 Gulf War. Military models are certified as accurate to within 20 feet, using the new Block 11R satellites. The standard GPS is called NAVISTAR GPS system. It is issued to special forces as the Rockwell Collins AN/PSN-11 Portable Lightweight GPS Receiver (called the "plugger"). It is about the size of a brick and weighs less than three pounds. In addition to pinpointing ground location, it can also be used to store and calculate a variety of other information, including routes traveled and calculated routes ahead. It can also be used to guide missiles and bombs.

Glock 9 mm pistol

In 1986, SEAL Team Six discovered a serious weakness in the standard-issue Beretta 9 mm pistol. During a firing demonstration on the range, the rear portion of a Beretta broke away from the pistol and

The GPS use satellite triangulation to yield position fixes to within less than 100 meters. (U.S. Army)

struck its user in the face due to a design flaw in the slide system.

SEALs immediately began looking for a replacement pistol. The Austrian Glock 9 mm was tested as a possible alternative. Since a substantial part of the Glock was made of plastic, it was assumed it would fare better in a SEAL's corrosive saltwater atmosphere. However, except for corrosion resistance, the Glock showed itself to be significantly less reliable than the Beretta M9.

Team Six then selected the Sig-Sauer P226 pistol in 1987 to replace the Beretta M9. Other SEAL teams soon followed the example of Team Six. However, a variety of pistols may still be found among the teams.

See also BERETTA M9 9 MM PISTOL; SIG-SAUER P226.

Goldwater-Nichols Act of 1986

Section 187 of Title 10, U.S. Code ("Unified Combatant Command for Special Operations Forces") was added as part of the 1986 Goldwater-Nichols

Defense Reorganization Act, which restructured the Department of Defense. Its importance to special operations and to the Navy SEALs was that it created the U.S. Special Operations Command (USSOCOM), to coordinate all U.S. special operations warfare, including counterterrorism, sabotage, and other clandestine missions. It also provided standardized training and developed a common doctrine for all special operations forces.

The Gulf War of 1991, Operation Desert Storm, was USSOCOM's first test, which it passed. SEALs and other special warfare forces rescued downed American pilots, sabotaged enemy command centers, and stole enemy military equipment, proving again that elite, trained, well-equipped SpecOps troops help win wars.

See also OPERATION DESERT STORM; ORGANIZATIONAL STRUCTURE, SPECIAL OPERATIONS; U.S. SPECIAL OPERATIONS COMMAND (USSOCOM).

Golf Detachment

The first detachment of three officers and 15 enlisted SEALs sent to Vietnam for active combat duty was detailed as "Golf" (for "G") Detachment, or "Team Golf." The detachment, from SEAL Team One, arrived in Vietnam in February 1966 and was placed under the command of Commander, Naval Forces Vietnam and authorized to conduct field actions in the Rung Sat Special Zone, which covered all the major water approaches to Saigon from the South China Sea.

See also SEALS; VIETNAM WAR.

USS *Grayback*

The USS *Grayback* was a diesel-powered submarine built in the 1950s to accommodate a Regulus missile. Because it had a large hangar for the missile, SEALs proposed that the submarine be converted to carry and deliver SEAL delivery vehicles (SDVs). The *Grayback* was assigned to work full-time with the SEALs in the 1960s and continued until the introduction of dry-deck shelters permitted other submarines to accommodate SDVs and their crews.

See also ADVANCED SEAL DELIVERY SYSTEM (ASDS); DRY-DECK SHELTER (DDS); SUBMARINE OPERATIONS; OPERATION THUNDERHEAD.

Grenada

Grenada, an island in the Caribbean, was the site of the 1983 Operation Urgent Fury. Four SEALs were killed in the brief combat action during a parachuting accident.

See also OPERATION URGENT FURY.

grenades

The U.S. military issues almost a dozen types of this weapon. The most common is the M67 fragmentation grenade. There are also smoke, incendiary, concussion, tear gas, and concussion/stun grenades. SEAL units take along a supply of these weapons on every mission. They can be used in a variety of combat situations, from clearing a room to marking a landing zone.

ground laser target designator (GLTD)

The PAQ-10 GLTD is a man-portable device that uses a laser system to designate targets.

See also COMPACT LASER DESIGNATOR (CLD); TERMINAL GUIDANCE.

guerrilla warfare

Guerrillas are irregular combatant bands of partisans who, more often than not, operate in an enemy's rear area. Although they are often indigenous to the area, loosely organized, and poorly armed, equipped, and uniformed, that is not always the case. The National Liberation Front (NLF) in Vietnam fielded highly effective units during the Vietnam War. The Viet Cong were frequently farmers and artisans by day and soldiers at night. They had a firm military structure and organization.

In conducting warfare, the guerrillas' goal is to disrupt the enemy by hit-and-run tactics—blowing up rail lines, quick ambushes on small units, terrorism, destroying supplies, and other similar operations. Guerrilla warfare seldom achieves victory on its own; it must evolve into conventional warfare in order to win. However, it can be a great asset in ultimately achieving political and military ends.

Guerrilla warfare, as part of the unconventional warfare scenario, has been practiced in America by

Indians; by frontiersmen, Rogers's Rangers, and other patriots during the Revolutionary War; by guerrilla bands such as Quantrell's Raiders during the Civil War; by outfits like Merrill's Marauders in World War II; and by both the army Green Berets and the navy SEALs during the Vietnam War.

Navy SEALs are not guerrillas, but they are trained to operate if necessary as guerrillas. One of the missions specifically ascribed to Naval Special Warfare is unconventional warfare—training, leading, and equipping partisans and guerrilla forces behind enemy lines.

Gulf of Tonkin Resolution

Actions by U.S. Navy SEALs and their South Vietnamese counterparts were responsible to a large degree for the Gulf of Tonkin Resolution, one of the turning points in American history. The American public was not to find out until years later that the SEALs had been waging de facto war against North Vietnamese communists for nearly two years before an incident in the Tonkin Gulf provided President Lyndon Baines Johnson an excuse to make the war official.

In the spring of 1964, "Swift" and "Nasty" boats—with their 50-foot aluminum hulls, 80 mm mortars, 57 mm recoilless rifles, and light machine guns—were operating with SEALs along the North Vietnamese coast. SEALs under OP-34A, working out of China Beach near Da Nang, were responsible for training South Vietnamese commandos for actions against targets in the North. Although Americans were specifically prohibited from going ashore on these actions, they were already becoming involved in combat with the North Vietnamese. Claims about the strict "advisory" capacity of Americans in Vietnam no longer had much validity. A gradual process was leading inevitably to war.

Hanoi, in turn, beefed up its response to the commando operations by adding to its sentry force along the coast and running more aggressive boat patrols. The stage was set.

In June 1964, SEALs on Nasty boats came to the relief of South Vietnamese commandos trapped near the mouth of the Kien River, in order to provide fire support for the commandos' recovery.

At midnight on July 31, 1964, four SEAL Nasties shelled the North Vietnamese islands of Hon Me and Hon Nieu with 57 mm recoilless fire, destroying a gun emplacement, a communications station, and several buildings. The communists thought they were being shelled by a destroyer's five-inch gun—perhaps by the USS *Maddox,* then operating off the North Vietnamese coast in international waters.

In retaliation, three communist torpedo boats attacked the American destroyer in broad daylight, launching four torpedoes. The torpedoes missed. American aircraft blew one of the boats out of the water and severely damaged another. That same night, three Nasties firing 57 mm rifles shelled a North Vietnamese radar site and a security outpost near the Ron River. Hanoi was convinced that these boats were working from larger American vessels offshore.

Four nights later, at about eleven P.M. on 4 August, the USS *Maddox* and another destroyer, USS *Turner Joy,* suddenly reported they were under torpedo attack. There has been some doubt as to whether the incident actually occurred, or whether it was another incident like the 1898 explosion of the USS *Maine,* used to provide an excuse for escalating the war. Whatever the case, the engagements against U.S. destroyers of August 4, and the previous one of July 31, were portrayed as unprovoked attacks by the North Vietnamese against American ships operating in international waters. Hanoi complained about the shelling of its two offshore islands the previous week, but Washington denied there was any connection between the two incidents.

On August 5, planes from two American carriers delivered a devastating retaliatory strike against North Vietnamese installations. On August 7, Congress passed the Gulf of Tonkin Resolution, which authorized President Johnson to "take all necessary steps, including the use of armed force, to assist any member of protocol state of the Southeast Asia Collective Defense Treaty requesting assistance in defense of its freedom."

It was the equivalent of a declaration of war and served as the legal basis for the massive American involvement in Southeast Asia over the following eight years. From that point on, SEAL involvement in the war grew rapidly.

See also CHINA BEACH; OPERATION PLAN 34A (OP-34A); QUANG KHE NAVAL BASE.

H

Hagensen Pack

In German-occupied France during World War II, Adolf Hitler placed Field Marshal Erwin Rommel in charge of defending France against an Allied invasion. Rommel personally visited potential invasion beaches the Allies might use along the French coast and sketched out formidable defenses. Steel posts were driven into the sand, connected with barbed wire and reinforced by mortar and machine-gun emplacements. In the surf offshore were placed "Belgian Gates," heavy steel latticework barriers ten feet square and weighing three tons each, propped up by heavy steel braces.

American naval combat demolition units were confronted with the challenge of blowing up the Belgian Gates but not littering the area with steel, which would be as much a problem as the original obstacles. A young lieutenant named Carl P. Hagensen worked up a solution—a waterproof canvas haversack filled with plastic explosives. A hook on one end allowed the "Hagensen Pack" to be draped quickly over an obstacle, and a cord at the other permitted packs to be linked together. The packs were to be utilized in such a way as to drop the Belgian Gates flat so that landing craft could simply roll over them.

The Hagensen pack, designated the M-138 satchel charge, is still used by Navy SEALs today, little changed from the original.

See also BELGIAN GATES; EXPLOSIVES.

HAHO (high altitude, high opening)

HAHO is a method of military parachute insertion in which the jumper takes to the air at extremely high altitudes and opens his parachute right away, in order to "fly" to his target.

See also AIRBORNE.

HALO (high altitude, low opening)

HALO is a method of military parachute insertion in which the jumper leaves the aircraft at high altitudes and drops in freefall until activating his canopy at a low altitude. This permits a fast, clandestine insertion.

See also AIRBORNE; FREEFALL.

Hamilton, William H. (Bill)

On May 25, 1961, five weeks after the botched Bay of Pigs affair, President John F. Kennedy delivered before a joint session of Congress his famous "unconventional warriors for unconventional times" speech and ordered the Pentagon to set aside $400 million to beef up special operations. Lt. Cdr. William H. "Bill" Hamilton, commanding officer of Underwater Demolition Team 21, was with his team on winter training in St. Thomas when he heard the president's speech. He and other men on his team set about drafting a letter to the Chief of Naval Operations (CNO) proposing the creation of a new naval unit capable of operations not only at sea but on land and in the air. He little realized at the time that he would be selected to perform that very task.

Hamilton, a 1949 graduate of the Naval Academy and a protégé of Douglas Fane, had long been interested in the idea of establishing unconventional warriors within the U.S. Navy. Before joining the UDTs shortly before the Korean War, Hamilton had served as a carrier pilot and had had a number of friends in aviation. While with UDT-5 in Korea, he and other frogmen floated the concept of making UDT airborne. They experimented with the use of helicopters for inserting and recovering swimmers through such techniques as rappelling, "fast roping," and "helo casting." A few frogmen even parachuted out of Korean airplanes to receive jump training—until somebody broke a leg and the training was discontinued.

"It occurred to me that this was what Doug Fane and I had been looking for for years," he exclaimed after hearing Kennedy's speech. "I saw it as a great opportunity."

Hamilton's letter had fallen on fertile soil. Even before Kennedy's speech, the navy was giving serious consideration to the concept of naval commandos. The name SEAL, an acronym for Sea-Air-Land, was first used by the navy's Unconventional Activities Committee in a memo dated April 29, 1961. In May 1961, this committee recommended the formation on each coast of a commando unit that would focus on guerrilla and counterguerrilla operations—the Navy SEALs.

Capt. Harry S. Warren, who headed a special operations section for Adm. Arleigh A. Burke, CNO, contacted Hamilton. "We're going to cut orders for you," he said.

Hamilton found himself in the Pentagon with a $4.3 million budget and a one-man staff, charged with preparing for the creation of two SEAL teams, one on each coast. Though many career officers opposed the concept of getting into messy guerrilla operations and venturing up muddy inland rivers, Hamilton proceeded at a rapid pace. Much of his time in the latter half of 1961 was utilized answering questions: How big should SEAL teams be? What missions should they handle? How should they be armed? Who do we select for the teams? What should training be like? Where should it be conducted?

The first SEALs would have to come from the already-trained UDTs. The UDTs would then have to replace men pulled out for the SEAL teams. The UDTs were essential for any future amphibious operations. "The amphibian force had to continue to have the support of the UDTs," Hamilton pointed out. "That meant this [the SEALs] would be a new organization with new bodies, new billets, new money, new equipment and a new mission." The basic organization of the SEALs followed the UDT model. Each of the two teams would comprise 10 officers and 50 enlisted men, with a lieutenant in command. Each team would, at least initially, conduct its own training.

As early as June 1961, even before the teams were officially authorized, Hamilton summoned to his office his UDT-21 operations officer, Lt. Roy Boehm, a crusty and outspoken former boatswain's mate. "I want you to select and train men as a nucleus for a Special Operations force to be incorporated into the Underwater Demolition Units," he said. "Roy, do you know what this means? We've somehow been granted *carte blanche* to create the finest band of unconventional warriors in the world. President Kennedy has taken a lot of flak for the Bay of Pigs. He's not going to let it happen again. He's caught up in the unconventional warfare concept and has authorized us to do it the way we want. All he wants to see is results. I'm putting it in your hands because I think you're the most capable man in UDT to do it. You *always* get the job done."

Part of Hamilton's genius lay in selecting the right man for the right job. It was Boehm, more than any other individual involved in the creation of the Navy SEALs, who stamped the commandos with the mark of excellence. For the rest of that year, supported by

Lieutenant Commander Hamilton, Boehm selected his plankowners and sent them for skill training in everything from hand-to-hand combat to cracking safes.

On January 7, 1962, the navy made its final decision. Backdated to January 1, 1962, the U.S. Navy SEALs were commissioned. Lieutenant Boehm received the first orders as acting commander of SEAL Team Two. Lt. Dave Del Guidice was appointed commander of SEAL Team One in California.

Lieutenant Commander Hamilton went on to a Pentagon assignment. He later served as officer in charge of the navy's Marine Mammal Program; as head of OP-06D "Red Cell," a program designed to test the security of the navy against terrorists; and as head of the CIA's Maritime Department.

See also BOEHM, ROY; DEL GUIDICE, DAVID; SEALS.

harbor breakout

"Harbor breakout" refers to clearing mines from a harbor prior to departure by ships. SEALs have formed a close working relationship with the navy's Explosive Ordnance Disposal (EOD) units and are often cross-trained in EOD.

See also EXPLOSIVE ORDNANCE DISPOSAL (EOD).

hardhat diving

In "hardhat diving," the diver receives his supply of air from the surface through a long umbilical hose. The diver wears a rigid helmet and an air-holding weighted diving suit which, together with his umbilical, restricts his activities to within a certain radius of his surface air supply. Before swimmers could become true undersea warriors, they had to free themselves of such limitations by carrying their own self-contained air supply. Although the hardhat diving suit was one of the steps toward SCUBA (Self Contained Underwater Breathing Apparatus), SEALs are not trained in hardhat diving.

See also DIVING, HISTORY OF.

Hawkins, Thomas L. (b. 1944)

Among the new equipment developed by and for underwater demolition teams (UDTs) and SEALs during the 1960s and 1970s were swimmer (now SEAL) delivery vehicles, or SDVs. These were tiny, "wet" submarines. Occupants had to wear breathing rigs while operating in the SDVs, since the subs were flooded with water. Depending upon the model— and there have been several, up to and including the modern Advanced SEAL Delivery System (ASDS)— an SDV could transport two to four swimmers plus a pilot and a navigator. It could travel faster and farther than a man could swim and haul a greater payload of demolitions or other materials.

Lt. Cdr. Thomas L. Hawkins became one of the navy's most enthusiastic supporters of the use of SDVs and was involved in the development and fielding of the little craft from the beginning. His work led to the commissioning of specialized SDV teams (SDVTs) in support of SEAL missions; he served as one of the first commanders of SDVT-2.

Hawkins graduated from college in 1966 and won a commission in the U.S. Navy through the officer aviation program in Pensacola, Florida. He left the flight program, disillusioned, and went straight to UDT training at Little Creek, Virginia. He was to remain involved in naval special warfare for the remainder of his career.

He is fond of telling stories about early experimentation with SDVs. One of his stories focuses on a simulated demolitions attack on a flotilla of destroyers anchored in Chesapeake Bay. "I went on board and the admiral offered me coffee," he recalls. "I said, 'Admiral, you have seven ships anchored here. At the slack tide, we'll bring an SDV out of that channel over there. These guys are going to come over here and systematically hit that ship, that ships, that ship . . . They will put an inert limpet mine on each ship.'

"This guy gives me the ho hum. I told him, 'At eight o'clock, you're going to see the first flare go off over there. I would like you to alert all your sonar operators, tell everyone manning the gunnels to be aware, try to catch us.'

"The first flare went off at eight o'clock. All of a sudden he had seven destroyers lying on the bottom. He became concerned." Hawkins then advised the admiral that the SEALs and their SDVs would be back the next night to do the same thing all over again—and they did.

One frightening incident points out the inherent danger SEALs face in their continuing bid for excellence in training and equipment.

In 1975, SDVT-2 was in Puerto Rico for winter training. Lieutenant Commander Hawkins was about to become the team's commanding officer. He and two SEAL petty officers took a Mark 8 SDV out into Vieques Channel at night to test-operate a new radio system for the Operational Test and Evaluation Force. SDV pilot Rick Brown and navigator Frank Fitzko occupied the front two seats at the controls, while Hawkins sat directly behind them. They were each wearing a Mark XV UBA, a closed-circuit mixed-gas underwater breathing apparatus with a six-hour air supply.

The seas were rough, and the radio malfunctioned. Rick Brown dove the boat to a depth of about 20 feet to avoid the surface churn and set a coarse back to the piers at the naval station. They collided with a sunken wooden barge, driving the boat's bow planes in it like a dart into a dart board. Worse yet, the crash jammed the control console back into the canopy release handle. They couldn't get out of the boat to bob to the surface, and they could not notify anyone of their predicament, because the radio was out.

"[There was] not enough life support to get us to daylight," Hawkins explains. He predicted the three of them would be dead, drowned, before sunrise. "We took turns prying and banging at [the canopy], trying to make a hole big enough to squeeze through. . . . By now, we had been three for more than an hour. We still had air for awhile longer. But we've tried everything."

"The only thing I can think of," suggests Brown, "is to try to break those bow planes off." It was a last desperate attempt to escape the barge that held them underwater. Time was running out.

"[Brown] started doing what you would do in your car if you're stuck in the sand," Hawkins said. "He started rocking the boat, fast forward, fast reverse . . . We can only keep trying to break free as long as the batteries last. We decided we were just going to do that until the batteries went dead. We didn't have any choice. We had tried everything else. We were basically down there on our own.

"He went forward-reverse, forward-reverse, forward-reverse. The boat vibrates from the screw trying to move it, but it doesn't budge. I don't know how long this went on. It seemed like forever. Frank and I can't do anything to help. We just sit there. . . .

"And then, something gives. The boat moves. Just a little bit forward. A little back. We can feel it starting to move. Then it goes way back. It breaks free and pops to the surface. Our ears feel the relief of pressure as we go up."

See also ADVANCED SEAL DELIVERY SYSTEM (ASDS); SEAL DELIVERY VEHICLE TEAMS (SDVTS).

heavy SEAL support craft (HSSC)

During the Vietnam War, SEALs used a variety of boats in coastal and riverine operations in the southern Mekong Delta area of South Vietnam. Among them were the converted World War II–era LCM (landing craft, mechanized), Mark 6. SEALs knew it under various names, the most common being Heavy SEAL Support Craft (HSSC), or "Mike boat." It rode very low in the water due to its armament and armor.

To convert the LCM to a HSSC, the troop well was cut down and the entire boat coated with armor plate. Weapons stations along the sides gave it tremendous firepower, including 50-caliber machine guns, M-60 machine guns, 40 mm automatic grenade launchers, and an 81 mm mortar in the bow. Some boats went additionally armed with a 7.62 mm minigun in the bow tub and a 106 mm recoilless rifle mounted on top of the overhead. The craft easily carried a full SEAL platoon, their equipment, and even additional personnel. Team One used it a great deal during early operations in the Rung Sat area. The boat, however, was loud and slow and offered a big target. It did not take the enemy long to figure out that SEALs were the only units using it in Vietnam.

On October 7, 1966, SEAL Team One suffered its greatest loss in a single engagement when its Mike boat was ambushed on the Long Tau River. Viet Cong on either bank opened up with small arms, automatic weapons, light machine guns, and mortars. Had the LCM not been converted to an armored HSSC, it would not have lasted a minute under the heavy fire.

Nineteen SEALs were aboard the Mike boat. Although the open hull section provided an excellent battle platform, it was vulnerable to overhead attack. An enemy mortar round made a direct hit in the open section, wounding 16 of the 19. Three were hit so badly they were forced to retire afterward for medical reasons.

Although battered and bleeding, the SEALs valiantly repulsed the attack. Intelligence reports later credited the SEALs with having accounted for 40 enemy dead.

Six months later, on the Vam Sat River, another SEAL Mike boat was ambushed. Again, the VC used mortars. A round, fixed with a proximity fuse, exploded directly over the open hull. Twelve SEALs were wounded and two killed. One of the wounded later died of his injuries.

After that, SEALs stopped using the Mike for support operations. It was used primarily after that for insertions and extractions, communications, and logistical support.

Heckler and Koch P11 ZUB underwater weapon

This underwater-firing pistol developed by H & K entered underwater demolition team and SEAL service in 1976 to replace the Underwater Defense Gun, Mark I Mod 0. Although little is known publicly about its actual functioning, since its operational information remains partially classified, in general it operates much the same as the earlier

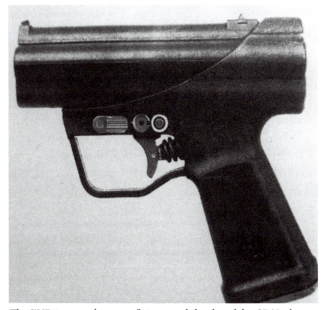

The ZUB is an underwater firing pistol developed for SEALs by H&K. (Kevin Dockery)

Mark I. Like the Mark I, it fires finned dart projectiles, five to a cylinder. Each projectile has its own individual barrel.

It is a lighter weapon than its predecessor, weighing only 2.65 pounds, and is electrically fired, with batteries, instead of with a propulsion charge. It can also be reloaded underwater, giving it a rate of fire of about 10 rounds per minute. It has a marginally greater lethal range than the Mark I—about 98 feet in the open air and from 32 to 49 feet at a depth of 60 feet. It is virtually silent.

Heckler and Koch acknowledges only that the weapon exists; the firm provides very little information about it.

See also UNDERWATER DEFENSE GUN, MARK I MOD 0.

helicopters

From its first sustained use in combat operations by the United States during the Korean War, the helicopter has become a general war workhorse, as much for the SEALs as for other units in the armed forces. This was especially true during the Vietnam War, when SEALs used helicopters nearly as much as they used boats for insertions, extractions, assaults, resupply, and reconnaissance.

The 1986 Goldwater-Nichols Act, which placed all special operations forces under a single joint command, also made available the assets of the entire military to special warfare. Helicopter models change and improve as mission requirements change, but two of the primary helicopters currently used by the SEALs and their support elements are the CH-60H Seahawk and the HH-60G Pave Hawk, operated by the Air Force Special Operations Command, a component of the U.S. Special Operations Command (USSOCOM).

The primary wartime mission of these birds is combat search and rescue, infiltration, exfiltration, and resupply of special operations forces in day, night, or marginal weather conditions. Night-vision goggles and forward-looking infrared assist low-level night operations and night water operation missions, which are performed by specially trained crews. The basic crew for either bird normally consists of a pilot, copilot, and three crewmen. The aircraft can also carry eight to ten troops. Two .50-caliber machine guns can be mounted in the cabin door, as well as two crew-served 7.62 miniguns in the cabin windows.

The helicopter became a general war workhorse, as much for the SEALs as for other units in the armed forces. SEALs here prepare to board a special operations Pave Hawk during Operation Desert Storm. (U.S. Navy)

In addition to the Seahawk and Pave Hawk, SEALs sometimes utilize other rotary-winged aircraft, such as the UH-60 Black Hawk, MH-53J Pave Low IIIE, OH-6A Cayuse, the AH-63 "Little Bird," CH-47 Chinook, and even an occasional UH-1 "Huey" left over from the Vietnam War. Hueys were used extensively in Vietnam and became an enduring and recognizable symbol of that war.

See also BLUE HAWKS; PAVE HAWK HELICOPTER (HH-60G); REDWOLVES; SEAHAWK HELICOPTER (CH-60H); SEAWOLVES.

hell box

The "hell box" is an electrical generator for setting off an explosive electrical firing train.

See also EXPLOSIVES.

Hell Week

Motivation Week, the true term for "Hell Week," is a period during Phase One of the Basic Underwater Demolition/SEAL (BUD/S) training course in which trainees are driven to their physiological and psychological limits.

See also BASIC UNDERWATER DEMOLITION/SEAL (BUD/S) TRAINING.

helo casting

As early as 1947, Francis Douglas "Red" Fane had experimented with the possibility of inserting and extracting swimmers from hovering helicopters. During the Korean War, a protégé of Fane's, William H. "Bill" Hamilton, and another Underwater Demolition Team Five officer, John Reynolds, continued these experiments. Hamilton and Reynolds asked Marine helicopter pilots based at Atsugi, Japan, to drop some frogmen into the ocean and pick them up again. Reynolds explained how it worked:

> We wanted to determine how fast the helicopter could fly and still have the swimmer enter the water in workable condition. We kept increasing the speed. People would skip like a stone across the water. . . .
>
> In the first group of tests, we had all our gear on: swim fins, masks, knives, explosives. When we hit the water, naturally, it tore everything off. So we made a pack of equipment, with a flotation bladder. The guy had a knife on his leg, that was about it. He'd go in holding his nose and his ass. We'd drop equipment at the same time in a flotation device.
>
> We spent a lot of time developing that technique. How high should the helicopter be? How fast should it go so the swimmer hits the water in a reasonable fashion? What kind of angle should the person take? Most of the momentum was forward rather than down. We were flying about twenty feet (above the water) at twenty five to thirty knots. We developed a pretty good technique for getting a person into the water.

The technique of "helo casting," as it became commonly known, is still used by special operations forces, although infrequently. In one of the most usual arrangements, a bar is attached to the helicopter so that the "caster" can swing out and hang momentarily to the side and below the helicopter before letting himself fall into the water. The trick is to let go at the optimum moment in order that the feet knife into the water smoothly.

Low-flying helicopters can usually avoid radar. Even if they are spotted at night, it is difficult for an observer to see a SEAL team being inserted, as the method is swift and silent, and the aircraft never stops moving.

Extracting swimmers from the water, however, proved a challenge to Hamilton and Reynolds.

"Well," Reynolds explained, "we figured we'd get a rubber loop on a ladder. We'll attach the ladder with bungee springs to the helicopter so it has some spring to it. The chopper will come along dragging this loop. The guy will do his thing, climb up the ladder into the helicopter."

> It was a disaster. Just as he was going to get the loop, it would hit a wave and bounce over him. Or he'd get the loop and he'd get about halfway up the ladder and the next man would hit the loop and it would fire the fellow who was on the ladder right off.

The only solution was for the helicopter to hover with a ladder hanging while the swimmers climbed it, a slow and dangerous process in enemy country. The problem of quick recovery from the water by helicopter remains as big challenge as it did 50 years ago.

See also FANE, FRANCIS DOUGLAS; HAMILTON, WILLIAM H.; OPERATION THUNDERHEAD

Higgins boat

"Andrew Higgins," said President Dwight Eisenhower, "is the man who won the war for us. If Higgins had not designed and built those LCVPs, we never could have landed over an open beach. The whole strategy of the war would have been different."

Andrew Jackson Higgins would likely have remained a small, if successful, Louisiana boatbuilder if the Japanese had not attacked Pearl Harbor. As it was, however, with his rapid design and production capability he manufactured 20,094 boats for military use during World War II. His designs landed more Allied troops during the war than all other types of landing craft combined. His LCVP (Landing Craft, Vehicle and Personnel) was widely used by naval combat demolition units and underwater demolition teams for their scouting and beach clearing operations.

During the 1930s, Higgins Industries had perfected a "Eureka" model workboat for use in the

"Helo casting" was developed by SEALs and U.S. Army Green Berets for inserting troops clandestinely into waters along hostile shores from low-flying helicopters. (U.S. Navy)

swamps and marshes of southern Louisiana. Its deep vee-hull forward gave way to a reverse-curved section amidships and two flat planing sections aft, flanking a semitunnel that protected the propeller and shaft and permitted the boat to operate in only eighteen inches of water and actually to push up on land. These features contributed to the boat's adaptation as a landing craft.

Higgins designed and produced two basic classes of military craft. One class consisted of high-speed patrol-torpedo (PT) boats, antisubmarine boats, dispatch boats, 170-foot supply vessels, and several other specialized patrol craft.

The second class consisted of various types of landing craft—the Landing Craft, Personnel (LCP); Landing Craft, Mechanized (LCM); and the LCVP. Although all these boats were "Higgins boats," the LCVP, generally known as *the* Higgins boat, could land a platoon of 36 men with their equipment, or a jeep and twelve men, then extract itself quickly, turn around in shallow surf, and return to sea for more men and equipment. The LCVP was the most common of the Higgins boats used by frogmen.

In spite of the large number manufactured, authentic Higgins boats became so scarce after the war that when the National D-day Museum tried to find one for display, it ended up building one, as no original could be found.

Ho Chi Minh Trail

Rather than a single road or trail, the "Ho Chi Minh Trail" was a network of trails and small roads along which the North Vietnamese infiltrated troops and supplies into South Vietnam during the Vietnam War. The trails, often camouflaged and all but invisible from the air, meandering into and through the neighboring countries of Laos and Cambodia, posed a continuing problem for American fighting men. Special operations people, including SEALs and army Special Forces, were often used in interdiction efforts to prevent war materiel from reaching Viet Cong and North Vietnamese forces in the South by this route.

See also SEALORDS.

"hunter"

The term "hunter" originated during the Vietnam War. Calling a teammate a "hunter" was the greatest compliment one SEAL could pay another. It meant the SEAL did much more than was asked of him. Rather than wait for the enemy, a hunter went out and found him in his own backyard.

"Hush Puppy"

"Hush Puppy," a Vietnam-era term, described several different models of "noise-suppressed" pistols used by special operations people and CIA agents. The name, as SEAL chief petty officer James Watson explains it, came from the pistol's official use—silencing yapping village dogs.

> When we originally asked for a suppressed pistol—the powers that be did not want the term "silencer" used—we were asked what we wanted it for. Since killing men with a suppressed handgun was considered somehow "unsportsmanlike," we told them the weapon was wanted to shoot dogs. Since the weapon was intended to silence dogs, and any other vermin who happened to get in front of it, the pistol was named the Hush Puppy. Because of that name, after a while, all silencers came to be called Hush Puppies.

One of the earlier-model "silenced" pistols was a noise-suppressed High Standard Model D military pistol manufactured during World War II for the Office of Strategic Services (OSS). It was a .22-caliber long rifle with an effective range of about 20 yards. The design of the suppressor was such that even when fired with high-speed ammunition, the bullet was slowed to below the speed of sound, which eliminated any sonic "crack." It was very effective and could be fired near enemy troops without their hearing the sound or recognizing it as a gunshot. Several thousand of them were manufactured during the war and were still in use by the Vietnam War.

Beginning in 1966, the Naval Surface Ordnance Center in White Oak, Maryland, began work to develop a noise-suppressed pistol suitable for the SEALs' special needs. In order for it to be interoperable with NATO, the Ordnance Center envisioned a 9 mm round rather than the .22 of the old High Standard. Technicians adapted the Smith and Wesson Model 39 to accept the suppressor formerly used by the CIA on the Walther P-38. It was developed as the 9 mm Pistol Mark 22 Mod O.

"The pistol was quiet," SEAL Richard Marcinko recalls, "especially with its slide held shut during firing by the slide lock. I always used the weapon as a single shot anyway, as the subsonic ammunition we had then wouldn't work the slide ideally for semiautomatic fire."

When fired with the special subsonic ammo designed for it, the sounds was unnoticeable at 50 yards. As the suppressor system only lasted for about two dozen rounds of special ammo and about six rounds of standard-velocity 9 mm, the accessory kit came equipped with additional suppressor inserts. The weapon became available for issue in 1967. It was, essentially, the first silenced pistol to be called a "Hush Puppy."

By the late 1970s, the Vietnam-era Mark 22s were wearing out. A German design, the Heckler and Koch P9S, first appeared to be a likely replacement. Using an extension barrel, the P9 was fitted with a stainless steel QualaTech suppressor designed by Mickey Finn. The QualaTech suppressor required only periodic cleaning and minimum maintenance, as compared to the Mark 22 kit. After three years of testing with 10 different weapons, however, the H & K lost out to the Beretta M92S-1. The new Berettas were available for issue in 1982 and could be adapted to a Mark 3 noise suppressor.

At about the same time, other new "Hush Puppies" were being introduced to and used by various SEAL units. In 1991, the U.S. Special Operations Command (USSOCOM) notified the firearms industry that SpecOps required a new handgun. Colt responded with the .45-caliber USSOCOM Colt Offensive Handgun Weapons System (OHWS) with suppressor. A laser aiming module was mounted on the frame of the OHWS, underneath the muzzle. It was secured with a quick-release system and contained a flashlight as well as visible and infrared lasers.

Heckler and Koch offered its own OHWS .45-caliber based on technologies the company had developed in its Universal Self-Loading Pistol. This new line of pistol included a plastic polymer frame, machined steel slide, and mechanical recoil-reduction system. Knights Armament Corporation provided the suppressor.

Both it and the Colt OHWS candidate met the requirements of 30-decibel noise reduction and 75 percent flash reduction over the unsuppressed system. Both were considered by the SEALs for adoption.

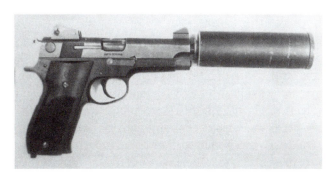

SEALs applied the term "Hush Puppy" to any pistol equipped with a noise suppressor. This is the 9 mm Mark 22. (Kevin Dockery)

In August 1992, the H & K was selected for further development under the second phase of the OHWS program. In mid-1995, phase three production began, with a requirement for 7,500 pistols, designated in its production model as the Mark 23 H & K Offensive Handgun Weapons System. The first production of Mark 23 pistols was delivered to the U.S. Special Operations Command on May 1, 1996, for operational deployment. The weapons began arriving at the SEAL teams shortly thereafter.

The Mark 23 is the current "Hush Puppy" for Special Operations, although other noise-suppressed pistols can be found.

Hussein, Saddam (b. 1937)

Saddam Hussein, the president of Iraq, commander in chief and field marshal of its armed forces, was the power and motivation behind Iraq's invasion of Kuwait in August 1990 that touched off Operation Desert Storm, the so-called War in the Desert.

See also OPERATION DESERT STORM.

hydrographic survey

In a hydrographic survey by U.S. Navy SEALs, swimmers search out natural or man-made obstacles in the waters off a beach and mark or neutralize them in preparation for an amphibious assault.

See also BEACH CLEARANCE; SEALS; UNDERWATER DEMOLITION TEAMS (UDTS).

hyperbaric chamber

The hyperbaric chamber is more commonly known as a "decompression chamber."

See also DECOMPRESSION CHAMBER.

hyperventilation

A "free diver" without underwater breathing apparatus or an air line to the surface may increase his time under water by deep-breathing prior to a dive, thus overloading his body tissues with oxygen and lowering his carbon dioxide content. Francis Douglas "Red" Fane was one underwater demolition team swimmer who perfected the technique. After hyperventilating, he could stay underwater up to five minutes at a time, long enough to dive 100 feet and swim underneath a submerged submarine from one side to the other. Modern U.S. Navy SEALs also practice the technique.

hypothermia

Hypothermia is a dangerous condition in which a cold environment lowers an individual's body temperature. SEALs and other divers must always contend with the threat, since lengthy unprotected submersion in water even as warm as 80 degrees Fahrenheit may produce hypothermia. SEALs use both wet and dry suits to counteract exposure to lowered temperatures and preserve body heat.

See also DRY SUIT; WET SUIT.

I

Ilo Ilo Island

Tiny Ilo Ilo Island at the mouth of the My Tho River in South Vietnam went down in SEAL lore as an example of enemy intractability. Ilo Ilo was almost legendary as a Viet Cong stronghold when the first SEAL "advisers" arrived in-country in 1962, and it was still a stronghold at the beginning of the end of concentrated SEAL activities in Vietnam in 1969.

The island was only about a half-mile long by a quarter-mile wide, surrounded on all sides at low tide by about 500 yards of soupy mud. A narrow canal ran into the heart of the island, through a savage terrain of streams, banks, thickets, swamps, and mudflats. The highest point of land on the island was only about two feet above the waterline. Most of the land above the mud flats was covered with nearly impenetrable mangrove thickets. A couple of small hamlets on the island provided aid and comfort to the enemy.

SEALs launched a number of operations against the island, beginning in 1963 and 1964 when Lt. Roy Boehm, the *first* SEAL, "advised" a company of Lien Doc Nguoi Nhai (LDNN), South Vietnam's version of SEALs.

Boehm and a small contingent of his LDNN, along with a company of ARVN (Army of the Republic of Vietnam) soldiers, penetrated the island to "de-infest" it of VC. Brief firefights between ARVN patrols and VC elements sparked throughout the day.

Late in the afternoon, Boehm and his LDNN came upon six VC junks beached on the flats, guarded by a lone sentry in the mangroves. Boehm cut the sentry's throat, then led his Vietnamese frogmen across the flats to the junks. About 10 VC opened fire from the cover of the largest boat, a motor craft equipped with a cabin. One LDNN was wounded, but all the VC died in the following exchange of fire. Friendly forces moved out; the enemy moved back in.

The island was still infested three years later when Lt. Richard Marcinko led his SEALs onto the island in search of a VC medical training facility. Marcinko's platoon first considered penetrating the island the easy way, via the canal, but "Dynamite Dick," as Marcinko was known, chose the more difficult route instead—fortunately, for as it turned out, the canal was heavily booby-trapped. The SEALs inserted at low tide and had to cross the flats by lying on their backs in the gooey mud and kicking themselves through it, a technique learned at BUD/S (Basic Underwater Demolition/SEAL training).

Once in the tangle of the jungle, the commandos came upon a small *baheo*—a little bamboo elevated shelter stashed with medical supplies. Among the medicines was a logbook containing the names of local VC, a big intelligence find. There were two more good-sized *baheos* nearby, in front of which six guerrillas gathered around a fire to cook their rice and chat. The SEALs killed five of them in a surprise attack. The sixth ran off into the mangroves and escaped. He returned shortly with some of his comrades.

Marcinko and his men fled the island under cover of 81 mm mortar fire from a Mike boat waiting on the river. Before they withdrew, they made a discovery that explained how the VC managed to cross the mud flats surrounding the island—odd-looking "mud shoes" made of strips of rubber inner-tube woven into a bamboo snow shoe–like frame.

As far as the SEALs knew, Ilo Ilo Island was still crawling with VC guerrillas when the war ended. It seemed that no matter how many times they were attacked, mortared, ambushed, and driven off, they came right back.

improvised explosive device

An improvised explosive device (IED), also referred to as a "kitchen table demolition," is a charge made from common household or other easily obtainable ingredients. SEALs are trained in their manufacture.

See also EXPLOSIVES.

inflatable boat, large (IBL)

The IBL is an inflatable boat whose special operations service began during World War II.

See also INFLATABLE BOATS.

inflatable boat, small (IBS)

The IBS, like its larger brother, the IBL, is an inflatable boat whose service with special operations began during World War II.

See also INFLATABLE BOATS.

inflatable boats

The history of inflatable boats, now used by U.S. Navy SEALs in a variety of configurations, goes back as far as 800 B.C., when the Assyrian king Ashurnasirpal II ordered troops to cross a river using greased, inflated animal skins. Similar vessels were made in ancient China. It was not until 1840, however, that an Englishman, Thomas Hancock, designed inflatable craft; he described them in his book, *The Origin and Progress of India Rubber Manufacture in England*.

Initially, inflatable boats were used by navies for transporting torpedoes and other cargo, as well as for utility purposes. U.S. Navy underwater demolition teams (UDTs) utilized two basic types of inflatable boats during World War II. These boats survived to be used by SEALs and UDTs during the Vietnam War and may still occasionally be found in service.

The Inflatable Boat, Large (IBL) is an eleven-man rubber boat over fourteen feet long, almost eight feet wide, and weighing over 400 pounds without crew or cargo. Its little brother, the Inflatable Boat, Small (IBS), is twelve feet long, six wide, and weighs about 300 pounds. Both boats were used during World War II and Vietnam for everything from clandestine scouting missions to utility transport. Until recent times, when the school switched to the CRRC (combat rubber raiding craft), BUD/S (Basic Underwater Demolition/SEAL) trainees were well acquainted with the inflatable boats through drills and evolutions with them.

The CRRC is a more modern cross between the IBS and IBL and in fact is sometimes known by either nomenclature. It is also known as a "rubber duck," or as a "Zodiac," in recognition of its manufacturer. It was originally designed as a lifeboat for World War II use, then modified slightly and improved with synthetic materials. Combat loaded, it weighs about 265 pounds, is fifteen feet long and has a six-foot beam. Powered by a 55 hp outboard with an 18-gallon fuel bladder, it has a range of about 65 miles doing a speed of 20 knots.

It is commonly used for clandestine surface insertions and extractions of lightly armed amphibious forces of SEAL fire teams—four or five men. It is one of the most versatile boats in the SEAL and boat-crew inventories. It can be tossed out of an airplane or helicopter, chucked over the sides of larger boats, or launched from either surface or submerged submarines. At times it can be considered disposable in combat operations.

Rigid-hull inflatable boats (RHIBS or RIBS) have evolved into the boats most used by SEALs. They are high-speed, high-buoyancy, extreme-weather craft whose primary mission is the insertion and extraction of SEAL tactical elements. They are actually a cross between standard fiberglass boats and inflatables. They offer fiberglass hulls with a V-shaped cross section to provide stability, a rigid motor mount, and firm footing. Only the gunwale section is inflatable.

They presently come in three variants. The 24-foot RHIB, the smallest, weighs about 10,000 pounds fully loaded. It is powered by a single Volvo inboard engine/outboard-drive power plant and is rated at a maximum speed of 28 knots and a range of about 175 nautical miles. It mounts a radar and an M-60 machine gun. The 30-footer is quite similar to the smaller boat, except that it has two engines with water-jet drives and has a higher rated maximum speed of 32 knots. It weighs approximately 15,000 pounds in combat weight and has a range of 150 nautical miles. The largest of the RHIBs is the 33-footer that can accommodate an eight-man SEAL combat element, a larger one if necessary. It can reach speeds up to 40 knots with a range of 250 miles. It mounts radar and two weapons—an M-60 machine gun or a Mark 19 grenade launcher.

The RHIBs are extremely seaworthy. Lightly loaded, they have operated in winds of 45 knots and state six seas with waves cresting up to 20 feet.

Ingram M10 submachine gun

Enemy contact is something to be avoided in most reconnaissance work. But when contact is unavoidable, the SEAL philosophy is to spray the greatest volume of fire possible, then "get out of Dodge." The Ingram M10 (MAC 10, for Military Armament Corporation) submachine gun, in its various caliber configurations—.45 ACP, 9 mm parabellum, .380 ACP—was designed for close-in defense. It is a high-volume weapon whose 32-round 9 mm magazine, or 30-round .45 magazine, can be emptied in two seconds.

The MAC 10 came to the SEALs in the early 1970s, when the teams were looking for a 9 mm submachine gun to supplement their Smith and Wesson Model 76s. Less than two feet in length and weighing only 8.82 pounds fully loaded with a 32-round box magazine *and* a noise suppressor, the 9 mm M10, the most popular of the three calibers, was a very compact submachine gun indeed, almost a machine pistol. Its advantages were its small size, which gave a SEAL scout swimmer an advantage; its rapid rate of fire; and the fact that it could be fitted with a noise suppressor.

Disadvantages included, curiously enough, its rapid rate of fire (a SEAL had only a two-second burst before having to reload) and its relatively poor accuracy. Some Special Forces troopers jokingly referred to it as a "phone booth gun," meaning you had to be in a phone booth with your target in order to be sure of hitting it.

The MAC 10 has been largely replaced in SEAL arsenals by the Heckler and Koch MP5 submachine-gun family.

See also MP5 HECKLER AND KOCH SUBMACHINE GUN.

insertion/extraction

It is frequently crucial to the success of a SEAL mission that the commandos enter an area unobserved. The departure of a team at the end of a mission also requires the same care, secrecy, and sometimes speed. With good reason, then, SEALs have devised a variety of insertion and extraction techniques that support the meaning of the SEAL acronymn—Sea-Air-Land.

SEALs may be delivered and picked up by any variety of special or commercially available watercraft, ranging from submarines and SEAL delivery vehicles to "rubber ducks" or speedboats. They may be dropped offshore or into adjacent waters by a technique known as "cast and recovery." An alternative to inserting from a watercraft is to swim in, either underwater with underwater breathing apparatuses or on the surface.

If delivery by water is unfeasible, SEALs may walk in, or ride in using a variety of conveyances, including fast-attack vehicles, motorcycles, military vehicles, or on occasion, even sports cars. There are several occasions of SEALs using horses, wagons, even an ox cart.

If no other clandestine method of insertion is available, SEALs turn to the air. If an aircraft can land in an area of operations, all the better. However, insertion by air generally means a parachute.

Airborne, waterborne, and land methods are frequently combined in order to place SEALs where they need to be and to recover them afterward. As in so many aspects of special operations, flexibility is the key.

See also ADVANCED SEAL DELIVERY SYSTEM (ASDS); AIRBORNE; CAST AND RECOVERY; FAST-ATTACK VEHICLE (FAV); HAHO (HIGH ALTITUDE, HIGH OPENING); HALO (HIGH ALTITUDE, LOW OPENING); HELICOPTERS; SEAL DELIVERY VEHICLE (SDV); SPIE (SPECIAL PROCEDURES, INSERTION/EXTRACTION); STABO (STABILIZED TACTICAL AIRBORNE BODY OPERATIONS); SUBMARINE OPERATIONS.

intelligence

For SEAL purposes, *intelligence* is defined as the collection, processing, integration, analysis, evaluation, and interpretation of available information concerning terrain, weather, and the enemy. The birth of the SEALs, through naval combat demolition units and underwater demolition teams, came about primarily through the navy's need for accurate intelligence about prospective beach landing sites. The very first mission of the very first SEALs, 40 years ago, was reconnaissance—intelligence gathering. Barely had the SEALs been commissioned than teams were being dispatched to Cuba to scout prospective invasion sites and to gather information on Soviet nuclear missiles being brought secretly into the island nation.

In spite of all the wonderful, expensive technology devoted to intelligence gathering, the billions spent on cameras and spy systems for aircraft and satellites, there is still no substitute for a man on the ground who can take a close-up "look-see" at a potential target. Overhead sources provide only essential planning information; a "recon" can fill in the intelligence gap. A landing zone may look entirely different from the air than from the ground. Sophisticated camouflage can conceal enemy weapons from spies in the sky.

Recon operations to gather intelligence are just as important now as they were in World War II, Korea, or Vietnam. SEALs still get tasked with recon operations and have made them their particular art form.

Some recons are small and covert, such as the hydrographic beach surveys SEALs conducted during Operation Desert Storm. Others may be *deep reconnaissance* or *strategic reconnaissance,* also conducted during Desert Storm, which typically require operators to travel covertly overland or be inserted covertly from the air. Such intelligence studies can be conducted in the water, on the beach, or far inland in large-scale, long-term studies of terrain, towns, and tactical units. However they are done, their purpose is to gather and provide intelligence for the theater commander in support of his operations.

See also BRUHMULLER, WILLIAM N., II; CUBAN MISSILE CRISIS; OPERATION DESERT STORM; HYDROGRAPHIC SURVEY; MISSIONS.

Intelligence Collection and Exploitation Program (ICEX)

ICEX was the term originally applied to the program of targeting Viet Cong infrastructure during the Vietnam War. It evolved almost immediately into the "Phoenix Program."

See also PHOENIX PROGRAM.

Iran Ajr

The *Iran Ajr* was an Iraqi ship captured by U.S. Navy SEALs caught laying mines in the Persian Gulf prior to Operation Desert Storm.

See also OPERATION EARNEST WILL.

Iranian hostage crisis

On November 3, 1979, Iranian militants seized the U.S. embassy in Tehran and took 63 Americans hostage. That precipitated a 444-day crisis during which a catastrophic rescue attempt ended in the death of five Americans. SEALs were involved in the rescue attempt.

See also OPERATION EAGLE CLAW.

isolation

SEAL elements preparing for a mission or operation are placed into isolation while they conduct planning. They may neither leave the area nor have unauthorized outside contact. This is a matter of security for both the SEALs and their mission.

See also MISSION PLANNING.

Iwo Jima

In spite of the bloody pounding the U.S. Marines took to dislodge the Japanese defenders from the island of Iwo Jima, the four underwater demolition teams—UDTs-12, 13, 14, and 15—that surveyed the invasion beaches prior to and during the landing suffered few casualties. One man was wounded at Futatsu Rock, and one man was missing and presumed lost. However, after the men of UDT-15 had completed their portion of the mission and were safely back aboard their destroyer, a Japanese Betty bomber dropped two bombs on the ship. Eighteen frogmen were killed, along with a marine observer attached to the team. Twenty-three others suffered wounds and burns, along with 11 of the ship's crew members. It was the worst disaster suffered by the UDT teams in the Pacific War and was second only in single-mission losses to those suffered at Omaha Beach during the D-day Normandy invasion.

See also USS BLESSMAN.

Janos, James (b. 1951)

James Janos is better known to the public under his professional name, Jesse "The Body" Ventura. As a member of UDT-12, Janos served in Southeast Asia during the waning years of the Vietnam War before being discharged in 1974. He became a professional wrestler and performed for many years in the ring before finally retiring in the 1980s. Briefly becoming an actor, he is best known as the man who carries and fires the minigun in the Arnold Schwarzenegger film *Predator*. He then went into politics to become Governor Jesse "The Mind" Ventura of Minnesota.

Jedi

"Jedi" was the nickname sometimes applied to the members of counterterrorist SEAL Team Six. It derived from the "Jedi warrior" characters in the *Star Wars* movies of the 1970s and '80s.

See also SEAL TEAM SIX.

USS *John Marshall*

The USS *John Marshall* (SSN 611, originally a Polaris submarine, SSBN 611) was converted to carry a dry-deck shelter when the USS *Grayback* no longer sufficed as a platform for SEAL delivery vehicles.

See also DRY-DECK SHELTER (DDS); USS *GRAYBACK*.

Joint Personnel Recovery Center (JPRC)

The JPRC was a unit formed under MACV-SOG, which was tasked with maintaining intelligence on allied prisoners of war in Vietnam and for launching rescue efforts.

See also "BRIGHT LIGHT"; MACV-SOG.

Joint Special Operations Command (JSOC)

Headquartered at Pope Air Force Base, North Carolina (at Fort Bragg), JSOC is an all-services planning and coordination cell, the primary mission of which is to study the techniques and requirements of all special operations forces components, including those of the naval special warfare community. It operates under the overall umbrella of U.S. Special Operations Command.

See also ORGANIZATIONAL STRUCTURE, SPECIAL OPERATIONS.

junk

A "junk" is a small traditional Chinese watercraft whose origins date back thousands of years. It may be powered by either sail or motor. Thousands of them, ranging from those just large enough for one person to craft of fourteen tons, ply the South China Sea and its tributaries. Junks were utilized during the Vietnam War by both sides, primarily for transporting supplies and equipment. U.S. Navy SEALs sometimes dressed in the typical "black pajamas" of the Vietnamese peasants and used the boats to disguise their mission movements.

One unique variant on the traditional boat is the use of plaited bamboo. In A.D. 975 military commander Tran Ung Long noticed that some of the Vietnamese fishermen could actually walk on water, in plaited bamboo baskets. He ordered boats made of bamboo in order to cross the river to reach his foe.

SEALs found that Viet Cong utilizing such craft were sometimes able to escape from rigid-frame boats in the shallow waters of the Mekong Delta. The flexible bamboo absorbs the shock of operating in shallow waters and, by spreading out over the surface of the water, permits a more shallow draft, allowing the junks to continue on their way.

See also JUNK FORCE.

junk force

During the Vietnam War, South Vietnamese military units used wooden or bamboo-hulled indigenous craft called "junks" for river operations against the Viet Cong and North Vietnamese army. Americans called them, informally, "junk force" or "Vietnamese junk forces."

Very early in America's involvement in the war, the U.S. Navy discovered that far more arms and supplies were getting to the Viet Cong from the North along Vietnam's 1,200-mile coastline than were coming overland via the Ho Chi Minh Trail network. Some 300 vessels of the South Vietnamese navy and the Vietnamese Junk Force were tasked with controlling coastal shipping. It was a formidable task, as on any given day there could be 50,000 sampans, junks, and trawlers in South Vietnamese waters.

The February 16, 1965, battle in Vung Ro Bay, in which an enemy trawler was surprised offloading supplies and was sunk after a fierce battle, led to Operation Market Time, the largest inshore blockade operation undertaken by the U.S. Navy since the American Civil War. It was carried out in conjunction with Vietnamese junk forces. SEALs in the Mekong Delta often conducted operations with the junk forces against the Viet Cong.

See also RIVERINE WARFARE.

K

Ka-Bar knife

Three varieties of the famous Ka-Bar combat/utility knife were manufactured during World War II, one of them designed especially for the underwater demolition teams (UDTs).

The first knife issued to the early UDTs, a design dated November 1943, was the USN Mark 1 Ka-Bar, standard throughout the navy. It was 10.13 inches long overall, with a 5.25-inch blade, and it weighed 0.42 pounds. The design was a shaped aluminum pommel over a stacked leather washer grip, with a small, flat steel guard. It greatly resembled the general style of hunting knives popular on the civilian market at the time. So many Mark 1s were produced that several cutlers were involved, each one modifying the design slightly to his own manufacturing methods. The general style of the knife, however, remained the same.

A fiber-reinforced gray plastic scabbard was issued to the UDTs, because leather sheaths were quickly rendered useless by constant exposure to salt water. A drawback of the Mark 1 was the weakness of the small blade, especially since it was widely used as a pry-bar.

The Mark 1 Ka-Bar was originally adopted by the U.S. Marine Corps as a multipurpose tool that would also serve as a fighting knife. The Camillus Cutlery Company and Union Cutlery were among at least five different manufacturers who produced more than a million of the knives during the war. The Mark 2 was a heftier, larger version of the Mark 1. It was a foot long overall, with a seven-inch blade, and a weight of 0.63 pounds. The blade had flat sides, parallel to within a few inches of the tip, and an edge grind that didn't quite come to midpoint. A fuller, or groove, ground into each side of the blade strengthened and lightened it. The Mark 2 design became so popular that it was eventually demanded by all the services, including the Coast Guard.

Since the blades of both the Mark 1 and Mark 2 were made of carbon steel, they soon rusted after exposure to salt water. The most exposed were the knives used by UDTs. To help minimize the corrosion, Union Cutlery produced a modified Mark 2 especially for the UDTs. It was called the Bright Mark 2.

The Bright was a Mark 2 modified. The first model had no fullers ground into the blade, and all the metal parts were bright chromed. The "production" model was a standard, fullered blade with a pinned pommel. Only a few hundred of the special UDT knives were made, and today they are rare items.

UDTs continued using the Mark 1s and Mark 2s throughout the 1940s and 1950s. A few may even be found among modern SEAL teams.

Kaine, Francis Riley (Frank)

Frank Kaine, after whom the Naval Special Warfare Command building at the Naval Special Warfare Center, Coronado, California, is named, was a leader in naval special warfare from World War II into the Vietnam War era. He became known as "MacArthur's Frogman," because of the faith Gen. Douglas MacArthur placed in the naval combat demolition units (NCDUs) that surveyed MacArthur landing beaches from Biak to Borneo.

Lieutenant (junior grade) Kaine was recruited early in the war by Draper Kauffman. He went through Kauffman's bomb-disposal school in Washington before attending the first NCDU class, which began in June 1943. From this first class came the four NCDUs that were the beginning of demolition forces for the Atlantic theater. In addition, Kaine's NCDU-2 ("Kaine's Killers") and Lt. Lloyd G. Anderson's NCDU-3 formed the nucleus of six NCDUs that served with the Seventh Amphibious Force, in MacArthur's command. Each NCDU consisted of five enlisted men and one officer.

Most of the other NCDUs working the Pacific merged with underwater demolition teams. The NCDUs under MacArthur, however, remained individual units throughout the war.

While other forces were moving north across the Central Pacific, MacArthur's forces were moving from Australia through the New Hebrides toward the Philippines. "MacArthur's Frogman" stood before the army's 32d Division and explained how he and his small group of swimmers could scout out invasion beaches and help American invaders avoid the fate of the Marines at Tarawa. "I guess we were convincing, because from then on, every landing they had, they had some of our units in it." Prior to each landing, MacArthur conferred with his generals and admirals, then summoned his young lieutenant to advise about the condition of invasion beaches.

Kaine directed 36 NCDU operations during the war, starting with the Admiralty Islands, and personally participated in a third of them: Aitape, Tanahmerah Bay, Hollandia, Biak and Nunfoor, Leyte, Mindoro, Lingayen Gulf, Palawan, Saransk, and Brunei Bay.

After the war ended, Kaine remained in naval special operations, conducting pioneer experiments with the skim boat and the Aqua Ho motor. He attained the rank of captain and served during the Vietnam War as commander of Special Warfare Group, Pacific.

See also AQUA HO MOTOR; BEACH CLEARANCE; NAVAL COMBAT DEMOLITION UNITS (NCDUS); SKIM BOAT.

Kauffman, Draper L.

Draper Kauffman, known as "the father of naval combat demolition," founder and head of the Navy Bomb Disposal School, was given the responsibility for launching the navy's underwater demolition program. He trained the first naval combat demolition units (NCDUs), which saw action in both the Atlantic and Pacific theaters of war, and led underwater demolition teams (UDTs) from Saipan to Okinawa. He was preparing for the invasion of Japan when the war ended. Both the NCDUs and the UDTs are considered direct forerunners of the U.S. Navy SEALs.

A very slender man who stood six feet tall, Kauffman graduated from the U.S. Naval Academy, class of '33, but failed to receive a commission because of poor eyesight; he wore thick Coke-bottle lenses. Instead, he went to work for a steamship line. In 1939, he spent two months at the company's offices in England, two in France, and two more in Germany, where he attended speeches delivered by Adolf Hitler. To him, Hitler was a scary man. He thought war was inevitable; he feared the West might lose it.

Shortly after war broke out in September 1939, he signed up as a volunteer with the French ambulance corps. He was taken prisoner by the Germans in 1940 when he and another ambulance driver attempted to penetrate their lines to recover wounded French soldiers. Eventually released because he was an American, he worked his way down to Lisbon, across the South Atlantic to Brazil, then up to Boston.

He enlisted in the British navy and soon volunteered to become a Royal Navy bomb disposal officer. He worked disarming German bombs throughout the Nazi blitz against Britain in the winter of 1940–41 and into the spring of 1941. By this time, the United States considered his experience in EOD (explosive ordnance disposal) too valuable to waste. Although his eyesight had not improved, he was finally commissioned in the U.S. Navy and was tasked with setting up an American bomb-disposal school.

The Navy Bomb Disposal School came into existence at the Washington Navy Yard in January 1942. For the next year and a half, Kauffman turned out bomb-disposal experts, first at the navy yard and then at American University in northwest Washington, D.C. His final exams for graduation from the school required nearly 30 hours of hard work, designed to test how well the men worked under the pressure of fatigue and to screen out those who didn't measure up. This reliance on physical stress as a testing point remains an important part of today's Navy SEALs. Today's SEALs are also experts on explosives, a direct link to Kauffman's bomb-disposal experts of half a century ago.

As early as January 1943, the United States began to experiment with clearing prospective invasion beaches of man-made obstacles. On June 6, 1943, Adm. Ernest J. King, Chief of Naval Operations, issued authorization for navy combat demolition training to commence in order to cope with the obstacles Hitler would undoubtedly use to hinder landings in Europe.

Kauffman was selected to head up NCDU training. In a hurried meeting in Washington, he was shown pictures of obstacles being built on French beaches and was told to "put a stop to that." He set up shop at Fort Pierce, Florida, a short distance from the old former casino occupied by the Amphibious Scouts and Raiders. His first volunteers came mostly from Navy construction battalions (Seabees), with the officer cadre raided from the bomb-disposal school.

His extensive program was designed, first of all, to toughen the men for demanding duty. His theory, based on the operations and training of the Amphibious Scouts and Raiders, postulated that a

man should be capable of ten times the physical effort he thought he was. Training commenced with a grueling week intended to weed out the less committed. It is still a part of SEAL training and is still known as "Hell Week." "The men had sense enough to quit—and left us with the boys," went one comment.

By April 1944, a total of 34 NCDUs had been deployed to England in preparation for Operation Overlord, the amphibious landing at Normandy. Other NCDUs were dispatched to the South Pacific, where all, with the exception of NCDU-2 and NCDU-3, which were assigned to Gen. Douglas MacArthur, were eventually assimilated by the underwater demolition teams.

Feeling his mission at Fort Pierce completed, Kauffman requested a transfer to a field unit. Adm. Richmond Kelly Turner, principal commander of the amphibious invasion of Tarawa and the Gilbert Islands, thought Kauffman was the man to advance further the UDT program in the Pacific. In April 1944, Turner had Kauffman transferred to the UDT school at Maui, where he took an advanced UDT course and then assumed command of UDT-5 in time for the invasion of Saipan.

Saipan, in the Mariana Islands, was coveted as a forward air base for the newly developed U.S. B-29 bomber. Operating out of Saipan, the B-29 would be able to reach mainland Japan with a full bomb load and return.

To meet Admiral Turner's requirements, the UDTs developed several new methods of operations. Daylight reconnaissance was one of these. That eliminated the use of rubber boats; the men were expected to swim. The "buddy system" and the "cast and recovery" technique for rapidly inserting and recovering swimmers were other innovations. UDTs were well on their way to becoming sea commandos.

Promoted to captain, Kauffman was later given responsibility for preparing for the marine landing on Kyushu, the southernmost of the main Japanese islands. He feared the teams would suffer a two-thirds casualty rate. For this scenario, each prospective beachhead had 10 UDT teams assigned. Three teams would go in first, followed by two more layers of three, and a single team in reserve. He intended to get the job done, no matter how many casualties his teams took.

The atomic bombing of Hiroshima and Nagasaki ended plans for the great invasion and brought victory over Japan. Kauffman went on to attain the rank of admiral and was commander of U.S. naval forces in the Philippines during the Vietnam War.

See also AMPHIBIOUS SCOUTS and RAIDERS, EXPLOSIVE ORDANCE DISPOSAL (EOD), KING, ERNEST J., NAVAL COMBAT DEMOLITION UNITS (NCDUS); NAVY BOMB DISPOSAL SCHOOL; UNDERWATER DEMOLITION TEAMS (UDTS).

Kennedy, John F. (1917–1963)

President John F. Kennedy has long been recognized as the impetus behind the creation of U.S. special operations forces, including Navy SEALs, and the redirection of American forces away from sole reliance on nuclear warfare and toward a security policy that included limited-war, and guerrilla-style operations.

On April 17, 1961, less than three months after JFK assumed the presidency, American-trained Cuban exiles landed in Cuba to overthrow dictator Fidel Castro—and suffered a devastating defeat at the Bay of Pigs. Among the lessons learned from that disaster was that the United States had difficulty carrying out operations that were too big to be kept secret but smaller than an all-out commitment of forces.

During World War II, Kennedy had served as an officer on a U.S. Navy PT boat in the South Pacific. That background provided him firsthand knowledge of how small groups of dedicated and well-trained men can exert an effect far out of proportion to their numbers. He recognized the needs for forces that could successfully wage guerrilla war as well as conventional war.

On May 25, 1961, he delivered to a joint session of Congress one of the most important speeches of his presidency. He not only set a goal of putting an American on the moon before the end of the decade but he also called for a major restructuring of the nation's military forces. "I am directing the secretary of defense to expand rapidly and substantially, in cooperation with our allies, the orientation of existing forces for the conduct of non-nuclear war, paramilitary operations and sub-limited, or unconventional wars. In addition, our special forces and unconventional warfare units will be increased and reoriented."

He ordered the Pentagon to take more than $400 million from other programs to beef up the military's special operations forces. The navy immediately prepared to comply with the directive by starting to design shallow-draft boats for operations in a riverine-type environment, and by launching studies to establish the best kind of unit to perform naval guerrilla warfare. The U.S. Navy SEALs were officially born on January 1, 1962.

President Kennedy died by an assassin's bullet in Dallas, Texas, on November 22, 1963. The accused assassin, Lee Harvey Oswald, was in turn assassinated on November 24 by Jack Ruby. Ruby died of natural causes before standing trial.

See also BAY OF PIGS; BOEHM, ROY; CUBAN MISSILE CRISIS; HAMILTON, WILLIAM H.; SEALS.

Kerry, Joseph R. (Bob) (b. 1943)

Lt. (j.g.) Bob Kerrey was the first SEAL to win the Congressional Medal of Honor, the nation's highest award for valor. He was serving with SEAL Team One, Delta Platoon, in Vietnam. Two other SEALs also won the medal during the Vietnam War.

In March 1969, two Viet Cong defectors showed up in the coastal city of Nha Trang with information that the VC had a secret base on Ham Tam Island, in Nha Trang Bay. From this base, sappers were being sent out to attack U.S. and South Vietnamese targets; intelligence agents were also being infiltrated from this base into spy networks within the South Vietnam government and military. The defectors warned that the SEALs would have to move quickly if they hoped to have any chance of capturing key officials and seizing the names of members of the spy network.

In the predawn of March 14, "Kerrey's Raiders," led by Lt. Kerrey, were dropped off from a small boat near the island. The raiding party consisted of Kerry, six other SEALs, a Vietnamese frogman, and the two defectors. They managed to swim ashore undetected in the moonless night. Without ropes, they scaled a sheer 350-foot cliff in the darkness in order to approach the enemy camp from above and behind.

The camp appeared to be sleeping. Kerrey assigned half his team to keep an eye on the drowsy

VC while he and the other half removed their boots and set out to check the rest of the camp barefooted.

Despite all their precautions, the SEALs were spotted and came under heavy automatic fire. The VC were more heavily armed than Kerrey had been led to believe. During the fierce firefight, a grenade sailed out of the darkness and exploded at Lieutenant Kerrey's feet. It blew him backward off his feet and into a rock field.

Although severely wounded, the young lieutenant maintained command. He radioed in the other half of his team and positioned it to deliver a withering crossfire against enemy positions. Seven VC were killed, others fled, and still others were captured. The SEALs took control of the camp and summoned helicopters to medevac the wounded squad leader, along with enemy prisoners.

The raid proved every bit as valuable as the SEALs hoped. It netted many documents and a list of VC agents in the area. Kerrey became the first SEAL to win the Congressional Medal of Honor for his bravery while under fire and while wounded. The citation, signed by President Richard M. Nixon, stated, "The havoc wrought to the enemy by this very successful mission cannot be overestimated. The enemy who were captured provided critical intelligence to the allied effort."

The lower part of Kerrey's right leg was partly blown off and left mangled by the exploding grenade. It later had to be amputated below the knee.

After Vietnam, Kerry went into politics. He was governor of his home state of Nebraska from 1983 to 1987, a U.S. senator from 1989 to 2001, and Democratic candidate for president of the United States in 1992.

See also MEDAL OF HONOR.

King

King was the name of a legendary SEAL scout dog used during the Vietnam War.

See also SCOUT DOGS.

King, Ernest J. (1878–1956)

The ninth Chief of Naval Operations (CNO) and Commander in Chief, U.S. Fleet, during World War II, Adm. Ernest J. King assured himself of a place in the history of naval special warfare by his role in establishing early forerunners of the U.S. Navy SEALs.

After graduating from Annapolis fourth in his class (1901), King began an early career described as "rather ordinary." He was remembered primarily in a number of commands as "meaner than hell," a man with an abrasive personality who "seemed almost to pride himself on the fact that he had earned his rank solely on his merits as a professional naval officer, rather than as a result of the friendship of others."

His career was resurrected by the war that started in Europe in the spring of 1939. Then-CNO Adm. Harold Stark appointed him commander of the Atlantic Fleet. There King ably managed the undeclared war with Germany's U-boats.

The morning after the Japanese attack on Pearl Harbor, Stark called him to Washington. Soon thereafter, King was running the Navy, first as commander in chief of the U.S. Fleet, then with the additional title of Chief of Naval Operations. He was the first man to combine both jobs. King's strategic brilliance earned him the complete confidence of President Franklin Roosevelt. "No fighter ever won his fight by covering up—merely fending off the other fellow's blows," he declared. "The winner hits and keeps on hitting even though he has to be able to take some stiff blows in order to keep on hitting."

During his tenure as head of the U.S. Navy in World War II, King issued directives establishing the Beach Jumper program, the naval combat demolition units (NCDUs), and "Amphibious Roger," all important steps in naval special warfare and in the eventual formation of the Navy SEALs.

Inspired by the success of British commandos in employing deception techniques on raids against the Nazis, he issued a secret letter on March 5, 1943, in which he charged the Vice Chief of Naval Operations with the recruitment of 180 officers and 300 enlisted men for the Beach Jumper program. His announcement stated, "The Navy is requesting volunteers for prolonged, hazardous, distant duty for a secret project." The project: "To assist and support the operating forces in the conduct of Tactical Cover and Deception in Naval Warfare."

Three months later, on June 6, 1943, he issued a second directive, to establish a special unit to cope with the obstacles that Hitler would undoubtedly order built to hinder landings in Europe. The directive provided men for "a present urgent require-ment," the building of an NCDU for assignment to the amphibious forces. He selected Draper L. Kauff-man to head the program. The first NCDU class began immediate training at Fort Pierce, Florida.

Shortly thereafter, King again looked toward spe-cial warfare when he ordered 120 officers and 900 men be trained for "Amphibious Roger." He looked upon Roger to form the core of what he envisioned as a "guerrilla amphibious organization of American and Chinese operating from coastal waters, lakes and rivers employing small steamers and sampans" to help bolster the work of the Sino-American Cooperation Organization (SACO). Only three groups of Amphibious Roger actually saw service; they conducted surveys of the upper Yangtze River in the spring of 1945 and a detailed three-month survey of the Chinese coast from Shanghai to Kit-chioh Wan, near Hong Kong.

Beach Jumpers, NCDUs, and Amphibious Roger all contributed to the eventual birth, growth, and development of the U.S. Navy SEALs.

Admiral King died on June 15, 1956, after several years of failing health.

See also AMPHIBIOUS ROGER; BEACH JUMPERS; KAUFFMAN, DRAPER L.; NAVY COMBAT DEMOLITION UNITS (NCDUS); UNDERWATER DEMOLITION TEAMS (UDTS).

Kistiakowsky, George (1900–1982)

Dr. George Kistiakowsky is best known in naval special warfare as the scientist who designed the explosive "linear demolition charge," and better known worldwide as one of the developers of the atomic bomb.

Born in Russia in 1900, he fought in the infantry and tank corps with the White Army against the Bolsheviks during the Russian civil war following the 1917 revolution. He fled to Germany when the communists came to power. There he studied chem-istry at the University of Berlin, earning his Ph.D. in 1925. He moved to the United States and joined the faculty at Harvard.

When World War II began, he studied explosives for the National Defense Research Committee. While in this position he often visited the training com-pound of Draper L. Kauffman's NCDU (Navy Com-bat Demolition Unit) at Fort Pierce, Florida, where

navy demolition experts were experimenting with various uses of explosives. Because of his propensity for careening around the compound at the controls of a tank, he was known to the NCDU men as "the Mad Russian."

It was his idea to stuff blocks of tetryl, a power-ful yellow powder explosive, into floatable rubber tubes. The snake-like tubes full of charges could be towed by a swimmer, manipulated in the water, and wrapped around an obstacle. His original con-cept was later used to build "linear demolition charges" to clear obstacles and blast trenches on the ocean floor.

In late January 1944, he joined the Manhattan Project and disappeared from the NCDU compound. It was not until after the war that most frogmen who had known him learned he had joined Dr. Robert Oppenheimer as one of the major developers of the atomic bomb. It was under his leadership that scien-tists were able to develop the complex explosive "lenses" needed to compress a plutonium sphere uniformly to achieve critical mass.

Kistiakowsky returned to Harvard after the war and advised several presidents on arms control and foreign policy. He retired from Harvard as professor emeritus in 1972 and died in 1982.

See also EXPLOSIVES.

kitchen table demolitions

"Kitchen table demo" is what special operations troops call improvised explosive devices (IED), or explosives that may be manufactured from common household or farm products.

See also EXPLOSIVES.

Korean War

The Korean War was the first war in which a world organization, the United Nations, played a military role. It began on June 25, 1950, when troops from Communist-ruled North Korea invaded South Korea. Sixteen UN countries sent troops to help the South Koreans; 41 other countries sent military equipment or food and other supplies. The United States sent more than 90 percent of the troops and war equipment. It became one of the bloodiest wars in history, with nearly a million civilians casualties. About 580,000 U.S. and South Korean troops and about 1,600,000 Communist troops were killed or wounded.

The underwater demolition teams (UDTs) of World War II, which had been considerably reduced in numbers, were used to some large degree during the war. It was in Korea that the UDTs began evolving toward more well-rounded commandos that would eventually lead to the birth of the Navy SEALs.

The war ended on July 27, 1953, with the signing of a truce. A permanent peace treaty has never been signed.

See also BUCKLEW, PHILIP H; HELO CASTING; OPERATION CHROMITE; OPERATION FISHNET.

Kwajalein Island

One of the world's largest atolls (rings of coral islands), Kwajalein lies in the Marshall Islands 2,443 miles southwest of Honolulu, Hawaii. Japan fortified the atoll and built airstrips and a seaplane base on it. The United States captured it in February 1944 and used it as a navy base for the rest of the war.

The Kwajalein assault was the first test for newly formed underwater demolition teams (UDTs) and the site where frogmen began working out their tactics.

See also ACHESON, BILL; LUEHRS, LEWIS F. TURNER, OPERATION FLINTLOCK; RICHMOND KELLY.

L

Lambertsen, Christian J.

Christian J. Lambertsen was a medical scientist who became known as "the father of U.S. combat swimming" for his invention of the Lambertsen Amphibious Respitory Unit (LARU) and his work in diving physics.

In the years preceding World War II, a number of people worldwide experimented with methods by which human beings could live and move freely about under seas and rivers. In 1940, a little more than a year before Pearl Harbor, Christian, at the time a 23-year-old medical student at the University of Pennsylvania Medical School, developed out of his studies in human physiology a remarkably sophisticated self-contained breathing system that would permit swimmers to operate underwater for long periods of time.

The Lambertsen Amphibious Respiratory Unit, or LARU, as it became known, consisted of a small bottle of pure oxygen, a container of soda lime, and a rebreather bag, all of which were rigged to a mask to permit the diver to breath underwater. At the beginning of a dive, the swimmer released a small amount of oxygen into the rebreather bag. As he breathed, the air he exhaled channeled through the soda lime, which filtered out the carbon dioxide; then it returned as purified oxygen to the rebreather bag. More oxygen was supplied as needed.

The system was truly self-contained and closed-circuit, as it gave off neither bubbles nor sound.

In those early days before the World War, the U.S. Navy's only divers were in the salvage community, hardhat divers tethered to the surface by air hoses, communications lines, and safety ropes. Lambertsen demonstrated his LARU to the navy, but it was simply not interested. Lambertsen turned to a new organization—the Office of Strategic Services, originally made up of men from all four branches of the U.S. military. His proposal that the OSS, a fast-moving outfit that combined intelligence gathering with guerrilla operations behind enemy lines, develop a combat swimmer corps was eagerly adopted. Called to active duty as an army officer when the war began, Lambertsen was put in charge of equipping and training about 100 "operational swimmers" of the OSS Maritime Unit.

Training of OSS swimmers was conducted at Camp Pendleton and Catalina Island in California and at Nassau in the Bahamas, where they worked with British divers. Unlike underwater demolition teams (UDTs), who worked at that time on the surface under cover of naval gunfire and air strikes, the Maritime Unit was trained in the use of the LARU in order to operate underwater at night, by stealth. The unit had several missions among which were: to sneak into harbors and sabotage enemy shipping; to gather intelligence in behind-the-lines operations; and to deposit saboteurs, intelligence agents, and raiders onto hostile shores and then pick them up again.

OSS swimmers were organized into three teams of about 30 men each. One of these units was sent to Maui and attached to UDT-10 in June 1944 in preparation for the advance on Japan. The UDTs readily adopted swim fins after the OSS showed them how to use them, but they had little use for the LARU. In actions at Kwajalein, Eniwetok, and Saipan, the UDTs had developed proven methods of beach reconnaissance that did not require swimming underwater. "This was not unintelligent," Lambertsen observed philosophically. "Someone is unlikely to use his stealth weapon when his cruisers are back in shape."

Gen. Douglas MacArthur soundly rejected Lambertsen's offer to send another OSS element to the South Pacific. MacArthur disapproved of the OSS's unconventional and unorthodox methods. Instead of working the Pacific, Lambertsen's operational swimmers went to Southeast Asia, where they were attached to the British army on the Arakan coast of Burma. Even there, the team was involved in only one operation—the reconnaissance of an island in advance of a British landing.

Although OSS swimmers participated in a limited number of live operations, Lambertsen was responsible for a remarkable list of developments in equipment and tactics for combat swimmers during his year and a half with the unit. Many of these innovations were to become standard with postwar UDTs and, later, the U.S. Navy SEALs.

> He invented a speaking device built into a face mask that permitted two-way voice communications between divers at ranges of up to 75 yards.
> He designed an underwater compass to use at night and over long distances.
> He devised a neutral-buoyancy container that permitted a swimmer to tow as much as 30 pounds of explosives or equipment underwater.

> He worked with other OSS members in the development of the "limpet mine," which could be attached magnetically or with glue to the hull of a ship.
> He collaborated with the British to devise tactics for their use of underwater X-craft.
> He anticipated the use of dry-deck shelters by his suggestion that the navy design a compartment on the deck of a submarine that could contain submersible craft and be used for launching and recovering them.

After the war ended, he returned to the University of Pennsylvania Medical School, but he retained his interest in underwater breathing. He was working with the army, teaching soldiers tactics for mining bridges and using small boats, when Lt. Cdr. Francis Douglas "Red" Fane found him in 1948. Fane persuaded him to come to Little Creek, Virginia, and work with him in training UDTs as that program gradually moved toward more unconventional tactics.

At Little Creek, Fane and Lambertsen developed still more new tactics for sea warriors. Among these were exit and reentry procedures for submarines; location and pickup of underwater swimmers by means of the submarine's sound gear; local communications between underwater swimmers and personnel inside a submarine.

Lambertsen's LARU system, he admitted, had serious limitations that required correction. If the lines became clogged, the diver suddenly found himself in danger of suffocating or drowning. If water got into the soda-lime canister, a choking "caustic cocktail" could erupt inside the diver's face mask. Too much oxygen might also be lethal, as it destroyed red blood cells, attacked the swimmer's neurosensory and nervous system, and caused "oxygen poisoning."

Experimenting with the latter problem, Lambertsen and Fane worked out a set of rules for breathing pure oxygen that would permit divers to work at certain depths for prescribed periods of time without adverse effects. In the early 1950s, Lambertsen modified his LARU to accommodate mixtures of nitrogen or helium with an elevated oxygen content to allow operations at greater depth and range without the hazards of oxygen poisoning. He then introduced the FLATUS I, a semiclosed SCUBA that continually added a small volume of mixed gas, rather than pure oxygen, to the rebreathing circuit.

It was semiclosed in that very small amounts of inert gases not consumed by the diver were continually exhausted as bubbles.

"Things began to go bad when the French came over and commercialized the Aqua-Lung—what people now think of as SCUBA," Lambertsen wrote. "There are many SCUBAs. It is a term I devised: self-contained underwater breathing apparatus. Most people think it is all air—take a breath and blow it away. That has very little military usefulness. And yet it was so easy that Fane got so happy with the ease of doing things that way that he just more or less rolled over and had his people use it. They became a bunch of skin diver types. That's when that long, nearly fifteen-year period of almost stagnation began. And it was largely because they went from a rapidly advancing technical system to where they were satisfied to train large numbers of people with open circuit apparatus. . . . It was not effective operationally. It made bubbles. . . . Certainly from the standpoint of surface detection, sonar and radar detection, those big tanks and all the rest of that just were not sensible."

It was not until much later, after the creation of Navy SEALs, that attention again focused on the development of advanced versions of bubble-free underwater breathing apparatus. Today's SEALs use a mixed-gas, closed-circuit underwater breathing apparatus, such as the Mark XV, not much different from the LARU Lambertsen designed in 1940.

Lambertsen went on to become the founder of the Institute for Environmental Medicine at the University of Pennsylvania and was involved in underwater physiology into the 1990s.

See also DIVING, HISTORY OF; FANE, FRANCIS DOUGLAS; OFFICE OF STRATEGIC SERVICES (OSS); UNDERWATER CLOSED-CIRCUIT BREATHING APPARATUS; UNDERWATER DEMOLITION TEAMS (UDTS).

Lambertsen Amphibious Respiratory Unit (LARU)

The LARU was a closed-circuit breathing apparatus invented for military divers by Christian J. Lambertsen shortly before World War II and developed for use by the Office of Strategic Services (OSS) Maritime Unit.

See also LAMBERTSEN, CHRISTIAN J.

landing craft

World War II in the islands of the Pacific gave rise to a whole new array of landing craft and ships, several of which were utilized by underwater demolition teams (UDTs) and at least one type of which survived in a modified form to be used by Navy SEALs during the Vietnam War.

The troop-carrying vessels ranged from small landing craft like the LCP (Landing Craft, Personnel) or the LVT (Landing Vehicle, Tracked), which was equipped with tank treads to allow it to crawl right up on the beach, to the LCI (Landing Craft, Infantry), which carried 200 soldiers. The LCVP (Landing Craft, Vehicle and Personnel) was big enough to carry a jeep and a squad or platoon of men. The LCM (Landing Craft, Mechanized) and the later LCT (Landing Craft, Tank) carried bulldozers, medium tanks, and heavy trucks to landing sites.

The LST (Landing Ship, Tank) and the LSD (Landing Ship, Dock) were the largest of the landing craft and were seagoing. The LST carried everything from troops and tanks to cargo and other smaller landing craft. The giant LSD had room for troops and other landing craft up to an LCT in size. It sometimes doubled as a repair ship.

Higgins Industries of Louisiana designed and produced more landing craft during the war than all other companies combined. In recognition of this fact, its LCVP was commonly known as "the Higgins Boat" and was the one generally used by UDTs during their pre-invasion recons and clearances when they were not utilizing rubber boats or other smaller craft.

During the Vietnam War, SEALs fighting in the Mekong Delta area of South Vietnam converted World War II–era LCMs into what became known as a Heavy SEAL Support Craft (HSSC), or more generally as a "Mike Boat."

See also HEAVY SEAL SUPPORT CRAFT (HSSC); HIGGINS BOAT.

LC-2

In addition to carrying a rucksack during a mission, SEALs and other special forces soldiers wear load-bearing gear, generally known as LC-2. The LC-2 is essentially oversized suspenders attached to a belt.

Clipped to the rig is a variety of pouches and holders to carry ammunition magazines, grenades, canteens, pistol and holster, small short-range radios, compass, sheath knife, field medical dressings, and a day's rations. In a pinch, the SEAL can drop his heavy ruck and still have emergency weapons and supplies in his LC-2 for survival and combat.

See also ALICE; BASIC LOAD.

Leap Frogs

The U.S. Navy SEAL Parachute Demonstration Team is nicknamed the "Leap Frogs." The team is stationed at the Coronado Special Warfare Center, California.

See also CHUTING STARS.

Lebanon

Lebanon is a small country at the eastern end of the Mediterranean Sea and at the western end of Asia, bordered by Egypt on the south and Syria on the east and north. Political differences between Lebanese Christians and Lebanese Muslims and their PLO (Palestine Liberation Organization) allies have often erupted into bloody battles. A civil war began in the 1970s that has continued on and off since then. Syria sent thousands of troops into Lebanon in 1976 to help the government restore order.

It can safely be said that hardly anyone knows at any given time what is going on inside the country. Terrorist groups abound. Christians and Muslims are constantly at each other's throats. The 1980s were a particularly unsettled period. PLO terrorists under Yasser Arafat made raids against Israel, and Israel retaliated with attacks against PLO, then based inside Lebanon.

In June 1982, a large Israel force invaded Lebanon, laid siege to PLO forces in western Beirut, and drove the PLO out of the southern part of the country.

The United States became involved soon thereafter, sending marines to the war-torn capital on a "peacekeeping" mission. So many factions warred against each other in Beirut that it took a score card to keep tabs on them. Syrian troops began rocketing U.S. aircraft. In October 1983, an Islamic Jihad

bombing of a U.S. Marines barracks in Beirut killed 241 marines.

Later the next month, Lt. Cdr. Michael J. Walsh and a platoon of SEALs from Team Four arrived in Beirut. For the next weeks, Walsh and his SEALs set up escape and evasion networks in the mountains in case American pilots were downed, established a countersurveillance program, and plotted possible targets among Syrian and PLO strongholds for American warplanes.

The Naval Special Warfare Task Force, which included the SEALs, helped coordinate evacuation of all Americans and certain other nationalities from the besieged nation before the year ended. The SEALs left with the evacuation, followed by the remainder of American troops still in the country.

Lemoyne, Irve C. (Chuck) (d. 1997)

Chuck LeMoyne was one of the first SEALs to attain the rank of admiral in a career that spanned more than 35 years in Naval Special Warfare.

He was a member of UDT-21 and UDT-22 and, in 1967, platoon commander of SEAL Team One in Vietnam. He monitored the PRUs (provincial reconnaissance units) in the Mekong Delta from January to September 1968. He was referred to as "Sir Charles" by Rear Adm. Thomas Richards, commander of the Naval Special Warfare Command, because of his gentlemanly manner.

LeMoyne was among the first military leaders to call for integrating all special operations forces from the different services into a single command. He is remembered most for establishing and commanding the Naval Special Warfare Command in 1987. He later served as deputy commander of U.S. Special Operations Command (USSOCOM), deputy to the officer in charge of all U.S. special operations. He held that position in 1989 during Operation Just Cause, the U.S. invasion of Panama, in which four SEALs were killed at the Paitilla airfield.

A number of senior ranking SEALs took the position that the four SEALs had been killed needlessly, attempting a mission outside their scope. LeMoyne assumed a different stand.

> We had a mission that was appropriate to us, we trained, prepared to do it, and we went in and did it. . . . I would like to have done it without suffer-

ing those casualties. We were not able to do that. I attribute that to the vagaries, the uncertainties of war. After the SEALs got hit, hit very hard, the end result was they stayed right on the target, they overcame the opposition, they accomplished what they were sent there to do and did that very well.

LeMoyne retired from the navy in 1996. He died on January 4, 1997, after a six-year battle with cancer.

See also NAVAL SPECIAL WARFARE COMMAND; OPERATION JUST CAUSE; PROVINCIAL RECONNAISSANCE UNITS (PRUS); U.S. SPECIAL OPERATIONS COMMAND (USSOCOM).

Leyte Gulf

The United States thwarted Japanese efforts to halt the American invasion of the Philippine Islands in 1944 in a series of World War II naval actions known as the Battle of Leyte Gulf. Underwater demolition teams (UDTs) surveyed the beaches prior to the Leyte invasion. Some of the frogmen witnessed the famous scene in which Gen. Douglas MacArthur fulfilled his promise to return.

Japanese had captured the island of Leyte early in 1942. On October 20, 1944, U.S. forces began landing there as a first step to recovering the Philippines. UDT-6, 8, and 10 took part in the difficult survey of potential landing beaches prior to the invasion. UDT-8 suffered heavily. Six of its men were wounded by enemy fire during the hydrographic survey; one of them eventually died. UDT-6 and 10 suffered no casualties.

Several men of UDT-8 were sent ashore to represent the frogmen when General MacArthur went ashore shortly after the Sixth Army stormed onto Leyte's east coast. He had made a famous promise to the Filipino people in 1942 when the Japanese captured the islands and forced him to flee to Australia: "I shall return."

MacArthur waded through water that came up to his knees and stepped before a Signal Corps microphone already erected on the sand. "People of the Philippines," he broadcast, "I have returned. By the grace of Almighty God our forces stand again on Philippine soil. . . . The hour of your redemption is here."

The landing also precipitated the greatest naval action of all times, as the Japanese attempted to hold onto the Philippines. Adm. William F. "Bull" Halsey's Third Fleet and the U.S. Seventh Fleet engaged Japanese admiral Toyoda Soemu's fleet in a four-day sea battle in Leyte Gulf. The Americans destroyed all four of Soemu's aircraft carriers, three of his nine battleships, 10 of 23 cruisers, and nine of 63 destroyers. The battle marked the first time the Japanese used kamikaze pilots.

Libya

The regime of Mu'ammar Gadhafi, leader of Libya since 1969, was targeted by U.S. Navy SEALs at least twice because of its support of international terrorism. Neither operation, though planned, was ever executed. The U.S. State Department refuses to comment, but SEALs involved confirm the fact.

U.S. intelligence uncovered evidence in the early 1980s that Gadhafi had dispatched assassins to American soil to murder President Ronald Reagan and other American leaders. Although the information was later learned to be false, it was taken seriously at the time. The Reagan administration wanted to send a message to Gadhafi, but it wanted the warning to be nonattributable.

A small group of SEALs from Little Creek, Virginia, were summoned to a secure intelligence building at the Norfolk Navy Base and ordered to make plans to destroy two diesel-powered submarines supplied to Libya by the Soviet Union. The plan they drafted proposed that the SEALs board a foreign merchant ship that would feign engine trouble and ask permission to enter the Libyan harbor. As the ship limped into harbor under cover of darkness, the SEALs would lower an SDV (SEAL delivery vehicle) into the sea. They would place limpet mines on the two subs, set the timers, and retreat back to sea, where a submerged submarine would pick them up. The SDV would be sunk. Gadhafi might know the U.S. had done it, but he would not be able to prove it.

The proposal went to the Chief of Naval Operations by secure phone, but the go-ahead never came.

A few years later, in 1986, SEALs developed an even more ambitious plan to attack Libyan terrorist training facilities. SEALs using SDVs would enter Libyan waters and go ashore to destroy the facilities.

The plan was rejected. The Reagan administration was determined to avoid any actions in which Americans might be seized and held by a hostile power. If caught, the SEALs might have been executed as spies. After all, Jimmy Carter had lost the White House because of the long hostage crisis in Iran. Instead of using SEALs, Reagan employed overt power. On April 14, 1986, Air Force F-111 bombers flying from England and navy bombers from the U.S. aircraft carriers *America* and *Coral Sea* hit targets on Benghazi and Tripoli, killing 20 people. Among the dead was Gadhafi's adopted infant daughter.

Although Libya's and Gadhafi's international reputations have improved since then, Libya is still suspected of exporting international terrorism. SEAL lieutenant commander Michael J. Walsh reported in the 1990s that Libyans were providing funds for subversive activities in Ecuador through the Libyan embassy in Panama.

See also TERRORISM.

Lien Doc Nguoi Nhai (LDNN)

Lien Doc Nguoi Nhai, Vietnamese for "Soldiers Who Fight under the Sea," were the South Vietnamese equivalents of the U.S. Navy SEALs or underwater demolition teams. During the Vietnam War, U.S. SEALs trained, "advised," and led the LDNN in combat.

After a fact-finding mission to South Vietnam in October 1961 by President John Kennedy's chief military adviser, Gen. Maxwell Taylor, the United States responded by increasing military aid to the country and adding to the number of American advisers in Vietnam; by deploying American support forces to Southeast Asia; and by adopting specialized counterinsurgency measures. The U.S. Navy presence in Vietnam increased from 79 men in 1959 to 154 in early 1964. A number of these advisers in 1963 and 1964 were SEALs, whose mission was to train and advise newly formed LDNN units in guerrilla and counterguerrilla operations in rivers, canals, harbors, and adjacent land areas.

Lt. Roy Boehm, the man most instrumental in forming the U.S. Navy SEALs, was one of the first LDNN advisers sent to South Vietnam. He received orders on July 6, 1963, assigning him to the U.S.

Military Assistance Advisory Group, Vietnam (MAAG-V). He described his first encounter with his new unit of "frogmen."

> About 20 of the 42 Vietnamese assigned to my LDNN appeared . . . at an old rock quarry training camp outside Nha Trang. Only about seven or eight seemed to have had any combat experience at all. . . . Khe was the senior enlisted man, a wiry 22-year-old of less than 100 pounds in weight with a hawklike face as wizened and wise as an emperor's monkey. He stood back, aloof, while the other Viets giggled and held hands. Most of them wore only remnants of uniforms. Some were barefooted or wore shower shoes purchased from the local military PX. Their equipment was almost in the same shape—rusted unmaintained M-14s and carbines, French-made open-circuit Aqua-Lungs frozen, rotted and unworkable. Many had lost their weapons, forgotten to bring them, or maybe sold them to the VC. . . .
>
> I resolved to make SeaAirLand commandos patterned after the SEALs out of my Vietnamese, rather than straight UDT frogs. SEALs were more versatile when it came to guerrilla tactics.

He thus established the early SEAL pattern for the training of LDNN, a pattern that later U.S. SEAL advisers such as Lieutenant Bill Early and Chief James D. Watson maintained. The LDNN never reached the proficiency of the U.S. SEALs, nor did they earn the enemy's respect and awe to the degree commanded by their American counterparts. Nonetheless, Vietnamese SEALs were among South Vietnam's crack combat units. Nguyen Van Kiet, the only Vietnamese to receive the U.S. Navy Cross, was working with the SEALs when he won it.

U.S. SEALs began their tenure in South Vietnam working with the LDNN; they ended it working with the LDNN. By the fall of 1972, the U.S. SEAL presence in Vietnam had dwindled to three officers and nine enlisted men. Most of these SEALs were assigned to patrolling the Demilitarized Zone region with LDNN troops to keep track of North Vietnamese army forces and identify targets for bombing attacks.

light patrol boat (PBL)

The PBL is a light patrol boat used by SEALs. It is essentially a Boston Whaler.

See also BOSTON WHALER.

Light SEAL Support Craft (LSSC)

In May 1967, engineers asked SEALs serving in Vietnam to describe what would be the best boat to support their operations in the Mekong Delta. They then returned to the United States where they designed, built, and tested the Medium SEAL Support Craft (MSSC) and the Light SEAL Support Craft (LSSC). The HSSC (Heavy SEAL Support Craft), a converted WWII–era LCM (Landing Craft, Mechanized), was already in service in Vietnam. The LSSC and the MSSC were introduced into the Vietnam War in June 1968. By early 1969, SEAL Team Two had 12 of them in operation.

The LSSC was 26 feet long. With a beam of nine feet six inches, it fit in the cargo hold of a C-130 aircraft. It was driven by twin 300 hp gasoline-powered inboard Ford Interceptor engines and twin outdrives. Its ceramic armor could withstand .30-caliber and even .50-caliber armor-piercing rounds. The boat turned within its own length and reached a speed of about 30 knots carrying a crew of three boatmen and a SEAL squad of seven. It was normally armed with two M-60 machine guns and a 40 mm grenade launcher. Besides radar, it was also equipped with an integral communications system and a storage area.

The MSSC specifications were similar to those of the LSSC as far as power, armor, and armament were concerned. The difference was that it was ten feet longer and capable of supporting a SEAL platoon rather than the squad for which the LSSC was designed.

A two-boat mobile support team to operate the boats was attached to each SEAL platoon in Vietnam. Both the LSSC and MSSC were seaworthy enough to be used along the coast as well as on canals and rivers. In a normal operation, a boat dropped off SEALs at their objective after dark, waited in the vicinity while they went "sneaking and peeking," then picked them up again at a predetermined extraction point. Often the boat provided a necessary service as a radio relay station, since the SEALs' PRC-77 radio had a range of only a few miles, depending upon terrain.

A chief petty officer veteran of a mobile support team describes how the boats and SEALs worked together: "We usually left about sundown, transited to our op area, making false insertions along the way. We dropped off the SEALs and then made a few more false insertions so the enemy never really knew where we left them. Sometimes we just put the guys aboard a sampan, towed them along behind us, and cut them loose to drift ashore while we continued on. We even had a few where the SEALs jumped off the boat and swam in to the bank."

Both the LSSC and MSSC were largely phased out of the SEAL inventory with the end of the Vietnam War.

See also "MIKE BOAT"; SEAL TEAM ASSAULT BOAT (STAB).

light stick

A "light stick" is a flexible plastic tube containing chemicals that, when mixed, illuminate. SEALs use them as lights or beacons, as signals, and on airborne operations to orient themselves to each other in the sky.

lightweight video reconnaissance system (LVRS)

The LVRS was developed to take some of the risk out of long range reconnaissance patrols behind enemy lines. The system consists of small still-frame video cameras which can be seeded in an enemy-controlled area. The camera then relays constant images back to a workstation up to six miles away. The imagery can also be transmitted via SATCOM or other radio links to commands far from the operational area.

limpet mine

The limpet mine is an explosive designed so that swimmers can attach it magnetically or with glue to the hull of a ship.

See also EXPLOSIVES; LAMBERTSEN, CHRISTIAN J.

Lindsay, James J.

Gen. James J. Lindsay, U.S. Army, was the first commander of the U.S. Special Operations Command (USSOCOM), which consolidated all special operations forces from all services under a single command in order to pool talents and resources for planning, training, and executing missions. USSO-

COM arose as a result of Operation Urgent Fury, the action against Grenada in 1983. Because of loss of helicopters, confused communications, misuse of Army Special Forces, and the deaths of four SEALs in that operation, the Senate Armed Services Committee urged the creation of a new overall special operations command. The existing Joint Special Operations Command included only highly specialized units, such as the Army's Delta Force and the Navy's SEAL Team Six. USSOCOM, as created by the Goldwater-Nichols Act of 1986, would include all SpecOps forces, including the Army Green Berets and the Navy SEALs.

The U.S. Special Operations Command, headquartered at MacDill Air Force Base, Tampa, Florida, was officially commissioned on April 16, 1987, with General Lindsay, a former Green Beret, as its commander. He served until after Operation Just Cause, the action against Panama in 1989, the first mission carried out by the SEALs under USSOCOM.

See also GOLDWATER-NICHOLS ACT OF 1986; ORGANIZATIONAL STRUCTURE, SPECIAL OPERATIONS; U.S. SPECIAL OPERATIONS COMMAND (USSOCOM).

"Little Bird" AH-6J helicopter

The AH-6J helicopter is a small observation-type helicopter used for special operations and counterterrorism missions. Its restricted range and load capacity limits its operations and utility in actual combat.

See also HELICOPTERS.

"Little Bird" MD-530 helicopter

The MD-530 helicopter, like the other "Little Bird," the AH-6J, is primarily used by SEALs on counterterrorism missions, not as a combat helicopter.

See also HELICOPTERS.

Little Creek, Virginia

U.S. Naval Special Warfare encompasses two major combat resources—Naval Special Warfare Group One, stationed in Coronado, California, and Naval Special Warfare Group Two, on Chesapeake Bay near the Atlantic at the Naval Amphibious Base, Little Creek, Virginia, part of the Norfolk Naval Base complex.

Little Creek was an amphibious training site during World War II. Underwater demolition teams were trained there and at Coronado following the war. It was also at Little Creek that the first SEALs were trained and commissioned in 1961–62. Initially, each team of SEALs—Team One on the West Coast, and Team Two on the East—conducted its own training. Following the commissioning of the Naval Special Warfare Command on April 16, 1987, however, all BUD/S training became centralized at Coronado.

Naval Special Warfare Group Two at Little Creek, like its mirror image at Coronado, is made up of three SEAL teams (Teams Two, Four, and Eight), a special boat squadron, and a SEAL delivery vehicle team. It is responsible for all potential battlegrounds and beaches from the Baltics to Cape Horn, including Europe and Latin America.

The Little Creek Naval Amphibious Base is also responsible for the Special Warfare Development Group. This is the SEAL "think tank," where new tactics, communications systems, dive equipment, and weapons are tested and evaluated. The Development Group also concocts special-operations tactics for air, ground, and maritime forces in and out of naval special warfare, especially concerning terrorism.

See also BOEHM, ROY; BASIC UNDERWATER DEMOLITION/SEAL (BUD/S) TRAINING; CORONADO; ORGANIZATIONAL STRUCTURE, SPECIAL OPERATIONS; SEALS.

LOLEX (low-level extraction)

LOLEX is a risky tactic in which a cargo airplane flies close to the surface and drops (extracts) a load off its tail ramp or out its cargo hatch. The technique has been used for unloading boats to SEALs already in the water and, occasionally, with the right terrain, for delivering supplies to land units. There are even reports of SEALs being delivered this way onto the ocean while strapped into a boat. "It is not one of those things you want to practice," commented SEAL Jack Macione. "You practice it with dummies. But when you have to, you do it."

low-intensity conflict (LIC)

Low-intensity conflict (LIC) is a modern term applied to warfare that is considered less than full-scale, open hostilities. Unconventional warfare and guerrilla warfare are aspects of LIC.

See also CENTRAL INTELLIGENCE AGENCY (CIA).

Luehrs, Lewis F.
During the World War II invasion of Kwajalein, Navy ensign Lewis F. Luehrs and Seabee chief petty officer Bill Acheson, both underwater demolition team members, swam in under enemy fire to perform a beach reconnaissance—and forever changed the shape of naval special warfare by introducing naval combat swimming.

See also ACHESON, BILL; KWAJALEIN.

Lundberg, Kevin E. (d. 1983)
Kevin E. Lundberg was one of four SEALs killed on October 23, 1983, during an airborne operation in support of Operation Urgent Fury against Grenada.

See also OPERATION URGENT FURY.

M4A1 carbine

The M4A1 carbine is essentially a shortened, lighter version of the standard-issue M16A2 battle rifle issued to the U.S. infantry.

See also M16 RIFLE.

M16 rifle

The M16 is the main battle rifle of the U.S. armed forces. The current model, the M16A2, is the standard by which all military rifles of the future will be judged. It was first purchased by the Defense Department in December 1961 as the AR-15, then adopted by the Secretary of Defense as the 5.56 mm M16. The navy purchased 240 of them in October 1964, primarily for special operations use. By early the next year, the U.S. Army was purchasing thousands of the XM16E1 model for maneuver battalions in Vietnam. With some modifications—forward bolt assist, a bolt closure mechanism on the upper receiver—the M16A1 has remained the U.S. standard battle rifle for nearly thirty years.

In Vietnam, the M16A1 was modified for Navy SEALs to make it easier to transport underwater and to prepare for immediate use by combat swimmers. Modifications consisted of coating many of the working parts of the weapon with Kal Gard to prevent corrosion; drilling a hole in the lower receiver extension tube and stock to let water drain off; installing an O-ring on the end of the buffer assembly; and attaching a blast suppressor. Permitting rapid drainage of water from the system and increasing protection from the corrosive effects of seawater allowed the weapon to be carried at depths of 200 feet without damage.

Manufactured by Colt and Fabrique National Manufacturing, Inc., the 5.56 mm M16A2 rifle is a lightweight, air-cooled, gas-operated, magazine-fed, shoulder or hip-fired weapon designed for either semiautomatic or automatic fire through the use of a selector switch. It is 39.63 inches in length and weighs a mere 8.79 pounds with a fully loaded 30-round magazine. It fires at a cyclic rate of 800 rounds per minute and has a maximum range of 3,600 meters, although it is most effective at a range of 200 meters or less. Nearly four million have been manufactured to date.

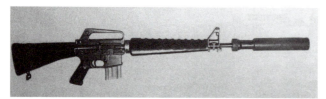

The M-16 is the main battle rifle of the U.S. armed forces. Here, it has been "SEAL-proofed" by adding a Navy Mark 4 noise suppressor. (Kevin Dockery)

Available for the weapon is the M203 grenade launcher, which attaches to the rifle and fires 40 mm grenades.

In the 1970s, the original blast suppressor was replaced by the KAC (Knight's Armament Company) model, which provides greater noise suppression and durability. It is also "SEAL-proof," in that it is completely self-draining within eight seconds after being removed from water.

The M16A2 is also produced as a shortened carbine version, the Colt Model 1723, which is particularly favored by SEALs and other special operations units. The M4A1 is essentially a M16A2 with a collapsible metal tube buttstock, a shorter barrel, and a modified sight deck.

See also M203 GRENADE LAUNCHER; M4A1 CARBINE.

M-60 fuse lighter
The M-60 fuse lighter is a device for igniting a time fuse in initiating a blasting charge.

See also EXPLOSIVES.

M60 machine gun
The M60 general purpose machine gun is a two-man, crew-served weapon. However, SEALs consider it a hand-held platoon-level fire support weapon, to be operated by a single soldier. Two of these 7.62 mm weapons are assigned per eight-man squad; opposing forces often claim to have engaged a much larger unit, since machine guns are normally assigned to platoon-sized elements.

The M60 evolved as a result of design work at the end of World War II to replace the Browning light and heavy machine guns. It came into the U.S. Army in time for the Vietnam War.

It weighs approximately 23 pounds and is belt-link fed, with a cyclic rate of fire of 550 rounds per

minute and a maximum effective range of 1,800 meters if mounted on a tripod.

The gun has been improved following the Vietnam War into the M60E1. The M60E1 differs from the original version in that a bipod has been attached to the rear of the gas cylinder, the rear sights have been modified, and a die-cast feed cover and a new feed tray have been added. A hanger assembly for the use of a 100-round ammunition "bandoleer" box enables the gunner to lay down fire while on the move.

M-138 satchel charge
The M-138 satchel charge is a self-contained pack of explosives created by Navy Lieutenant Carl P. Hagensen for use of the naval combat demolition units against obstacles at Normandy during World War II's D-day. Called the "Hagensen Pack," it is still used by modern SEALs.

See also EXPLOSIVES; HAGENSEN PACK.

M203 grenade launcher
The M203 grenade launcher fits beneath the barrel and foregrip of either an M16, M14, or Colt 727 rifle. The launcher consists of a 40 mm aluminum tube, trigger, and perforated metal heat shield. A lever on the left side releases the launcher's barrel, which slides forward for loading with a single round. This barrel accepts all manner of special-purpose

The M-203 fits beneath the barrel and forward grip of an M-16 rifle. It fires 40 mm grenades. Here, a grenade is being loaded. (Kevin Dockery)

ammunition: fragmentation grenades, smoke bombs, tear gas, high-explosive antitank (HEAT) rounds, parachute flares, buckshot, and incendiaries. With it a skilled SEAL grenadier can slam a round through a window at a range of 150 meters or lay down area fire at 400 meters.

M249 squad automatic weapon (SAW)

A standard light machine gun used by special operations forces.

See also SAW.

MacArthur, Douglas (1880–1964)

Gen. Douglas MacArthur was commander of Allied forces in the Southwest Pacific during World War II. Although he considered the unconventional and unorthodox methods of the OSS (Office of Strategic Services) extreme and refused to allow the guerrilla unit to operate under his command, he embraced Lt. Francis Riley "Frank" Kaine and a small number of NCDU (naval combat demolition unit) swimmers attached to his command in Australia. Kaine became known as "MacArthur's frogman." MacArthur's endorsement of the NCDU and underwater demolition teams helped cement the role of combat swimmers within the U.S. Navy.

See also ALAMO SCOUTS; KAINE, FRANCIS RILEY; LEYTE GULF; OFFICE OF STRATEGIC SERVICES (OSS).

Machen, Billy W. (d. 1966)

Radarman Second Class Billy W. Machen was the first SEAL to be killed in a firefight in the Vietnam War. He died on August 19, 1966. Ten months before, Cdr. Robert J. Fay, a frogman with the underwater demolition teams, became the first UDT/SEAL casualty of the war, when he died during a mortar attack against the Da Nang Air Base on October 28, 1965.

On August 18, 1966, Machen's eight-man patrol, operating in the Rung Sat Special Zone, destroyed two large Viet Cong rice caches. American helicopter pilots spotted several VC boats in the same area the next morning. The SEAL squad went to investigate. "Jeez, I'm not real crazy about this daytime stuff," Machen commented.

The patrol reached a clearing and halted. Machen, the point man, went ahead to check out things. Suddenly he opened fire on hidden enemy forces, triggering a VC ambush before the rest of the patrol entered the kill zone. Machen went down in a hail of fire, dying almost instantly.

The rest of the patrol suppressed the fire of 30 to 40 VC, recovered Machen's body, and retreated to be extracted by helicopters. SEALs are proud of the fact that they have never left behind a fallen comrade.

Machen was posthumously awarded the Silver Star. His gallant actions, said the citation, prevented further losses from his patrol.

Macione, Jack

Lt. Jack "Blackjack" Macione made one of the greatest intelligence finds of the Vietnam War, perhaps *the* greatest find—and it occurred on his first day in-country, in July 1967.

He debarked from a DC-6 at Tan Son Nhut airport in Saigon after a flight of 18 hours. There he was met by Lt. Henry "Jake" Rhinebolt. Rhinebolt was the officer in charge of the SEAL contingent in Vietnam and the man whom Macione would be relieving after his "breaking in" period.

Rhinebolt said he had a "hot mission." He had only that day received intelligence that a high-ranking Viet Cong courier had been walking south from North Vietnam for the past several weeks. He would be arriving this very night at a location on the shores of the South China Sea. The SEALs intended to nab him. "Come on, Jake, you gotta be shitting me," was Macione's immediate reaction. "This guy is walking south. He could be anywhere in a couple thousand square miles of jungle. And we're going to find him?"

At approximately two A.M., two squads of SEALs made an insertion into an inland waterway off the sea. The squads split up to approach a hootch (a native building) from two different directions. Macione was patrolling as "tail end Charlie," the last man in his squad.

He heard a sudden noise behind him on the trail. He grabbed HM1 (Hospitalman First Class) Paul T. Schwartz, ahead of him. They turned in time to see dim shapes approaching. At first, they thought the arrivals were members of the second squad joining up with them; they had somehow lost radio contact with each other. The first guy in the approaching file ducked a branch and bumped into Macione. He was wearing a conical hat. A VC!

Using his limited Vietnamese, Macione ordered the guy to put up his hands. The VC swung his rifle around and fired at point-blank range. Macione managed to deflect the rifle barrel as the weapon discharged.

Schwartz opened up with his shotgun. A firefight erupted, everyone shooting back and forth in the dark, tracers flying. Macione spotted the dark outline of a head floating downstream in the canal, escaping out with the tide. After ascertaining that it was not another SEAL, he put a round into the head, and it sank.

The brief firefight subsided as quickly as it began. Macione jumped into the edge of the waterway to cover his squad's waterside flank. Complete silence prevailed for the next two hours as the SEALs held their position to keep from blundering into an enemy's hasty ambush.

Macione felt somebody grab him underwater. He whirled around to find a knapsack floating against him. Attached to the knapsack was the same VC he had shot in the head two hours ago. The tide had taken the body out and brought it right back in. Incredibly, it was the very man, the VC courier, whom the SEALs had set out to kill or capture.

Among other important intelligence items, the knapsack contained marked locations of six major arms caches in the area and the names of over 100 VC agents who had inserted themselves into jobs with U.S. agencies and the South Vietnamese government in Saigon. It was the greatest intelligence find of the war up to that point and may have been the greatest of the entire war.

"Can you imagine?" Macione recalls, awed. "I had just come twelve thousand miles, didn't have anything to wear or put on. I go down the river, and it's the guy we're looking for. And if he'd been one foot either way in the jungle we never would have seen him. If we'd been fifteen seconds one way or the other we wouldn't have run into each other."

Before he retired, Macione served with the underwater demolition teams and Navy SEAL teams for over 23 years. He participated in 700 combat missions and has the distinction of being the only Navy SEAL to have earned three Purple Hearts in a single day.

See also AIRBORNE; DOMINICAN REPUBLIC INTERVENTION.

MACV-SOG

President Lyndon Baines Johnson authorized covert operations against North Vietnam on January 24, 1964, when he established MACV-SOG (Military Assistance Command Vietnam—Studies and Observation Group), one of the most highly classified and elite military units in Southeast Asia. SEALs, U.S. Army Special Forces and other special operations personnel were involved with SOG from the beginning.

SOG masked a number of covert and overt activities within its various operations sections. OPS-31 ran maritime operations, OPS-32 covered air operations, OPS-33 was psychological warfare, OPS-34 headed espionage and sabotage, and OPS-35 conducted direct raids into North Vietnam. OP-80 was established in September 1966 to keep track of American prisoners of war and facilitate their recovery under the code name "Bright Light." SEALs ran a number of Bright Light missions during the Vietnam War.

Beginning in early 1964, SEALs attached to SOG under the code name OP-34A trained and sometimes accompanied South Vietnamese commandos on coastal raids against North Vietnam.

SOG penetrations into neighboring countries were conducted throughout most of the war. Penetrations into Laos and, later, Cambodia aimed at disrupting enemy supply columns as well as gaining intelligence on supply movements along the multitentacled Ho Chi Minh Trail.

A typical cross-border SEAL SOG mission began at the large air base of Nakhon Phanom on the Thai border with Laos. The United States had set up a major electronic monitoring system at the base; it used sensors to track enemy movements. Four or five SEALs would be inserted by helicopter to a "cool" landing zone—where the sensors indicated no recent enemy activity. The SEALs would then work their way through the jungle to the nearest hostile supply trail, set up observation on it for varying lengths of time, then "boogie" out when they had seen enough. Occasionally they rigged explosive booby traps on the trail.

SOG and SEALs with it were also involved in the Phoenix Program, another highly controversial covert operation, run by the CIA to disrupt and destroy the Viet Cong infrastructure in the South.

Because of lingering political sensitivities, many SOG actions during the Vietnam War are still classified Top Secret.

See also "BRIGHT LIGHT"; CHINA BEACH; GULF OF TONKIN RESOLUTION; PHOENIX PROGRAM; PROVINCIAL RECONNAISSANCE UNITS (PRUS); SEALS.

Maiale

Maiale, Italian for "pig," or "pork," was the name given a World War II–era manned torpedo. Manned torpedoes were the predecessors of SEAL delivery vehicles (SDVs). The Maiale was developed by the Italian lieutenants Tesco Tesci and Elios Taschi with the goal of disabling the British fleet that dominated the Mediterranean. It was essentially a 22-foot-long torpedo containing 660 pounds of explosives in a detachable warhead. Two men rode it like a horse to steer it, each wearing goggles, a bulky rubber suit, and carrying his own air supply. It traveled at a speed of about two and a half miles per hour, had a range of 10 miles, and could submerge to a depth of 100 feet.

On the night of December 18–19, 1941, six Italians led by Lt. Luigi de la Penne and his copilot,

Maiale, *Italian for "pork" or "the pig," was the term applied to World War II–era manned torpedoes used by the Italians. Here, Navy Underwater Demolition frogmen recover one of the manned torpedoes. (National Archives)*

Emile Bianchi, sunk two British battleships and a tanker at anchor at Alexandria, leaving the British without a battleship in that area for a year. All six were captured by the British. Other Italian swimmers, however, continued operations until Italy signed an armistice agreement in August 1943. Maiale riders were credited during those three years with sinking or damaging ships totaling 150,000 tons.

See also ADVANCED SEAL DELIVERY SYSTEM (ASDS); CHARIOTS.

Mao Tse-tung (Mao Zedong) (1893–1976)

Mao Tse-tung became the Communist leader of China after his defeat of Chiang Kai-shek and the Chinese Nationalist Party in 1949. His writings, particularly on guerrilla warfare and the role of peasants in revolutionary wars, became influential worldwide. When Roy Boehm began training underwater demolition team men to become SEALs in 1961, Mao was one of the philosophical sources upon which he based his concept of commandos.

Boehm committed to memory the supreme maxim of unconventional warfare: *The front is everywhere.* He also memorized Mao's clear and concise philosophy:

> When the enemy advances, we retreat.
> When he escapes, we harass.
> When he retreats, we pursue.
> When he is tired, we attack.
> When he burns, we put out the fire.
> When he loots, we attack.
> When he pursues, we hide.
> When he retreats, we return.

See also BOEHM, ROY; SEALS.

Marcinko, Richard (b. 1940)

Richard Marcinko, underwater demolition team frogman and Navy SEAL who served during the Vietnam War, rose through the ranks to create and command both SEAL Team Six, the nation's most elite and classified counterterrorist unit, and the equally controversial "Red Cell" team. He was subsequently investigated (under the code name Operation Iron Eagle), court-martialed in 1990,

Marcinko was the controversial founder and first commander of the SEAL counterterrorist unit, SEAL Team Six. (U.S. Navy)

convicted of conspiracy and misuse of government funds, and sent to federal prison.

He published his autobiography, *Rogue Warrior,* in 1992, writing with professional journalist John Weisman. That book and a subsequent series of action adventure *Rogue Warrior* novels penned with Weisman made him the most famous SEAL in the navy.

See also "RED CELL"; SEAL TEAM SIX; TERRORISM.

Mark I STAB

The SEAL team assault boat (STAB) was the first specialized SEAL combat boat. It eventually evolved into the Mark II STAB, also known as the strike assault boat or light SEAL support craft (LSSC).

See also LIGHT SEAL SUPPORT CRAFT (LSSC); SEAL TEAM ASSAULT BOAT (STAB).

Mark 2 combat knife

The Mark 2 was more famous as the Ka-Bar. Dwindling supplies led to its replacement in 1982 by the Mark 3 combat knife.

See also KA-BAR KNIFE; MARK 3 COMBAT KNIFE.

Mark II Mod 0 sniper rifle

The navy increased the firepower of the elite SEAL team in 2001 with the addition of a new 7.62 mm semiautomatic sniper rifle from Knight's Armament Company of Vero Beach, Florida. The Mark II, Mod 0 is designed along the lines of the SR 25 Stoner special lightweight military competition rifle, also made by Knight's. The Mark II differs from the SR 25 in having a shorter (20-inch) barrel instead of the 25-inch barrel of the competition rifle.

The SEAL sniper rifle "system" includes a Leupold Tactical 3.5 to 10X variable scope, a 20-round magazine, and a quick-detachable sound suppressor serialized for individual rifles. Whereas most sniper rifles in the past, most notably the Winchester .306, were bolt action, the SEAL sniper has a semi-automatic feed.

Mark II STAB

The Mark I STAB was the first specialized SEAL combat boat. It evolved into the Mark II, better known as a light SEAL support craft (LSSC) or strike assault boat.

See also LIGHT SEAL SUPPORT CRAFT (LSSC).

Mark 3 combat knife

The Mark 3 Mod 0 combat knife, one of several used by SEALs during the unit's short history, was accepted from the Naval Weapons Support Center in Crane, Indiana, on October 21, 1982, to replace the Mark 2. A short-bladed Bowie, it was patterned after the AKM-47 bayonet used in the Soviet Union. The overall length is 10.88 inches including a six-inch blade. The blade has a very deep, concave clip point to ease the penetration of the knife into a target. The point of the blade, however, has proven to be a weakness, in that it is too thin and weak for prying and digging. SEAL knives are intended as utility tools as well as weapons.

See also KA-BAR.

Mark V Special Operations Craft (SOC)

The Mark V is the newest craft in the naval special warfare inventory. Its primary mission is as a medium-range insertion and extraction platform for special operations forces in a low-to-medium-threat environment. It is 82 feet long and capable of hauling 16 SEALs and their combat rubber raiding craft. Five gun stations aft can handle a variety of weapons, including the .50-caliber machine gun, the 25 mm chain gun, or the 7.62 mm minigun.

The Mark V SOC normally operates in two craft detachments with a mobile support team. The detachment is deployable on two U.S. Air Force C-5 aircraft into a theater area of operations within 48 hours of notification.

Mark VII Seal Delivery Vehicle (SDV)

The Mark VII was the U.S. Navy's first operative swimmer (later SEAL) delivery vehicle.

See also ADVANCED SEAL DELIVERY SYSTEM (ASDS).

Mark 8 flexible linear demolition charge

The Mark 8 is a linear explosive used for blasting paths through barriers like reefs or sand bars.

See also EXPLOSIVES.

Mark XV diving lung

The Mark XV (or 15) is the mixed-gas diving SCUBA currently used by U.S. Navy SEALs.

See also MIXED-GAS BREATHING; SEALS.

Mark 19 40 mm grenade launcher

The navy originally developed the MK 19 for use on its patrol boats, but it is now used by all the U.S. branches of the military. The weapon is a fully automatic, rapid fire grenade launcher capable of firing 60 40 mm grenades per minute. It is normally used on vehicles and at strongpoints.

See also M203 GRENADE LAUNCHER.

SS *Mayaguez*

"I told him we wouldn't go," said Lt. (j.g.) R. T. "Tom" Coulter, a platoon commander of SEAL Team One, Subic Bay, Philippines. "Nope, we're not going on that one. We're not going unarmed with a white flag after 30 Marines just got their ass blown off."

He was refusing a no-win mission handed to him by Rear Adm. R. T. Coogan, commander of Carrier Task Force 73. The mission was to recover a U.S. merchant ship, SS *Mayaguez,* that had been seized by communist Khmer Rouge forces. He faced a possible court-martial.

On May 12, 1975, two weeks after the fall of Vietnam, when the remnants of U.S. forces ignominiously withdrew from the rooftop of the U.S. embassy in Saigon, the 10,485-ton SS *Mayaguez* was sailing in the regular shipping lanes in the Gulf of Siam, about 60 miles off the Cambodian coast. At two P.M., communist Khmer Rouge fired a 76 mm shot across the merchantman's bow and took her and her 39-man American crew captive. The Khmer Rouge had wrested control of Cambodia away from its government in mid-April.

The pirates forced the *Mayaguez* to anchor off Kaoh Tang, a small island 30 miles from the Cambodian coast. President Gerald Ford denounced the seizure as an "act of piracy" and demanded immediate release of the ship. He ordered military action at 5:45 P.M. on May 14 when diplomatic efforts failed. He ordered the aircraft carrier USS *Coral Sea* and Rear Adm. R. T. Coogan, commander of Carrier Task Force 73, to retrieve the ship and crew.

SEALs at Subic Bay were alerted, but the decision was made to send in marines first. Eleven big CH-54 helicopters took off from a Thai base at U-Tapao. Three of the choppers lowered their Marines onto the USS *Holt,* a destroyer escort. The *Holt* served as a platform for assaulting the *Mayaguez.* The merchantman was boarded without firing a shot. The ship had already been abandoned by the pirates, who had taken the American crew with them.

A second Marine assault force arrived on the west and east beaches of Kaoh Tang to rescue the ship's crew. Marines met withering fire from machine guns, mortars, and rocket-propelled grenades. One helicopter crashed on the beach, another went down off shore, a third belly-flopped into the sea. The marines, pinned down on the beaches with heavy casualties, withdrew under the cover of naval gunfire and air support.

Three Marines were killed, and 44 more were wounded on the beach; 23 air force combat security police died when their helicopter crashed in Thailand enroute to the scene; 15 marines, navy men, and airmen were killed in the helicopter crashes and by other hostile fire.

It was now the SEALs' turn. Lt. (j.g.) Tom Coulter, another officer, and twelve enlisted men and their gear were flown from the Philippines to the USS *Coral Sea*. Rear Admiral Coogan explained that he wanted the SEALs to sail to the island in a boat carrying a white flag, retrieve the bodies of the marines and other casualties, and scavenge the black boxes and coding devices from the wrecked helicopters.

"He didn't order me to go. My option to him was, if he ordered us to do it, I had room on the front of the boat for him to come in with us. I said, 'We have room on the front of the boat for you, Admiral, if you want to wave the flag. But I personally don't think that's a very good idea.' He said, 'Well, no one asked you your opinion.' I said, 'Well, we're not going. We're not going in unarmed. That's not what we [SEALs] do.'"

Coulter proposed a workable alternative plan that saved him from a likely court-martial. The SEALs would swim in at night, do a strategic reconnaissance, recover the bodies and secret devices, and return to sea.

Before any plan could materialize, however, the Khmer Rouge inexplicably freed the 39 American crewmen of the *Mayaguez,* placing them aboard a Thai fishing vessel the pirates had previously seized. An American destroyer picked them up. *Mayaguez* and crew were safe, but the incident had cost the lives of 41 American servicemen, including three marines listed as missing in action. Nearly 50 had been more wounded.

The missing Marines would remain MIA for several years until U.S. diplomatic relations were restored with Cambodia.

McFaul, Donald L. (1957–1989)

U.S. Navy SEAL chief petty officer Donald McFaul was one of four SEALs killed in an ambush at Paitilla airfield in Panama during Operation Just Cause.

See also OPERATION JUST CAUSE.

McGuire rig

The "McGuire rig" is basically a webbing sling, or a series of slings, attached to a single rope. It was used during the Vietnam War for emergency helicopter extractions of SEALs and other personnel from terrain where a helicopter could not land.

The chopper hovered above the trees and dropped up to three slings on the same 150-foot rope to people on the ground. Persons to be extracted sat in the webbing slings and slipped their hands through wrist loops that prevented them from falling as they were being hoisted. The main problem with "the string," as it was sometimes called, was that the hands were not free to fire a weapon or use a radio. The rig was also uncomfortable and impaired blood circulation.

Extracted persons swinging through the air on the end of the rope were airlifted to a safe place and returned to earth. Later, winches were developed to hoist troops into the helicopter, saving them the harrowing, swinging flight across the sky.

The McGuire rig was invented by Charles T. McGuire, a sergeant major with Project Delta in Vietnam, circa 1964–65.

The McGuire was later replaced by the safer, more comfortable STABO rig.

See also STABO (STABILIZED TACTICAL AIRBORNE BODY OPERATIONS).

Medal of Honor

The Congressional Medal of Honor is the highest award for valor issued by the United States. Three Navy SEALs have been awarded it, all for heroism under fire during the Vietnam War. The three SEALs are Joseph R. "Bob" Kerrey, Thomas R. Norris, and Michael Edwin Thornton.

See also KERREY, JOSEPH R. "BOB"; NORRIS THOMAS R.; THORNTON, MICHAEL EDWIN.

Medium SEAL Support Craft (MSSC)

The MSSC was a 36-foot platoon-sized boat used by SEALs during the Vietnam War.

See also LIGHT SEAL SUPPORT CRAFT (LSSC).

Mekong Delta

That marshy lowland area of Vietnam south of the Annamite Range and the coastal lowlands where U.S. Navy SEALs and the "brown-water navy" conducted the majority of their operations during the Vietnam War was known as the Mekong Delta.

The delta encompasses the entire southern tip of the country. Average rainfall in the region measures 80 inches a year, and the average height of land above sea level is less than 10 feet. Two wide rivers split the delta and form the largest of a network of streams and canals that drain the lowlands into the South China Sea. The southernmost river, the Bassac, runs generally northeast to southwest; the Mekong, to the north, runs nearly west to east. Viet Cong used the streams and canals—arteries of flowing, thin mud that seep out of swamps and pools swarming with mosquitoes—to ferry men, arms, and ammunition into the major war zones north of Saigon.

The delta is a sleepy place where rice grows well, making it Vietnam's chief agricultural area, but it is also thousands of square kilometers of heat, wet rot, mangrove swamp, nipa palm, and jungle. It is alive with snakes, spiders, scorpions, crocodiles, jungle cats, and, during the Vietnam War, Viet Cong.

See also BROWN-WATER NAVY.

"men with green faces"

During the Vietnam War, Navy SEALs struck awe, terror, and an almost superstitious dread into the

Merrill's Marauders is looked upon as one of several predecessors of U.S. Special Operations forces. Here, General Fred Merrill (center) confers with soldiers during a "dangerous and hazardous" mission to penetrate the Japanese line in Burma. (National Archives)

hearts of the enemy in the Mekong Delta. Because they worked in the dark, attacking suddenly and unexpectedly, then disappearing back into the jungle, the SEALs seemed to many Viet Cong to be far more numerous and ferocious than they actually were. Because they painted their faces to blend into the darkness and jungle, SEALs became known as "the men with green faces."

Merrill's Marauders

In 1943, at the height of World War II, approximately 3,000 American soldiers answered President Franklin Roosevelt's call for volunteers for "a dangerous and hazardous mission" to penetrate Japanese lines in Burma. They became the 5307th Composite Unit (Provisional): six combat teams of 400 soldiers per team, along with a headquarters and an air transport command. Brig. Gen. Frank Merrill became their commander. The unit soon became known popularly as "Merrill's Marauders."

The Marauders trained in the jungles of Central India, then began a long, secret march up the Ledo Road and over the outlying spurs of the Himalayan Mountains into Burma. Without tanks or heavy artillery for support, they walked over 1,000 miles through extremely dense and almost impenetrable jungle. In five major and 30 minor engagements behind Japanese lines, they defeated veteran Japanese units, captured the only all-weather airfield in northern Burma, and completely disrupted enemy supply and communications lines.

Merrill's Marauders are looked upon as one of several predecessors of U.S. special operations forces.

"Mike boat"

The "Mike boat" was a converted World War II–era LCM (Landing Craft, Mechanized) used by SEALs during the Vietnam War as a heavy SEAL support craft.

See also HEAVY SEAL SUPPORT CRAFT (HSSC).

Miles, Milton E. ("Mary")

Many of the tactics and methods of operations used by SEALs working with South Vietnamese comman-

dos and native tribes such as the Montagnards and Nungs during the Vietnam War were pioneered by a navy guerrilla fighter during World War II—Cdr. Milton E. "Mary" Miles.

Shortly after the United States became involved in the war, Commander Miles was summoned to the office of the Chief of Naval Operations. Classmates at Annapolis had given him the unusual nickname of "Mary," after the silent screen star Mary Miles Mintner. Thus it was that Mary Miles received his orders: "You are to go to China and set up some bases as soon as you can. The main idea is to prepare the China coast in any way you can for U.S. Navy landings in three or four years. In the meantime, do whatever you can to help the navy and to heckle the Japanese."

Then a senior officer in his forties, Miles had lived in China for a time, knew the Chinese and their culture, and spoke the language. He quickly formed a working alliance with a Chinese warlord and set up a thriving training camp for guerrillas near K'un-ming, in the far south of China, outside the area of Japanese occupation. From this camp, dubbed "Happy Valley," he oversaw a network of naval units and raiding groups scattered widely across central and southern China. Many successful raids and guerrilla forays were launched from these camps.

He also formed an intelligence net along the Chinese coast to keep track of Japanese movements in and out of Chinese ports and to provide weather reports to American commanders in the Pacific.

In 1945, Philip H. Bucklew, the "father of naval special warfare," was assigned to join up with Miles's guerrillas, make his way to the China coast, and personally reconnoiter beaches on which Allied troops might be able to land. By this time Bucklew was an expert in amphibious operations, in which neither Miles nor any of the some 80 American soldiers, sailors, and marines with him had had experience.

No landings were ever made in China. "Happy Valley" and its satellite network of guerrilla base camps continued to operate against the Japanese until the end of the war.

See also BUCKLEW, PHILIP H., II.

mini–armored troop carrier (MATC)

The MATC is a 36-foot, all-aluminum hull craft designed for high-speed patrol, interdiction, and combat assault missions in rivers, harbors, and protected coastal areas. It has a large well for transporting combat-equipped troops, cargo, or gunners operating the seven weapons stations. Propulsion is similar to the PBR's (patrol boat, river) internal jet pump. The hydraulic bow ramp is designed to facilitate the insertion and extraction of troops and equipment. Crew size is normally four but can be modified depending upon mission.

minisubmarine

The SEAL delivery vehicle (SDV) is sometimes referred to as a minisubmarine, a not quite accurate term. An SDV is a "wet" submersible, meaning it does not have a dry interior, as a real submarine would.

See also ADVANCED SEAL DELIVERY SYSTEM (ASDS).

mission planning

The U.S. Navy SEAL community may be classified as a "service industry" that exists to solve problems for the U.S. government and its other armed forces. Before SEALs go anywhere, however, the mission has to be authorized. Most modern SEAL missions originate outside the Naval Special Warfare Command, sometimes in the Pentagon or even the White House. Wherever the mission originates, it eventually finds its way down to the operations section of either Naval Special Warfare Group One or Two, then to a SEAL team commander and the members of one of its platoons for mission planning.

There are two basic planning procedures, deliberate and ad hoc. The deliberate planning procedure may be a lengthy affair. It is often worked on in advance by the intelligence sections of naval special operations. A contingency plan of possible scenarios may already be developed and on the shelf. Both Operations Just Cause and Urgent Fury were at least partially planned months in advance of the actual missions.

In an ad hoc situation, SEALs may have no more than an hour or so to prepare and launch a mission. "The planning process can take anywhere from a couple of hours to a couple of months," one SEAL explained. "It depends on the magnitude of whatever you are trying to do, and the schedule for when you have to complete it."

Once the mission has been approved down to platoon level, squads are issued the *warning order,* generally by either the team leader or the platoon commander. Essentially, the warning order is a statement of what the SEALs are going to be doing and what they should do to prepare. It includes in general terms the situation, mission, special instructions, uniform, weapons, chain of command, and schedule, concluding with the time to expect the more detailed *patrol order,* which provides more specific instructions for subordinate leaders and individuals.

Squads actually to be launched on the operation, or that will be on standby, go into *isolation.* That means exactly that. They may be placed in a guarded compound—no chance to go home and kiss the wife and feed the dog, no phone calls, no outside contact that may compromise the operation.

The squads in isolation will be supported by operations, intelligence, supply, personnel, and other sections. These provide the SEAL unit with assets, such as weapons, dive gear, ammunition, demolitions, maps, boats, aircraft, food, anything required by the SEALs to complete the mission.

A *patrol order,* or *operations order,* is presented to the isolated SEALs in the five-paragraph format all U.S. military units have used since World War I. The patrol order details the *situation,* both from the enemy and friendly standpoints; the *mission;* the general *execution* (it's up to the squads to plan the specifics); *service and support* (beans and bullets); and *command* and *communications.*

Brainstorming begins immediately within the tasked SEAL unit. It may last for hours or days, even weeks or months, depending upon time constraints. The objective is to produce the mission plan, complete with contingency plans, that has the best chance for success. The squads may request any information available—satellite photos, sketches, area studies, intelligence briefings, human assets from the target region. If time permits, the mission leader may even reconnoiter the objective area. A prisoner, as has been done in the past, may even be snatched from the area of operations for questioning.

Planning is conducted from the center out—beginning with "actions at the objective," working forward from there to when the squads must exfiltrate and backward to when they must infiltrate. Rehearsals are conducted; they may be as elaborate as time and resources permit. Every man must know the plan and the part he plays in it.

The last step is the *briefback,* during which the unit presents to the commander its plan in detail and is subjected to questioning to make sure all individuals are prepared and ready to go. The commander may either approve the plan as designed, accept it with modifications, or tell the planners to go back and try again.

Once the plan is approved, the squads are ready to start the mission. The initial planning stage is over.

See also MISSONS; SEALS.

missions

While naval special warfare forces are under the operational control of the Commander in Chief, U.S. Special Operations Command, up to one-third of the nation's SEALs and special boat squadrons are "farmed out" at any particular moment in support of the Department of Defense's five war regional combat commanders in chief. The rest are in training or on standby for rapid air and sea deployment. As the eyes and ears of the fleet, SEALs are almost always first to enter a hostile area. They are a dedicated combat force, capable of being projected globally whenever or wherever a theater commander needs them.

Intelligence collection, raids and ambushes, combat search and rescue, training of foreign military forces, and counterterrorism and counternarcotics operations are all integral elements of the naval special warfare (NSW) mission. All U.S. special operations forces have been assigned a basic list of five mission profiles:

1. Direct action (DA): short-term seize, destroy, damage, or capture operations; attacks against facilities ashore or afloat; "prisoner snatch" operations; small offensive combat operations against hostile forces.
2. Special reconnaissance (SR): reconnaissance and surveillance operations; covert beach surveys; listening posts; observation posts.
3. Unconventional warfare (UW): training, leading, and equipping partisan and guerrilla forces behind enemy lines.
4. Foreign internal defense (FID): training, advising, and teaching the military, paramilitary, and law enforcement personnel of allied nations; professional development, normally in a noncombat environment.
5. Counterterrorist operations (CT): operations conducted against terrorist units and individuals; may be used as a direct response to terrorist operations or as indirect, preventive, or deterrence measures.

Because SEAL elements are compact in size, heavily armed, and highly maneuverable, they offer a unique combination of abilities in clandestine operations, swift and deadly attacks, and surgical application of force. A key element in their utilization is their capability to conduct missions against targets that larger, conventional forces could not approach undetected.

Missions may be launched from any number of platforms: nuclear submarines, various naval and nonnaval ships, floating barges or vessels of opportunity; combat submersibles or by underwater breathing apparatus; and from the air by helicopter, fixed-wing aircraft, or parachute. The majority of NSW operations originate from sea-based platforms; more than 80 percent of the sovereign nations of the world are directly accessible from the sea or river systems, and about half of the world's industry and population are located within one mile of an ocean or navigable waterway.

See also MISSION PLANNING; SEALS; SEAL TEAM MISSION STATEMENT.

mixed-gas breathing

SEALs have available to them three separate life-support systems for conducting underwater naval special warfare operations. The open-circuit compressed-air system, commonly known as the Aqua-Lung or SCUBA, is perhaps the least desirable; it emits bubbles that can be seen on the surface, and it makes noise.

The second system is the LAR V (Mark V) Draeger UBA (underwater breathing apparatus), which uses 100 percent oxygen in a rebreather arrangement. Because of the potential for oxygen poisoning, this system has a safe diving depth of 35 feet or less.

The third system, the Mark XV (15) Draeger, a self-contained, closed-circuit, mixed-gas UBA, is the one most frequently used by SEALs. Oxygen is mixed and diluted with other gases, normally air, to maintain a preset "partial pressure of oxygen"

(PPO$_2$) level. This preset PPO$_2$ level increases the depth and duration capability in comparison to the Mark V; deep, long-duration dives may still require diver decompression.

Although SEALs rarely dive deeper than 30 or 40 feet, the capability to do so was made available to them by mixed-gas breathing experiments conducted in the mid 1920s as a result of the need for submarine rescue and salvage at great depths.

Compressed air alone proved unsuitable at great depths because of the need for lengthy decompression afterward, as well as time limits at depth. Oxygen diving was dangerous below 30 fsw (feet of seawater). There was a driving need for a new diving medium.

In 1924, the U.S. Navy teamed with the Bureau of Mines in the experimental use of helium-oxygen mixtures. These experiments showed that such mixtures allowed diving to considerably greater depths, with none of the undesirable mental effects associated with oxygen—"rapture of the deep," or oxygen poisoning. Decompression time was also considerably shortened.

The Draeger Company of Lubeck, Germany, began experiments with the use of two tanks, one containing oxygen, the other compressed air. This mixture of 50 percent air and 50 percent oxygen allowed reasonable depths with a closed-circuit system. The work eventually resulted in the Mark XV (15) Draeger used today by Navy SEALs.

See also CLOSED-CIRCUIT BREATHING APPARATUS; DIVING, HISTORY OF; OXYGEN POISONING.

Mobile Riverine Forces (MRF)

U.S. Navy and U.S. Army forces joined in a concentrated effort during the Vietnam War to cut off enemy use of inland-waterway infiltration routes for resupply and troop replacement. The combined force was known as the Mobile Riverine Forces (MRF).

See also RIVERINE WARFARE.

mobile training team

Under the authority of their foreign internal defense mission profile, small detachments of SEALs as well as Army Green Berets are frequently deployed from home bases and sent as "mobile training teams" to foreign nations. An MTT mission, which usually lasts about six months, is designed to train large numbers of host-nation personnel.

For example, a SEAL MTT was sent to Turkey to establish an underwater demolitions training course. U.S. SEALs trained the Turkish military in demolitions, weapons handling, parachuting, diving, and other related skills. Graduates of the training then went on to become instructors at a Turkish school in underwater demolitions.

The first SEAL involvement in the Vietnam War was in the form of MTTs, setting up training schools for the South Vietnamese army and navy.

More recent examples of SEAL MTTs have been in Central and South America, where SEALs support the counter-drug war by training antidrug forces.

Mobility Six (MOB Six)

In 1978, SEAL lieutenant Norman J. Carley began training a special squad in SEAL Team Two to act as a counterterrorist reaction force. He called the squad "Mobility Six," or MOB Six. Two years later, MOB Six evolved into the counterterrorist SEAL Team Six.

See also CARLEY, NORMAN J.; SEAL TEAM SIX; TERRORISM.

MOLLE

MOLLE, or modular lightweight load-carrying equipment, system is an improvement over the old ALICE pack currently used by special forces. The MOLLE system is expected to shortly replace ALICE.

See also ALICE.

Momsen Lung

The Momsen Lung was a primitive early underwater-breathing apparatus developed by U.S. Navy lieutenant C. B. Momsen to allow trapped sailors to escape from disabled submarines. It was a simple device consisting of a mouthpiece attached to a small cylinder containing oxygen and a lime purifier. A canvas rig came down over the user's head, front and

The H&K submachine gun, a favorite for elite counterterrorist units around the world, including SEALs, is a compact German-manufactured weapon that comes in several versions. (Kevin Dockery)

back, with a full face mask. The device contained enough oxygen for up to three-fourths of an hour, depending upon how hard the user breathed.

The Momsen was given its first operational test in 1929, when 26 officers and men used it successfully to surface from an intentionally bottomed submarine. It was utilized for a number of years until submariners developed more effective and safer ways of escaping a sunken boat.

See also DIVING, HISTORY OF.

"Morning glory" operation

"Morning glory" was a term coined by SEALs during the Vietnam War to indicate arriving on a target at first light.

Morris, Stephen Leroy (d. 1983)

Petty Officer First Class Stephen Morris disappeared with three other SEALs after parachuting into high seas during the start of Operation Urgent Fury against Grenada in 1983. The four SEALs were the first combat casualties of the action.

See also OPERATION URGENT FURY.

MP5 Heckler and Koch submachine gun

The MP5 is a compact, German-manufactured submachine gun used by many elite units around the world, including the British SAS, German GSG 9, and the U.S. Navy SEALs. The MP5A3 made it into

the U.S. inventory in small numbers by the late 1970s. SEAL Team Six became the first SEAL team to use the MP5 as its standard weapon.

The MP5 is not a single weapon but a family of weapons with over a dozen different variations, all using the same basic action and operating system. All versions fire the parabellum 9 mm round at 800 rounds per minute, and all are capable of single-action fire. The weapon's unique roller-delayed blowback system operates the weapon in a fully locked breach position. This means the first round is fired from a locked chamber that provides life-and-death accuracy on the first shot.

The MP5A2, with a fixed butt stock, and the MP5A3, with a retractable one, are standard models; the MP5A4 and MP5A5 are newer models of the same design. The MP5 weighs about 7.54 pounds with one 30-round magazine and is less than 20 inches in length.

The MP5K is the shortest MP5 at 12.8 inches in length, without a butt stock. The 5SD series is composed of suppressed versions.

In addition to manufacturing the weapon, H & K produces a comprehensive line of accessories, including a tear gas canister launcher, rifle grenade launcher, removable telescopic sight, a subcaliber device to permit it to fire .22 long rifle ammunition, a noise suppressor, infrared sighting scope, replacement front grip with a built-in flashlight for aiming or illumination, a miniature laser sight built into the weapon for use with night-vision goggles, and a briefcase that can carry an MP5K and fire it while concealed.

Accuracy and reliability have made the MP5 submachine gun popular with SEALs. The weapon is used for a variety of purposes but primarily for close-quarters combat.

"murder ball"

"Murder ball" is a game of mayhem and brute force, something like football without any rules, played by UDT and SEAL trainees while in Basic Underwater Demolition/SEAL (BUD/S) training. Biting, gouging, and wrestling are allowed and encouraged. It was particular popular with the early UDTs, who passed it on to the SEALs. It is not as popular among modern trainees.

See also BASIC UNDERWATER DEMOLITION/SEAL (BUD/S) TRAINING.

N

"naked warriors"

It is unclear exactly when, where, or how the term "naked warrior" arose to describe men of the underwater demolition teams (UDTs). It came into general usage following the invasion of Kwajalein in World War II, when two UDT men, Ensign Lewis F. Luehrs and Chief Petty Officer Bill Acheson, stripped down to swim trunks worn underneath their uniforms and introduced swimming as the best method for surveying prospective beach-invasion sites.

Francis Douglas Fane brought the term into common acceptance in 1956 when he published his memoirs, *The Naked Warrior* (Naval Institute Press).

See also ACHESON, BILL; FANE, FRANCIS DOUGLAS; KWAJALEIN; UNDERWATER DEMOLITION TEAMS (UDTS).

"Nasty" boat

The famed PT boats of World War II lived on in reincarnated PTF (Patrol Torpedo, Fast) boats described in a U.S. Navy press release in 1963 as "designed to perform amphibious support and coastal operations . . . by the Navy's Sea-Air-Land (SEAL) teams in unconventional and paramilitary operations."

The navy bought 14 PTF "Nasty" boats from the Norwegian government and began deploying them to Vietnam in February 1964. They were called "Nasty" after a Norwegian bird. They operated from Da Nang and China Beach on coastal patrols to block the sea infiltration of war supplies from North Vietnam, to perform special raids on North Vietnamese fortifications, and to insert raiders and reconnaissance teams against the enemy. Nasties played a major role in the incident that led to the "Gulf of Tonkin Resolution" and President Lyndon Johnson's decision to send American combat troops to Vietnam.

Previous boats used by American unconventional forces along the Vietnamese coastline were not big enough or fast enough and had insufficient range to carry out the more ambitious raids planned against the North Vietnamese. The Nasty was 80 feet long with a shallow draft of only three feet seven inches; powered by two 18-cylinder British-built Napier-Deltic diesel engines each capable of generation 3,120 horsepower, it could run at speeds of 40 knots. It had room for a special boat unit crew, ten SEALs, and their provisions for up to 48 hours. It was armed at various times during the war with 20 mm and 40 mm guns, 81 mm mortars, 57 mm recoilless rifles, 3.5-inch rocket launchers, and flamethrowers.

Nasty boats proved unsuited for operations in the shallow rivers and tributaries in southern Vietnam. Other crews and their boats—notably "Swift boats" and PBRs (Patrol Boats, River)—were created to provide the U.S. Navy with special warfare capability in the Mekong Delta region. Most PTF "Nasty" boats disappeared from the navy's inventory before the Vietnam War ended.

See also CHINA BEACH; GULF OF TONKIN RESOLUTION; MACV-SOG.

National Liberation Front (NLF)

The NLF was the political and administrative arm of the guerrilla Viet Cong forces during the Vietnam War.

See also VIET CONG.

Naval Advisory Detachment

U.S. Navy SEALs involved in the covert MACV-SOG OP-34A missions at the beginning of the Vietnam War operated under the cover name of "Naval Advisory Detachment."

See also CHINA BEACH; MACV-SOG; OPERATION PLAN 34A (OP-34A).

Naval Amphibious School

The Naval Amphibious School, run by the Naval Special Warfare Center at Coronado, California, teaches a total of 24 scheduled classes in naval special warfare, including eight Basic Underwater Demolition/SEAL (BUD/S) courses a year. Classes range from "Special Warfare Craft Crewmen" and "Closed Circuit Diving Procedures" to such specialized courses, taught under varying circumstances and times, as dry-docking procedures, gunfire support, and operation of SEAL delivery vehicles.

See also BASIC UNDERWATER DEMOLITION/SEAL (BUD/S) TRAINING.

Naval Combat Demolition Training and Experimental Base

During the American landings on Kwajalein in World War II, Navy Seabee chief Bill Acheson and Ensign Lewis F. Luehrs, both underwater demolition team (UDT) members, made the historic decision to strip to swim trunks and conduct the beach survey and reconnaissance by swimming. The experiment was so successful that men of UDT-1 stripped to do the beach clearance for the marine landing on Eniwetok, directly to the west of Kwajalein. Prior to this, all NCDUs (naval combat demolition units) and UDTs had done their reconnaissance dressed in full combat gear and tethered to boats by safety lines.

The success of these two events prompted veteran UDTs in the Pacific to take another look at conducting beach recons during daylight hours by swimming. Less than three weeks after Kwajalein, veterans of that operation set up the new Naval Combat Demolition Training and Experimental Base at Maui, Hawaii. Training began in April 1944. It was intended to meet the specific needs of amphibious warfare in the Pacific. The break with previous beach training proved revolutionary.

The greatest difference was in the emphasis on developing strong swimmers. The use of rubber boats was minimized, as was dependence upon life-flotation belts. UDT frogmen began working both in the water and on the beach wearing only swim trunks, swim shoes, combat knives, and face masks.

Draper Kauffman, who had set up and commanded the NCDU training facility at Fort Pierce, Florida, was sent to Maui to assume command of the school. He reacted with shock at the changes he saw in training, but he soon took to the new concept. His first assignment after arrival at the school was to scout the beach for the invasion of Saipan.

See also ACHESON, BILL; KAUFFMAN, DRAPER L.; KWAJALEIN; NAVY COMBAT DEMOLITION UNITS (NCDUS); SAIPAN; UNDERWATER DEMOLITION TEAMS (UDTS).

naval combat demolition units (NCDUs)

Even though the first American amphibious assault in World War II, at Guadalcanal, had been a relatively easy one, virtually unopposed, the U.S. Navy foresaw the need for demolitions units to go in front of an invasion to clear away obstacles. The American invasion force getting ready to move into French North Africa was unable to wait while the navy formally trained such units; it required a stop-gap measure. In September 1942, 17 navy salvage personnel arrived at the Amphibious Training Base, Little Creek, Virginia, for a one-week emergency course on demolitions, explosive cable cutting, and commando raiding techniques.

This temporary 17-man unit was designated as a "naval demolition unit" (NDU). During Operation Torch on November 10, 1942, it succeeded in cutting cable and net barriers across the Wadi Sebou River in North Africa. Its actions enabled a U.S. destroyer to traverse the river and insert U.S. Rangers to capture the Port Lyautey airdrome.

The naval demolition unit was summoned once more, on July 10, 1943, during Operation Husky, the Allied invasion of Sicily. Volunteers were rushed through a demolition course and sent to join the invasion fleet off Italy. They waited patiently as the invasion began but were not needed. Most of this group returned stateside to become instructors for the newly commissioned Naval *Combat* Demolitions Unit (NCDU) training center at Fort Pierce, Florida. There would be no further need for stopgap measures once the first NCDU class graduated.

On June 6, 1943, Adm. Ernest J. King, who "wore dual hats" as Chief of Naval Operations (CNO) and Commander-in-Chief, U.S. Fleet, had issued a directive establishing the Naval Combat Demolitions Units. He had sent another directive at the same time giving Lt. Cdr. Draper L. Kauffman, founder and head of the Navy Bomb Disposal School, responsibility for launching NCDU training.

The first class assembled immediately. The men were drawn from three primary sources—the Navy Construction Battalions (Seabees), the Bomb Disposal School, and the Mine Disposal School. It was reasonably expected that these men were already familiar with explosives and basic demolitions.

From this first class came four NCDUs, which were the beginning of the demolition force of the Atlantic Fleet. An NCDU was arbitrarily set at one officer and five men, because training had determined that the most effective number in a single rubber boat was six. Each of these four teams was given a number, starting with NCDU-1. By April 1944, a total of 34 NCDUs had been trained and

deployed to England in preparation for Operation Overlord, the amphibious landing at Normandy.

Although NCDUs were primarily intended for use in the Atlantic theater, NCDU-2, led by Lt. (j.g.) Francis Riley "Frank" Kaine, and NCDU-3, under Lt. (j.g.) Lloyd Anderson, formed the nucleus of six NCDUs sent to the South Pacific to work with Gen. Douglas MacArthur and the Seventh Fleet. Three other NCDUs, sent to Hawaii for use in Adm. Richmond Kelly Turner's operations, blended into the underwater demolition teams (UDTs).

A total of 550 NCDU men assembled for the Normandy invasion. They were split into two groups for the American beach landings, one for Omaha Beach and one for Utah Beach. Cap. Thomas Wellings commanded the Omaha group; Lt. Cdr. Herbert Peterson commanded the Utah group. Some of the teams were enlarged into 13-man "gap assault teams" to go ahead of the invasion and clear away the ominous Belgian Gates and other obstructions implanted along the shore and in the water by German defenders. NCDUs were thus the first men to invade France.

There were 16 gap assault teams, one for each of the eight 50-foot-wide gaps that would be blown through to Utah Beach and one for each of the eight gaps of Omaha Beach. Working with the NCDUs were 26-man teams of army engineers, whose job was to take care of obstacles above the high-water mark while the navy men worked on those closer to the water or submerged.

By evening of D-day, 13 of the planned 16 gaps had been cleared and marked. America had a firm hold on Hitler's Fortress Europa. The cost was hideous to NCDU men who had gone ahead to clear the way. Thirty-one NCDU men died on Omaha Beach, and 60 were wounded, a casualty rate of 52 percent. Four were killed on Utah Beach and 11 wounded.

The Omaha NCDU unit received one of only three presidential unit citations awarded to the navy for the Normandy landing. The Utah Beach NCDUs received the only Navy Unit Commendation awarded.

Veteran NCDUs from Utah Beach participated in the relatively tame landings in southern France in August 1944. That was the last amphibious operation in the European theater of operations. The NCDUs, direct predecessors of Navy SEALs, were dispersed within months after the war ended.

See also BELGIAN GATES; BUCKLEW, PHILIP H.; D-DAY; FORT PIERCE, FLORIDA; HAGENSEN PACK; KAINE, FRANCIS RILEY; KAUFFMAN, DRAPER L.; KING, ERNEST J.; OPERATION HUSKY; OPERATION OVERLORD; OPERATION TORCH; TARAWA; UNDERWATER DEMOLITION TEAMS (UDTS).

naval demolitions unit (NDU)

The naval demolitions unit was created as an emergency stopgap measure during World War II while the first naval combat demolitions unit was being trained.

See also NAVAL COMBAT DEMOLITIONS UNIT (NCDU).

Naval Diving and Salvage Training Center (NDSTC)

The Naval Diving and Salvage Training Center, located at Panama City, Florida, serves as the center for all U.S. Navy diving. Completed in 1980, it offers a number of advanced diving courses, which SEALs frequently attend. It has trained thousands of selected U.S. and international students in all branches of the uniformed services. Some of the advanced courses SEALs may attend include Diver Explosive Ordnance Disposal (EOD), EOD Mixed-Gas Underwater Breathing Apparatus (UBA) Diving, Saturation Diving, and Master Diver.

Naval Special Operations Forces

Naval special warfare is composed of various naval special operations forces, including the two SEAL groups, one on each coast; special boat squadrons; naval psychological operations forces; mobile communications teams; and others.

See also NAVAL SPECIAL WARFARE.

Naval Special Warfare

The Naval Special Warfare Command (NAVSPECWARCOM) was commissioned on April 16, 1987, at the Naval Amphibious Base in Coronado, California. Its mission is to prepare naval special warfare (NSW) forces to carry out assigned missions and to develop maritime special operations strategy, doctrine, and tactics. The command, under a rear admiral, is responsible for the training, equipping, supporting, and operational control of all naval special warfare units.

Naval special warfare focuses on five principal mission areas of special operations: unconventional warfare (UW), direct action (DA), special reconnaissance (SR), foreign internal defense (FID), and combating terrorism (CBT). NSW is also involved in such collateral activities as security assistance, antiterrorism, counterdrug assistance, personnel recovery, and special activities (which may cover a wide range of unspecified assignments).

NSW units are organized, trained, and equipped to conduct special operations launched both from the sea and its tributaries. They are deployed in small units worldwide to support fleet and national operations.

NAVSPECWARCOM is the naval component of the U.S. Special Operations Command (USSOCOM). USSOCOM brought all components of U.S. military special operations under a single command. NAVSPECWARCOM in turn has subordinate commands, which include the Naval Special Warfare Center on the Naval Amphibious Base at Coronado, California; the Naval Special Warfare Development Group, at Little Creek, Virginia; Naval Special Warfare Groups One and Two, located respectively at Coronado, California, and Little Creek, Virginia; and naval special warfare command combat service teams (CSSTs), assigned to each naval special warfare group.

The Naval Special Warfare Center is a major component command of NAVSPECWARCOM. It is the schoolhouse for most naval special warfare training.

The Naval Special Warfare Development Group provides centralized management for testing, evaluating, and developing current and emerging technology applicable to naval special warfare forces. It also develops maritime, ground, and airborne tactics for NSW and conducts counterterrorism operations.

The two naval special warfare groups, NSWG-1 and NSWG-2, equip, support, and provide command and control elements and trained and ready SEAL and SDV (SEAL delivery vehicle) platoons and forces to meet mission requirements.

Naval special warfare command combat service support teams (CSSTs) are equipped and tasked for three primary mission elements—crisis-action planning and coordination; in-theater contracting, small purchase, and lease actions; and comprehensive forward operating base support and security. Their mission elements include responsibility for force embarkation, load planning, transport coordination, combat cargo handling, liaison, construction, support and maintenance of camps, and defensive combat planning and execution. This is the "beans and bullets" command that supports NSW forces in action.

From these subordinate commands, naval special warfare task groups and task units may be organized and tailored in size and composition for particular missions. They may operate in unilateral, joint (multiservice) or in combined (international) operations. Their job is to provide command and control, administration, and logistical support for assigned units.

The SEAL platoon is the largest operation element normally employed to conduct a tactical mission. Extensive preparation and rehearsal is required to conduct multiplatoon operations. A SEAL platoon of 16 SEALs is ordinarily commanded by a navy lieutenant.

Each of the two naval special warfare groups is commanded by a navy captain and consists of three SEAL teams. A SEAL team is composed of a headquarters element, eight operational SEAL platoons, and a SEAL delivery vehicle (SDV) team.

Special boat squadrons (SBRs) equip, support, and provide ready special operations ships, boats, and crews. SBR-1 is based at Coronado, California, on the West Coast; SBR-2 is at Little Creek, Virginia, on the East Coast.

U.S. naval psychological operations forces produce audiovisual products, documents, posters, articles, and other material suitable for psychological operations.

A mobile communications team is an operational component of the communications-electronics department of NSWG-1 and 2. It is responsible for providing operational communications support to SEAL teams, SDV teams, and special boat squadrons in deployed fleet and joint operations; for organizing, training, and integrating new equipment; for developing tactics for communications support; and for preparing, implementing, and reviewing communications plans in coordination with higher authorities.

See also CORONADO; GOLDWATER-NICHOLS ACT OF 1986; KENNEDY, JOHN F.; LITTLE CREEK, VIRGINIA; MISSIONS; NAVAL SPECIAL WARFARE FORCES; ORGANIZATIONAL STRUCTURE, SPECIAL OPERATIONS; SEALS; SPECIAL BOAT SQUADRONS.

Naval Special Warfare Command

The mission of Commander, Naval Special Warfare Command is to prepare naval special warfare forces to carry out assigned missions and to develop maritime special operations strategies, doctrine, and tactics.

See also NAVAL SPECIAL WARFARE; ORGANIZATIONAL STRUCTURE, SPECIAL OPERATIONS.

Naval Special Warfare Command Combat Service Support Team (CSST)

CSST, a major component under Naval Special Warfare Command, was designed to support special warfare operations.

See also NAVAL SPECIAL WARFARE; ORGANIZATIONAL STRUCTURE, SPECIAL OPERATIONS.

Naval Special Warfare Development Group (DevGru)

The navy felt Richard Marcinko's 1992 autobiography *Rogue Warrior* focused too much public attention on its counterterrorism force, SEAL Team Six. To escape the spotlight, Naval Special Warfare selected an innocuous-sounding title—Development Group, or DevGru—to replace "Team Six" and buried DevGru in the organizational charts. This allowed the navy to disclaim existence of a SEAL Team Six; DevGru remains the same Team Six, revamped somewhat but with essentially the same missions and responsibilities as before.

The U.S. government describes DevGru as having been established to oversee development of naval special warfare tactics, equipment, and techniques. This is only marginally true, although certainly this is part of its purpose. DevGru is a component not only of naval special warfare but also of the Joint Special Operations Command, Pope Air Force Base, North Carolina, which also has control of other counterterrorism units, like Delta Force and the 160th Special Operations Aviation Regiment.

Although the organization and strength of Dev-Gru is classified and can only be guessed at, the unit is believed to have 300 or more operatives, broken down into 16-man platoons, much like regular SEAL platoons. Teams are organized into four-team assault groups code-named by color—Red, Blue, Gold, and Gray. Each team specializes on a particular type of target, such as oil rigs, shipping, airplanes, or structures.

DevGru also maintains its own helicopter support unit and trains frequently with the 160th SOAR, especially in the area of ship assault. Reportedly, DevGru is one of only a handful of U.S. military units authorized by government to conduct preemptive actions against terrorists and terrorist facilities.

See also MARCINKO, RICHARD; "RED CELL"; SEAL TEAM SIX.

naval special warfare groups

Naval special warfare is broken down into two primary naval special warfare groups, one on each coast—Group One at Coronado, California, and Group Two at Little Creek, Virginia.

See also NAVAL SPECIAL WARFARE; ORGANIZATIONAL STRUCTURE, SPECIAL OPERATIONS.

Navy Bomb Disposal School

Draper Kauffman, known as "the father of naval combat demolitions," was founder and head of the Navy Bomb Disposal School, established at the Washington Navy Yard in January 1942. That today's SEALs are so proficient in explosives is a direct legacy of Kauffman's bomb disposal experts a half-century ago.

The Chief of Naval Operations closed the Navy Bomb Disposal School at the end of World War II. Today's Navy Explosives Ordnance Disposal evolved from the military and civilian bomb disposal units of that era.

See also EXPLOSIVE ORDNANCE DISPOSAL (EOD); KAUFFMAN, DRAPER L.

Navy Dive Tables

Navy Dive Tables, or "decompression tables," were designed by the navy to prevent caisson disease, or "bends," a condition caused by nitrogen buildup in joints and fatty tissue due to pressure at depth. The tables determine the rate at which a diver must decompress while surfacing.

See also BOYLE'S LAW; CAISSON DISEASE; DECOMPRESSION CHAMBER.

Navy Scouts and Raiders

The Navy Scouts and Raiders of World War II were better known as the Amphibious Scouts and Raiders.

See also AMPHIBIOUS SCOUTS AND RAIDERS.

Nguyen Van Kiet

Nguyen Van Kiet was the only Vietnamese to be awarded the Navy Cross for valor during the Vietnam War. He won it while on an operation with SEAL lieutenant Thomas R. Norris to rescue a downed American pilot.

See also NORRIS, THOMAS R.

night vision goggles (NVG)

Night vision is essential to any special operations soldier working under the cover of darkness. The primitive Starlight amplification scopes of the Vietnam War have largely been replaced by night vision goggles (NVGs). NVGs have become so sensitive and accurate that helicopter pilots wear them to attack ground targets at night.

The NVG being issued to special forces is the PVS-7D that can be worn either on the helmet or used like a pair of binoculars. The device amplifies ambient light from stars and other available light millions of times to present a clear though monochrome-green picture to the user. A small infrared light on the front of the PVS-7D provides lighting indoors or where there is no celestial lighting.

nitrogen narcosis

In the 1930s, hardhat deep-sea divers using compressed air in deep waters with correspondingly high pressures were discovered to become "intoxicated" and euphoric, sometimes to the point of losing judgment and a sense of place. This nitrogen narcosis, or "rapture of the deep," was linked to nitrogen in the air breathed under high pressure. Special breathing mixtures, such as helium-oxygen, were developed for deep diving.

nitroglycerin

Nitroglycerin is the most powerful explosive in common use. The use of explosives is an important part of SEAL operations.

See also EXPLOSIVES.

nonmagnetic SCUBA swimmers knife

Underwater mines, with their magnetically influenced fuzes, became increasingly common by the late 1950s and a distinct problem for explosive ordnance disposal (EOD) divers by the 1960s. A magnetic mine is ingeniously designed to explode in the proximity of metal. EOD equipment, therefore, had to be completely nonmagnetic, usually nonferrous, to prevent SEALs, underwater demolition team frogmen, and EOD divers from inadvertently setting off a mine when they approached it underwater to rig it with a charge and explode it in place.

Special nonmagnetic breathing equipment and other diving gear was available. However, diving knives were made of carbon steel and therefore unsuitable. In February 1961, the U.S. Navy issued a procurement contract for a specialized knife. By April 1962, the Imperial Knife Company of Providence, Rhode Island, had the "Nonmagnetic SCUBA Swimmers Knife" ready for use.

It was a "dagger" weighing slightly more than half a pound. It was twelve inches long overall, with a 7.31-inch blade of a gray oxide color and a molded fiberglass handle. It was constructed of Haynes Alloy 25 (copper-chromium-tungsten-nickel) and had no detectable magnetic signature.

Because of the relatively high individual cost of the knife—over $100 in 1962—it was reserved for special issue only. Only 1,100 of the blades were produced, each marked with a serial number and year of manufacture. They remained available for issue well into the 1990s.

Noriega, Manuel Antonio (b. 1934)

Panamanian dictator Manuel Noriega was ousted by U.S. forces during Operation Just Cause and seized to stand trial in the United States for drug trafficking. He was convicted and is currently serving a long prison term in a U.S. federal prison.

See also OPERATION JUST CAUSE.

Normandy Landing

On June 6, 1944, Allied troops landed on the Normandy beaches to drive the Germans out of occupied France. Amphibious Scouts and Raiders and Naval Combat Demolition Units (NCDU), both predecessors of modern U.S. Navy SEALs, participated in the landing. The NCDUs suffered the highest casualty rate, 52 percent, of any American unit involved in the landings.

See also BEACH CLEARANCE; BELGIAN GATES; D-DAY; NAVAL COMBAT DEMOLITION UNITS (NCDUS); OPERATION OVERLORD.

Norris, Thomas R. (b. 1944)

Two of the most remarkable feats of bravery performed by SEALs during the Vietnam War occurred after most American forces had been withdrawn and the few remaining SEALs were about to be extracted. Three SEALs won the Medal of Honor, the nation's highest award for valor, out of a total of 238 awarded during the conflict. Incredibly enough, Lt. Thomas R. Norris won his in April 1972 for his heroic rescue of two downed U.S. airmen and was then the subject of a rescue himself in October 1972 that resulted in the winning of a second SEAL Medal of Honor by Petty Officer Michael Edwin Thornton. The third Medal of Honor for SEALs in the Vietnam War went to Joseph R. "Bob" Kerrey.

In late March and early April 1972, the North Vietnamese army (NVA) rolled across the DMZ in a multidivisional Blitzkrieg-type attack. The target was the upper provinces of South Vietnam, the goal to topple the South Vietnamese government. The attack was backed by recently acquired Soviet armor and highly trained air defense troops firing surface-to-air missiles (SAMs). Although most U.S. ground troops had already been withdrawn,

America weighed in with heavy airpower. B-52s pounded the attackers to stop the so-called NVA Easter offensive.

In the midst of the battle, on April 2, an American EB-66 electronic-warfare plane escorting B-52s to jam enemy radar and locate SAM sites suffered a direct hit by a SAM. The plane's electronic warfare officer, Air Force lieutenant colonel Iceal Hambleton, was the only survivor. He parachuted far behind enemy lines in Quang Tri Province, in the middle of the NVA's main avenue of attack. The effort to recover Hambleton, who had worked in the Strategic Air Command (SAC) and possessed a wealth of information about U.S. missile forces and targets, grew into one of the most complicated and costly efforts of the entire war. Officials were determined that he not be captured and passed on to the Soviets.

A standoff ensued. American air cover kept NVA soldiers away from Hambleton, but the enemy had him surrounded. Several U.S. helicopters from F Troop, Eighth Cavalry Regiment, attempted a rescue. One UH-1 "Huey" was shot down. The survivors were captured and hustled across the border into North Vietnam. Another Huey crash-landed on a nearby beach. Two HH-3E "Jolly Green Giants" were badly hit but managed to limp back to crashland at the Phu Bai airbase; another went down and burned in a heavy pall of black smoke. Because of bad weather and heavy enemy fire, the Americans called off further helicopter attempts.

The downing of two OV-10 observation planes involved in the rescue attempt further complicated matters. One of their airmen, Capt. William Henderson, was captured hiding in bushes ten meters from the Song Mieu Giang River. Two other airmen, 1st Lts. Bruce Walker and Mark Clark, hid out separately in the same region as Iceal Hambleton. There were now *three* Americans requiring rescue.

Andy Anderson, a former Marine recon officer who now headed the final days of the Joint Personnel Recovery Center, known under the code name Bright Light, devised a plan whereby commandos on the ground would attempt to rescue the three flyers. He approached the Navy Advisory Group for help. Lt. Tom Norris volunteered his services and those of the Vietnamese SEAL LDNN (Lien Doc Nguoi Nhai) he advised.

On April 10, Anderson, Norris, and a squad of LDNN reached the ARVN (Army of the Republic of Vietnam) outpost closest to the downed airmen. It was an old French bunker complex along Route 9, which led to Laos. It was manned by an understrength platoon of ARVN Rangers and two tanks.

Anderson had already devised a plan that involved coordination between FAC (forward air control) planes and the desperate airmen in the jungle. The plan had been passed along to the downed Americans through their emergency radios, using an ingenious method of code talk that prevented compromise. Using this code, each man was directed to move toward the Song Mieu Giang River.

Hambleton, for example, was an avid golfer. His code involved golf and the layout of different courses he had played. In this manner, he was advised of the safest route to proceed toward the river while avoiding large concentrations of enemy forces. An overhead FAC pilot acted as his spotter. "Make like Esther Williams and head for the Big Muddy," were the instructions he received for one leg of his hazardous journey.

On the ground, Norris and his LDNN frogmen were entrusted with going up the river to rescue the Americans when they arrived at their pinpointed objectives. The first rescue went off successfully on the night of April 10. Norris and four LDNN frogmen crept a mile and a half through enemy patrols, jungle, and swamp to rescue Lieutenant Clark. Lieutenant Walker was killed by the NVA in his attempts to evade before Norris and his men could reach him. That left only Hambleton still in danger. Norris intended to make another foray for him as soon as conditions permitted.

The NVA pounded the ARVN outpost during the day of April 11, killing five South Vietnamese and wounding 15 others. Shrapnel struck Anderson above the left eye; he was ordered evacuated. The ARVN outpost continued to hold out.

On the night of April 13, Norris decided to make a last effort to find Hambleton and bring him out. Two other attempts in previous days had failed. This time Norris would take with him only one other man, a Viet LDNN named Nguyen Van Kiet, whom he trusted literally with his life.

As soon as darkness fell, the SEAL and the frogman donned the clothing and cone hats of Vietnamese fishermen and set out up the Song Mieu Giang River in a small sampan. Hambleton, who had carefully nursed the batteries of his emergency radio, was instructed to move to a pickup point on the river. By this time he had been on the ground 11 days, starving and all but exhausted.

Norris and Nguyen paddled close to the river bank, in the shadows of the jungle. They stopped whenever they detected signs of the enemy. Several times they requested air strikes to clear the way. Hambleton was waiting for them, having been "golf course"–guided to his pickup point. The two rescuers had him lie in the bottom of the sampan, where they covered him with banana palm fronds. Almost three hours had passed.

The little boat and its heroic occupants had almost reached the ARVN outpost when they suddenly came under fire by heavy automatic weapons. All aboard would have been lost had not U.S. Air Force "fast movers" come in swiftly to strafe and bomb the enemy forces into silence. Norris and Nguyen made it safely back to the outpost with Hambleton.

Lieutenant Colonel Hambleton's rescue became the stuff of legend, from which a movie, *BAT-21* (Hambleton's call sign), was made. It starred Gene Hackman as Hambleton and Danny Glover as the FAC who shepherded him to the river where SEAL Norris and Nguyen picked him up.

President Gerald R. Ford signed Lieutenant Norris's Medal of Honor citation: "By his outstanding display of decisive leadership, undaunted courage, and selfless dedication in the face of extreme danger, Lieutenant Norris enhanced the finest tradition of the United States Naval Service."

Nguyen Van Kiet became the only Vietnamese in the war to receive the U.S. Navy Cross. The citation was signed by Secretary of the Navy J. William Middendorf II: "Due to Petty Officer Kiet's coolness under extremely dangerous conditions," it stated, "and his outstanding courage and professionalism, an American aviator was recovered after an eleven-day ordeal behind enemy lines. His self-discipline, personal courage, and dynamic fighting spirit were an inspiration to all, thereby reflecting great credit upon himself and the Naval service."

See also BRIGHT LIGHT; NGUYEN VAN KIET; THORNTON, MICHAEL EDWIN.

North Vietnamese Army (NVA)

U.S. forces fighting the Vietnam War were confronted by two main enemy forces—the North Vietnamese army (NVA) and South Vietnamese guerrilla forces known as Viet Cong. The NVA were recruited and trained in North Vietnam and sent south as a conventional army to fight American and South Vietnamese. The SEALs primarily fought against the Viet Cong.

O

obstacle-avoidance sonar

Like other submarines, the odd little vessel called a SEAL delivery vehicle (SDV) is visually blind. It operates subsurface for fast, covert SEAL insertions and is powered by rechargeable silver-zinc batteries. It must therefore rely on sensors and instrumentation to navigate safely. A computerized doppler navigation sonar displays speed, distance, heading, depth, and other piloting data. The obstacle-avoidance sonar, coupled with the inertial navigation system, allows the SDV operator to cruise around underwater without crashing into submerged cliffs and other obstacles. All its electronics are housed in a dry, watertight instrument panel.

See also ADVANCED SEAL DELIVERY SYSTEM (ASDS).

"Octopus"

"Octopus" is the term applied to the hoses and mouthpiece assembly of an underwater breathing apparatus.

Office of Strategic Services (OSS)

The Office of Strategic Services (OSS) in World War II was much more like modern SEALs than were the underwater demolition teams (UDTs) of that day. That was especially true of the OSS Maritime Unit, which can be considered one of the ancestors of today's SEALs; it exerted the most direct effect on contemporary UDTs and upon the subsequent development of the SEALs.

The super-secret OSS was organized in 1942 under the direction of the Joint Chiefs of Staff. Its mission was to gather and analyze information and conduct psychological and guerrilla warfare. Maj. Gen. William J. "Wild Bill" Donovan became its commander. After the war ended in 1945, its functions were divided between the Department of State and the War Department. The Central Intelligence Agency (CIA) was formed in 1947 to unify all government intelligence agencies.

During the OSS's three years of existence, it used military agents and operators for behind-enemy-lines missions in France, China, Burma, and, in more limited numbers, in the Pacific. Gen. Douglas

MacArthur refused to allow the OSS, with its unconventional and unorthodox methods, to operate under his command in the Southwest Pacific.

OSS swimmers of the Maritime Unit were organized into three teams of 30 men each. Their training was far superior in many ways to that of the UDTs. They were highly skilled in scouting and raiding techniques, underwater work, and land and sea sabotage. They were familiar with both U.S. and foreign weapons, were airborne, and were adept at hand-to-hand combat. In addition, their water skills could not be matched by the UDTs. Christian J. Lambertsen, who invented the LARU (Lambertsen Amphibious Respiratory Unit), a closed-circuit underwater breathing apparatus (UBA), was an OSS member for a year and a half and personally taught swimmers the use of his UBA and of swim fins.

The summer of 1944 might be considered a turning point for the UDTs and their influence upon naval special warfare. In June, Wild Bill Donovan offered Adm. Chester Nimitz one of his 30-man swimmer units for use in the Pacific. The unit, under the command of Lt. Arthur Choate, was dispatched to Maui with all its underwater and diving equipment. It merged with UDT-10, and Lieutenant Choate was made commander of the team.

Choate's first contribution to underwater work was to change the attitude of the UDTs toward swim fins and to teach their use not only for swimming but also for scrambling about on coral and on the beaches. This was all new to the UDTs; up to this point they had been swimming barefoot or in sneakers. Lt. Cdr. John T. Koehler, commanding officer of the Maui UDT school, quickly put out an order for every pair of swim fins in Hawaii.

Although the UDTs quickly adopted the fins, they didn't take to the LARU. That would come later in the emergence of naval special warfare.

The OSS swimmers with UDT-10 were involved in several missions before the war ended. Other OSS swimmers of the Maritime Unit, however, participated in a single operation and then only in a minor, supporting role: a team attached to the British 14th Army on the Arakan coast of Burma conducted an uneventful preliminary reconnaissance of an island before a British landing.

See also USS BURRFISH; CENTRAL INTELLIGENCE AGENCY (CIA); DIVING, HISTORY OF; DONOVAN, WILLIAM J. "WILD BILL"; LAMBERTSEN AMPHIBIOUS RESPIRATORY UNIT (LARU); LAMBERTSEN, CHRISTIAN J.; MACARTHUR, DOUGLAS.

Okinawa

The assault on Okinawa in World War II was by far the largest operation in the history of the underwater demolition teams (UDTs). Nearly a thousand swimmers from eight UDT teams were put into the water to survey the beach and blow obstacles prior to the amphibious landing. Only one frogman was killed.

See also UDT-16; UNDERWATER DEMOLITION TEAMS (UDTS).

Olson, Norman H. (b. 1931)

Norman Olson received a bachelor of science degree and a commission in the Naval Reserve from the U.S. Merchant Marine Academy, Kings Point, New York, prior to entering the navy for a 30-year career. He served at sea on three amphibious ships and held every single operational and administrative position in Underwater Demolition Team-21. He also commanded UDT-11 in Vietnam during the war and held various other positions and commands in naval special warfare. He was the first and only SEAL officer to command a major shore establishment (Naval Amphibious Base, Little Creek, Virginia). He also served as the first Chief of Staff of the Joint Special Operations Command.

In 1956, he commanded the first detachment of UDT men to go to parachute jump school. After attending HALO (high altitude, low opening) parachute school, he became very active in sport parachuting, eventually accumulating more than 2,300 parachute jumps. He was the founder of the Navy Parachute Demonstration Teams (the Chuting Stars and the Leap Frogs), and the founding director and curator for the UDT/SEAL Museum at Fort Pierce, Florida.

After retiring from the navy as a captain, Olson served as director of security for the Reagan-Bush presidential campaign, director of industrial security for the Electric Boat Division of General Dynamics Corporation, and founding director for the UDT/SEAL Museum. In 1998, the UDT/SEAL

Museum Association created the "Captain Norman H. Olson Distinguished Achievement Award," to be presented annually to one or more recipients for service to the museum and naval special warfare.

See also AIRBORNES; CHUTING STARS; LEAP FROGS; OPERATION JACKSTAY; UDT/SEAL MUSEUM.

Omaha Beach

"Omaha Beach" was the code name for one of two beaches assigned to the Americans for the Normandy D-day invasion of France in June 1944. The other was Utah Beach. Swimmers of the naval combat demolition units (NCDUs) went ahead to clear the way of obstacles. Thirty-one NCDU swimmers died on Omaha Beach, and 60 were wounded, a casualty rate of 52 percent, making Omaha Beach the site of the worst single day in the history of naval special warfare.

See also AMPHIBIOUS SCOUTS AND RAIDERS; BEACH CLEARANCE; BELGIAN GATES; BUCKLEW, PHILIP H.; D-DAY; NAVAL COMBAT DEMOLITION UNITS (NCDUS); NORMANDY LANDING; OPERATION OVERLORD.

OP-06D

OP-06D was the nomenclature assigned to the SEAL unit established to test the security of naval bases against terrorist attacks. It was better known as "Red Cell."

See also RED CELL.

OP-80

Formed under the auspices of MACV-SOG, OP-80 was the unit tasked with maintaining intelligence on allied prisoners of war and launching recovery efforts during the Vietnam War. It was better known as "Bright Light."

See also "BRIGHT LIGHT."

Open-Circuit Breathing Apparatus

There are two basic types of SCUBA (self-contained underwater breathing apparatus), "closed-circuit" and "open-circuit." The open circuit utilizes a tank of compressed air and a valve, hose, and mouthpiece assembly that furnishes air to the diver on demand. A valve opens on intake of breath to furnish air, then closes on exhalation to expel the released air into the water through an escape valve. SEALs rarely use an open-circuit system on missions, because it emits bubbles and noise, which can attract enemy attention.

See also AQUA-LUNG; CLOSED-CIRCUIT BREATHING APPARATUS; COUSTEAU, JACQUES-YVES.

operational security (OPSEC)

Due to the often clandestine nature of special warfare activities, operational security (OPSEC) is vital in keeping an enemy or a target confused about or ignorant of pending developments and strategies. SEALs are security conscious during all phases of planning, training, preparation, and support.

OPSEC consists of signal security, physical security, and information security, all of which are related and must be considered simultaneously.

Signal security protects operations information through communications and electronics security—communications codes, secure-voice equipment, proper procedures, radio silence, antenna positioning, and other such measures.

Physical security is implemented by using security forces, barriers, sensors, and secure containers to deny or limit access to facilities, areas, materials, documents, or personnel.

Information security prevents disclosure of operational information by restricting access to or the release of written, verbal, graphic, or electronic information.

At the beginning of a mission, a SEAL team may be "isolated." All security measures are placed into effect from the initiation of a mission until its conclusion to prevent a possible leak that could alert the enemy.

Operation Blue Spoon

Shortly before midnight on Tuesday, December 19, 1989, guests sleeping at the Marriott Hotel on the south side of Panama City were suddenly awakened by the crackling stutter of rifle fire from the nearby Punta Paitilla Airfield. U.S. Navy SEALs were engaging Panamanian forces, prematurely as it turned out, in the opening act of Operation Just Cause.

Several factors precipitated the massive American assault. Noriega had been under U.S. criminal indictment since February 1989 on charges of drug trafficking and money laundering. On December 15, 1989, Panama's National People's Assembly, made up almost entirely of Noriega henchmen, passed a resolution declaring that a state of war existed between Panama and the United States. When, on the next evening, troops of the Panamanian Defense Forces shot and killed a U.S. marine in downtown Panama City, then arrested a second marine and his wife, whom they tortured, President George Bush ordered that a planned option for the invasion of Panama be implemented.

A plan for a massive military takeover of Panama, code-named Operation Blue Spoon, had already been drafted during the Reagan administration. Gen. Colin Powell, chairman of the Joint Chiefs of Staff, and Gen. Thomas Kelley, director of operations for the Joint Special Operations Command (JSOC), now used Blue Spoon as the foundation for a military operations against the small Central American country. Defense secretary Dick Cheney coined a new name for the planned operation—Just Cause.

The plan had three basic goals: to remove or neutralize military resistance to U.S. forces; capture General Noriega; and restore order to the country and install a stable, democratically elected government. It would be applied swiftly and with such overwhelming force at so many locations that Noriega and his followers would be removed or eliminated without grave danger to either the country or its ordinary citizens.

A total of 27 targets were picked, requiring 27,000 American troops, including a 4,150-man special operations force. Integrated into the plan were U.S. Army Rangers and U.S. Army Special Forces (Green Berets); Delta Force, along with its helicopters and psychological-warfare units; Air Force AC-130 aircraft, Pave Low special operations helicopters, and Air Force combat air controllers; and the U.S. Navy SEALs. For the most part, commandos of the various services would be assigned missions compatible with their skills and characters.

SEALs were tasked with two parts of the operation. They were to disable the *Presidente Porras,* a

65-foot patrol boat that Noriega might use in an attempt to escape to sea when the action began, and they were to capture Punta Paitilla Airport in southern Panama City to prevent Noriega from fleeing in a Learjet he kept there.

H-hour was set at 1 A.M., December 20, 1989. The fight at the Paitilla Airfield was to be remembered as the single worst disaster in SEAL history.

See also OPERATION JUST CAUSE.

Operation Chromite

The amphibious landing at Inchon on September 15, 1950, during the Korean War was given the code name Operation Chromite. UDT-1 and UDT-3 (underwater demolition teams) provided swimmers who went in ahead of the landing craft, scouted mudflats, marked shallow points in the channel, cleared fouled propellers, and searched for mines. In addition, four UDT frogmen acted as wave guides for the marine landing.

See also KOREAN WAR.

Operation Crossroads

The end of World War II saw the underwater demolition teams (UDTs) drastically reduced in size and number. Without the necessity for conducting beach clearances in advance of amphibious landings, there seemed to be little need for frogmen. One use the navy apparently found for swimmers involved Operation Crossroads, part of the development of nuclear weapons.

Few records are publicly available of that top-secret era, but it is known that a few members of UDTs were assigned to Crossroads to assist in the testing of nuclear weapons. They participated in the preparation and measuring of the beaches at Bikini Atoll, where two test bombs were exploded in July 1946. It is reported that the frogmen were "instrumental" in the pre- and postblast surveys.

Operation Desert Shield

Desert Shield was the code name for the initial "defense of Saudia Arabia" phase of the Persian Gulf War against Iraq. It began on August 7, 1990, and ended on the evening of D-day, January 17, 1991, when the second-phase air raids of Operation Desert Storm began.

See also OPERATION DESERT STORM.

Operation Desert Storm

The planning and buildup phase of the Persian Gulf War against Iraq, Operation Desert Shield, ended when the actual war, Operation Desert Storm, began on D-day, January 17, 1991. U.S. Navy SEALs played a critical role from the very beginning until the "Southwest Asia cease-fire" campaign began on April 11, 1991. During the 163 days of Desert Shield and the 42 days of Desert Storm, SEALs conducted over 270 missions in support of coalition forces. It was the first time SEALs had been called upon to serve as an integral part of a much larger force involved in a major conventional war.

By 1991, U.S. special operations forces had been active in 18 of America's military involvements since 1975, most of them still classified Secret. The Persian Gulf War was the first major military action in the post–cold war world. When Saddam Hussein of Iraq decided to attack Kuwait and take over its oil empire with 100,000 troops at 2 A.M. Gulf time on August 2, 1990, he overwhelmed and conquered his little neighbor within 12 hours.

The conflict had developed in three phases. First was the buildup of tension in the area following the end of the 1980–88 Iran-Iraq war, leading to a border dispute between Iraq and Kuwait and the subsequent invasion. The second phase was the forming of the allied coalition and the buildup of forces in the Kuwaiti theater of operations. This was the Desert Shield phase. Desert Storm, the final phase, began with the air war and ended with the 100-hour ground war that defeated Hussein and drove him from Kuwait.

Within a short time after Iraq invaded Kuwait, SEAL reinforcements were being deployed to the detachment assigned to the Middle East squadron based in Bahrain. By August 11, a contingent of 105 West Coast SEALs and support personnel were on the ground in Saudi Arabia setting up a base camp on the coast south at Dhahran. Eventually, American forces in the Gulf would number more than 540,000, of whom some 9,000 were from the

Special Operations Command, including four SEAL platoons, one SEAL fast attack vehicle detachment, one high-speed special boat unit, one SEAL delivery vehicle team, and one joint communications support element. Until then, however, the Dhahran SEALs were virtually the only American fighting men standing between Hussein and further conquest.

The U.S. Navy had a number of duties to perform: seize and maintain control of the Persian Gulf; protect friendly ships; block Iraqi trade; clear mines in the Gulf; prepare for an amphibious assault and execute it; fly recon and combat sorties; transport much of the heavy armor, supplies, and troops for the buildup; and, finally, launch an attack and soften up hard enemy defenses. SEALs were involved in most of these missions.

Very early in the buildup, SEALs trained a force of Saudi SEALs and marines in close air support techniques. They dealt directly with Kuwaiti resistance fighters, training the underground and making clandestine deliveries of weapons and equipment. Their high-speed boats conducted patrols for signs of enemy infiltration and attack. They conducted special recon missions along the Kuwaiti border with Saudi Arabia, made hydrographic recons of Kuwaiti beaches in anticipation of an amphibious landing, effected hull searches of incoming ships to check for timed mines, ran night harbor security patrols and antimine sweeps, and took part in many practice amphibious landing exercises. In addition to all this, they participated in 118 combat search and rescue missions, took enemy prisoners of war on three occasions and seized an oil platform, a ship, and the island of Qaruh.

Once he occupied Kuwait, Saddam Hussein had ordered the closing of all embassies in Kuwait City. The United States had refused to shut down its embassy. Iraqi soldiers surrounded it, laying siege and holding U.S. personnel as virtual hostages. Detachments from SEAL Team Six were sent to the gulf to prepare for a possible rescue, since the American embassy was only across a street from the water, a few hundred yards away.

SEAL commandos disguised as locals slipped into the capital to take a firsthand look at the situation. They collected information on where the hostages were likely hiding inside the compound and how best to assault it. They were considering a possible airborne infiltration with a seaborne insertion of combat support swimmers when Hussein unexpectedly released the hostages in December 1990.

The air war began on January 17, 1991, with the launch of naval cruise missiles against Baghdad, followed by repeated coalition air strikes for the next 39 days and nights. Prior to release of the first missile, however, several SEAL detachments silently infiltrated Kuwait and Iraq by air and sea and set up hidden observation posts in view of carefully selected targets. Armed with electronics devices known as compact laser designators, they "painted" high-priority targets with laser light. The reflected light was invisible to observers but guided aircraft "smart bombs" directly to their bull's-eyes.

During the air war itself, SEALs were one of the most active parts of the U.S. combat team. They were first to have face-to-face contact with the enemy and first to capture Iraqi prisoners of war.

The Iraqis occupied seven oil platforms in the Durrah oil field in the northern Persian Gulf. When two helicopters from the USS *Nicholas* were fired upon from four of these platforms, the *Nicholas* and the Kuwaiti ship *Istiglal* returned fire. SEALs then boarded the platforms, secured them, and captured the surviving enemy soldiers and a large amount of weaponry and equipment. Five Iraqis were killed in the engagement and 23 captured. There were no American casualties.

Within the following days, SEALs from the USS *Curts* captured an enemy vessel gone dead in the water from air strikes and took 51 more Iraqi prisoners. SEALs seized an oil terminal, taking another 16 prisoners, then secured the island of Qaruh, a Kuwaiti island close offshore in the Gulf. Three Iraqis were killed on Qaruh and 29 captured. Using their fast boats, SEALs rescued 20 Iraqis whose ship had been sunk, then picked an American F-16 pilot from the sea after his plane went down.

A U.S. naval pilot flying over the tiny island of Umm al-Maradim saw spelled out on the sand with stones the message SOS WE SURRENDER. "Not knowing whether it was a trick or an actual surrender," explained a naval officer, "of course we sent in the SEALs." The island proved to be deserted. Left behind were antiaircraft emplacements and stocks of ammunition. SEALs blew them up in place.

As SEALs had made first contact with the enemy, they likewise found themselves in the first ground combat of the war. By January 31, the air assault had been under way for about two weeks, but action on the ground had so far been limited to sporadic artillery duels. But on that day, four SEALs manning an observation post in a cavelike bunker on the coast, just south of the Kuwaiti border, were spotted by civilians, who must have snitched on them to the Iraqis.

The evening was eerily quiet until about 10 P.M., when the SEALs suddenly detected the growl of a tank coming toward them. The steel monster lumbered onto a berm about 150 yards away and opened fire. The first round was illumination; it exploded in a brilliant sun directly over the SEALs' heads. The next rounds were HE (high explosives), bursting all over the terrain.

It was obvious from the fire pattern that the tank hadn't pinpointed the SEALs' location. The SEALs were armed with heavy machine guns and 40 mm grenades, no match for their armored foe. Wisely, they chose retreat over valor. Their first impulse, being SEALs, was to head for the water. They suppressed that thought and made a dash for it south across the desert in their jeeplike Humm-V. The tank was no match for the Humm-V's speed. These four SEALs were the last Americans to leave the border area before the ground war began three weeks later.

The ground war kicked off at 4 A.M. on February 24. One of the most important and successful SEAL missions of the campaign was led by Lt. Tom Deitz on the night before D-day. He and his platoon had scouted the Kuwaiti coastline for a likely amphibious landing site for the 17,000-Marine assault force waiting on ships in the Gulf. However, on the night of 23 February, Deitz and his men were assigned to launch a diversion to make the Iraqis think the long-anticipated assault was coming from the sea when it was actually thundering across the desert from out of Saudi Arabia. The SEALs planted explosive charges in the beach surf, then sped back and forth off shore firing machine guns and grenades. They were credited with tying down at least two Iraqi divisions, which could not be used against the actual assault.

SEALs of Team Six were moved out by helicopter to Kuwait City when the offensive began. As coalition ground forces closed in on the city, they fast-roped down from hovering choppers onto the roofs of U.S. embassy buildings. Marine units quickly reinforced the SEALs to secure the compound. To everyone's amazement, the American flag was still flying.

SEALs in expensive ($40,000) fast attack vehicles, high-speed dune buggies, patrolled the streets around the embassy until President George Bush ordered all coalition forces to suspend offensive combat operations at midnight on February 28. Iraq had been driven out of Kuwait and defeated in only 100 hours of ground combat.

During Desert Shield and Desert Storm SEALs had suffered no losses and sustained no casualties, although they had often operated deep inside enemy territory. The most important lesson of the war for the SEALs, said Cap. Ray Smith, commander of Naval Special Warfare Task Group, Central, was that they had proved they could work effectively with other forces in a major conventional conflict and, in spite of their small numbers, contribute significantly on the battlefield.

See also DEITZ; TOM, OPERATION DESERT SHIELD.

Operation Desoto

Special U.S. Navy patrols were assigned as Operation Desoto to eavesdrop off the Vietnam coast on enemy shore-based communications prior to the Gulf of Tonkin incident. SEAL missions under OP-34A, along with the Desoto missions, led to the Gulf of Tonkin incident and the introduction of U.S. combat forces into Vietnam.

See also CHINA BEACH; GULF OF TONKIN RESOLUTION; MACV-SOG; OPERATION PLAN 34A (OP-34A); QUANG KHE NAVAL BASE.

Operation Eagle Claw

On November 3, 1979, Iranian militants seized the U.S. embassy in Teheran and took 63 American diplomatic personnel hostage. Eight days later, the Joint Chiefs of Staff charged U.S. Army major general James Vaught with forming a task force to plan a military hostage rescue, under the code name Operation Eagle Claw. Lt. Cdr. Richard Marcinko, former commander of SEAL Team Two, was one of two navy representatives assigned to the task force.

He recalled that at least two SEALs were involved in the mission.

Army colonel "Chargin' Charlie" Beckwith was selected to lead the rescue. He had conceived and built an elite, highly trained outfit to fight terrorism and conduct surgical behind-the-lines operations. It was called SFOD-D, Special Forces Operational Detachment Delta—or, more commonly, Delta Force. This would be the elite unit's first operational mission. The plan that finally evolved from the task force assigned Delta to make the hostage snatch, with support from both the air force and navy.

It was a complicated plan, whose intricacies ultimately contributed to the disaster that occurred in the Iranian desert. It called for U.S. Navy RH-53D Sea Stallion helicopters to fly from a carrier in the Arabian Sea deep into Iran, to an isolated spot code-named "Desert One." There, they would rendezvous with C-130 cargo planes carrying the 132 Delta Force soldiers, plus their equipment and fuel for the choppers.

From Desert One, choppers would insert Delta teams on the outskirts of Teheran under cover of darkness. The soldiers would hole up during daylight hours, sneak into the city that night, storm the embassy and escort the hostages to waiting choppers, fly back to waiting C-141s at the secured airfield at Manzaniyeh, and then get quickly out of the country.

Neither the military nor the CIA had reliable contacts or assets inside Iran. One of the task force's goals was to infiltrate as many operatives into the country as it could. Dick Meadows, a highly decorated former Green Beret and now a civilian consultant for Delta Force, and a party of Special Forces soldiers clandestinely entered Teheran under various cover stories. Several of the soldiers spoke foreign languages, including Farsi, Iran's official language. Their job was to act as a reception committee for the invading Delta Force.

Meadows's orders were to make his way through the chaos of the city, establish a safe house, locally procure covered trucks to transport the rescue force once it was inserted by helicopter, and guide rescuers from the landing zone to their assault positions near the embassy.

The two SEALs involved in the operation, both of whom have remained unidentified to the present time, had worked for Marcinko when he commanded Team Two. One was a first-generation American who had grown up speaking German at home. He slipped into Iran posing as a German businessman. The second SEAL penetrated the capital by assuming the disguise of a monk. Information procured by the two commandos about the embassy compound proved invaluable to rescue planning. Neither was ever recognized with medals, commendations, or promotions.

On the night of April 24, 1980, Operation Eagle Claw was launched. Of the eight Sea Stallion helicopters that lifted off the carrier USS *Nimitz,* one had mechanical problems en route and had to abort. Two others flew into sandstorms and got lost.

In the meantime, C-130s carrying Delta Force had already arrived at the refueling point, Desert One, in Iran. Murphy's Law, which states that anything that *can* go wrong *will,* reared its troublesome head. An Iranian bus driving by the site was stopped and detained, along with its 45 or so passengers. Then along came a gasoline tanker truck. Troopers blew it up, but the driver jumped out and escaped by flagging down a passing motorist. Presumably, he was hightailing it to Teheran to sound the alarm.

When the surviving navy helicopters arrived, Colonel Beckwith determined that their numbers were insufficient to effect the rescue. He decided to abort the mission, refuel the choppers, and scramble the entire force out of Iran and back to Egypt or the *Nimitz.* That was when disaster struck.

As one of the choppers was maneuvering to refuel, it collided with a parked EC-130 refueling craft, into which a Delta element had just loaded. Chopper and airplane immediately exploded in a blue flame that could be seen for miles across the desert. Five soldiers were killed, and eight were injured. The survivors, carrying their dead and wounded, piled into the remaining C-130s and got off the ground immediately.

Agents waiting in Teheran were left behind and had to exfiltrate on their own. Meadows actually caught a commercial flight out. The SEAL posing as a monk was on the ground only a couple of days; he had already left the capital before the Desert One tragedy. Being the typical self-reliant type, he walked 600 miles to the Turkish border, where he crossed safely.

This was America's only rescue attempt during the hostage crisis. The hostages were held at the embassy for 444 days, until they were inexplicably released hours after the inauguration of President Ronald Reagan on January 20, 1981.

Operation Earnest Will

U.S. Navy SEALs were present and active in the Persian Gulf long before Operation Desert Storm initiated the Persian Gulf War against Iraq in 1991. From 1987 to 1989, at the end of the war between Iran and Iraq, SEALs participated in a special operations task force to prevent Iranians from seeding mines in the seaway used by the world's oil tankers. The operation was code-named Earnest Will.

Staging out of a pair of rented barges, the task force, composed of U.S. Army helicopters, navy special boat units (SBUs), and SEALs, patrolled the water for mines and boarded and searched ships suspected of planting them. Each of the barges was large enough to support attack and cargo helicopters, landing facilities, and dockage for SBU boats. SEALs were rotated in and out of the gulf over the two and a half years that the operation lasted.

The primary action of the period involving SEALs occurred when the *Iran Ajr* was discovered laying mines. The ship fired upon a U.S. Army helicopter when ordered to stop. The ship and crew were captured by SEALs without casualties.

See also IRAN AJR.

Operation Fishnet

By the summer of 1952, the Korean War had stalemated and turned into a war of attrition. United Nations blockades had severely cut the flow of supplies into the North. China was experiencing near famine and had little food to send to her soldiers in Korea. A great deal of the North Korean diet, both for civilians and the military, therefore came from fish netted out of the sea. American underwater demolition teams (UDTs) operating in the war zone were ordered to launch Operation Fishnet, to remove or destroy all North Korean fishing nets they could find. The idea was to starve the enemy armies.

UDTs working along the coast on reconnaissance or demolition raids made note of the locations of nets. Later, other UDTs went over the side to destroy or confiscate them. Many were given to South Korean fishermen.

UDT-5 made the first foray of Operation Fishnet in July 1952, near the North Korean port city of Wonsan. It was not completely successful. The frogmen hacked away at two nets without attracting attention. However, starting on a third net, they were spotted by enemy soldiers ashore, who opened fire on them. They managed to escape without casualties under covering fire from their transport boat and a South Korean patrol boat.

Two months later, in September, commandos from UDT-3 made a similar Fishnet raid 15 miles south of the Manchurian border. Using small rubber boats, they rowed so close to shore that one group was startled by soldiers crossing a wooden bridge almost above their heads.

In the meantime, other members of the team radioed the code phrase "Key West," meaning they had located a net. It was about 300 feet long and supported by cork, pieces of wood, and clusters of glass balls. It was anchored to shore by a steel cable encased in hemp. Enemy soldiers on the beach had built a bonfire in order to keep warm. The fire turned out to be a godsend, as it helped frogmen see what they were doing while concealing them in the shadows on the sea.

They destroyed the net by dragging sections of it into their rubber boat and ripping it with knives. Bolt cutters were brought in from a landing craft that waited nearby in support, and the anchor cable was cut. The frogmen were busy rigging two explosive charges to the net when shots rang out. They lit time fuses and headed for sea. They heard the charges going off as they reached their landing craft.

It is unclear exactly how effective Operation Fishnet was, if at all. Chief Petty Officer James L. "Gator" Parks, UDT-1, remembers that a number of fishnets were confiscated or destroyed during the year.

We would do this all up and down the coast of North Korea," he says. "I think we were very effective. We cut a lot of fishnets up, I know that. We went in one night and sank some sampans, too, with demolition charges. None of that stuff seemed to be guarded to any extent at all. You could actually see people up on the beach. Either we were doing our job pretty well, or they weren't paying much attention. . .

We got a lot of bad publicity from the [North] Koreans because we were "criminals" coming in and cutting their fishnets and starving their people. It was rumored they had rewards out for us.

Plans were made for a renewed assault by UDTs on the nets at the height of the 1953 fishing season. However, an armistice ended the fighting on July 27, 1953.

See also KOREAN WAR.

Operation Flintlock

The World War II attack on Kwajalein beginning on January 31, 1944, code-named Operation Flintlock, came a little more than two months after the near disaster at Tarawa. It was very much an experiment in using the newly formed underwater demolition teams (UDTs) in combat. At Tarawa, due to lack of intelligence about the invasion beaches, more marines had drowned trying to get to the beaches than were killed by the Japanese on the island. A cry went up for a new type of scout unit. Adm. Richmond Kelly Turner seized the few teams of naval combat demolition units (NCDUs) that were not assigned to Europe for D-day and made them the nucleus of his new unit. In this way, the UDTs came into existence. Kwajalein was almost an ideal site for the fledgling UDTs to work out their tactics.

The Kwajalein atoll lies in the Marshall Islands, about halfway between Hawaii and the Philippines. Analyzing Japanese radio transmissions, U.S. Navy intelligence experts learned that the bulk of Japanese forces had been moved to outlying islands, leaving Kwajalein lightly defended. U.S. commanders decided to skirt the outlying islands and cut straight for Kwajalein and its nearby twin island, Roi-Namur.

The army's Seventh Division would assault Kwajalein, while the Fourth Marine Division attacked Roi-Namur. UDT-1 was assigned to scout and clear the army's beachhead; UDT-2 was assigned to the marines.

Accompanied by marine scouts, UDT-2 conducted a night reconnaissance of Roi-Namur and reported back that the beaches were suitable for landing. At Kwajalein, UDT-1 likewise planned a night beach recon, but at the last moment Admiral Turner ordered two daylight approaches instead, one on the morning tide and one on the evening. He was concerned about a log wall under construction by the Japanese, as well as the possibility of other surprises hidden in the water that a nighttime beach survey might miss.

Hidden coral reefs forced the scout boats to stay too far offshore to permit an accurate assessment of the beaches. Frogmen wore full combat gear, including life vests and boots, and were under strict orders to stay attached to the boats by lifelines when they were in the water. However, two of the UDTs—Seabee chief petty officer Bill Acheson and Ens. Lewis F. Luehrs—stripped down to swim trunks and dove in to conduct the reconnaissance as swimmers. Information obtained by these rogue swimmers caused Admiral Turner to change his tactics for the invasion.

As dawn broke on February 1 and the invasion began, UDTs led the way against both islands to clear obstructions and blaze a trail. Both teams brought with them a promising new secret weapon—small wooden landing craft called "Stingrays," which were in effect remote-controlled floating bombs. They were designed to speed unoccupied toward enemy defenses, where they could be exploded by radio to clear a path for following troop craft.

At Roi-Namur, the first Stingray, loaded with five tons of dynamite, headed into the haze of bombardment smoke that hung over the island and surrounding waters. It failed to explode. Not only that, but it suddenly returned and attempted to ram invader boats. Only quick action by three UDT men prevented disaster. They sped alongside the drone and jumped into it to cut the explosive firing train. A second drone also malfunctioned. It sped toward the beach as it was intended, but then it made a tight circle and charged the boat from which it was supposedly being controlled. Fortunately, the TNT it contained did not explode.

UDT-1 at Kwajalein was having the same problem. Of three drones launched, one promptly sank, while the engines on the other two quit, leaving the boats wallowing in the waves. Stingrays were never again used in the Pacific War.

The major lesson learned by the UDTs at Kwajalein was that the task of destroying enemy underwater defenses and other obstacles would have to be done by men, and that swimmers in the water were more effective at this and in reconnoitering beaches than were men in boats.

See also ACHESON, BILL; KWAJALEIN; LUEHRS, LEWIS F.; STINGRAY; TARAWA; TURNER, RICHMOND KELLY; UNDERWATER DEMOLITION TEAMS (UDTS).

Operation Game Warden

Operation Game Warden was the code name assigned to Vietnam War operations that deployed river patrol boats and hovercraft to prevent enemy use of waterways.

See also RIVERINE WARFARE.

Operation Giant Slingshot

Operation Giant Slingshot was one of the operation code names under the SEALORDS program during the Vietnam War.

See also SEALORDS.

Operation Husky

The invasion of Sicily on July 10, 1943, code-named Operation Husky, marked a point of departure in the development of what eventually became the U.S. Navy SEALs.

The disastrous invasion of Tarawa in the Pacific, barely seven months previously, on November 20, 1942, had taught the U.S. Navy a valuable lesson—that amphibious assaults were high-risk operations that require careful preparation. Information about Tarawa island, its defenses, and its approaches had been severely limited. Hydrographic data had been sketchy, tidal data almost nonexistent. Conventional landing craft carrying marines had come to a halt against coral reefs 500 yards offshore. More marines had drowned attempting to reach shore than later died fighting the Japanese on the island.

The Tarawa debacle led to a scramble to develop special teams to scout beaches for amphibious assaults in both the European theater of war and in the Pacific. A special emergency team of demolition men was created at the Dynamiting and Demolition School at Fort Bragg, Virginia, for the express purpose of assisting amphibious operations against Italy. Lt Fred Wise, a Seabee, was in charge of the 13-man volunteer team. This team and a handful of other demolition men were trained as quickly as possible and then shipped to the Mediterranean in time for Operation Husky, the invasion of Sicily. This unit received a name—Naval Demolition Unit (NDU).

On July 10, 1943, nearly 1,400 ships and over 1,800 landing craft disembarked nearly 500,000 soldiers in a 150-mile-wide front on Sicily. A landing of that scale had never been attempted before, and has not been since, even at Normandy.

NDU scout boats preceded the landings of the first waves to locate channels and then signal their locations by blinker or hooded lights. Swimmers placed markers on the beaches to guide in additional boats after sunrise. Scout boats also sought channels and buoyed them to guide in the landing craft that followed.

An American, Philip H. Bucklew, the "father of naval special warfare," was also active in Operation Husky. In the spring of 1942, the British had formed a secret unit called Combined Operations Pilotage Parties (COPP) in preparation for expected amphibious landings. COPP used two-man kayaks in their scouting forays and conducted their missions under cover of night. Bucklew, along with Amphibious Scouts and Raiders, helped the NDUs scout the Sicilian beaches and guide soldiers of Gen. George Patton's Seventh Army ashore on the southern coast.

Five men of the COPP were lost at sea. Four others were captured by the Germans. Two got lost and had to paddle 80 miles to the island of Malta. No Americans of the NDUs were lost.

See also BUCKLEW, PHILIP H.; COMBINED OPERATIONS PILOTAGE PARTIES (COPP); NAVAL COMBAT DEMOLITION UNITS (NCDU); NAVAL DEMOLITION UNITS (NDU); TARAWA; UNDERWATER DEMOLITION TEAMS (UDTS).

Operation Iron Eagle

Operation Iron Eagle was the code name for the criminal investigation of SEAL Richard Marcinko, who commanded controversial SEAL Team Six and the Red Cell.

See also MARCINKO, RICHARD; "RED CELL"; SEAL TEAM SIX.

Operation Jackstay

U.S. forces in Vietnam in early 1966 were still trying to learn how to fight a guerrilla war in a challenging terrain of tidal rivers, mangrove swamps, and jungles. Operation Jackstay, which began on March 26, 1966, and ended on April 7, was the SEALs' first amphibious operation in Vietnam. They conducted it in conjunction with Underwater Demolition Team 11 and the Fifth Marine Regiment.

In preparation for a marine landing, swimmers of UDT-11 were put ashore from the APD USS *Weiss* at 0330 on March 26 to reconnoiter beaches on the southern tip of Long Thanh Peninsula, a point in the Rung Sat Zone that jutted out into the waters of the South China Sea. The marines' quarry were Viet Cong forces operating against shipping near the mouth of the Saigon River.

"It was a horrible experience," recalls UDT-11's commander, Lt. Norman Olson. "We got put in—you've got to understand the UDTs had no SEAL training whatsoever. The SEALs had had small arms training and did all this land warfare stuff. The UDTs by and large didn't do that. . . . That was a very ill-conceived operation. . . . [O]ur whole team could have been wiped out. We weren't trained for that."

U.S. Marines went ashore at 0715. At the same time, SEALs from Detachment Golf and Force Reconnaissance marines moved into the denseness of the Rung Sat jungles to set up surveillance points. SEALs reported VC moving so close to their positions they could hear them breathing. The first enemy casualties were four VC who stumbled onto American SEALs and were ambushed.

During the two weeks that followed, SEALs, UDT frogmen and marines routed the VC from the area and destroyed a considerable number of bunkers and amounts of munitions. In spite of Lieutenant Olson's misgivings at the beginning of the operation, neither the SEALs nor UDT suffered any casualties. Jackstay was hailed as a success.

See also GOLF DETACHMENT; RUNG SAT SPECIAL ZONE.

Operation Just Cause

American special operations forces, recently consolidated under the U.S. Special Operations Command, played a major role in Operation Just Cause, the successful U.S. effort in 1989 to unseat Panamanian dictator Manuel Antonio Noriega and bring him to justice in the United States on charges of money laundering and drug trafficking. Of 27,000 American troops eventually committed to the effort, 4,150 were a combination of SpecOp forces—U.S. Army Rangers and Special Forces, the antiterrorist Delta Force, and the U.S. Navy SEALs. SEALs were tasked with two major missions, one of which was the ill-fated assault on the Paitilla airfield that resulted in

American Special Operations forces played a major role in the successful U.S. effort to unseat Panamanian dictator Manuel Antonio Noriega in 1989. Four SEALs were killed in the operation to bring Noriega to justice in the United States on drug charges. Here, Noriega is shown boarding an aircraft for the United States following his capture. (Department of Defense).

the most SEALs ever lost in a single engagement in the nearly three decades of their existence.

Planning for the invasion, under the code name Operation Blue Spoon, actually began more than a year previously, on a contingency basis, because of the increasing tension between the United States and Noriega. As commander of the Panamanian Defense Forces (PDF), he had been the de facto ruler of Panama since 1981. He was indicted in absentia by a U.S. federal court in February 1988 on charges of drug trafficking and money laundering but continued in power in Panama. On May 7, 1989, he overturned by force the results of a democratic election to remain in control. On December 15, Panama's National People's Assembly, most of whose members were handpicked Noriega appointees, named him "maximum leader" and officially installed him as head of the government. That same meeting declared that a state of war existed between Panama and the United States.

The next night, December 16, Panamanian troops shot and killed U.S. Marine lieutenant Robert Paz, who had gotten lost driving with other officers to a local restaurant. Another American officer and his wife, who witnessed the shooting, were arrested, beaten, and brutalized.

According to treaties signed in 1979, the United States had the right to defend the Panama Canal against outside threats. President George Bush ordered that Operation Blue Spoon be converted into action as Operation Just Cause. He designed three goals: the quick neutralization or removal of military resistance, the capture of Manuel Noriega, and the installation of a stable, democratically elected government. Gen. Colin Powell, chairman of the Joint Chiefs of Staff, and his director of operations, Gen. Thomas Kelley, proposed to accomplish these goals by applying such overwhelming force so swiftly and at so many locations simultaneously that Noriega and his followers would be removed and his 23,000-man PDF and "Dignity Battalions" neutralized without causing grave damage to Panama or its largely friendly population.

Twenty-seven targets were scheduled to be hit at H-hour, 1:00 A.M., on December 20, 1989. It would be the largest airborne operation since World War II. Special operations forces would pave the way. Army Rangers would parachute onto military airfields to seize them; Green Berets would form blocking forces; Delta would rescue an imprisoned American citizen, Kurt Frederick Muse, from the Modelo Prison and then seek to capture Noriega in Panama City. SEALs were assigned to put out of action the 65-foot PDF patrol boat *Presidente Porras,* which Noriega might use in an escape attempt. Their other major mission was to disable Noriega's Learjet at the Paitilla airfield to prevent the dictator's escape by that method.

SEAL Team Two drew the *Presidente Porras.* Cdr. Norm Carley, skipper of Team Two, was in charge of Task Unit Whiskey, a contingent of 21 SEALs selected for the missions. At 2300 on December 19, two night-black "rubber duck" CRRCs (combat rubber raiding craft) set out from Rodman Naval Station, site of a permanent SEAL base on the western side of the canal at Panama City. It was only a mile across the canal to Pier 18, the main pier jutting into Balboa Harbor, to which the *Presidente Porras* was tied.

In the first CRRC were Commander Carley, Lt. Edward Coughlin, Petty Officer Tim Eppley, boat coxswain George Riley, and machine gunner Chris Kinney. There were also five men in the second rubber boat: Petty Officer Randy Beausoleil, Petty Officer Chris Dye, coxswain Scott Neudecker, communications specialist Mark Dodd, and automatic weapons man Pat Malone.

Ashore at the Rodman facility but still within range of the objective, a fire support team manned .50-caliber heavy machine guns, automatic grenade launchers, and 60 mm mortars, all preregistered on likely targets around Pier 18 and equipped with night sights.

Two PBRs (Patrol Boat, River) would remain afloat on the canal with the task unit's remaining SEALs, ready to retrieve the SEAL saboteurs afterward or to intervene should the vulnerable "rubber ducks" be attacked.

At the last moment, kickoff time was moved up to 11:00 P.M. from 11:30 P.M. Using 35 hp motors, the two CRRCs and their crews quietly zigzagged across the canal to a mangrove swamp just north of Pier 18. The motor on one of the boats malfunctioned en route, and the boat had to be towed the rest of the way. The high-performance outboard engines were simply not designed to run at such slow speeds. Although the SEALs had brought along a spare motor, Carley elected not to replace the engine because of the noise it would cause.

The ten SEALs sat silently hidden in the dark swamp while mosquitoes feasted on their blood, waiting for H-hour. They received word that the entire operation had been moved up from 1:00 A.M. to 12:45 A.M. because of a security leak. However, it was too late to readjust the timers on the explosives contained in the 20-pound Hagensen Packs. They were already set to go off at 1:00 A.M., and 1:00 A.M. was when they would go off.

At shortly before midnight, Commander Carley motored the first dive team, Eppley and Dye, to within about 150 yards of Pier 18. The swimmers slipped from the rubber boat into the water with their Hagensen Packs. Using Draeger rebreather systems, which emitted no bubbles, they swam about 20 feet beneath the oily surface of the bay as they made their way by compass board to the pier.

In the meantime, Carley went back for the second pair, Coughlin and Beausoleil. Once he had returned with them and eased them into the water, he towed the other disabled boat back to Rodman. The underwater saboteurs would be retrieved by PBRs underneath the Bridge of the Americas.

The *President Porras* was tied up perpendicular to a floating concrete dock between boats of the Panama Canal Control Commission. The two swimmer-team pairs, about five minutes apart, swam to the pier and surfaced beneath it. They worked their way through the pilings to the other side, where they once again submerged. Each team did a "shallow-water peek," coming almost to the surface in order to identify the target, then going under again when it was positively identified.

The war began before the swimmers accomplished their mission. General Noriega had somehow ascertained that the Americans were preparing to attack him. His troops were alert and jumpy all over Panama. In Balboa Harbor, boats cranked up their engines in hopes that spinning props would discourage frogmen. Grenades were dropped into the water to explode. An American unit became engaged in a firefight with Panamanians on the shore near the pier.

Undeterred, the SEAL swimmers attached their explosives to the hull of the *Porras* using their Mark 138 Mod 1 Hagensen Packs, each containing a total of 20 pounds of C-4 explosives, equipped with Mark 39 arming devices and Mark 96 detonators. It took each team less than two minutes to rig its charge. The first team departed the target at 12:13 A.M, the second at 12:17. The timers were set for 0100.

By the time the explosives went off, the swimmers were far enough away to be safe, but they were still shaken by the powerful blast. Both 1,020 hp diesel engines from the *Presidente Porras* were hurled completely out of the craft. Even as battles erupted throughout the capital and surrounding suburbs, PBRs fished the teams out of the water and returned them unharmed to the Rodman Naval Station.

At the same time that Team Two was engaged in taking out Noriega's patrol boat, SEAL Team Four, led by Cdr. Tom McGrath, was concentrating on the Paitilla airfield. McGrath was the same officer who had been involved in Operation Thunderhead, the ill-fated attempt to rescue prisoners of war from Vietnam nearly two decades earlier. He would remain offshore with a seven-man command and control unit during the operation; he chose Lt. Cdr. Pat Tuohy to lead the assault force ashore. Tuoy, a former enlisted man, also had a disastrous past with the SEALs; he had been involved in the fatal parachute drop made during Operation Urgent Fury against Grenada in 1983.

Punta Paitilla Airport was a private facility with an airstrip that ended at the very shore of Panama Bay. It was known that Noriega kept a personal Learjet hangared there, and it was believed that he might attempt to reach it in order to flee once the operation began. Three SEAL Team Four platoons—Golf, Bravo, and Delta, approximately 50 men—would make a landing to put the jet out of commission. Originally, the plan called for the SEALs to move up to the hangar and use night-vision scopes on rifles to disable the plane's nose gear and fuel tanks. New orders required them actually to enter the hangar and slash the airplane's tires. "That was a major change in the rules of engagement," one SEAL commented.

That change, plus the Ranger-type landing, whereas SEALs were accustomed to working in small units and using stealthy movements, would later be considered major contributors to that night's tragedy.

U.S. Navy patrol boats dropped 16 CRRCs loaded with the SEAL assault force into Panama Harbor about a mile offshore from the airfield. With the SEALs were two air force combat air controllers, whose job was to communicate with an AC-130 gunship orbiting overhead as instant air cover.

The rubber boat armada, led by Lieutenant Commander Tuohy, moved in close offshore and anchored near the dimly lighted seaward end of the runway. As swimmer scouts eased over the side of one boat to reconnoiter, Tuohy received word that H-hour had moved up from 1:00 A.M. to 12:45. A sense of increased urgency ensued, heightened by further news that a Panamanian helicopter had just taken off from Colon, 35 miles away, and that in it might be Noriega heading for Paitilla and his Learjet.

The SEALs landed at the end of the runway. The hangar was at the other end, about 1,200 to 1,400 yards away. Golf Platoon broke into two squads, code-named Golf One and Golf Two, and took the point. Golf One, commanded by Lt. Tom Casey, took the right flank; Golf Two and its commander, Lt. (j.g.) Mike Phillips, took the left flank. Approximately 200 yards behind Golf followed Bravo and Delta Platoons. Bravo took the left rear flank, while Delta moved up on the right.

The night was dark enough to provide some concealment. However, Golf was only about a quarter of the way up the runway when war erupted. Tracers began arcing and sailing all over the city. The SEALs felt terribly exposed. Their chances of achieving surprise had been lost.

They glimpsed men running toward the hangar. Through night-vision scopes, they saw a number of other armed men hiding behind barrels and heavy metal doors inside the hangar, only about 30 yards away now. Panamanian security forces triggered the deadly ambush before the lead Golf squad had time to react and seek cover.

Lieutenant Casey's Golf One took the brunt of the initial fire. His entire command of nine men was mowed down around him. Only Casey himself, miraculously, remained unscathed. The cries of the wounded blended into the hellish rattle of automatic weapons fire.

Chief Petty Officer Donald L. McFaul, 32, one of the most experienced men in the platoon, had been hit in the head and killed. Petty Officer Christopher Tilghman, 30, was already dead on the tarmac, lying among the wounded.

Lieutenant Phillips of Golf Two shifted the aim of his squad to provide a curtain of fire in front of Golf

One. Standard tactics called for the SEALs to pull back, carrying their wounded and dead. However, Casey was the only man still on his feet. He couldn't drag back eight men alone.

Phillips sent two men scurrying across the tarmac to help in the withdrawal. They and Lieutenant Casey began dragging the dead and wounded toward the rear. Golf Two SEALs, lying prone on the concrete, poured withering fire into the hangar.

"Grenades!" Phillips shouted, meaning the 40 mm projectiles fired from M203 grenade launchers attached to M-16 rifles. The hangar filled with exploding blossoms of flame from a rainstorm of the lethal little missiles.

In the midst of the firefight, Lt. (j.g.) John Patrick Connors, 25, led his Bravo Platoon squad storming up the runway and took up a position between the two Golf squads. Connors and another of his men were hit, but not badly. They returned fire with 40 mm grenades. Then, as Connors raised up to fire, he took an AK-47 round and was killed instantly.

At least three SEALs now lay dead in the carnage. The rest of the SEALs moved up and formed a perimeter around the dead and wounded. The firefight lasted a furious 15 minutes before the PDF forces inside the hangar, approximately 20 soldiers, pulled out, dragging their own casualties. During the entire firefight, SEALs could hear their AC-130 gunship circling above them. The air force techs kept radioing for help but failed to receive a response from the bird. Somehow, their ground-to-air communications had failed. When they finally raised Howard Air Force Base, the fight was already over.

An officer listening in on satellite communications back at Fort Bragg, North Carolina, was amazed at how calm Lieutenant Commander Tuohy sounded as he talked to an army general circling overhead. "I could hear everything Pat Tuohy said. I could hear he said he had two KIA, [killed in action] three KIA. Seven WIA [wounded in action]. Need a helicopter. Just as calm as he could be. The general asked if he wanted to withdraw over the beach to the water. He said, 'Sir, my orders were to seize the airfield and hold it until relieved and those remain my intentions, over.' Just as calm. . . . [W]hat I heard in those radio transmissions bespoke a very brave man."

One hour and twenty minutes passed after the shooting stopped before army medevac choppers, held on the ground because of the heavy air traffic, arrived from nearby Howard Air Force Base to pick up the SEAL dead and wounded. By that time, a fourth SEAL, Second Class Petty Officer Isaac Rodriguez III, 24, had bled to death. Eight were wounded. SEALs had suffered the first official casualties of Operation Just Cause. The surviving SEALs held the airfield for another 37 hours until relieved by Army Rangers.

Elsewhere in the city, other SEAL teams, including SEAL Team Six, carried out several small, specialized actions, none of which compared to those against the Paitilla airfield and against *Presidente Porras*. In proportion to their numbers, Special Operations suffered the heaviest casualties of the operation—eleven killed and 129 wounded of a total American casualty number of 23 KIAs and 255 wounded.

All objectives of Operation Just Cause were attained, including the capture of Manuel Antonio Noriega. He sought refuge at the Vatican embassy in Panama City during the night of fighting but finally surrendered to American forces on January 3, 1990. He was convicted of charges against him and is presently incarcerated in a federal prison in the United States.

See also OPERATION BLUE SPOON.

Operation Market Time

Operation Market Time was the code name assigned to Vietnam War operations designed to prevent enemy seaborne infiltration into South Vietnam.

See also RIVERINE WARFARE.

Operation Overlord

Operation Overlord was the code name assigned to the invasion of Normandy on June 6, 1944, in which Allies began the drive for the final defeat of Nazi Germany. Naval combat demolition units cleared the way for the landings and suffered the greatest percentage of casualties of any unit participating in the invasion.

See also AMPHIBIOUS SCOUTS AND RAIDERS; BEACH CLEARANCE; BELGIAN GATES; BUCKLEW, PHILIP H.; D-DAY; HAGENSEN PACK; KAUFFMAN, DRAPER L.; NAVAL COMBAT DEMOLITION UNITS (NCDUS); OMAHA BEACH.

Operation Plan 34A (OP-34A)

During the beginning stages of the Vietnam War, U.S. Navy SEALs participated in covert activities against North Vietnam. Those activities were given the top-secret code name "OP-34A."

See also CHINA BEACH; GULF OF TONKIN RESOLUTION; MACV-SOG.

operation planning

"Operation planning" or, more commonly, "mission planning," refers to planning conducted by SEALs in preparation for a mission.

See also MISSION PLANNING.

Operation Restore Hope

Somalia, the easternmost country on the mainland of Africa, was in 1993 the site of the bloodiest and fiercest firefight in which U.S. forces had been involved since the end of the Vietnam War.

Plagued by famine, disease, and war, the country had been under brutal military rule since 1969. When the current dictator, Gen. Mohammed Siad Barre, was ousted in January 1991, the nation fell into civil war. Two warlords, Mohammed Farah Aidid and Mohammed Ali Mahdi, battled for control of Mogadishu, the capital. Famine swept the land. Thousands died from hunger and violence.

On August 22, 1993, the United States directed the deployment of a joint special operations task force (JSOTF) to Somalia to support U.S. efforts at peacemaking. That was the beginning of Operation Restore Hope. More than 28,000 American troops were promised to help the United Nations provide food and stability to the nation. By this time, Aidid controlled most of Mogadishu and was a central contributor to the continuing civil war. One of the goals of Restore Hope was to capture Aidid.

By August 28, JSOTF, referred to as Task Force (TF) Ranger, had set up headquarters at the Mogadishu International Airport. TF Ranger was made up of special operations groups from the 75th Army Rangers, special operations Blackhawk helicopters, Army Special Forces, Delta Force, Air Force special tactics personnel, and a squad of SEALs from Team Six.

During August and September 1993, task force personnel conducted six missions into the capital to capture Aidid. He escaped each time and remained at large. His ragtag guerrilla troops in the city, growing increasingly bolder and more aggressive, took to sniping at American troops.

On October 3, 1993, at 3:32 P.M., TF Ranger launched its seventh mission to capture either Aidid or his lieutenants, this one directly into his stronghold. The assault force consisted of about 160 men, three surveillance birds, a spy plane, 19 other aircraft, and twelve vehicles, including three five-ton trucks and nine wide-bodied combat Humvees.

Helicopters airlifted a Ranger assault force, the mission of which was to "fast rope" onto the target—a former hotel in the downtown area—and capture Aidid or his officers, who were supposed to be inside the hotel. The ground convoy moved out three minutes later with trucks to haul back the prisoners and assault force. Heavily armed Humvees provided fire support for the convoy. With the convoy were four Team Six SEALs, led by Chief Signalman John Gay.

As they entered the city the raiders came under heavy fire, more intense than during previous missions. Gay, who was riding the left rear seat of the third Humvee in the convoy, heard a shot. The round pounded him hard on his right hip. Incredibly, his Randall knife had deflected the bullet; medics dug several bloody knife fragments out of Gay's hip and quickly bandaged him.

In the meantime, the helicopter assault force had reached its objective at the hotel and captured 24 Somali "Sammies" of Aidid's leadership cadre. Rangers were involved in fierce street fighting by the time the convoy arrived. Hundreds of Aidid's men poured rifle and automatic fire down from rooftops and out of alleys.

The convoy loaded the prisoners and Rangers into the trucks and was starting back to the airport when Somalis shot down an MH-60 Blackhawk with a rocket-propelled grenade (RPG). The chopper crashed three blocks away.

One six-man element from the convoy fought its way to the downed Blackhawk and set up security while an MH-6 assault helicopter and a 15-man combat search and rescue (CSAR) team evacuated the Blackhawk survivors. The CSAR bird was itself hit, but the pilot managed to nurse it safely back to the airport.

The situation worsened. Ground fire struck two more MH-60s, bringing one of them down. A Somali mob overran the site and killed everyone except the pilot, whom the Somalis took prisoner. The second Blackhawk, although hit broadside by an RPG, made it to a safe area of the city before it crash-landed.

The ground convoy, its trucks full of detainees and Rangers, attempted to reach the crash site but became lost among the narrow, winding alleyways. Withering small-arms fire inflicted a number of casualties on the Rangers before the convoy gave up the attempt and began fighting its way back toward the airport.

It met a second rescue convoy on its way out; The two convoys merged to fight their way back to safety. Chief Gay's Humvee led the retreat. By this time the vehicle was riddled with bullets, emitting smoke, rapidly losing power, and running on three rims. The interior was smeared and splattered with blood. It contained Gay, himself wounded, eight wounded Army Rangers, and one dead Ranger. Another wounded Ranger rode the hood; there simply was not room inside for him. The battered convoy reached the airfield around 6:00 P.M.

A quick-reaction force from the U.S. 10th Mountain Division, supported by helicopter gunships, penetrated the city to reinforce and bring relief to pinned-down air crewmen and blocking forces. This reaction force soon found itself also pinned down.

A second quick-reaction force, consisting of Rangers, 10th Mountain Division soldiers, and Malaysian armored personnel carriers finally reached the battle sites at 1:55 A.M. on October 4. Casualties were loaded onto the armored personnel carriers, which also provided rolling cover as the entire force withdrew.

The main force reached safety at 6:30 A.M..

A total of 16 Americans were killed and 83 wounded in Mogadishu on October 3 and 4. Somali casualties were estimated to be well over 1,000. In one of the most disturbing scenes of the episode, which appeared internationally on TV and in other media, a Somali mob dragged by a rope through the streets the mangled and mutilated body of an American Blackhawk airman.

On December 8, 1993, U.S. Navy SEALs and U.S. Marine Force Recon teams conducted the initial reconnaissance for a marine landing at Mogadishu. TV cameras were on the beach to record one of the most widely publicized "assaults" in history. The event was unopposed.

The United States eventually withdrew from Somalia, after suffering one more dead American and 17 more wounded, having achieved only limited, if any, success. Aidid was never captured.

Operation Thunderhead

"Thunderhead" was the code name given to a "Bright Light" mission to rescue American prisoners from the infamous Hoa Lo prison (also known as the Hanoi Hilton) in Hanoi, North Vietnam. SEALs used in it a SEAL delivery vehicle for the first time in a combat situation. The operation was the most highly classified POW effort of the Vietnam War.

In late 1971, the American escape committee at the Hanoi Hilton devised a "mole plan" by which POWs proposed to tunnel from the Hilton to the Red River, then float down the river to the Gulf of Tonkin, where they would be picked up by U.S. search and rescue helicopters. They managed to smuggle details of the plan out of the prison through coded communication with high-flying U.S. spy aircraft. Secretary of Defense Melvin Laird gave his approval to the plan in January 1972 but stipulated that the tunneling had to be dropped. The POWs would have to escape to the river by another route. That could be done, came the reply from the prison, again using signals to communicate.

Two men intended to make the escape attempt—Airmen John Dramesi and James Kasler. They would break out of the prison when the Red River reached flood stage in early spring, steal a boat, and float it down the river to the Gulf of Tonkin. If they were unable to get a boat, they would simply use driftwood.

"We secured lots of supplies," Kasler later explained. "We made Vietnamese costumes and even the style of hats they wore. We saved bread and rice for food and stole anything else we could use. The Vietnamese were careless about leaving stuff lying around."

"We used lime mixed with the heavy toilet paper to form a cardboard-like material," Damesi added. "We hid our supplies in the holes in the ceilings and covered them with this stuff. We then used charcoal to blend the cardboard into the color of the walls. We had a ladder, mirrors and other supplies. I even had a key to the cell door hidden in the ceiling."

On May 4, 1972, SR-71 aircraft flying high over Hanoi produced a pair of sonic booms, a pre-arranged signal to the Hanoi Hilton that all was ready to support the escape. Operation Thunderhead had begun. Navy men would be waiting at the mouth of the Red River from June 1 to 15 to rescue the escaping prisoners.

The cruiser USS *Long Beach,* in international waters in the Gulf of Tonkin, acted as the command post for the operation. Thunderhead planners designated a small island called "Point Delta" at the mouth of the Red River as the main rendezvous point. U.S. SEALs would be deposited on the island to look for the POWs and recover them. Daily reconnaissance flights would keep a sharp lookout for the red and yellow flag that the fleeing POWs would use as a signal that they were on their way.

The first problem occurred on the night of June 4. The submarine USS *Grayback* launched a 19-foot SDV containing four SEALs from SEAL Team One—Lt. Melvin S. Dry, Lt. (j.g.) John C. Lutz, Fireman Tom Edwards, and Warrant Officer P. L. Martin. Dry and Martin were to be delivered to the island to hide and watch for the POWs while Lutz and Edwards returned with the SDV to the submarine. This was the first SDV to have gone into service with the U.S. Navy.

The river current was so strong the men could make little headway. The vehicle's batteries died halfway to the island, and the SEALs found themselves adrift in the open ocean. A search and rescue helicopter plucked them out of the brine the next morning. The SDV was sunk to prevent its falling into enemy hands.

The following night, June 5, the helicopter from the cruiser *Long Beach* that had picked the SEALs out of the ocean airlifted them to a rendezvous with the *Grayback.* They were to "helo-cast" into the water, then dive down to the submarine for entry.

The SEALs stepped out of the chopper doors into the darkness. Lieutenant Dry struck a heavy floating piece of debris that crushed his throat, killing him instantly. Lutz, Martin, and Edwards followed him

out quickly, in that order, unaware of what had happened to him. Edwards suffered a broken rib because the helicopter was hovering too high. The other two SEALs were uninjured.

To complicate matters even further, the USS *Grayback* radioed an urgent message at almost the same time the SEALs were bailing out of the chopper into the sea: "Do not deliver my package. I say again, do not deliver my package." An NVA patrol boat was approaching; the submarine had to move. It was already too late for the SEALs, who were already in the water. One of them was dead, and one was injured. They remained in the water until they were rescued by a helicopter at dawn.

Thunderhead operations continued until June 15, when they were called off. It was later learned that the POWs had called off the escape attempt themselves, because it was too risky and could cause NVA retaliation against the remaining POWs.

See also ADVANCED SEAL DELIVERY SYSTEM (ASDS); "BRIGHT LIGHT"; DRY, MELVIN S.; USS *GRAYBACK.*

Operation Torch

Amphibious Scouts and Raiders, direct ancestors of the U.S. Navy SEALs, participated in their first combat mission during Operation Torch, the Allied landing in North Africa in 1942.

See also AMPHIBIOUS SCOUTS AND RAIDERS.

Operation Urgent Fury

The U.S. invasion in 1983 of the tiny Caribbean island of Grenada, Operation Urgent Fury, ended four years of Marxist control. It was the first time since before World War II that an avowed communist government was replaced by a pro-Western one. The action resulted in the deaths of four SEALs, the first combat deaths of SEALs since the Vietnam War.

Grenada, in the southeastern Caribbean, is a small island of approximately 133 square miles with a population of about 110,000 people. It became independent from Britain in 1974. In 1979, Maurice Bishop seized power, established the leftist Provisional Revolutionary Government, and then turned to Cuba and the USSR for support. The United States became concerned, in this Cold War era, when Bishop with Cuban aid began constructing a 9,000-foot-long runway, capable of accommodating strategic bombers from the Soviet Union.

On October 13, 1983, Bernard Coard, the deputy prime minister, sized power in the name of the Provisional Revolutionary Army (PRA) and placed Bishop under house arrest. Coard wanted Grenada to convert to a communist government right away. This second coup signaled an expansion of Soviet power in the Caribbean, which had been held in check since the Cuban missile crisis.

On October 19, in the capital at St. George's, the PRA opened fire on a crowd that had forcibly freed Bishop and other members of his former government, killing over 50 people and wounding that many more. Bishop and four of his ministers and three of his supporters were taken to nearby Fort Rupert and shot. A shoot-on-sight curfew was extended to the entire island.

About 1,000 Americans currently lived on the island, of whom some 600 were students at St. George's University Medical School. The U.S. State Department held an emergency meeting. On October 14, the National Security Council ordered the Joint Chiefs of Staff to prepare for a military rescue of U.S. citizens on the island. President Ronald Reagan expanded the mission to taking over the island and rescuing Grenada's former governor general, Sir Paul Scoon, who was being held under house arrest by the new regime. Joint Task Force 120 was assembled, and Vice Adm. Joseph Metcalf was placed in command of what was code-named Operation Urgent Fury. The operation was to be carried out in complete secrecy, no press notified.

It was to be the most massive American invasion since the Inchon landing of the Korean War, involving 13 ships, hundreds of fixed-winged aircraft and helicopters, and more than 7,000 men. Overall command fell to the navy. Elements of the invasion force consisted of parts of SEAL Teams Four and Six; U.S. Army's Delta Force; the First and Second Ranger Battalions; the 82d Airborne Division; the First Special Operations Wing of the Air Force; and the 22d Marine Amphibious Unit (MAU). All four services would be operating together for the first time since the Vietnam War.

The general plan called for the marines to make an amphibious landing to take the northern half of the island, while Rangers and elements of the 82d Airborne secured the southern half by parachuting onto the airfield at Point Salines, at the island's southern tip. SEALs were tapped to perform four crucial missions:

1. The first of these was the Salines airfield mission. Operators from SEAL Teams Four and Six and a team of four Air Force combat control team (CTT) members were tasked to pave the way for the airdrop on Salines, going in on the night of October 23, 1983. The invasion would launch in the early hours of October 25.
2. SEAL Team Four would provide SEALs to reconnaissance the marines' proposed beach landing site, near Pearls Airport on the northern end of the island.
3. SEALs of SEAL Team Four were assigned to capture the Beauséjour radio station at St. George's on the night of 24/25 October in conjunction with the invasion and to keep the station off the air until U.S. forces took over.
4. SEAL Team Six would assault Government House, near St. George's, and rescue Governor General Sir Paul Scoon from house arrest.

During the late afternoon of October 23, 12 SEALs in two C-130 aircraft were flown to a point about 40 miles northwest of Point Salines, where they were to parachute into the ocean to rendezvous with a destroyer, the USS *Caron*. The four-man Air Force CTT waited aboard the destroyer to link up with the SEALs.

The SEALs each jumped with more than 100 pounds of weapons, ammunition, and equipment. Also dropped were a pair of blunt-nosed fiberglass Boston Whaler assault boats with 175 hp outboard engines. The SEALs intended to secure their boats, motor to the destroyer, pick up the CTT, and head for the Point Salines airfield. The CTT would emplace radio beacons at the airstrip to guide in the MC-130 Combat Talon aircraft that would airdrop Rangers at dawn on October 25.

Although the parachute jump was supposed to be made at dusk, it was dark by the time the doors opened and the SEALs tailgated out of the C-130s into the night. The waters were rough and the winds high. Master Chief Engineman Johnny Walker recalls that the seas were six to eight feet and the wind was about 20 knots. He hit the water hard, losing much of his equipment, and became immediately separated from the boats and his teammates. Wind reinflated his parachute and dragged him through the water, nearly drowning him before he managed to cut free with his knife.

Other SEALs were not so lucky. Caught in the sea in a pitch-black night, four of the twelve jumpers simply vanished and became the first casualties of the operation. They were Machinist's Mate First Class Kenneth John Butcher, Quartermaster First Class Kevin Lundberg, Hull Technician First Class Stephen Leroy Morris, and Senior Chief Engineman Robert Rudolph Schamberger. One of the boats was also lost.

The survivors ultimately found the remaining Whaler and regrouped on the destroyer. They assembled with the Air Force CTT and attempted to complete their mission that same night. Bad fortune continued to plague them. En route to the island, they spotted a Grenadian patrol boat approaching and cut power. Overloaded, the boat was swamped with seawater. The motor refused to start again. The boat drifted out to sea on a strong outboard tide. The SEALs and Air Force techs were rescued several hours later.

The next night, October 24, now over 24 hours behind schedule, the SEALs and CTTs made another attempt to infiltrate Point Salines. On the final run into the beach, the boat swamped and capsized. The airmen lost all their radio beacon equipment in the surf. The mission had failed. The small force once again swept out to sea, to be rescued a second time. The Rangers would have to make their combat jumps unassisted by beacons.

In the meantime, that same Monday night (October 24), at 2200 (10:00 P.M.), the 22d Marine Amphibious Unit sent in a SEAL element led by Lt. Michael Walsh to scout invasion beaches for the marine landing on the island's northern end. The SEALs used raiding boats to carry them close to shore, then switched to inflatable rubber boats for the landing. They beached in a driving rainstorm after conducting a hydrographic survey of offshore waters. They found themselves, undetected, within listening distance of a Grenadian work party digging defense emplacements.

By 0200, the SEAL team had completed its mission and radioed back to waiting marines that reefs offshore made the landing site unapproachable except by very shallow-draft vessels. Admiral Metcalf changed his plans. Instead of making an amphibious assault, the marines would be helicoptered onto Grenada and landed at Pearls Airport and at nearby Grenville.

Marines began choppering ashore at 0520, Tuesday, October 25, in coordination with Rangers paradropping onto Point Salines in the south. Parachutes were still in the sky over the unfinished airfield, gunfire spattering from Grenadian and Cuban forces, when an eight-man SEAL unit from Team Four landed in a rubber boat north of the airport. It quickly made its way toward the Beauséjour radio station. Radio Free Grenada was a 75,000-watt transmitter built from Soviet-supplied equipment and capable of blanketing a large area of the Caribbean. It lay less than a mile from the sea, on a hill overlooking St. George's below.

The element of surprise had already been lost. The radio station was in full operation, broadcasting an appeal to resist the American invasion, when the SEALs captured it and a handful of Grenadian soldiers. Hearing the station go off the air and surmising the reason, a unit of the Grenadian army hurried to investigate.

Lt. Donald K. Erskine, commander of the radio mission element, dispatched a SEAL security team to the road leading past the radio station, on either side. The team north of the station, armed with an M60 machine gun and a light antitank weapon, ambushed a truck heading south filled with PRA militia, killing five, wounding several others, and scattering the remainder into the bush.

A reaction force led by a Soviet-built BTR-60 armored personnel carrier roared up from Fort Frederick to retake the station. A SEAL sent a rocket into the BTR's turret, disabling the gun. Four of the SEALs, including Lieutenant Erskine, were wounded in the action, none of them with injuries that were immediately life threatening.

Seeing that defending the station was hopeless, the SEALs destroyed the transmitter and made a dash for the sea. They hid out in the bush until after dark that night, then swam out toward the invasion fleet and turned on strobe lights. Helicopters quickly arrived to hoist them to safety.

SEAL Team Six, under Cdr. Robert Gormly, had been selected for the primary SEAL mission—the rescue of Governor General Scoon and his staff from house arrest at Government House, on the outskirts of St. George's. This mission too had its foul-ups.

Two "Night Stalker" Black Hawk helicopters were supposed to deliver the 23-man SEAL force to Government House, one landing in the backyard and the other in the front. Because of an overall delay, it was nearly daylight when the two choppers took off on the rescue mission. When they arrived at the house, they discovered trees growing on the mansion's lawns; they could not land. Grenadians around the house compound opened a withering fire on the helicopters.

The chopper at the rear of the house was hardest hit. Thirteen of the SEALs in it nonetheless managed to fast-rope to the lawn. Commander Gormly was unable to get out of the helicopter. The SEALs also left their damaged radio, which meant they had no communications with their tactical operations center.

SEALs in the second helicopter, unable to get out, returned to the fleet for further assignment. That left the rescue up to thirteen SEALs, with Lt. John Koenig in charge. They fought their way across the lawn and into the mansion, where they found Scoon, his wife, and nine staff members hiding in the basement. Koenig set up defensive perimeters both inside the house and on the grounds outside. The plan had called for Scoon and his staff to be freed and taken to helicopters waiting outside to be flown to safety. The inability of the choppers to land, however, called for an alternative plan.

Koenig and his SEALs prepared to hold out against overwhelming odds until another rescue helicopter or the marines arrived. The loss of their radio had put them out of touch with the rest of the invasion force. Surrounded by enemy plinking rounds at them, they could do nothing except hold on and wait. The siege continued throughout the day, with intermittent attacks by Grenadian forces. One of the SEALs, a sniper, picked off a number of enemy by moving from window to window upstairs. Fortunately, the mansion was located on a hilltop, which provided the SEALs excellent fields of fire across the lawn.

The PRA commander called up three APCs and ordered an attack on the mansion. SEAL lieutenant Bill Davis discovered to his surprise that the phone system was still in operating condition. He dialed the airfield at Salines, where American Airborne and Rangers were already in control, and asked for gunship protection. Two Sea Cobras responded to the summons for help. Both were shot down by antiaircraft emplacements from Cuban military headquarters at Fort Frederick. Three Marines died. An AC-130 Spectre gunship, with 20 mm Vulcan cannon and machine guns, then took to the sky to watch over the SEALs. Its massive firepower destroyed one APC and stopped the attack. It circled over Government House for the rest of the day and throughout the night, out of range of ground fire, but prepared to stop any further movements against the SEALs.

Lieutenant Bobby McNabb recalls an incident during the night. "The only night shoot I saw," he says, "was when we called in a strike on an APC on my side. He was probably fifty to seventy-five yards away. He wasn't shooting at us. He was trying to hit the plane. You could hear the plane, kind of see it outlined up there. The plane shot the 20 mm at him. Every time one of those rounds hit, they kind of give off a spark. Well, he was hitting dead on top of the APC. The Spectre hit the APC so many times it had a hellish glow over the top of it. You could see the bodies getting blown about. Oh, man, it was brutal."

In the meantime, A-7 fighter bombers from the carrier USS *Independence* knocked out antiair defenses around St. George's and in the process also helped prevent any organized attack against the Governor's mansion. Admiral Metcalf ordered the 22d MAU's Company Golf, held in reserve, to be carried around the island and landed under cover of darkness at St. George's to relieve the SEALs.

While Golf was landing at Grand Mal Bay, Fox Company, already on the island, crossed by helicopter and landed next to Grand Mal. At 0300 on May 26, the two marine companies linked up and, reinforced with five M60A1 Abrams tanks, descended upon the governor's mansion. The PRA soldiers besieging Government House fled. The SEALs inside the house were relieved at 0712, and the governor and his staff were quickly evacuated. The SEALs had suffered no casualties during the day and night of battle.

With the arrival of the marines and tanks in St. George's, the invasion action was over, except for the mopping up. Fighting continued for several days, but most of the defenders either surrendered or fled into the mountains. SEALs in a pair of fast recon boats patrolled the water around the island, interdicting small craft that were attempting to effect the escape of officers and soldiers of the Provisional Revolutionary Army.

In mid-December, U.S. combat forces went home, and a pro-American government took power in Grenada. Official casualties for the operation were 19 Americans dead, including the four SEALs, and 123 wounded. Forty-nine Grenadians and 29 Cubans had been killed; several hundred had been wounded.

Organizational Structure, Special Operations

Naval special warfare is only one slice in a broad spectrum of special operations forces within the U.S. military. Partly by design, partly by tradition, SpecOps forces are isolated and aloof from the rest of the military and, especially, from the public.

During the cold war, because of the horror associated with a potential all-out nuclear war, the U.S. military began reorienting itself away from what is called "high-intensity combat" to "low-intensity conflict" (LIC). LIC meant conflict on a small, controlled level, conducted by teams of specialists like the Navy SEALs and the Army Green Berets.

The Goldwater-Nichols Act of 1986 restructured the military and helped redefine warfare after the bloody, embarrassing lessons of the failed Iranian hostage-rescue mission (Operation Eagle Claw) and the invasion of Grenada (Operation Urgent Fury). Under this act, in a policy known as "jointness," all special forces units within the military were integrated under a single command. Previously, each branch had operated independently, with its own missions, men, radio frequencies, logistics train, and command structure.

The new chain of command within special forces looks like this:

National Command Authority (NCA)

All military assets, including special operations, fall under the highest level of command authority, which consists of the president of the United States, secretary of defense, and under it, the chairman of the Joint Chiefs of Staff.

U.S. Special Operations Command (USSOCOM)

Headquartered at MacDill Air Force Base, Florida, USSOCOM is one of the best funded and most secure elements in the U.S. forces structure. It integrates special operations assets from all services into one organization, with a single commander and a basic set of missions. Each special forces branch contributes to the overall pool its talents and resources for planning, training, and executing missions.

Joint Special Operations Command (JSOC)

JSOC is USSOCOM's planning and coordinating cell, headquartered at Pope Air Force Base, North Carolina, contiguous to Fort Bragg. Its principal mission is to study the techniques and requirements of the various SpecOps communities to make sure all efforts are coordinated. Each branch of the military contributes its own resources, through its subordinate command.

U.S. Army Special Operations Command (USASOC)

The U.S. Army contributes to USSOCOM its Special Forces (Green Berets), a regiment of Rangers, the Delta counterterrorist unit, and a special operations aviation unit called Task Force 160 (TF 160), plus psychological civil affairs and signal units. Most are stationed at Fort Bragg, North Carolina.

Air Force Special Operations Command (AFSOC)

AFSOC, headquartered at Hulbert Field, Florida, provides special aircraft and crews to insert and extract army and navy combat elements and to support them with airpower. It owns and operates special versions of the C-130 Specter gunships, CH-53 and CH-60 Pave Hawk and Pave Low helicopters, within the First Special Operations Wing.

U.S. Navy Special Operations Command (NAVSOC)

NAVSOC contributes through its Naval Special Warfare Command its SEALs, special boat squadrons, and the U.S. Marine force reconnaissance units.

See also NAVAL SPECIAL WARFARE.

OSS Maritime Unit

One of the origins of today's SEALs can be found in the creation of the Maritime Unit by the top-secret Office of Strategic Services (OSS) during World War II. The OSS Maritime Unit was much more like modern U.S. Navy SEALs than were the underwater demolition teams of the day.

See also OFFICE OF STRATEGIC SERVICES (OSS).

oxygen poisoning

Oxygen toxicity or oxygen poisoning, the danger of breathing 100 percent oxygen under pressure, was discovered in the 1870s by French physiologist Paul Bert. He demonstrated in laboratory experiments with animals that breathing oxygen under pressure could cause poisoning of the central nervous system, convulsions, and even death.

In spite of Bert's discovery, divers remained unaware of the damage of oxygen toxicity. The seriousness of the problem became apparent during the early years of World War II, when large numbers of combat swimmers were being trained in the use of closed-circuit underwater breathing apparatus. Research on the problem continued in the U.S. Navy after the war and led to the setting of depth and time limits on divers using pure oxygen.

These limits proved operationally restrictive. The Navy Experimental Diving Unit reexamined the entire problem of oxygen poisoning in the 1980s. This led to the navy going almost exclusively to mixed-gas diving.

Modern SEALs rarely use pure oxygen in their dive training and missions, finding that mixed-gas rebreather systems are safer and more than meet their mission needs.

See also AQUA-LUNG; BOYLE'S LAW; CAISSON DISEASE; CLOSED-CIRCUIT BREATHING APPARATUS; DIVING, HISTORY OF; LAMBERTSEN, CHRISTIAN J.; MIXED-GAS BREATHING.

P

Painter, William (d. 1963)

Lt. (j.g.) William Painter was a "plankowner" of SEAL Team Two, the first SEAL team commissioned into the U.S. Navy in 1962. He was also the SEALs' first loss due to death in training or combat.

Painter was a member of a mobile training team dispatched to Turkey in 1963 to train Turkish frogmen. On May 21, during training in the Bosphorus on buoyant ascents, he donned an Aqua-Lung to go underwater with the students, the better to observe them. He surfaced from his first dive, submerged a second time, and was never seen again. His body was never recovered, although SEALs and others conducted an extensive search of the area.

Paitilla Airfield

When the United States invaded Panama in the 1989 Operation Just Cause to oust and arrest strongman Manuel Antonio Noriega, Navy SEALs were assigned two primary missions. One of these entailed disabling a Learjet at Paitilla airfield, in which Noriega might attempt an escape. Four SEALs were killed in the effort.

See also OPERATION JUST CAUSE.

Panama

In 1989, the U.S. military invaded Panama to oust and arrest the dictator Manuel Antonio Noriega. SEALs were assigned two primary missions during Operation Just Cause, resulting in the deaths of four of them at Paitilla airfield in Panama City.

See also OPERATION JUST CAUSE.

parakeet operations

Parakeet was the term SEALs applied to missions during the Vietnam War wherein they snatched and took prisoner enemy agents or important enemy officers or political cadres. The name came from the way such operations were conducted.

SEALs discovered that a single helicopter flying over Vietnam was such a common sight that it was virtually ignored. SEALs thereby began using single helicopters to disguise their intent. Working on reliable intelligence as to the location of a particular target, a squad of SEALs would load into a lone chopper, "parakeet" in suddenly on the suspect while he was sleeping or otherwise occupied, and haul him away. Parakeet operations helped build the fearsome SEAL reputation in Vietnam that no enemy, anywhere, was safe from the dreadful "men with green faces."

patrol boat, coastal (PBC)

The twelve PBC cyclone-class ships assigned to naval special warfare are the largest platforms the special boat squadrons have ever had. They are assigned to the naval special warfare groups at Coronado and Little Creek but are likely to be forward based. Coastal patrol and interdiction are their primary missions, with special operations support as a secondary mission. Working in low-intensity environments, the ships' operational missions include long-range SEAL insertions and extractions, tactical swimmer operations, intelligence gathering, operational deception, and coastal and riverine support. They normally operate in pairs for mutual support.

The PBC, with its crew of four officers and 24 enlisted personnel, and room for nine passengers (SEALs or coastal law-enforcement personnel), has an overall length of 170 feet, a 25-foot beam, a draft of 7.8 feet, and a displacement of 328 tons at full load. The hull is steel, with an aluminum superstructure. Powered by four Paxman diesels, each generating 3,350 horsepower, it reaches a maximum speed of more than 30 knots and can cruise at twelve knots on twin engines for a maximum range of 3,000 nautical miles.

It is the most heavily armed of naval special warfare craft. Armament includes a Mark 38 25 mm rapid-fire gun; a Mark 96 25 mm rapid-fire gun; a Stinger antiaircraft missile station; and four pintles to support any combination of .50-caliber machine guns, M-60 machine guns, or Mark 19 grenade launchers. It is also equipped with a chaff decoy launching system for antiship missile defense, along with a rubber boat and swimmer retrieval system.

The commander of a PBC is usually a surface warfare officer, not a SEAL.

patrol boat, river (PBR)

The patrol boat, river (PBR) was designed for high-speed riverine patrol operations and SEAL

The PBR was designed for high-speed riverine patrol operations and SEAL insertion and extraction during the Vietnam War. (U.S. Navy)

insertions and extractions during the Vietnam War. More than 500 of the boats were built after they were first introduced into the Vietnam conflict in 1966. Only a few remain in the current navy inventory.

Constructed of reinforced fiberglass with ceramic armor protecting vital crew areas, the PBR was 32 feet long with a beam of 11 feet seven inches. It weighed eight and three-quarters tons and was powered by twin 215-horsepower GM diesel engines with two Jacuzzi-type waterjet pumps for propulsion. It has a range of approximately 300 nautical miles at a full speed of 24 knots. It can operate in shallow, debris-filled water of as little as two feet in depth and is so maneuverable that it can turn 180 degrees at full power within its own length.

It has a crew of four and carries six passengers. One of the most heavily armed boats of its size, it comes with a twin-mounted .50-caliber machine gun, a stand-mounted .50-caliber and a Mark 19 40 mm grenade launcher, with options for additional .50-calibers or 40 mm grenade launchers, 60 mm mortars, or M-60 machine guns.

Its relatively quiet operation and surface search radar system make the PBR an ideal craft for shallow-water patrol and interdiction.

Lt. Roy Boehm, the *first* SEAL and first acting commander of SEAL Team Two in 1962, was assigned to the Naval Amphibious School at Coronado, California, in 1966 to build and develop a training program for the PBRs and Vietnam's first riverine operations. He had just returned from a tour in Vietnam himself as an adviser for the Lien Doc Nguoi Nhai, South Vietnamese frogmen. Not since the American Civil War had an American river force sustained river combat operations. PBR "river rats" working in Operations Game Warden and Market Time made more regular contact with the enemy than any other outfit in the war zone while suffering fewer casualties per capita.

See also OPERATION GAME WARDEN; OPERATION MARKET TIME.

Pave Hawk helicopter (CH-60G)

One of the current primary helicopters used in SEAL missions, the CH-60G Pave Hawk is a twin-engine, medium-lift helicopter operated by the Air Force Special Operations Command (AFSOC), a component of the U.S. Special Operations Command (USSOCOM). Equipped with all-weather radar that enables the crew to avoid inclement conditions, the Pave Hawk has primary wartime missions of infiltration, exfiltration, and resupply of special operations forces in day, night, or marginal weather conditions. Other missions include combat search and rescue. During Desert Storm, Pave Hawks provided emergency evacuation coverage for SEAL teams penetrating the Kuwaiti coasts before the coalition invasion.

The basic crew of the Pave Hawk is a pilot, copilot, flight engineer, and two crewmen. It is equipped with a rescue hoist with a 200-foot cable and a 600-pound lift capacity. Armament consists of two crew-served 7.62 mm miniguns mounted in the cabin windows. Two .50-caliber machine guns may also be mounted in the cabin doors. It can carry eight to ten troops in addition to the crew.

See also HELICOPTERS.

The Pave Hawk is one of the current primary helicopters used in SEAL missions. (U.S. Special Operations Command)

Persian Gulf War

The 1991 war in which the United States led a coalition of forces against Iraq, after Iraq invaded neighboring Kuwait, was known by a variety of names, among which were: the Persian War; Gulf War; Iraqi War; Desert War; "The Mother of All Battles"; War in Southwest Asia; the Persian Gulf War; and Desert Storm.

See also OPERATION DESERT STORM.

Phoenix Program

As early as 1961, Sir Robert Thompson, who served in the British embassy in Saigon, South Vietnam, declared that the guerrilla Viet Cong (VC) infrastructure should be the primary target of any counterinsurgency effort in Vietnam. The United States attempted to heed his advice. In July 1967, the Central Intelligence Agency (CIA) launched its Phoenix Program, which targeted the VC infrastructure in hopes of "neutralizing" key members and thereby strangling the communist revolution. According to William Colby, a CIA official who for a time oversaw Phoenix and later became CIA director, the program as of May 1971 had resulted in the deaths of at least 20,000 VC suspects.

SEALs participated in Phoenix primarily through the provincial reconnaissance units (PRUs) they "advised" in the Mekong Delta. The PRUs were the most effective action arm of the Phoenix Program.

"The way to make a difference was not to set ambushes in free-fire zones, but to attack the VC infrastructure," said SEAL Robert A. Gormly, who participated in Phoenix. "We were fighting an ideology. Killing young men and women who had been forced, by terrorist means, into serving their communist masters wasn't going to defeat the ideology. . . . The communist movement in the South was much like a giant lizard. Its head was the small group of dedicated communists who formed the political infrastructure. Its tail was the military force. Each time we hacked off a portion of the tail and proclaimed that we had seriously damaged the creature, the head of the lizard grew more tail. Our strategy all along should have been to go after the head. . . . Phoenix Program went after the head of the lizard."

It has to be understood that terrorism in South Vietnam was a major crime, as it was and is today in the United States and other nations. The Vietnam War was more than a war fought between opposing soldiers; it was also a law enforcement problem. Phoenix grew out of previous projects designed to attack the communist-led insurgency from a law enforcement prospective.

The forerunner of Phoenix, known as Phung Hoang among the Vietnamese, was the Intelligence Collection and Exploitation Program (ICEX), developed by the CIA in the mid-1960s with the aim of putting the Viet Cong political organization under pressure. By the time ICEX evolved into the more elaborate Phoenix Program, it was neutralizing 800 VCI every month through VC defection, prisoner snatches, and ambushes.

Although Phoenix was launched in 1967, Vietnamese cooperation remained minimal until July 1968, when South Vietnam issued a presidential decree formally directing that the network be set up. Its implementation fell under the joint directorship of MACV (Military Assistance Command Vietnam) and the CIA, working with the Vietnamese military, paramilitary, and police.

Phoenix offices were set up in Saigon, with branch offices down to provincial and district level. The overall goal of the program was to identify individuals through a census program, remove VC leadership that had infiltrated the government at all levels, and then replace these traitors with a cadre loyal to the Saigon government. It was an all-encompassing program whose tactics were designed not only to crush the Viet Cong but to intimidate communist sympathizers. Tactics relied heavily on both violence and propaganda, often intertwined to enhance the effectiveness of each.

In close cooperation with South Vietnamese police and intelligence and army units, U.S. managers of the program gathered intelligence on VC operatives, prepared "black lists" of suspects in each village or province, and then dispatched elite military units to apprehend or execute the targets.

The PRUs operated as the major enforcement arm of Phoenix. PRUs varied in size from a reinforced platoon to near battalion size. The units were made up of Vietnamese, many of whom were *chieu hoi* (VC and NVA turncoats), Montagnards, and Chinese. Armed and paid by the CIA as a mercenary army, the PRUs were indigenous military action groups led by American "advisers." While a few were advised by the U.S. Army soldiers and Marines, most advisers were Army Green Berets and Navy SEALs.

The PRUs in the Mekong Delta were the most effective of all the South Vietnamese troops. By the end of 1968, the IV Corps (Delta) area PRUs were almost entirely advised by SEAL personnel. SEAL advisers accompanied PRUs on an average of 15 Phoenix missions a month. Most of these missions involved prisoner snatches, ambushes, and intelligence gathering.

"The agency (CIA) people I worked with were interested in results," said SEAL Frank F. Thornton. "They didn't want to know what I was doing or where I was, only that I was accomplishing the mission."

Although Phoenix developed an unsavory reputation as a "band of bloodthirsty assassins" back in the United States, that was not necessarily the reality. Some PRUs did, in fact, act as assassination teams. However, the idea of eliminating the VC infrastructure was not to kill as much as it was to capture. "Dead men tell no tales." Intelligence garnered from seized individuals could be used to move up the ladder to higher-level targets. SEALs working with the PRUs developed an extensive intelligence network throughout the Delta, which helped make the Phoenix Program the best in Vietnam for eliminating the VC infrastructure.

"Primary operations was to snatch," said Thornton. "Jumping off the skids of a helicopter onto a hooch [hut] rooftop doesn't give people inside much time to react. Sneaking into a building in the middle of the night, shining a penlight into an individual's face to identify him, then silently snatching him up and extracting builds a reputation among the people left behind. It soon became known if you're a VC sympathizer or part of the chain of command, you will be found out and disappear. Almost mystical powers are attributed to men who conduct such operations among superstitious people."

Kevin Dockery described a "parakeet" mission to seize a prisoner. "Moving through an open area of rice paddies during the early evening after last light," he said, "the SEALs completed the entire operation in an hour. From a house in Phuo Khanh village, the SEALs abducted a suspected VC squad leader and liaison man. Exfiltrating quietly, the SEALs left no mark of their passage or what happened to the villager who had suddenly 'disappeared.'"

When working with PRUs, SEALs often wore the familiar "black pajama" garb of the Viet Cong. They put a lot of effort into learning to walk, move, and think like the VC. Their main objective was to blend in with the environment, to crawl about the jungle and Delta marshes as the VC did.

"We killed three regional-level officers," said SEAL Michael J. Walsh, describing a typical operation in which the objective was to kill important officials and obtain intelligence. "Two of them would be equivalent to two-star generals. The documents we captured were so sensitive we weren't even allowed to know what they contained. The stuff was flown out of the country that evening, and it went right to the Pentagon. We received a Top Secret message back that simply said, 'Thanks.'"

Although the Phoenix Program officially ended in September 1972, when *Phung Hoang* was crossed out of reports, it nonetheless continued under a new name. The Special Police Investigative Services (SPIS) targeted the VC infrastructure in the same way Phoenix had until the withdrawal of U.S. forces from Vietnam in 1975.

"I'm telling you, that worked," insisted Mike Walsh. "[Y]ou'll see that at the end of the war the Viet Cong were saying, 'What really hurt us was that Phoenix Program.'"

See also COLBY, WILLIAM EGAN; PROVINCIAL RECONNAISSANCE UNITS (PRUS).

photography
Formerly, special operations forces used conventional photography to record enemy site locations and potential targets during reconnaissance missions. Digital photography can now send nearly real-time recon data back to command authorities. A digital camera takes pictures with a photosensitive computer chip. The image is then converted into a computer file that can be loaded onto a computer and uploaded by a SATCOM (satellite communications) system to virtually anywhere in the world. SEALs use a mix of commercial digital camera gear ranging from Casio devices to high-tech Kodak/Nikon units.

Phung Hoang
Phung Hoang was the Vietnamese name for the top-secret CIA Phoenix Program, which targeted guerrilla enemy infrastructure during the Vietnam War.

See also PHOENIX PROGRAM.

"Pinlon"

"Pinlon" was the code name used by SEALs for the Havana Harbor area during the Cuban missile crisis and events leading up to it. SEALs made a number of covert reconnaissance missions into Cuba as the crisis began and played itself out.

See also CUBAN MISSILE CRISIS.

plankowners

On January 1, 1962, the first U.S. Navy SEAL team was commissioned at Little Creek, Virginia. The original members of that team were known as the "plankowners" of the U.S. Navy SEALs. These are the plankowners of the U.S. Navy SEALs:

Officers:
   Gordon Ablitt
   Roy H. Boehm
   John F. Callahan
   Joseph DiMartino
   David H. Graveson
   Tex Hager
   William Painter
   Dante M. Shapiro
   Charles C. Wiggins

Chief Petty Officers:
   James C. Andrews
   Rudolph E. Boesch
   Donald Stone

Enlisted Men:
   Harry M. Beal
   Bennie Benzschawel
   Pierre Birtz
   Wayne Boles
   Ron Brozak
   William Bruhmuller
   Charles Bump
   William E. Burbank, Sr.
   A. D. Clark
   John W. Dearmon
   George W. Doran
   James F. Finley
   Samuel R. Fournier
   Ronald G. Fox
   William H. Goines
   William T. Green
   Tom Iwaszczuk
   Stanley S. Janecka
   Charles W. Jessie
   Rex W. Johnson
   Michael D. Kelly

   Claudius H. Kratky
   Louis A. Kucinski
   James P. MacLean
   Richard D. Martin
   Frederick McCarty
   Mike McKeawn
   Melvin F. Melochick
   Tom Murphy
   Richard Nixon
   Bob Peterson
   John Ritter
   Paul T. Schwartz
   Bobby G. Stamey
   Joseph Taylor
   John D. Tegg
   James C. Tipton
   James T. Tolison
   Robert A. Tolison
   Erik Tornblom
   Jim Wallace, Jr.
   James D. Watson
   Leonard A. Waugh
   Harry R. Williams

See also BOEHM, ROY.

point man

During a combat ground movement or an underwater operation, the SEAL who takes the lead position of the element is known as the "point man." His responsibility is to keep alert for danger, obstacles, and other hazards.

Post-BUD/s training

"Tadpoles" who graduate from the Basic Underwater Demolition/SEAL course have not necessarily completed training. Most go on to post-BUD/S training in airborne operations, the Special Operations Medical Course, and other specialty schools. In fact, a SEAL is always in training as long as he remains with the teams.

See also BASIC UNDERWATER DEMOLITION/SEAL (BUD/S) TRAINING.

Pre-BUD/S School

Most candidates for SEAL training must first complete a five-day pretraining course, a pre-BUD/S school, at the Naval Special Warfare Center at Coronado, California, to help prepare them for Basic Underwater Demolition/SEAL (BUD/S) training and to eliminate candidates who are not serious about it.

See BASIC UNDERWATER DEMOLITION/SEAL (BUD/S) TRAINING.

Presidente Porras

Presidente Porras was a 65-foot patrol boat in which it was feared Gen. Manuel Antonio Noriega would attempt to escape when the United States invaded Panama in 1989. Destroying or disabling the boat was one of two primary missions assigned to the SEALs.

See also OPERATION BLUE SPOON; OPERATION JUST CAUSE.

primacord (primadet)

Both "primacord" and "primadet" are names applied to detonating cord.

See also EXPLOSIVES.

Prince

Prince was the name of one of the best-known scout dogs used by SEALs during the Vietnam War.

See also SCOUT DOGS.

Provincial Reconnaissance Units (PRUs)

Funded and advised by the U.S. Central Intelligence Agency, the Phoenix Program utilized the Provincial Reconnaissance Units (PRUs) as its major enforcement arm in its mission against the Viet Cong and its political organization, the National Liberation Front (NLF), during the Vietnam War. U.S. Navy SEALs, especially toward the end of the program, were heavily involved as "advisers" to PRU units in the Mekong Delta.

See also PHOENIX PROGRAM.

PTF (Patrol Torpedo, Fast) boat

President John F. Kennedy's 1962 mandate that gave birth to the U.S. Navy SEALs meant naval special warfare required a high-speed, shallow-draft boat that could operate in a hostile coastal environment and insert, support, and extract SEALs. As the commanding officer of the newly commissioned Naval Operations Support Group One (now Naval Special Warfare Group One), Capt. Philip H. Bucklew went looking for such a craft.

The development of the PTF began with two aged post–World War II PT boats, which were modernized and redesignated as PTFs on December 21, 1962. These two boats began SEAL support operations at Little Creek, Virginia, but never saw combat duty. Instead, the navy turned to the Norwegian Tjeld (Nasty)–class torpedo boat, purchased a fleet of fourteen, designated them as PTFs, and sent them to war in Vietnam in February 1964.

See also "NASTY" BOAT.

Quang Khe naval base

The North Vietnamese naval base at Quang Khe was one of the most urgent targets for SEALs and their South Vietnamese commandos operating out of China Beach under the top-secret OP-34A program prior to active U.S. involvement in the Vietnam War.

As early as 1961, the Central Intelligence Agency was conducting secret intelligence-gathering missions and sabotage operations against the North Vietnamese. In January 1964, the program was transferred to the Defense Department and was placed under the control of a cover organization called MACV-SOG (Military Assistance Command Vietnam—Studies and Observation Group). SEALs attached to SOG operated under the innocent name of Naval Advisory Detachment but were actually SOG operatives under OP-34A. Their major role was the training of South Vietnamese commando forces to be inserted into North Vietnam by boat and parachute on intelligence-gathering and sabotage missions.

Using Nasty and Swift boats, SEALs and their Vietnamese commandos began increasing their raids along the coast. They also turned to offshore bombardment, as well as clandestine commando inser-

tions. At the same time, Gen. William C. Westmoreland, commander of MACV, brought U.S. coastal patrols closer to shore in order to provide cover and communications assets to SEAL OP-34A missions; the patrols moved from 20 miles offshore to within four miles of the North Vietnam coast. Operation Desoto was the code name given to the special U.S. Navy patrols designed to eavesdrop on enemy shore-based communications. Destroyers outfitted with sensitive electronic interception equipment were used.

The Quang Khe naval base, located 75 miles north of the Demilitarized Zone, 120 miles north of the SEAL base at China Beach, near Da Nang, was a high-priority target. It was not only the staging base for small enemy boats smuggling arms south to Viet Cong units but also a base for the formidable 83-foot Chinese-made "Swatow" motor gunboats, which posed a danger both to guerrilla operations along the coast and to the America Desoto patrols offshore.

SEALs twice sent in Vietnamese frogmen to sabotage the Swatows. The first attempt in mid-February 1964 failed. A second attempt was scheduled for early March. SEAL Cathal L. "Irish" Flynn was a SEAL adviser at China Beach. "They really had a tough job to do," he said. "They had to go across a sand bar, go up a river a certain distance, dogleg left, swim accurately in on those patrol boats and put two limpets on each boat. It looked like a really tall order."

Four selected Vietnamese frogmen conducted a rehearsal on a river similar to that at Quang Khe. But the frogmen inserted to conduct the actual mission never returned. North Vietnam radio claimed to have killed one frogman and captured three others. Swatow operations at Quang Khe continued.

Missions such as these against the North Vietnamese coastline, along with the Desoto operations offshore, led to the perception by the North of a concerted effort by the United States to escalate the war. The North soon instigated the incident at the Gulf of Tonkin, which President Lyndon Johnson used as a pretext for sending combat troops to Vietnam.

See also CHINA BEACH; GULF OF TONKIN RESOLUTION; MACV-SOG; "NASTY" BOATS.

Qurah Island

The Iraqi invasion of the neighboring nation of Kuwait led to Operation Desert Storm, the war against Iraq. U.S. Navy SEALs recaptured the first Kuwaiti soil of the war on January 14, 1991.

The air war against Iraq had barely begun when Iraqi soldiers on the tiny island of Qurah, 16 miles off the coast of Kuwait, fired upon patrolling helicopters from the frigate USS *Curts*. The helicopters returned the fire and killed three of the enemy. The Iraqis immediately raised white flags of surrender.

SEALs were detailed to go in and capture the surviving enemy. Using helicopters and boats, the SEALs stormed the island, becoming the first ground troops to retake Kuwaiti soil. They met virtually no resistance. Twenty-nine Iraqi soldiers surrendered with their weapons, explosives, and night-vision devices.

See also OPERATION DESERT STORM.

R

radios

Communications within the SEALs, as within all special operations, continues to expand expontiatially with new technology. SEALs will use in the field whatever works, old or new. Their communications gear will often be a mix of the tried-and-true and the advanced.

For short-range tactical communications, SEALs are equipped either with the Motorola PRC-126 Saber-series radio or the new Multiband, Intro-Team Radio (MBITR) system. The Saber is small enough that it can be worn on a SEAL's combat harness, leaving his hands free. Range is about six miles under good conditions.

The MBITR communicates across a much wider band of frequencies, including VHF-FM, VHF-AM, and UHF-AM/FM. The range is similar to the Saber.

Long-range communications are normally based around one of several lightweight satellite communication (SATCOM) systems. The current state-of-the-art special operations radio is the AN/PRC-137F Special Mission Radio (SMRS) which has a built-in encryption device. It can be hooked up to a Morse code keypad, a microphone, or a laptop computer. An accompanying small solar panel provides the SEAL communications specialist with the ability to recharge radio batteries, even in a hostile environment.

The major problem with SATCOM systems is that an available satellite transponder is not always overhead. Therefore, long-range communications in the field uses as a backup the old reliable TRQ-43 High Frequency radio sets which bounce high frequency signals off the upper atmosphere. When equipped with an encryption device, the "Turkey 43," as the radio is called, can fire off secure radio messages from one point to almost anywhere else in the world.

See also COMBAT SURVIVOR EVADER LOCATION SYSTEM (CSEL); GLOBAL POSITIONING SYSTEM (GPS); U.S. SPACE COMMAND (SPACECOM).

raid

Raids are a special form of attack designed to destroy installations or facilities critical to the enemy's operation, or to accomplish some other specific battle goal. They are characterized by surprise, speed, flexibility, and concentration of forces. A raid is best conducted by small special operations units, such as the Navy SEALs, Army Rangers, or Delta Force.

Rangers

The U.S. Special Operations Command (USSO-COM) integrates special operations units from all services into one command organization. The U.S. Army contributes Special Forces (Green Berets); the U.S. Army Ranger regiment; the First Special Forces Operational Detachment—Delta (Delta Force); a special operations aviation unit; plus psychological, civil affairs, and signal units.

The Rangers have the longest history and are considered the finest light infantry force in the world. The present 75th Ranger Regiment traces its ancestry back to 1756, when Maj. Robert Rogers

recruited nine companies of American colonists to fight for the British during the French and Indian War. Ranger philosophy and doctrine date back to that era. The lineage of the Rangers is the basis for all other modern U.S. special operations forces, including the Navy SEALs.

See also ORGANIZATIONAL STRUCTURE, SPECIAL OPERATIONS; ROGERS'S RANGERS.

rappel

There are two basic methods of rappelling, or descending from a precipitous height by use of a rope.

The first method, the "double rope" system, requires the rappeller to bring the doubled rope between his legs, over his shoulder, and across his chest. As he descends backward down the obstacle face, he uses one hand to steady himself on the uphill line while utilizing the other hand on the downhill side as a "brake."

The second, more common, method is to use a special "saddle" secured around the rappeller's waist and hips, to which is attached a D-ring that secures the rope while allowing it to slide freely through a single hitch in the ring.

SEALs practice both methods, both from helicopters and as part of mountaineering work. Sometimes they rappel the "Australian" way, facing downhill on the rope and literally racing down the obstacle.

Col. William R. Darby was the first commander of modern U.S. Rangers. (U.S. Army)

"rapture of the deep"

Divers at certain depths and pressures sometimes experience disorientation and confusion. This condition, known as nitrogen narcosis or "rapture of the deep," was discovered to be the result of breathing nitrogen in compressed air.

See also NITROGEN NARCOSIS.

recompression chamber

The hyperbaric chamber is sometimes known as a decompression chamber or as a recompression chamber, depending on its function at a particular time. It is used in the treatment of caisson disease, or "bends," by "recompressing" the diver to his previous atmospheric pressure and gradually bringing him back to normal pressure.

See also CAISSON DISEASE; HYPERBARIC CHAMBER.

SEALs practice rappelling from a UH-1B "Huey" helicopter. (Charles W. Sasser)

recovery site

As part of their mission planning, SEALs either designate, or have designated for them, a "recovery site" from which they can be extracted should it become necessary to go into E & E mode (escape and evasion). The area selected should be accessible to aircraft or to ground or sea rescue forces.

See also ESCAPE AND EVASION (E&E); MISSION PLANNING.

Recovery Studies Division

Recovery Studies Division was the official name for the unit formed under MACV-SOG (Military Assistance Command Vietnam—Studies and Observation Group), whose mission it was to maintain intelligence on allied prisoners of war and mount rescue

attempts. It operated throughout the Vietnam War. It was more familiarly known as "Bright Light."

See also "BRIGHT LIGHT."

"Red Cell"

"Red Cell" resulted from the efforts of Vice Adm. J. A. "Ace" Lyons, Jr., then Vice Chief of Naval Operations for Plans, Policy and Operations, and it was brought both to fruition and destruction by Cdr. Richard Marcinko. It was a specialized unit formed primarily of SEALs from the counterterrorist SEAL Team Six. Its mission was to test security at U.S. naval installations.

On October 23, 1983, 241 marines and navy personnel were killed in their barracks in Beirut, Lebanon, when terrorists drove a truckload of TNT through the front of the building. Admiral Lyons vowed to prevent a repetition of the tragedy. He proposed to create a special team to test the security of key naval installations against the threat of sneak terrorist attack. He described his plan in a memorandum to the Chief of Naval Operations:

> I have established the Red Terrorist Cell under the Code of OP-06D. This cell will plan terrorist attacks against U.S. naval ships and installations worldwide. They will identify the vulnerabilities of the targets and plan the attacks within the known capabilities, ethnic characteristics of the terrorist factions and the political objectives of the sovereign states involved. In conjunction with the attack scenario, this group will also recommend actions which can be taken which will either inhibit or so complicate any planned terrorist action that they will not occur.

Richard Marcinko, who had won a Silver Star during the Vietnam War and later founded SEAL Team Six, had just been replaced as commander of Team Six. Marcinko and Lyons had cultivated a friendship that went back several years. Although Lyons selected Marcinko to build Red Cell, he brought in Capt. Bill Hamilton as the titular commander, because of Marcinko's abrasive personality. Hamilton was the same officer who in 1961 was charged with establishing the SEALs. He was named head of OP-06D, with Marcinko as his deputy.

The Red Cell originally comprised 14 men—three officers and 11 enlisted men—and was classi-

Red Cell, established under the code OP-06D, was formed to test security at U.S. naval installations worldwide and prevent terrorist attacks such as the bombing of this U.S. military barracks in Saudi Arabia in 1996. (Department of Defense)

fied above Top Secret. Most of the men came from SEAL Team Six, now commanded by Marcinko's replacement, Cdr. Robert Gormly. The organization reported directly to the Chief of Naval Operations (CNO), through the Vice CNO of Plans and Operations, Admiral Lyons.

Lyons's plan called for the Red Cell to make mock terrorist attacks over a period of several years against about 50 naval bases, in the hope that exposed weaknesses would prompt navy leaders to beef up security and therefore protect the facilities from real terrorist attacks. The exercises under Marcinko were frighteningly realistic. Although advance warnings were given of each "attack," they proved acutely embarrassing to installation commanders whose security was breached.

In an early test of the Red Cell concept, Marcinko and an enlisted man were dispatched to the Charleston, South Carolina, naval base.

Although they dressed in scroungy clothing, were unshaven, and wore long hair, they drove unchecked through the gate. They utilized the next several days penetrating secure nuclear storage areas and even going aboard nuclear-powered submarines. They were never challenged.

On another operation, the Red Cell tested the security of Air Force One, which was housed at Point Mugu Naval Base, its home when President Ronald Reagan vacationed at his California ranch, 125 miles to the south. The entire team eluded marines and naval security patrols to infiltrate the base via poorly secured rear gates and fences. Marcinko and company videotaped themselves placing "explosives" in the air intakes of F/A-18 Hornet jets; "destroying" the main Point Mugu communications antennas; setting off smoke grenades in the main headquarters building; racing a car up and down the flight line, pursued by jeeploads of security personnel; and "kidnapping" dependent women and children at the off-base Mugu cafeteria. The Red Cell operators then stole a weapons carrier, loaded it with a 500-pound simulated bomb concealed beneath a tarp, and left it at the Bachelor Officers' Quarters over a weekend. On the third day, they drove the vehicle and bomb to an area near Air Force One, climbed out, activated the "explosive," and walked away.

The realism of Marcinko-directed exercises led to a number of bitter complaints. A middle-aged petty officer had been forced to do jumping-jacks and pushups. A security officer had been kidnapped from his home and held hostage in a motel room. A naval civilian employee filed a lawsuit against the Red Cell, claiming he had been abused and his ribs broken.

"There were always a lot of rumors because [Marcinko] and his colleagues were coming to do [an] exercise," said Capt. George Vercessi, a naval public affairs officer assigned to the team to improve its image. "He would say things to shock or get your attention. He'd go into a briefing and say, 'We won't break any skin. We won't draw any blood. No broken teeth. Everything else is mine.' He would tell the women, 'We're not going to pull the skirt over your head and tie your hands behind your back.' He wanted to get attention. He enjoyed twisting tails."

Apparently, Marcinko twisted too many tails. When he was up for promotion to the rank of captain, the CNO and other top officials, including the president of the United States, were deluged with complaints describing Marcinko as a maverick, unfit for command. Partly as a result of these letters, and partly because of actual irregularities in the books of SEAL Team Six when Marcinko was commander, the Naval Investigative Service opened a probe, under the code name Operation Iron Eagle.

On April 3, 1986, Marcinko was dismissed from the Red Cell. He was court-martialed in January 1990 and convicted of conspiracy, bribery, conflict of interest, and making false claims against the government, all connected with his extralegal methods of obtaining equipment and materiel for his team. He served over a year in a federal penitentiary, where he penned his best-selling autobiography, *Rogue Warrior.*

With professional author John Weisman, he also wrote a number of other "Rogue Warrior" books,

including one entitled *Red Cell* that purported to tell, under the guise of fiction, the true adventures of the unit. However, the closest Red Cell ever came to a real-world operation, other than its "attacks" on naval bases, was when the CNO, Adm. James Watkins, tapped Marcinko to accompany him as bodyguard on an uneventful trip to the Persian Gulf.

Capt. Tom Tarbox took over the Red Cell for a brief period after Marcinko was relieved. In the end, however, after less than five years of life, the unit was dissolved. Its responsibilities, still secret, were absorbed by DevGru (Naval Special Warfare Development Group) and other counterterrorist units.

See also HAMILTON, WILLIAM H.; NAVAL SPECIAL WARFARE DEVELOPMENT GROUP (DEVGRU); OPERATION IRON EAGLE; SEAL TEAM SIX.

Redwolves

The Navy Seawolf helicopter units formed to support SEAL units during the Vietnam War were disbanded in 1972. Four years later, in 1976, two new helicopter groups were created to work with the SEALs. They were the "Redwolves" on the East Coast, meant to support Naval Special Warfare Group Two at Little Creek, Virginia; and the "Blue Hawks" on the West Coast, assigned to support Naval Special Warfare Group One, at Coronado, California.

See also SEAWOLVES.

relative work

"Relative work" is the term used to describe parachutists guiding off each other while in the air.

See also AIRBORNE.

ribbon charge

A ribbon charge is a special explosive for cutting door locks and hinges and other similar applications.

See also EXPLOSIVES.

rigid-hull inflatable boat (RHIB or RIB)

The RHIB, or RIB, is an inflatable water craft widely used on SEAL missions.

See also INFLATABLE BOATS.

riverine forces

Evolving out of the Vietnam War, riverine forces included personnel and craft fighting in the rivers and swamps of the Mekong Delta.

See also RIVERINE WARFARE.

riverine warfare

U.S. Navy SEALs were a vital part of riverine warfare, a joint U.S. Army/Navy effort to prevent enemy use of inland waterways during the Vietnam War.

Riverine warfare was not something new to Southeast Asia, nor was it exactly new to U.S. military forces. During the American Civil War, the Union operated navy gunboats on the Ohio and Mississippi Rivers and other inland waterways. "Nor must Uncle Sam's web feet be forgotten," said Abe Lincoln in 1863. "At all the watery mar-

gins they have been present. Not all on the deep sea, the braced bay, and the rapid rivers, but also up the narrow muddy lagoon and wherever the ground was a little damp, they have been and made their tracks."

During the Indochina War of 1946–54, the French created combat water units called Dinassauts to operate in Vietnam's hostile streams. In 1955, after the French pulled out, the newly formed Vietnamese navy established river assault groups (RAGS) to patrol the inland waterways. By 1964, RAGS possessed over 200 craft.

The Mekong Delta, just south of Saigon, encompasses the entire southern tip of the country. During the early years of the American phase of the Vietnam War, Viet Cong (VC) guerrillas ferried men, arms, and ammunition through thousands of north-south canals and across two wide rivers, the Bassac and the Mekong, into the war zones north of

Riverine forces, a joint U.S. Army/Navy effort to prevent enemy use of inland waterways, were developed during the Vietnam War. Here, a riverine task force chugs up a canal in the Mekong Delta, supported by a UH-1 "Huey" gunship. (U.S. Army)

Saigon. Prior to 1965, operations against this infiltration were the responsibility of the South Vietnamese forces. From December 1965 onward, however, America took over. The U.S. Navy established a river force code-named Operation Game Warden (Task Force 116) to operate in conjunction with the U.S. Navy's Operation Market Time (Task Force 71). Market Time was designed to cut off VC seaborne infiltration. The U.S. Navy River Patrol Forces (also known as riverine forces, or the brownwater navy) were the largest American river force since the Civil War.

Game Warden proved effective, but the navy decided that what it really needed was a mobile combat unit with enough firepower to patrol, engage, and wipe out known VC sanctuaries. Between August 1966 and November 1967, 17 million cubic tons of silt were dredged in order to create a base on the My Tho River for a new Mekong Delta Mobile Afloat Force (MDMAF), which soon became known as the Mobile Riverine Force (MRF). It comprised a naval component (Task Force 117) and the Second Brigade of the U.S. Army's Ninth Infantry Division.

The MRF spawned both new tactics and new weaponry. In addition to Swift boats and PBRs (Patrol Boats, River), the riverine forces utilized floating armored troop carriers with steel slats, monitors, command and control boats, and "Zippos" armed with flamethrowers and other heavy weapons. The MRF often moved down waterways in formation, like an armored penetration. During the last six months of 1967 it killed over 1,000 VC, largely concentrating on Long An and Ding Tuong Provinces in the Mekong Delta, with special attention to the Rung Sat Special Zone around Saigon.

Because the Delta, and the Rung Sat Special Zone in particular, were the special provinces of the U.S. Navy SEALs, the SEALs often worked with the riverine forces or received their support in their own special brand of riverine warfare.

By the end of 1968, the objectives of Market Time on the coast and Game Warden and the MRF in the Delta had largely been achieved. The VC moved to exploit a new infiltration route—from across the Cambodian border. To counter this, Market Time, Game Warden, and the MRF units were welded into a combined force under the code name SEALORDS.

See also BAILEY, LARRY W.; BOSTON WHALER; COLBY, WILLIAM EGAN; HEAVY SEAL SUPPORT CRAFT (HSSC); JUNK; JUNK FORCE; LIGHT SEAL SUPPORT CRAFT (LSSC); MACIONE, JACK; MEKONG DELTA; NORRIS, THOMAS R.; PATROL BOAT, RIVER (PBR); PTF (PATROL TORPEDO, FAST) BOAT; RUNG SAT SPECIAL ZONE; SEALORDS.

Rivero, Horacio (1910–2000)

Horacio Rivero was the first Hispanic four-star admiral in the U.S. Navy. He served as Vice Chief of Naval Operations and Chief of Allied Forces, Southern Europe. He is most remembered by the SEALs as a vocal opponent during their early years. As Vice CNO, Rivero sent out a memo decreeing that the navy not become involved in any shallow-river warfare. That same year, SEALs were sent to Vietnam.

When the suggestion was made that SEALs should wear jaunty black berets like the green berets of Army Special Forces, Rivero retorted, "We call them white hats in the navy. I don't know any black berets and I want that term wiped out." The black beret eventually became standard uniform headgear for SEALs.

In fairness to Rivero, he later became a strong supporter of the SEALs in Vietnam.

Rivero retired from the navy in 1972 and served as ambassador to Spain before returning to live in his homeland of Puerto Rico. He died there at the age of 90 in 2000.

Rodriguez, Issac, III (1965–1989)

Petty Officer Isaac Rodriguez, III was one of four SEALs killed in combat during Operation Just Cause against Panama in 1989.

See also OPERATION JUST CAUSE.

Rogers's Rangers

Maj. Robert Rogers recruited nine companies of American colonists in 1756, known as Rogers's Rangers, to fight for the British during the French and Indian War. Ranger techniques and methods were the stock in trade of American frontiersmen, but Rogers was the first to incorporate them in a permanently organized fighting force. These tactics form the basis of much of modern special operations. His "Standing Orders" were written in 1759 but apply just as well to today's unconventional warfare and to the SEALs, Green Berets, and other SpecOps troops who wage it as they did to operations conducted by Rogers and his men.

Rogers's Standing Orders

1. Don't forget nothing.
2. Have your musket clean as a whistle, hatchet scoured, sixty rounds powder and ball, and be ready to march at a minute's warning.
3. When you're on the march, act the way you would if you was sneaking up on a deer. See the enemy first.
4. Tell the truth about what you see and what you do. There is an Army depending on us for correct information. You can lie all you please when you tell other folks about the Rangers, but don't never lie to a Ranger or officer.
5. Don't never take a chance you don't have to.
6. When you're on the march we march single file, far enough apart so one shot can't go through two men.
7. If we strike swamps or soft ground, we spread out abreast, so it's hard to track us.
8. When we march, we keep moving till dark, so as to give the enemy the least possible chance at us.
9. When we camp, half the party stays awake while the other half sleeps.
10. If we take prisoners, we keep 'em separate till we have had time to examine them, so they can't cook up a story between 'em.
11. Don't ever march home the same way. Take a different route so you won't be ambushed.
12. No matter whether we travel in big parties or little ones, each party has to keep a scout twenty yards ahead, twenty yards on each flank and twenty yards in the rear, so the main body can't be surprised and wiped out.
13. Every night you'll be told where to meet if surrounded by a superior force.
14. Don't sit down to eat without posting sentries.
15. Don't sleep beyond dawn. Dawn's when the French and Indians attack.
16. Don't cross a river by a regular ford.
17. If somebody's trailing you, make a circle, come back onto your tracks, and ambush the folks that aim to ambush you.
18. Don't stand up when the enemy's coming against you. Kneel down, lie down, hide behind a tree.
19. Let the enemy come till he's almost close enough to touch. Then let him have it and jump out and finish him off with your hatchet.

Source: Department of the Army. *Special Forces Handbook.*

rope-sling recovery

The rope-sling recovery method of snatching swimmers out of the sea into a speeding boat was developed by World War II underwater demolition teams. The sling, or "scoop," used by modern SEALs is not a rope but instead a thick rubber loop. As the boat comes roaring past, each swimmer snags the loop held out by a boatman. It is attached to a huge bungee cord that jerks the SEAL out of the water and into the boat.

See also CAST AND RECOVERY.

rubber duck

SEALs commonly refer to an inflatable rubber boat as a "rubber duck."

See also INFLATABLE BOATS.

Rung Sat Special Zone

Saigon (now known as Ho Chi Minh City) lies about 40 miles inland from the South China Sea. A delta area composed of a huge mangrove swamp crisscrossed by meandering streams lies between the capital and the sea to the east and the mouths of the Mekong River to the south and east. During the Vietnam War, this was known as the Rung Sat Special Zone, a major area of operations for the U.S Navy SEALs.

Control of the zone was critical for both sides. Americans needed it because their supply ships had to be able to move safely up and down the river to Saigon. For the Viet Cong, it was a major transit route from the huge Mekong River Delta to the south of Saigon to the war zones of the north. The struggle for the zone continued throughout the war.

S

safe area

An enemy-free area within an enemy zone of control is called a "safe area" by special operations forces.

safe house

In special operations, a "safe house" refers to a location, generally a sympathizer's house, where an operator may hide out during a covert mission into enemy territory and expect to receive support and concealment.

Saipan

A number of important developments occurred in the evolution of underwater demolition team (UDT) tactics during the battle to wrest Saipan from the Japanese in June 1944. Saipan is a rocky island in the Pacific, 13 miles long and five miles wide.

The disaster at Tarawa, in which hundreds of U.S. Marines died floundering in treacherous and exposed waters before they ever reached the beach, pointed out the need for beach reconnaissance prior to an amphibious assault. This need led to the development of NCDUs (naval combat demolition units) and UDTs, which eventually evolved into the U.S. Navy SEALs.

At first, the demolition units were required to wear complete uniforms (including boots), life vests, and to remain tethered by line to their boats. During the Kwajalein invasion of January 31, 1944, however, Ens. Lewis F. Luehrs and Chief Petty Officer Bill Acheson performed the first swimming reconnaissance of an enemy beachhead. This success led to swimmers' conducting beach surveys two weeks later at Eniwetok, an island directly to the west of Kwajalein.

After the Marshall Islands campaign, UDT teams returned to Hawaii to prepare for further action. Under Lt. Cdr. John T. Koehler, commanding officer of UDT-2, and Lt. Cdr. Draper L. Kauffman, commanding officer of UDT-5, swimming programs were begun. The entire concept of UDT was being revolutionized. Swimming became the primary method of conducting the job. Each man had swim fins, swim shoes (to protect against coral), swim trunks, a dive mask, gloves and kneepads, a knife and life belt, first aid packet, two grease pencils, and four plexiglas plates on which to record data while in the water.

Several new methods of operations were also developed for application at Saipan. First of all, men were expected to rid themselves of dependence upon being taken to the target by rubber boats, and instead to swim to their targets. They would do this, for the first time, in broad daylight.

Adm. Richmond Kelly Turner, the amphibious fleet commander, summoned Kauffman to his flagship. "Now, the first and most important thing is reconnaissance for depth of water, and I'm thinking of having you go in and recon around eight." Kauffman assumed he meant eight in the evening. "Well, Admiral, it depends on the phase of the moon."

"Moon? What the hell has that got to do with it? Obviously, by eight o'clock, I mean 0800."

Kauffman expected 50 percent casualties.

Another development had to do with the way swimmers were deposited into the water. A short time previously, Ens. Wade Theyer and Lt. Tom Westerlin had developed the "cast and recovery" method of rapidly inserting frogmen from a boat and recovering them afterward. Kauffman's UDT-5 would use it for the first time at Saipan.

The "buddy system" was another advancement. Each man was assigned a combat buddy; they were expected to look out for each other. When the beach reconnaissance at Saipan began on June 14, one man of a buddy team was injured while swimming in to the reef. His partner performed first aid, completed their assignment, then returned to tow the wounded man a mile farther out to sea and safer waters. Both were rescued.

Under the cover of ships firing salvos, the UDT men swam to within 50 feet of the beach. The information they obtained changed the basic plan for the operation. Also, apparently, bobbing heads in the sea were extremely difficult targets. Of some 200 UDT swimmers in the water, only one man was killed, and a very few were wounded.

Saipan was the site of important changes in seaborne warrior tactics. Cast and recovery, the buddy system, and other tactics first used at Saipan are still taught and used by Navy SEALs.

See also ACHESON, BILL; CAST AND RECOVERY; KAUFFMAN, DRAPER L.; NAVAL COMBAT DEMOLITION UNITS (NCDUS); TARAWA; UNDERWATER DEMOLITION TEAMS (UDTS).

USS *Sam Houston*

The USS *Sam Houston* was one of two Polaris type submarines first converted to carry dry-deck shelters (DDSs) for the SEALs.

See also DRY-DECK SHELTER (DDS); USS *GRAYBACK*.

San Clemente

San Clemente, a rocky, brush-choked island about 60 miles off the California coast, is used for BUD/S (Basic Underwater Demolition/SEAL) training. It is there that the final phases in explosives, small-unit combat tactics, reconnaissance, patrolling, rappelling, swimming, and range firing of specialized SEAL weapons are conducted. Use of the island, controlled by the U.S. Navy, dates back to the World War II era. Underwater demolition teams first camped in tents while undergoing training. World War II–era one-story buildings soon replaced the tents, replaced in turn in recent years by new masonry buildings.

The island training phases are especially demanding on officer trainees, who are required not only to undergo all training given to enlisted men but also to act as officers in planning training operations and leading them.

In March 1988, Hospital Corpsman Third Class John Joseph Tomlinson died of hypothermia while undergoing training off the island's shore.

See also BASIC UNDERWATER DEMOLITIONS/SEAL (BUD/S) TRAINING.

sanitary weapon

A weapon whose origin and ownership cannot be traced back to any particular military or nation is called a "sanitary weapon" in SpecOps speech. SEALs are sometimes required to undertake clandestine missions, the detection of which could cause serious international repercussions. They are thus "sterilized" to the point that their clothing, equipment, weapons, and even their bodies cannot be traced back to the United States.

"If you are captured, the U.S. will disavow all knowledge" is more than a cliché in some circumstances.

saturation diving

When the blood and tissues of a diver have absorbed all the gases they can hold at a particular depth—when he is *saturated*—he can remain at that depth for as long as necessary without a corresponding lengthening of his decompression period. For example, a diver working for an hour at 200 fsw (feet of seawater) requires three hours and 20 minutes of decompression. That same diver, once saturated can spend, five days at 200 fsw and undergo only a single decompression when prepared to surface, as opposed to the conventional method of spending 40 days making one-hour dives with long decompression periods after each dive.

SEALs are rarely involved in "saturation diving," although they must be prepared for it if necessary.

SAW (squad automatic weapon)

Special operations forces have adopted the M249 squad automatic weapon (SAW) as their standard light machine gun. Based upon a Belgian design from Fabrique Nationale, the weapon weighs only 22 pounds. It fires 5.56 mm ammunition, the same as the standard-issue M16 or M4 battle rifles. It fires from either a belt or the same 30-round magazine the M16 uses. The gun can be fired from the shoulder, from a bipod, or it can be mounted to vehicles.

At the present, the M249 fires the standard ball and tracer rounds issued to line units, which limits its penetration power against light vehicles or sandbagged positions. However, a new generation of ammunition is now in the experimental stage—an armor-piercing round that can penetrate over an inch of armor plate.

See also M60 MACHINE GUN.

Schamberger, Robert Randolph (d. 1983)

Chief Petty Officer Robert Schamberger was one of four SEALs killed parachuting into the sea off the coast of Grenada during Operation Urgent Fury in 1983.

See also OPERATION URGENT FURY.

scout dogs

Of the many innovations SEALs contributed to special warfare, one of the most intriguing experiments had to do with the use of scout dogs in Vietnam, where they were used for scouting, tracking, sentry duty, flushing out the enemy, and detecting mines and booby traps. SEAL plankowner Bill Bruhmuller, SEAL Team Two, was one of the early pioneers of the use of dogs in combat by SEALs. "When we first went to Vietnam," he reminisces, "we didn't know the terrain or anything like that. I got the idea of maybe having a scout dog would be a pretty good idea. We heard about the army using them to great success. Our CO, who was Bill Early, agreed to give it a try."

Bruhmuller attended canine training at the Norfolk, Virginia, police department with a big, black shepherd named Prince. Prince, said Bruhmuller, was the perfect SEAL. He worked hard, and he played hard. When Bruhmuller and his team were shipped to Vietnam in 1967, Prince accompanied them. On his first night in-country, at a SEAL base near Tre Noc on the Bassac River in the Mekong Delta, he tracked down a Viet Cong who had been trying to sneak through the perimeter wire.

Team Two eventually ended up with three or four scout dogs. The men rigged special harnesses to allow the dogs to parachute. A dog in harness would be attached to the chest of a jumper, who would release the dog on a lowering line just before he reached the ground. Most of the dogs readily adapted to parachuting. One, however, refused even to go near an airplane after his first jump.

The SEALs took the dogs on nighttime patrol and on ambushes. Prince in particular was excellent on night duty. He would detect an approaching enemy long before the SEALs were aware of danger.

However, the dogs' usefulness in the waterlogged Mekong Delta, where most SEALs operated, proved to be limited. The dogs' legs were simply not long enough to propel them through the muddy swamps, and they sometimes had to be carried. Also, their sense of smell was limited because of the water.

Bo Burwell, who served with SEAL Team Two in the Delta, had previously operated as a dog handler with a marine reconnaissance unit in more suitable terrain farther north. His dog, King, service number K9-37, saved his life on at least two occasions. On the first occasion, King picked up the trail of a VC waiting in ambush and tracked him down. The 110-pound shepherd attacked the 120-pound Vietnamese and ripped out his throat, killing him. On the second occasion, King alerted on a booby trap and prevented Burwell from walking into the trip wire.

King was killed while on a scouting operation with another marine company. A command-detonated Claymore mine exploded directly at his feet. The mine wounded a number of marines, but the dog took most of the blast, saving in his last action at least some of his fellow Americans.

As for Prince, he served a second tour of duty under SEAL handler Mike Bailey. He was wounded once in action but remained in service to save his SEALs several times by giving advance warnings of enemy presence. One afternoon during a patrol rest-and-listening halt, Prince wandered off and returned tossing around a Chinese communist hand grenade, playing with it, much to the chagrin of the SEALs. He then led the team to a large cache of enemy weapons.

On another occasion, the SEALs were a point element for a marine unit when Prince alerted to sand dunes directly ahead. "The dog is alerting to something over there," Bailey advised the marine commander. "Hard to tell what it is, but we need to go around this way." The marine officer chose to ignore the warning. He elected to continue past the sand dunes, where waiting VC ambushed him. The SEALs avoided the same fate by paying attention to the dog and going the other way.

See also BRUHMULLER, WILLIAM N., II.

SCUBA

The first workable, open-circuit, demand-type SCUBA (self-contained underwater breathing apparatus) was invented during World War II by two Frenchmen, Jacques Cousteau and Emile Gagnan. It utilized a pair of compressed air tanks, a mouthpiece, and a demand-valve regulator. It was patented in 1943 as the Aqua-Lung.

SCUBA has since evolved into two types—open-circuit (which emits bubbles, as the original did) and closed-circuit, which does not. SEALs primarily use closed-circuit SCUBA on missions.

See also AEROPHORE; AQUA-LUNG; CLOSED-CIRCUIT BREATHING APPARATUS; COUSTEAU, JACQUES-YVES; DIVING, HISTORY OF; LAMBERTSEN AMPHIBIOUS RESPIRATORY UNIT (LARU); LAMBERTSEN, CHRISTIAN J.; MIXED-GAS BREATHING; MOMSEN LUNG; OPEN-CIRCUIT BREATHING APPARATUS.

Scyllias (ca. 500 B.C.)

Breath-holding swimmers of ancient Greece are known to have dived for sponges and engaged in military exploits. The story of Scyllias, the most famous of these divers, was recorded by the historian Herodotus.

During a naval campaign about 500 B.C., King Xerxes I of Persia took Scyllias prisoner aboard his ship. When Scyllias learned Xerxes intended to attack a Greek flotilla, he jumped overboard with a knife. The Persians assumed he had drowned. Instead, he made his way among Xerxes fleet, using a hollow reed as a snorkel, and cut the ships loose from their moorings. Then he swam nine miles to rejoin the Greeks off Cape Artemisium.

Seabees

Members of the naval construction battalions established in December 1941 following the Japanese attack on Pearl Harbor were called "Seabees." The earliest Seabees were recruited primarily from the civilian construction trades and assigned to building bases, airstrips, bridges, roads, warehouses, hospitals, gasoline storage tanks, housing, and other structures to assist the war effort. When the naval combat demolition units and underwater demolition teams were organized to clear beaches, Seabees were heavily recruited for them because of their experience with demolitions.

Sea Bull newsletter

The Sea Bull was an unofficial single-sheet newsletter published monthly by members of SEAL Team Two during the Vietnam War. It was a folksy publication passing along news, gossip, and information, both official and unofficial.

Seafloat

During the Vietnam War, "Seafloat" was the mobile advanced tactical support base built on the Song Cau Lon River in Ca Mau Province at the extreme southern tip of Vietnam. It served as a base of operations for waterborne guard posts using Swift boats, various riverine units, and assorted SEAL and underwater demolition teams. At one point, about 30 Swift boats, one monitor, one heavy SEAL support craft, one medium SEAL support craft, one light SEAL support craft, two or three junks, three SEAL platoons, and about 40 Seafloat staff called the floating dry-dock home.

Seafloat was more than a floating dock for boats. It also included quarters for support and operational personnel, as well as maintenance and other support structures that could be disassembled and reassembled as the need arose. It was constructed in Nha Be in May and June of 1969, then towed south by sea, up the Song Bo De River, then even farther up the muddy, swift currents of the Song Cau Lon. Mike boats and a combat salvage boat set the anchor buoys against a ten-knot tidal current.

It remained in the heart of the U Minh Forest, a VC stronghold, until October 1970, when it was towed back out into the South China Sea—and disappeared.

Seahawk helicopter (CH-60H)

The CH-60H is the current fleet combat support helicopter. It provides the navy Combat Logistics Force with an at-sea vertical replenishment capability. It also serves as the primary search and rescue helicopter for amphibious task forces and provides other essential support to amphibious operations. Its secondary mission is special warfare support for special operations forces.

See also HELICOPTERS.

SEAL delivery vehicle (SDV)

The SDV is a small "wet" minisubmarine that can clandestinely transport SEAL swimmers underwater to an insertion point.

See also ADVANCED SEAL DELIVERY SYSTEM (ASDS); DRY-DECK SHELTER (DDS).

The SDV is a small "wet" mini-submarine that can clandestinely transport SEALs to an insertion point. Here an SDV has just been released underwater from a dry deck shelter attached to a submarine. (U.S. Navy)

SEAL Delivery Vehicle Teams (SDVTs)

SDVs (SEAL delivery vehicles) are fast, covert "wet" combat submersibles that offer SEALs the most clandestine means of infiltration available to any military force in the world. Without ever breaking the surface of the water, these minisubmarines can deliver SEALs to an area or provide them a platform from which to lay explosives or gather intelligence directly under an enemy's nose. The vehicles have their own support units, SEAL delivery vehicle teams (SDVTs).

Each of the two naval special warfare groups, one on each coast, is composed of three SEAL teams, one special boat squadron, and one SDV team, which operates and maintains the SDVs. An operator and navigator, both fully qualified SEALs, are assigned to operate each SDV during a combat assignment. The SDVT in each group is skippered by a navy commander, who has three operational SDV task units and a headquarters element under his command. SDVTs normally deploy aboard submarines but may also be deployed from shore or surface ships.

See also ADVANCED SEAL DELIVERY SYSTEM (ASDS).

SEALORDS

The SEALORDS program, SEALORDS being an acronym for "Southeast Asia Lake, Ocean, River, and Delta Strategy," was a determined effort by the brown-water navy, Navy Seawolves helicopters, SEALs, and the South Vietnamese navy and ground forces to cut enemy supply lines from Cambodia and disrupt Viet Cong base areas deep in the Mekong Delta during the Vietnam War. It was developed by Vice Adm. Elmo R. Zumwalt, Jr., who was appointed commander of naval forces in Vietnam in September 1968.

As early as 1964, Lt. Cdr. Philip H. Bucklew had been sent to Vietnam to determine whether most enemy resupply came in across the Cambodian border or from down the coastline in ships. He concluded that while some supplies came down the coast, most arrived across the Cambodian border via the Ho Chi Minh Trail network.

Operations Market Time and Game Warden were designed to use the deep-water and brown-water navy on the major waterways to interdict supply

The SEALORDS program was a determined effort by navy helicopters, SEALs, and the South Vietnamese military to cut enemy lines deep in the Mekong Delta during the Vietnam War. Viet Cong (VC) used sampans and other craft to smuggle war materiel to units fighting in Vietnam.

routes. Although both operations proved successful, a substantial flow of supplies still reached VC units in the Delta overland, from the Ho Chi Minh Trail through North Vietnam, Laos, and Cambodia. A like amount arrived through Cambodian ports on the Gulf of Thailand. From these ports, war materiel moved into the river network, especially the small tributary streams, and was thus distributed through the Mekong Delta for use by enemy forces all over Vietnam.

Admiral Zumwalt decided to do something about it. He launched SEALORDS, formally designated as Task Force 194, in October 1968. While Game Warden and Market Time continued to function, their operations were scaled down and their personnel and resources were increasingly dedicated to SEALORDS. Heavily armed PBRs (Patrol Boats, River) began operating along previously uncontested smaller rivers and canals with the support of naval aircraft, *Seawolves* helicopters, riverine assault craft, and SEALs.

SEALORDS forces acting under Operation Giant Slingshot intended to block supplies coming through Cambodia at a point known as the Parrot's Beak, west of Saigon. Allied forces began establishing patrol "barriers," often using electronic sensor devices, along waterways paralleling the Cambodian border.

In November 1968, PBRs and riverine assault craft managed to secure transportation routes in the operational area between the Gulf of Siam at Rach Gia and the Bassac River at Long Xuyen. SEALORDS forces also penetrated deep into the Giang Thinh-Vinh Te canal system and established waterway patrols from Ha Tien on the Gulf of Siam to Chau Doc on the upper Bassac. In December, U.S. naval forces pushed up the Vam Co Dong and Vam Co Tay Rivers west of Saigon, against heavy enemy oppositions, to cut infiltration routes from the Parrot's Beak. In January 1969, river forces established patrol sectors along canals westward from the Vam Co Tay to the Mekong River. Thus, by early 1969 a patrolled waterway-interdiction barrier extended almost uninterrupted from Tay Ninh northwest of Saigon to the Gulf of Siam.

SEALs were involved in SEALORDS operations from the beginning. By this time they had learned to establish their own intelligence networks and to operate on that information themselves.

On January 10, 1969, a seven-man SEAL squad from Sixth Platoon, SEAL Team One, was conducting a riverine support patrol along the Vam Co Dong River when it uncovered a large VC munitions cache. It seized 620 rounds of mortar, rocket, and recoilless rifle ammunition, 65 hand grenades, and 27,000 rounds of small-arms ammo.

In February, Fifth Platoon developed intelligence from an informant that VC were in control of a village near the My Tho River. A squad conducting a recon patrol on February 16 came upon five armed VC in a building. The VC fled; the SEALs opened fire and brought down all five. The building turned out to be a VC/NVA postal station filled with important enemy documents.

Operation Giant Slingshot ran for 515 days until the operation was turned over to the South Vietnamese in May 1970. SEALs and the other elements of SEALORDS slowed the flow of supplies to the VC in the Delta to a bare trickle. It was one of the more successful projects of the war.

See also BROWN-WATER NAVY; BUCKLEW, PHILIP H.; OPERATION GAME WARDEN; OPERATION MARKET TIME; SEAWOLVES.

SEAL Prayer

Lt. Cdr. E. J. McMahon, Navy Chaplain Corps, penned the following prayer for the U.S. Navy SEALs during the Vietnam War:

> Dear Father in Heaven, if I may respectfully say so, sometimes you are a strange God. Though you love all mankind, it seems you have special predilections too. You seem to love those men who can stand alone, who face impossible odds, who challenge every bully and every tyrant—those men who know the heat and loneliness of a Calvary. Possibly you cherish men of this stamp because you recognize the marks of your only Son in them. Since this unique group of men known as the SEALs know Calvary and suffering, teach them now the mystery of the Resurrection—that they are indestructible, that they will live forever because of their deep faith in You. And when they do come to heaven, may I respectfully warn you, dear Father, they also know how to celebrate. So please be ready for them when they insert under your pearly gates.
>
> Bless them, their devoted families and their country on this glorious occasion. We ask this through the merits of your Son, Christ Jesus the Lord. Amen.

SEALs

Commissioned in January 1962, the U.S. Navy SEALs are the navy's equivalent to the Army Green Berets in the theater of unconventional warfare.

In 1961, shortly after John F. Kennedy took office as president of the United States, he ordered the armed forces to increase their capability for limited and unconventional warfare. He also wanted the U.S. military to be able to train guerrillas for other

SEALs were commissioned in 1962 to engage in unconventional warfare in a maritime environment. Here, a SEAL climbs into a submarine. (U.S. Navy)

In a memo dated 29 April 1961, the committee first used the SEAL acronym, a contraction standing for *Sea, Air, Land,* and denoting the unconventional capabilities of the SEALs to operate in all environments.

Lt. Cdr. William H. "Bill" Hamilton, commander of Underwater Demolition Team 21, wrote a letter to the CNO following President Kennedy's speech of May 25, 1961, in which he outlined his plans for unconventional forces, proposing the formation of a naval commando force. Hamilton was immediately assigned to the Pentagon, given a $4.3 million budget, and ordered to build one. He, in turn, tapped Lt. Roy Boehm as the man actually to set up, structure, recruit, and train the first SEAL team.

The SEALs were formally authorized in December 1961 and commissioned on January 7, 1962, retroactive to 1 January.

See also BOEHM, ROY; CALLAHAN, JOHN F.; HAMILTON, WILLIAM H.; KENNEDY, JOHN F.; MISSION PLANNING; MISSIONS; NAVAL SPECIAL WARFARE; ORGANIZATIONAL STRUCTURE, SPECIAL OPERATIONS; SEAL TEAM.

Seal Tactical Training (STI)

Following the successful completion of Basic Underwater Demolition/SEAL (BUD/S) training, all new SEALs are sent to a SEAL Tactical Training course to learn counterterrorism tactics.

See also DEVGRU; "RED CELL", SEAL TEAM SIX.

SEAL team

The centerpiece of naval special warfare comprises the SEAL teams. The U.S. Navy Special Warfare Command supports two naval special warfare groups—Group One stationed at Coronado, California, and Group Two at Little Creek, Virginia. Each group commands three SEAL teams, a SEAL delivery vehicle team, and a special boat squadron.

SEAL Teams One, Three, and Four are based at Coronado, California, while Teams Two, Five, and Eight are at Little Creek, Virginia. Each team is staffed by about 225 men, of whom only 160 are actually members of the platoons. The others are support and logistics people from the fleet, such as parachute riggers, intelligence specialists, armorers, electronic technicians, personnel clerks,

countries and to conduct counterguerrilla operations. He authorized the Pentagon to take more than $100 million from other programs in order to beef up special operations forces.

Declared Vice Adm. Ulysses S. G. Sharp, deputy Chief of Naval Operations (CNO) for Plans and Policy, "Since this type of operation is held in such high regard in high places, we had better get going." Adm. Arleigh A. Burke, the CNO, began giving serious thought to the navy's role in this new kind of warfare. He formed the navy's Unconventional Activities Committee to look into it. In May 1961, the committee recommended the formation of a commando unit on each coast, to be focal points for navy involvement in guerrilla and counterguerrilla operations. The teams were originally known as special operations teams (SOTs).

and others, along with training and command-and-control personnel.

There are 10 platoons of SEALs in each team. A platoon is composed of two squads of eight men each; each platoon is commanded by a lieutenant. A squad can also be further divided into two fire teams of four men each.

See also CORONADO; LITTLE CREEK, VIRGINIA; NAVAL SPECIAL WARFARE; ORGANIZATIONAL STRUCTURE, SPECIAL OPERATIONS; SEALS.

SEAL team assault boat (STAB)

The first specialized SEAL combat boat, a mainstay of SEAL operations during the early stages of the Vietnam War, was known formally as the Mark I STAB.

Following the Cuban missile crisis, Lt. Jack Macione, a SEAL, saw the need for a good SEAL team boat.

"What I envisioned," he said, "was a lightweight, outboard-driven boat that would be helicopter-transportable and could go in back of a C-130 [aircraft]. You could pick it up and move it. . . . It would be very versatile. It would be a package boat, come as a kit. You would configure the boat in a matter of minutes or an hour or so for your mission configuration. I saw no reason this boat could not have the firepower of a destroyer plus the versatility of a high-performance craft."

During the missile crisis, SEALs utilized 26-foot fiberglass, trimaran-hulled boats in preparation for a possible invasion of Cuba. Lieutenant Macione, Lt. Larry Bailey and Petty Officer Bob Gallagher con-

The centerpiece of naval special warfare is the SEAL Team, which is trained to operate in all environments. (Charles W. Sasser)

verted this basic design boat into a boat specialized for use by SEALs in the waterways of Vietnam.

The finished product was 26 and a half feet long and seven feet wide, with a trimaran hull. Powered by twin Mercury outboards ranging from 100 hp to 150 hp, it had enough power to get up on its "step" in about five seconds. Fully loaded with a crew of three and 14 or 15 SEALs aboard, it could reach speeds of 50 mph or more. It was armored to withstand .30-caliber fire.

It could accommodate 10 heavy weapons, including .50-caliber and M60 machine guns, and as many as six 106 mm recoilless rifles. The 106 has the firepower of a five-inch gun on a destroyer, which means a STAB literally does carry the firepower of a destroyer. Equipped with a fixed fire-control system, all six big guns and the machine guns could all be fired by the coxswain in his Kevlar-protected pilot's cocoon. He controlled the speed of the boat with his right hand, steered the boat with his left, and fired the weapons with his left or right foot.

The STAB was parachute-deployable, was designed for LOLEX (low-level extraction) from an aircraft, and could be slung beneath a helicopter for transport. Macione also designed a wire cutter on the front of the boat to catch and cut any wires that the enemy might string across waterways.

SEAL Team Two took ten STABS with them to Vietnam in 1967, where the boats quickly proved their utility. The portability of the boat allowed SEALs to turn an old guerrilla trick against the VC.

The VC had developed the habit of placing sentries along tributaries to watch for boats going upstream. The boats had to eventually return downstream, at which time they were ambushed. SEALs began having themselves and a STAB helo-lifted up a tributary, from where they were dropped to float back downstream. This unexpected maneuver sometimes caught the enemy sunbathing, swimming, or playing cards on the riverbank. Mounted 7.62 miniguns and M60s on the boat made short shrift of the surprised enemy.

The STABS were used almost constantly. By 1969, most of them were wearing out and were being replaced with new boats called light SEAL support craft (LSSC), also known as the Mark II STAB. But this time the STAB was an acronym for "strike assault boat" instead of "SEAL team assault boat."

See also LIGHT SEAL SUPPORT CRAFT (LSSC); MACIONE, JACK.

SEAL Team Mission Statement

A statement published in Naval Warfare Information Publication (NWIP) 29-1, *SEAL Teams in Naval Special Warfare,* outlined the mission of the U.S. Navy SEALs when they were commissioned in 1962. The assigned mission of the SEALs was composed of three parts:

1. Development of a specialized navy capability in guerrilla/counterguerrilla operations to include training of selected personnel in a wide variety of skills.
2. Development of doctrinal tactics.
3. Development of special support equipment.

NWIP 29-1 also provided the SEALs their mission assignments. As the specific text of the publication is still classified, the mission statement can be generalized as follows:

1. To develop a specialized capability for sabotage, demolition, and other clandestine activities conducted in and from restricted waters, rivers, and canals. Specifically, to be able to destroy enemy shipping, harbor facilities, bridges, railway lines, and other installations in maritime areas and riverine environments. Also to protect friendly supply lines, installations, and assets in maritime and riverine environments from similar attack.
2. To infiltrate and/or exfiltrate agents, guerrillas, evaders, and escapees.
3. To conduct reconnaissance, surveillance, and other intelligence-gathering activities.
4. To accomplish limited counterinsurgency civic action tasks that are normally incidental to counterguerrilla operations. Possibilities include medical aid, elementary civil engineering activities, boat operations and maintenance, and the basic education of the indigenous population.
5. To organize, train, assist, and advise the United States, allied, and other friendly military or paramilitary forces in the conduct of any of the above tasks.
6. To develop doctrine and tactics for such operations.
7. To develop support equipment, including special craft.

See also MISSIONS.

SEAL Team Six

Chairman Mao Tse-Tung of China was a strong advocate of the use of terrorism to achieve political goals. "Kill one," he proclaimed, "and terrorize

SEAL Team Six conducts counterterrorism training aboard a U.S. Navy aircraft carrier. (U.S. Navy)

a thousand." Although terrorism in the political area is certainly not a recent development in human history, it became more prevalent in the twentieth century. Units to combat terrorism—counterterrorism teams—existed as early as the 1920s, when Colombia formed one to free hijacked passenger planes.

The modern form of counterterrorism (CT) got its start in the late 1960s to thwart Palestinian terrorists hijacking airplanes in the Middle East. Most countries, however, still lacked CT capabilities until after the 1972 Munich Olympics, during which the so-called Black September terrorists killed eleven Israeli athletes. Nearly every nation now has elite, highly trained CT elements.

Although the U.S. Navy's official involvement in CT goes back to the failed 1980 attempt to rescue American hostages from the U.S. embassy in Iran, SEALs by then had already begun counterterror training. Elements of SEAL Team Two on the East

Coast had even dedicated, unofficially, a two-platoon group known as MOB Six (Mobility Six) to extensive training in anticipation of a scenario requiring special CT training and tactics.

During the Iran hostage crisis, Cdr. Richard Marcinko was assigned to the Pentagon to work on followup rescue plans. He added what at the time was a nonexistent SEAL element to the joint task force plan. He promised that if his proposal were accepted, he would actually create such a specialized unit and have it in operation within six months.

Ronald Reagan's election as president in 1980 brought an end to the hostage crisis, but Marcinko's plan to create a SEAL CT element was nonetheless approved by Adm. Thomas Hayward, Chief of Naval Operations (CNO). Marcinko was picked to design, build, equip, train, and lead what later became known as the best counterterrorist force in the world. He called it SEAL Team Six, because the number would make the Soviets believe there were five other

SEAL teams somewhere, when there were actually only two others at the time. MOB Six was disbanded as soon as Team Six was formed. Many of its members transferred to Marcinko.

Marcinko wanted Team Six lean and mean, with a personnel complement of 75 enlisted men and 15 officers. Grooming standards were modified—long hair, earrings, beards, and mustaches—in order to permit the operators to pass as blue-collar workers anywhere in the world. He vowed the team would be available on a four-hour notice to deploy from its base at Dam Neck Fleet Combat Training Center, Virginia, to anywhere in the world.

Training emphasized realism for missions in a maritime scenario, such as ship boardings and oil-rig takedowns. Saying he considered "maritime" any operation on which the SEALs carried canteens of water, Marcinko placed Six in training for air ops, plane hijack recoveries, and structure takedowns. Training was conducted in both military and civilian facilities throughout the United States. The unit participated in exchange programs and joint training exercises with more experienced international teams, such as Germany's GSG-9, Great Britain's Special Boat Squadron, (SBS), and France's combat divers. Training included a tremendous amount of combat shooting and other specialized training.

True to his word, Marcinko had SEAL Team Six operational as of January 1, 1981, six months after he started. Its certification mission involved the recovery of a simulated stolen nuclear device from "terrorists" on Vieques Island, seven miles east of Puerto Rico. With 56 operators, Team Six performed a HAHO (high-altitude, high-opening) parachute drop and glided in for 10 miles under cover of darkness to the objective. The operation was declared a tremendous success.

A few years later, Team Six joined the FBI to stage a rescue training exercise on a Norwegian cruise ship, which had moored in Jacksonville, Florida, for refitting. Helicopters carrying SEAL Team Six operators came in downwind of the ship, flying low over the water to avoid detection. They flared up at the last instant, dropped off the assault teams, and were gone. Raiding craft simultaneously came alongside the ship, and SEALs climbed aboard using ladders and extendible painter poles. The entire ship was under attack within seconds.

FBI senior agent John Simeone, later deputy commander of the FBI's Hostage Rescue Team, declared it an impressive demonstration.

SEAL Team Six was involved in a number of operations, both overt and covert, throughout the 1980s and 1990s, including:

1. 1983—Rescue and evacuation of Governor Paul Scoon from Grenada during Operation Urgent Fury;
2. 1985—Deployment to the site of the *Achille Lauro* hijacking;
3. 1989—Took part in Operation Just Cause as part of Task Force White, which included SEAL Team Two. Its primary task, along with Delta Force, was the location and securing of Panamanian strongman Manuel Antonio Noriega;
4. 1990—Operated in Panama again as part of a secret operation code-named Pokeweed. Its goal was the apprehension of Colombian drug lord Pablo Escobar. Team Six was deployed ashore from the U.S. aircraft carrier USS *Forrestal* offshore, but the mission was unsuccessful, due to poor preassault intelligence;
5. 1991—SEAL Team Six reportedly recovered Haitian president Jean Bertrand Aristide under cover of darkness following the coup that deposed him;
6. 1991—Team Six began contingency planning for shooting down Saddam Hussein's personal helicopter with Stinger missiles. This operation never got beyond the planning stages;
7. 1997—Deployment to Bosnia to capture war criminals.

Scandals erupted in SEAL Team Six involving alleged bribery and misuse of government funds by Marcinko. He was eventually convicted of these charges. The publication of his autobiography *Rogue Warrior* in 1992 prompted the navy to avoid notoriety by changing the name of SEAL Team Six to Naval Special Warfare Development Group (DEVGRU, or DevGroup) and hiding it administratively within the chain of command. DevGru, however, continues, with essentially the same missions and responsibilities as SEAL Team Six.

See also ACHILLE LAURO; BOSNIA; MARCINKO, RICHARD; MOBILITY SIX (MOB SIX); NAVAL SPECIAL WARFARE DEVELOPMENT GROUP (DEVGRU); OPERATION DESERT STORM; OPERATION EAGLE CLAW; OPERATION JUST CAUSE; OPERATION URGENT FURY; "RED CELL"; TERRORISM.

sea mammals

Although U.S. Navy SEALs have not been directly involved with training sea mammals for war purposes, they are affected by the results in a number of ways. Dolphins and sea lions are being trained to take the place of human swimmers in detecting and disarming mines, sabotaging ships, and retrieving underwater items. Dolphins have even been trained to kill other swimmers, in a program called the "swimmer nullification system."

Throughout history, animals have been trained for warfare, most commonly dogs, horses, mules, and carrier pigeons. During World War II, the U.S. Army Air Corps contemplated unleashing thousands of kamikaze bats on Japan, each of then carrying an incendiary bomb.

The Navy Marine Mammal Program, much of which is still classified, began in 1960 and has been known under different titles over the years, most recently as the Naval Command, Control and Ocean Surveillance Center, Research, Development, Test and Evaluation Division. Naval research began with a single Pacific white-side dolphin for hydrodynamics studies. Researchers demonstrated that trained dolphins and sea lions could work unfettered in the open sea to perform tasks with great reliability.

Since then, dolphins, sea lions, and even whales have demonstrated their ability to recover objects from great depths of 650 to 2,100 feet, where divers without special submarines could never reach.

SEAL captain William "Bill" Hamilton was in charge of the marine mammal program at Naval Special Warfare Group One in Coronado, California, for over three years beginning in 1980. Bottle-nosed dolphins and sea lions were trained in harbor defense, mine countermeasures, and a "Quickfind" method in which seals were conditioned to find electronics packages from tests of missiles and other ordnance.

Marine mammals have been utilized on at least three occasions in combat situations. SEAL Rudy Boesch recalls seeing dolphins acting as harbor guards at Cam Ranh Bay in Vietnam in 1971. In 1987, dolphins were used to spot mines in tanker escort operations in the Persian Gulf. They then returned to the Gulf during Desert Storm, the war against Iraq, where they were utilized in harbor defense at Bahrain.

Details of the Marine Mammal Program remain sketchy, as it is the navy's policy not to discuss specific details other than to say it uses animals in undercover surveillance and to locate, mark, and retrieve objects.

Seawolves

U.S. Navy helicopter pilots during the Vietnam War were considered a vital part of the triad in the Mekong Delta known as the "SEAL package." This mutually supporting system consisted of SEALs, PBR (Patrol Boat, River) forces, and the Seawolves.

Shortly after SEALs and the "brown-water navy" began operating in the vast network of waterways in the Mekong Delta, it became apparent that they would need another partner, one in the air. The helicopter gunship appeared to be the answer. It could use its high visibility, speed, and maneuverability to gather intelligence on Viet Cong guerrilla movements, relay that intelligence to SEALs and riverine forces for action, then apply firepower where needed.

Since the navy had no suitable helicopters, the army supplied the navy 22 Utility Helicopter 1Bs (UH-1Bs, or "Hueys"). Four detachments of eight pilots, eight crewmembers, and two ships per detachment reported to Tan Son Nhut airfield near Saigon for training in mid-1966. Operations began in September; the navy pilots worked as part of an HC-1 detachment out of Vung Tau but were assigned to waterborne bases in the Delta. These bases were specially built barges with facilities for both PBRs and helicopters, and their crews.

It was during these first operations that the pilots came to be called "Seawolves" by their army counterparts. The name stuck.

Each chopper was armed with two seven-round 2.75-inch rocket pods, four fixed forward-firing M60 machine guns, and two flexible-mounted M60s, one each in the doors on each side. In addition to patrolling for intelligence and targets of opportunity, the Seawolves also infiltrated and extracted SEALs, provided air support and rescue for both SEALs and riverine forces, and were on call 24 hours a day as an emergency-reaction force. Pilots and crews "on call" often slept in their flight suits in order to be prepared for an immediate response to an emergency. The Seawolves gunships were never more than a few minutes away from any point in the Delta. More than one SEAL or PBR crew owes his life to the quick reactions, daring, and abilities of the Seawolves.

"There were some places where the army chopper pilots refused to go," said SEAL lieutenant Wilbur "Pat" Patterson. "We relied on the chopper pilots for insertion and retractions. The Navy Seawolves were the most aggressive pilots we had over there. They'd go in to anywhere, anytime."

Seawolves flew in two normal patrol formations. The "light helo fire team" formation consisted of two aircraft, while the "heavy helo fire team" was composed of three aircraft. Crews flew an average of 600 missions, 3,500 hours of flight time, per each year-long tour. A number of choppers were shot down by enemy fire, and their crews killed, before the Seawolves were disbanded in 1972. By that time, the Seawolves had nine operational detachments stationed in Vietnam in support of SEALs and riverine forces—at Nha Be, Binh Thuy, Dong Tam, Rach Gia, Vinh Long, and Vung Tau, with others stationed on mobile floating bases in the Delta.

See also BLUE HAWKS; OPERATION GAME WARDEN; REDWOLVES.

sensitive area

Any specific location or area that has become of intelligence interest either to the SEALs or other branches of the military or the U.S. government is known as a "sensitive area." During the Cuban missile crisis, for example, suspected missile sites were of particular intelligence interest and therefore designated "sensitive areas."

SERE school

Survival, Escape, Resistance and Evasion (SERE) courses are taught by all branches of the U.S. military to prepare service personnel for escaping and surviving if they are captured by enemy forces. SEALs now teach their own SERE course, through their Naval Special Warfare Center.

See also ESCAPE AND EVASION.

Shepherd, William "Bill" (b. 1950)

Although Navy SEALs are known for operating in virtually all environments—sea, air, and land—for-

mer SEAL-turned astronaut Capt. Bill Shepherd added a third element to that equation—space. After having served 13 years with the U.S. Navy SEALs, Shepherd became an astronaut in 1984 and subsequently went higher and farther than any other commando in history, flying three space shuttle missions as a mission specialist. "I always thought, kind of in the back of my mind, there was a lot of correlation between being in a spacesuit and some of the activities that you do when you're diving," he said.

On October 31, 2000, Shepherd and two Russian cosmonauts—Sergei Krikalev and Yuri Gidzenko—launched aboard a Russian rocket from Kazakhstan to rendezvous with the International Space Station orbiting at 17,180 miles per hour, 237 miles above the earth. Shepherd was the first commander of the space station's first crew. They were to test the station's components, conduct two space walks, and make connections between the modules.

The space station is being built by 16 different nations and is expected to be completed in 2006 after 46 rocket launches. When completed, the 500-ton orbiting station will house seven people at a time for three to six months. It will have more cabin space than a 747 jumbo jet.

After spending 141 days in orbit, Shepherd returned to earth on March 21, 2001. Astronauts, he said, have a lot in common with SEALs. Both must endure hardships and work well as a team.

shotguns

In a sudden, close encounter with the enemy, nothing beats the blast of buckshot from a 12-gauge shotgun to even the odds. SEALs prefer shotguns with a simple pump action. Semiautomatics are too likely to jam in damp and dirty conditions, making them undependable in combat.

An effective 12-gauge combat load contains nine pellets of No. 00 buckshot, each about one-third of an inch in diameter, approximately the size of a .32-caliber bullet. At a distance of 25 meters, the shot pattern covers a circle a little wider than a man's chest. A skilled shooter can fire five rounds within a few seconds, making a shotgun of any manufacture an incredibly accurate and lethal weapon for room clearance and other close-order combat.

A wide variety of munitions other than 00 can transform the shotgun into a versatile, multipurpose weapon. A "flechette" round fires 20 steel darts that can penetrate a steel helmet at 300 meters. A hardened lead slug is capable of penetrating a cast-iron engine block at 100 meters or of blowing a heavy door off its hinges. A room 12 feet square can be made uninhabitable by a single 12-gauge CS tear gas round.

Siebe, Augustus (1788–1872)

The German-born inventor Augustus Siebe, living in England, receives credit for developing the first effective standard diving dress, the prototype of hardhat diving rigs still in use today. It was a hardhat helmet sealed to a watertight, air-containing rubber suit connected to an air pump on the surface.

See also DIVING, HISTORY OF.

signal panel

SEAL members on mission carry a patch of cloth, a "signal panel," which can be displayed on the ground as a prearranged signal to friendly aircraft.

Sig-Sauer P226

Early in 1987, SEAL Team Six became dissatisfied with the officially issued Beretta M9 pistol because of failures in the slide mechanism. The team scouted around for a replacement and settled on the Sig-Sauer P226 9mm semiautomatic handgun manufactured in Switzerland. Because of Switzerland export restrictions, the Swiss Sig company allied with the Sauer company of Germany to produce the weapon and therefore make it available.

The other SEAL teams followed Team Six's example and also began replacing their Berettas with the Sig-Sauer. The initial request for 800 weapons was put out in October 1988. The SEAL teams have expressed their satisfaction with the P226 as their standard sidearm.

The weapons has two minor drawbacks: First, it is a very costly weapon. Second, the slide has a tendency to rust in spots after exposure to salt water.

The P226 fires 9mm parabellum (9×19mm) ammunition at a semiautomatic rate of fire of 40rpm. It comes equipped with a 15-round removable box magazine and weighs slightly more than two pounds fully loaded. It is 7.72 inches in length and has an effective range of about 50 yards.

Berettas and Sig-Sauers are both found in SEAL teams today, along with an assortment of other handguns.

See also BERETTA M9 9MM PISTOL.

skim boat

Following World War II, Francis Riley "Frank" Kaine developed an experimental boat as a faster and more efficient means of deploying swimmers for beach clearances and other underwater demolition team (UDT) missions. He called it a "skim boat." It was a hydrofoil that skimmed the surface of the water. Antenna sensors at the bow adjusted the hydrofoils for wave action. Although it could carry a single 200-pound man at speeds up to 40 knots, its use was abandoned, since it was unsuitable for UDTs who used the "buddy system."

See also KAINE, FRANCIS RILEY "FRANK."

"Sky Hook"

"Sky hook" is the term commonly applied to the Fulton surface-to-air recovery (STAR) system.

See also FULTON SURFACE-TO-AIR RECOVERY (STAR).

Smith, Raymond C., Jr.

Commander of Naval Special Warfare Task Group Central during Operation Desert Storm, Captain Smith was a 1967 graduate of Annapolis who missed the opportunity to command SEALs during the Vietnam War. An on-site commander of a multiplatoon special operations force during the Persian Gulf War, he led the first such unit to be sent overseas in the history of the SEALs. It was the largest deployment of SEALs since Vietnam. Of 540,000 troops shipped to the war zone, some 9,000 were of the Special Operations Command.

Shortly after Saddam Hussein's Iraqi forces invaded Kuwait on August 2, 1990, Captain Smith was appointed head of a SEAL task force, Naval Special Warfare Task Group Central. He was given 72 hours to select and load men and equipment and be ready to leave for the war zone.

The first contingent of 105 West Coast SEALs and support personnel arrived in Saudi Arabia nine days after the invasion. Smith set up headquarters at Ras al-Gar, 75 miles north of Dhahran. Eventually, his force numbered 260 men, including special boat units and support people. Only 60—four platoons—were SEALs.

This was the first time SEALs had served as an integral part of a larger force involved in a major conventional war. Decisions Smith made, along with the performance of his SEALs, helped define the future of naval special warfare. In laying out his concepts of employment, Smith vowed the SEALs would operate in their traditional small-unit roles and become enmeshed in none of the Ranger-like operations that had led to the disaster at the Paitilla airfield in Panama in 1989. "I wanted to do what we do well, and I wanted to make sure my boss knew what we could do," Smith said.

SEALs under Smith surveyed beach landing sites, ran reconnaissance patrols, assaulted enemy ships and strongpoints in small-unit format, and conducted other missions for which SEALs are prepared and known. SEALs proved they could work effectively in a conventional conflict and fit into a large force fighting a major war.

Smith and his task group returned to Coronado on March 11, 1991, having successfully conducted some 200 missions. His unit had suffered not a single casualty.

See also OPERATION DESERT STORM.

snorkel

A snorkel is a mouth tube that permits a skin diver to breath while swimming on the surface with his face underwater. It was the first and most crucial step in providing an air supply to permit a diver to stay underwater longer. The first snorkels, reeds or hollow tubes, date back to at least 500 B.C. when the Greek Scyllias was captured by a Persian naval force. He seized a knife and escaped by jumping overboard. Once in the water he used a hollow reed as a snorkel as he swam among the Persian fleet, cutting each ship loose from its moorings.

While snorkels allowed a diver to remain at least partly submerged for an extended period, permitting

more covert approaches to enemy strongholds, they proved to be severely limited. It might seem that a longer breathing tube would permit the diver greater depth and flexibility. Such was not the case. It is almost impossible to breath through a tube at a depth of over three feet, since the weight of the water exerts a pressure of nearly 200 pounds on the diver's chest.

Snorkels have very limited utility for SEALs. They use them to conduct routine chores, such as cleaning boat hulls while in the water or searching for items in shallow water. Snorkels have very little potential for combat missions.

See also DIVING, HISTORY OF; SCYLLIAS.

SOG SK2000 knife

During the Vietnam War, a knife was manufactured specifically for issue by Green Beret soldiers of the army's Fifth Special Forces Group who operated with the top-secret Studies and Observation Group (MACV-SOG). SEALs who worked for SOG were occasionally given one of the knives, designated as SOG SK2SS.

SOG Speciality Knife Company began manufacturing a loose duplicate of the rare Fifth SFG knife. It was redesignated as the SOG SE2000 when it was issued to SEALs. It was more a fighting knife than a general tool, as the shape of the tip and back edge, which could be sharpened, aided in penetration.

The knife weighed .78 pounds, was 12.31 inches long overall, and had a 7.06 inch blade. The blade was of stainless steel, with a molded, checkered handle with four finger grooves.

The SOG SK2000 was being considered in 1993 tests as the issue steel SEAL knife, but it was beaten out by Mission Knives of California. The company submitted its Multi Purpose Knife for the tests. It had a unique blade made of nearly indestructible titanium. SEALs turned to it as a better knife.

Somalia

Somalia is a small sub-Saharan country of Africa, the easternmost country on the continent, in which U.S. forces, including SEALs, were involved in one of their fiercest firefights since the Vietnam War.

See also OPERATION RESTORE HOPE.

space program

While the more glamorous SEALs often received the credit, the recovery of the space capsules of the Mercury, Gemini, and Apollo programs were all actually accomplished by specially trained frogmen of the underwater demolition teams (UDTs). UDT swimmers also helped in the weightlessness training of astronauts for the Skylab program.

The 1960s and 1970s were the glory days for the men of the UDTs. They were always the first into the water to greet the astronauts after splashdown. They saw themselves on TV, on the front pages of newspapers, in magazines, and even in the *Encyclopedia Britannica*. One team flew to Chicago on a private jet for a ticker-tape parade.

The National Aeronautical and Space Administration (NASA) was founded on October 1, 1958. The space program, Project Mercury, was introduced six days later. By 1963, Mercury had evolved into Project Gemini and then into the Apollo Program, during which a man would be landed on the moon. After reentry into the earth's atmosphere, the space capsules would deploy parachutes and land in the ocean.

The recovery of the capsule and astronauts followed a specific pattern, for which UDT frogmen trained rigorously. The recovery generally required three divers, all wearing wetsuits and SCUBA gear. They were flown to the floating capsule by helicopter, out of which they "helo-cast" into the waves.

Specially trained frogmen of the underwater demolition teams (UDTs) helped recover manned spacecraft during the early stages of NASA's space program. Here, UDT men recover astronauts James A. Lovell and Edwin E. Aldrin in 1966. (U.S. Navy)

The first man in the water attached a sea anchor to the capsule. A sea anchor, similar to a parachute, is deployed to drag in the water and prevent the capsule from being pushed along by the wind. The other two men of the team then put the flotation collar on the capsule as a precaution to keep it afloat. After the flotation device was secured, rubber boats were dropped with which to recover the astronauts. The capsule hatch was then opened. The astronauts clambered from their spacecraft into the rubber boat, from which they were transferred to a waiting aircraft carrier. The frogmen remained with the capsule until it was also recovered.

Christopher O. Bent, UDT-21, vividly recalls the first Apollo spacecraft launched from Cape Kennedy atop a newly developed Saturn booster in February 1966. It was an unmanned, suborbital, full-scale test. Bent was the first member of the recovery team dropped into the water at the recovery site north of Ascension Island, midway between Brazil and Africa. His job was to attach the sea anchor. It was fully dark when the helicopter put him in.

While attaching the parachute anchor, he spotted a large shark nearby. Thinking quickly, he swam into the parachute canopy and pulled it completely around his body until only his face mask and eyes showed. His quick action possibly saved his life.

Chief Petty Officer Michael Bennett participated in July 1969 in the recovery of *Apollo 11*, aboard which were the first men to walk on the surface of the moon, Neil Armstrong, Edwin "Buzz" Aldrin, and Michael Collins. The *Encyclopaedia Britannica* has a picture of a helicopter and a frogman jumping from the helicopter into the water next to the command module; Bennett was the jumper.

Because scientists were worried that astronauts might bring back some unknown disease or life form, an elaborate procedure was established for their recovery. Frogmen were responsible for the first phase of the isolation phase.

The UDTs bathed the command module around the hatch with a Betadine solution before opening it. The hatch was opened, and the astronauts donned BIG (biological isolation garment) suits. Swimmers washed down the astronauts as they sat in the rubber boat. The spacemen were then picked up by helicopter and whisked off to an aircraft carrier, where they were held in further isolation for the presumed incubation period of any bugs.

UDT seaman Luco W. Palma and Petty Officer Third Class Roger C. Banfield were members of UDT-13 assigned to recover astronauts James A. Lovell, Jr., Jack Swigert, Jr., and Fred Haise, Jr. from their ill-fated *Apollo 13* mission. The craft had lost power and was rapidly running out of life-supporting air when the astronauts managed to return to earth on April 17, narrowly averting disaster. They landed in the Pacific near Samoa.

The recovery went even more quickly and smoothly than normal. The astronauts were lifted from the Moon landing module, which they had had to use for reentry to Earth, and were delivered to a waiting aircraft carrier. (However, bad luck seemed to follow UDT-13, as it had already plagued *Apollo 13*. Five months later, Luco W. Palma was killed and Roger Banfield wounded by a 105 mm artillery-shell booby trap in Vietnam. UDT-13 also suffered one other death and eight other serious wounds in Vietnam within a few months following the recovery.)

Men of the UDTs played one other vital role in the space program during this same era. UDT divers in the summer of 1968 were assigned to train Skylab astronauts in weightlessness. Weightlessness in space is very similar to weightlessness underwater. The frogmen trained the astronauts how to work in the lab underwater.

Eventually, a SEAL went into space. Commander Bill Shepherd, a former member of SEAL Team Two and a 28-year veteran of naval special warfare, was sent into space in 2000 as the first commander of the *International Space Station*.

See also SHEPHERD, WILLIAM BILL.

special boat squadrons (SBR)

Aside from the SEALs, the other major part of the U.S. Naval Special Warfare Command (SPECWAR-COM) comprises the special boat squadrons (SBRs). The idea behind the SBRs was to provide SEAL teams with dedicated "organic" mobility, along with the ability for special surface patrol and surface strike missions. The squadrons are commanded by SEALs but manned largely by dedicated professionals within special warfare who have the naval career specialty of "combat craft crewman." Like the SEALs, they are all strictly volunteers.

There are two special boat squadrons within naval special warfare. SBR-1 is based at Coronado, California, and SBR-2 at Little Creek, Virginia. Each exists to equip, support, train, and provide crews and special operations ships and craft for special operations activities. Each SBR is composed of special boat units (SBUs) and Cyclone-class Patrol, Coastal (PBC) ships. Crews are trained and equipped to operate a variety of surface craft either on the seas and coastal areas or on rivers, inland streams, and waterways.

SBUs list their mission as to employ, operate, and maintain a variety of surface combat craft; to conduct and support naval and joint special operations, riverine warfare, coastal patrol and interdiction; search and rescue operations; surveillance; harassment; interdiction of maritime lines of communications; deception operations; armed escort and small-caliber gunfire support; and infiltrating and exfiltrating troops.

Special Boat Squadron One at Coronado maintains operational and administrative control of Special Boat Unit Eleven, SBU-12, and four Cyclone-class PCs.

The two SBUs at Coronado consist of some eight rigid-hull inflatable boat detachments, with two boats and crews per each detachment, along with five Mark V special operations craft detachments and two Patrol Boat, River (PBR) detachments. This configuration may change from time to time.

SBR-2 at Little Creek commands SBU-20 and SBU-22, along with nine Cyclone-class PCs.

SBU-20 consists of a headquarters element, 13 RIB detachments, and five Mark V special operations craft detachments. Again, each detachment consists normally of two boats and crews. SBU-22 is composed of a headquarters element, two PBR detachments, two mini-armored troop carrier detachments, and two Patrol Boat, Light (PBL) detachments. SBU-22 is mainly a reserve organization; it draws over 70 percent of its strength from naval reservists.

SBU-26, based in Rodman, Panama, comes under the administrative control of SBR-2 but is under the direct operational control of SPECWARCOM. It consists of a headquarters element and 10 PBL detachments. It concentrates on a riverine environment in support of the Southern Command (SOCOM) theater of operations.

See also NAVAL SPECIAL WARFARE; ORGANIZATIONAL STRUCTURE, SPECIAL OPERATIONS.

Special Forces, U.S. Army (Green Berets)

The Green Berets, so- called because of their distinctive headgear, are part of the U.S. Army's contribution to the U.S. Special Operations Command. USSOCOM integrates assets from all the military services, including the Navy SEALS, into one organization.

U.S. Army Special Forces and the U.S. Navy SEALs are similar in many respects, especially in that they share a joint heritage and are both dedicated to conducting unconventional and guerrilla warfare. The two organizations regularly exchange cross-branch training in such areas as foreign weapons, improvised munitions, parachute training, water and boat training, and other aspects of unconventional warfare. When the Navy SEALs were formed in 1962, they adapted many Green Beret tactics and techniques to their own special requirements.

The Special Forces heritage can be traced back through World War II's Office of Strategic Services (OSS), the Ranger battalions, the "Devil's Brigade," and "Merrill's Marauders" to Rogers's Rangers during the French and Indian War. SEALs share part, if not all, of this unconventional heritage.

Army Special Forces, as they exist today, began with activation of the 10th Special Forces Group on June 19, 1952. Members of the Special Forces were sent to Vietnam in 1956. Special Forces remained active in the war until the Fifth Group was withdrawn in 1971. The first Medal of Honor awarded for heroism in Vietnam went to a Special Forces captain, Roger H. C. Donlon. Special Forces earned 16 more Medals of Honor during the course of the war, a number that, as with the SEALs, was far out of proportion to their numbers involved in the war.

See also U.S. SPECIAL OPERATIONS COMMAND (USSOCOM).

special forces operational base (SFOB)

A provisional organization set up within a friendly area to provide command, administrative, training, intelligence, and logistical support for unconventional units operating within the area, as well as for indigenous unconventional warfare forces sponsored by that special warfare unit, is referred to as an SFOB (special forces operational base). The SFOB will normally be under an army Special Forces component

commander of the joint unconventional warfare task force (JUWTF) operating in the area.

special operations teams (SOTS)

SEALs were originally called "special operations teams" (SOTs) during their preorganization stages in 1961.

See also SEALS.

special police investigative service (SPIS)

During the Vietnam War, MACV-SOG (Military Assistance Command Vietnam—Studies and Observation Group) set up the top-secret Phoenix Program to target the infrastructure of the National Liberation Front and the Viet Cong. This controversial program was ostensibly discontinued, although in reality it simply continued under a new name— Special Police Investigative Service.

See also PHOENIX PROGRAM.

special warfare insignia

The U.S. Navy authorized a special forces insignia for its underwater men in the fall of 1970. Underwater demolition teams (UDTs) and the SEALs had different badges. Each had an anchor in the center, with a trident and a flintlock musket behind the anchor. The SEAL insignia, more commonly called a "trident," added an American eagle perched astride the trident.

A few years later, in the early 1970s, the two insignias were combined. Thereafter both SEALs and UDTs wore the SEAL insignia.

SPIE (special procedures, insertion/extraction)

During the Vietnam War, special operations units experimented with techniques for lifting men from jungle clearings that were too small for a helicopter landing zone. Two of these techniques worked particularly well—SPIE (special procedures, insertion/extraction) and STABO (Stabilized, Tactical, Airborne Body Operations). Both became standard procedures for extracting SpecOps troops from spots otherwise inaccessible to even a helicopter, such as

SPIE was a technique developed during the Vietnam War for lifting men from jungle clearings too small for a helicopter to land. (U.S. Navy)

with a safety rope to prevent their drifting apart when airborne.

"spook boats"

In the 1970s, fleet sailors began using the term "spook boats" to describe those submarines to which dry-deck shelters (DDS) were attached. A DDS contains and launches SEALs and their SEAL delivery vehicles. CIA agents, SEALs, Green Berets, and other covert operatives are commonly referred to as "spooks."

See also ADVANCED SEAL DELIVERY SYSTEM (ASDS); DRY-DECK SHELTER (DDS); SUBMARINE OPERATIONS.

spy satellites

Spying from space got its start in 1960, when the United States launched a 300-pound orbiting satellite to take photographs of the Soviet Union. Since then, satellites have become among the military's most valuable tools for sensing enemy targets, movements, locations, buildups, and other activities. Satellites have become so sophisticated that virtually every populated inch of the earth now comes under surveillance, with such resolution that the numbers on a vehicle license place can be read. A half-dozen military satellites were mustered into service in 1990 and 1991 to serve U.S. forces during Operation Desert Storm. The exact number of spy satellites, their functions and capabilities, remain classified.

SEALs use images from space in planning missions against selected targets.

STABO (Stabilized Tactical Airborne Body Operations)

STABO is a rope method for extracting special operations personnel by helicopter from areas too small or inaccessible to allow a helicopter landing.

See also SPIE (SPECIAL PROCEDURES, INSERTION/EXTRACTION).

starlight scope

The starlight scope uses magnified ambient light from the stars, the Moon, and other sources to pro-

small clearings in the forest, the sides of mountains, boats, or even from the tops of trees.

Developed by the navy, SPIE is a single-rope technique in which any number of men wearing harnesses similar to parachute harnesses hook up in line on a single rope and are pulled into the air by a hovering helicopter, to which the rope is attached. The single rope technique prevents the men from colliding with each other, while leaving their hands free to fire weapons. SEALs commonly use this technique.

STABO is a favorite of army Special Forces. It is a technique similar to SPIE, except that each man hooks into a different rope. If more than one trooper is hoisted at a time, they are connected vide a reasonable degree of night-vision. It can also be adapted as a night scope for a weapon. Other night-vision devices can be worn, like large glasses to aid night vision for pilots and special warfare operators on night missions.

Stingray

Underwater demolition teams (UDTs) experimented with remote-controlled boats filled with demolitions during their beach-clearance operations in the South Pacific during World War II. The experiments with "Stingrays" were largely unsuccessful.

See also OPERATION FLINTLOCK.

strategic combat operations

Strategic combat operations are defined as the science and art of conducting a military campaign on a broad international or global level. SEALs are rarely, if ever, involved in strategic operations, because of their specialized mission capabilities and limited troop size. Instead, they focus on tactical combat operations.

See also COMBAT TACTICS.

strike assault boat (STAB)

The STAB is more commonly known as the Mark II light SEAL support craft (LSSC), or SEAL team assault boat.

See also LIGHT SEAL SUPPORT CRAFT (LSSC); SEAL TEAM ASSAULT BOAT.

submarine operations

Although SEALs may use a variety of techniques to insert themselves into a mission, the most stealthy method of all is by submarine. At any one time, SEALs may be deployed in submarines operating around the world, waiting for their unique services to be required. There are three basic methods by which a SEAL unit may be deployed from a submarine.

If an intended insertion point is screened in some way from observation by the enemy, and if sea conditions permit, the submarine can surface and launch the SEALs in rubber raiding craft.

If the SEALs must launch submerged, the easiest way is the dry-deck shelter (DDS) method. The DDS is a chamber that bolts onto the deck of the vessel and operates on the same principle as a submarine lockout chamber. However, it is far larger, big enough to accommodate an entire SEAL platoon with all its gear and its SEAL delivery vehicle (SDV), and it is a lot faster than the alternative. The DDS also converts to a hyperbaric chamber for treating divers who suffer from the painful, potentially fatal condition known as decompression sickness, or caisson disease.

To its skipper's relief, a submarine can remain five miles or more offshore to deploy SEALs by DDS and SDV, whereas it must move much closer to the beach to insert them by either of the two other methods.

The third method is to insert swimmers directly from the submarine. A U.S. submarine has a small chamber, the "escape trunk" or "lockout chamber," forward of the sail. It is a spherical space about six feet across, large enough to accommodate up to five swimmers at a time. It serves two functions: first, to allow trapped submariners to escape a boat sunk in shallow water; second, to deploy and recover combat swimmers.

The process begins with the swimmers donning wetsuits, combat equipment, and SCUBA or rebreather equipment, as needed. It is also quite possible for them to ascend without underwater breathing apparatus; SEALs train for "free ascent," or "blow and go." They can be recovered the same way, by simply drawing in a deep breath and diving down to enter the chamber.

Cramped and uncomfortable, the SEALs climb into the chamber. It is sealed, and water slowly begins to enter. Mouthpieces and air hoses inside the chamber allow the SEALs to breathe using the sub's air supply until the chamber is full of water and the outer lock opens for them to swim into the open sea.

A SEAL explains the procedure: "You get into there, you've got all this weight on you, you close the bottom hatch, you stand there, doubled over—tanks on your back, equipment in your arms—three to five people jammed in there. Then somebody has to find a way to reach over to the valve so you can start to flood the chamber."

In a typical insertion, one man will lock out first, alone. He will retrieve the rubber boats from their storage in the sail locker on deck, inflate them, and let them float to the surface on a long tethering line, which he secures to the submarine. He then signals the submarine's skipper either by flashing a light signal at the periscope, if the captain is willing to expose it, or by rapping on the boat's hull with the handle of his knife. The next batch of divers immediately enters the chamber and prepares to be expelled.

This entire activity takes place normally in darkness, almost entirely by touch, and requires quite a long time. It is usually conducted in cold, high seas; hypothermia and seasickness may prove a problem. The depth is usually around 40 feet.

If SEALs are to be extracted by submarine, the same process is followed, only in reverse. After exchanging the proper signals, the SEALs either take their boat or swim out to deep water to the rendezvous. They dive down to the lockout chamber, seal it, drain it of water while they breathe using the chamber's air supply system, and reenter the sub.

Submarines often spend weeks at a time working with SEALs in training exercises. During the Vietnam War, underwater demolition team members and SEALs carried out a number of hazardous beach reconnaissance missions and even fought battles ashore after locking out of submarines. SEALs were inserted by submarine on a missile reconnaissance of Cuba during the Cuban missile crisis in 1962.

See also ADVANCED SEAL DELIVERY SYSTEM (ASDS); BOEHM, ROY; CUBAN MISSILE CRISIS; DRY-DECK SHELTER (DDS); USS *GRAYBACK*; "SPOOK BOATS"; OPERATION THUNDERHEAD.

subskimmer

The subskimmer is a British boat that can operate not only as a speedy surface craft but also as a submersible, either partially or completely below the water. U.S. Navy SEALs can call on a variety of small boats for their use during missions, including the subskimmer.

The subskimmer is a four-commando inflatable craft powered by a 90 hp engine that permits a surface top speed of 25 knots and a range of 70 nautical miles. When partially submerged, the boat uses its snorkel-equipped outboard engine. In this mode, it

The British subskimmer can operate on the surface as well as below the water. U.S. Navy SEALs can call upon a variety of small boats for their use during missions, including the subskimmer. (Defense Boats, Ltd.)

has a maximum speed of about two knots, to prevent the wake from stripping away the divers' face masks. When fully submerged, the vessel is driven by a pair of battery-powered electric motors.

The batteries possess enough power for about six hours underwater, enough to support an undetected underwater approach and withdrawal from a target. The boat is partially deflated in order to submerge, then reinflated with an electric pump for surface operations.

Sun Tzu (Sunzi) (400–320 B.C.)

Sun Tzu was an outstanding military genius of China. A native of the state of Ch'i (Qi), he fled to the neighboring state of Wu on account of a rebellion. There, he wrote *The Art of War* in 13 chapters for Ho La, the ruler of Wu and was subsequently made a general.

The Art of War is considered the first and most authoritative treatise on the conduct of warfare. Sun Tzu's tactics are studied and practiced today by SEALs and other practitioners of warfare.

Swift boat (fast patrol craft, PCF)

The 50-foot Swift boat, or fast patrol craft, was a modified oil-rig crew boat utilized by SEALs and their boat crew support during the Vietnam War. The Swift's high speed and shallow draft allowed it to operate in the shallow rivers and tributaries of Vietnam or off the coast. Lightly armored, its best defense was its speed and maneuverability. It was armed with a twin .50-caliber machine gun turret on top of the main cabin and an M60 machine gun mounted amidships.

The Swift served throughout Vietnam. Most were left behind with the South Vietnamese navy when U.S. forces pulled out.

swim fins
Enlarged frog-foot-shaped footwear worn by SEALs and other divers to increase speed and maneuverability underwater, swim fins were patented by a Frenchman, Louis de Corlieu, in 1933. First called "swimming propellers," they were popularized worldwide by an American entrepreneur, Owen Churchill. Churchill's first year of production of swim fins was in 1940. Initially only 946 pairs were sold, but in later years of the war, tens of thousands were sold to Allied forces for use by underwater demolition teams and other water forces.

See also DIVING, HISTORY OF.

swimmer delivery vehicle
The SEAL delivery vehicle, a type of "wet" minisubmarine used for the clandestine delivery of sea commandos, was originally known as the *Swimmer delivery vehicle*.

See also ADVANCED SEAL DELIVERY SYSTEM (ASDS).

swimmer propulsion unit
Since World War II and Italian-manned torpedoes, frogmen have continued their attempts to increase

Using the idea of manned torpedoes, Navy SEALs experimented with a variety of small powered underwater vehicles to increase their speed. SEAL George Callison experiments with a "sea sled" while with the Underwater Test and Evaluation Unit in the U.S. Virgin Islands. (U.S. Navy)

their underwater speed by the use of small powered vehicles. U.S. Navy underwater demolition team frogmen experimented with various devices during the 1950s and 1960s to increase the speed of a swimmer from one or two miles per hour up to three or four. Most of these experiments involved battery-powered "underwater propulsion units," onto which a diver hung with both hands while the little torpedo-shaped device towed him through the water.

Swimmer propulsion units, though still available, are rarely used by modern SEALs. The advanced SEAL delivery system, a type of wet minisubmarine which can carry up to eight swimmers, has proven to be far more effective and practical.

See also ADVANCED SEAL DELIVERY SYSTEM (ASDS) CHARIOTS; MAIALE.

T

Tachen Islands

In 1955, while the United States was still protecting the Chinese Nationalist government on Taiwan against the mainland Chinese communists, Taiwan decided that its occupation of the Tachen Islands, near the mainland, was untenable. The Nationalist government wanted to send ships to the islands to evacuate its troops but was afraid of being attacked by the Beijing government. Taiwan called on America for help.

The U.S. Seventh Fleet undertook the mission of protecting the evacuation. In February 1955, Underwater Demolition Team 11 was sent to chart a safe passage for the evacuation ships in deep water while the fleet hovered offshore as a protective screen. The Nationalist Chinese evacuated without communist interference, and the American frogmen blew up all installations and supplies on the islands that might be useful to the mainland Chinese.

tactical combat operations

Tactical combat operations are defined as the science and art of handling troops in the presence of the enemy or for immediate objectives. SEALs have become experts in the tactics of unconventional warfare.

See also COMBAT TACTICS.

tactical operations center (TOC)

The center for control of operations within an area of operations is called the TOC. It is the nerve center for all activity by subordinate units. Within the SEALs, it will typically consist of a commander, operations officer, intelligence operatives, and support personnel. Its size and number depends upon the size and number of units operating within the command.

See also MISSIONS; SPECIAL FORCES OPERATIONAL BASE (SFOB).

Tarawa

In SEAL legend, the World War II battle of Tarawa is looked upon as the birth of the underwater demolition teams, predecessors of the Navy SEALs.

Tarawa was the first step in the U. S. Navy's strategy to hop from island to island northwest across the Pacific toward the Japanese home islands, building air and naval support bases as it went. Prior to the invasion, hydrographic information about the islands and coral atolls of the Pacific was extremely limited. Invasion planners led by Rear Adm. Richmond Kelly Turner, amphibious fleet commander, were forced to depend upon information obtained from previous occupants of the islands, from old charts and tide tables provided by the British (some dating back to 1841), and from photo surveys by U.S. airplanes and submarines.

Turner expected five feet or more of water over the reefs surrounding Tarawa. However, D-day for the invasion, November 20, 1943, happened to fall upon the neap tide, when winds sometimes caused the level of the water to rise and fall unpredictably, often several times within a few hours.

The first waves of U.S. Marines, using tracked landing craft, available only in limited numbers, made it to shore with minimal problems; there they engaged Japanese troops, who put up an unexpectedly stiff resistance. The neap tide, however, caused the water level suddenly to fall. Subsequent waves of marines in flat-bottomed landing craft ran solidly aground on the coral, which in many places was covered with less than two feet of water. Combat-laden marines had to wade several hundred yards to shore through a maze of shallows and sudden deep dropoffs. Tanks sank, taking with them all aboard. Men carrying over 100 pounds of weapons and equipment dropped into deep holes and drowned. Japanese defenders ashore blazed away at the waterlogged Americans.

The U.S. Marines lost 1,027 dead and another 2,242 wounded out of an invading force of 16,800. More marines drowned attempting to wade ashore at Tarawa than were killed fighting the Japanese for the island.

The losses caused a tremendous uproar back in the United States and within the navy command and control staff. Almost immediately after the battle, Admiral Turner sent out an urgent order for the creation and utilization of special teams of men trained to scout out enemy beaches, remove natural and man-made obstacles, and guide invading forces ashore.

Actually, training of such units had already begun. The Amphibious Scouts and Raiders and the naval demolition units were already being used in the European theater and had seen action in Africa and in Italy. Naval combat demolition units (NCDUs) were in training in Fort Pierce, Florida. Admiral Turner requested NCDUs be sent to the Pacific to be the vanguard of his amphibious forces for the next step in the island-hopping campaign—Saipan.

NCDUs in the Pacific quickly merged into underwater demolition teams (UDTs). The SEALs were commissioned in 1962. Twenty years later, UDTs merged with the SEALs to become a single command under naval special forces.

See also ACHESON, BILL; AMPHIBIOUS SCOUT AND RAIDERS; BUCKLEW, PHILIP H.; D-DAY; FORT PIERCE, FLORIDA; KAINE, FRANCIS RILEY; KAUFFMAN, DRAPER L.; KWAJALEIN; LANDING CRAFT, NAVAL COMBAT DEMOLITION UNITS (NCDUS); NAVAL DEMOLITION UNITS (NDUS); OPERATION FLINTLOCK; OPERATION TORCH; SAIPAN; UNDERWATER DEMOLITION TEAMS (UDTS).

target acquisition

"Target acquisition" refers to the detection, identification, and location of a target in sufficient detail to permit the effective employment of weapons against it. Targets can be acquired in a number of different ways—by spy aircraft, spy satellites, ground assets, reconnaissance teams, or other direct intelligence. SEALs conducted a number of target-acquisition missions during Operation Desert Storm.

Task Force 194

U.S. forces during the Vietnam War were confronted with the problem of enemy supplies crossing the Mekong Delta for use by Viet Cong units throughout Vietnam. The U.S. Army and Navy, working with the South Vietnamese, formed SEALORDS (Southeast Asia lake, ocean, river, and delta strategy) to interdict resupply and reinforcement lines in the northern Delta. SEALORDS was formally and officially known as Task Force 194, composed of Army Special Forces, riverine and junk forces, and U.S. Navy SEALs.

See also SEALORDS.

Task Unit Whiskey

During Operation Just Cause against Panama in 1989, U.S. SEALs were assigned two major missions. One of these was to disable the patrol boat *Presidente Porras,* which dictator Manuel Antonio Noriega might use in an escape attempt. Task Unit Whiskey was the code name assigned to this particular SEAL unit.

See also OPERATION JUST CAUSE.

terminal guidance

During wartime, SEALs may be called upon to locate specific enemy targets for attack by supporting aircraft, artillery, or missiles. Over the years, special ops have used a lot of different gear to help them designate and plot terminal guidance (TG) targets. The 16-pound Compact Laser Designator (CLD) was used by special forces during the Gulf War. The need for a lightweight TG device led to the development of the Litton PAQ-10 Ground Laser Target Designator (GLTD).

The GLTD is about the size of two shoe boxes taped together. It weighs under 12 pounds and is equipped with 10X sighting optics and a laser rangefinder/designator which can sight, range, and designate targets up to six miles away. An aircraft equipped with a laser spot tracker can home in on the laser spot produced by the GLTD and apply ordnance with amazing accuracy. GLTD also provides guidance for laser-guided bombs and missiles.

See also COMPACT LASER DESIGNATOR (GLD).

terrorism

According to the FBI definition, "Terrorism is the unlawful use of force or violence against persons or property to intimidate or coerce a government, the civilian population or any segment thereof, in furtherance of political or social objectives." "Kill one and terrorize a thousand," was the way Chairman Mao put it.

Terrorists prey on fears to gain their objectives, whatever they may be—the release of prisoners, money, or ublicity for political gains. They depend upon the sudden death of small groups of people or of individuals to strike terror into the hearts of the entire population. The power of such terrorists has been increased dramatically in an age of mass media and live-feed satellite, when the bombing of a bus in Israel is seen in Tulsa, Oklahoma, five minutes later. Weapons of mass destruction—

nuclear devices—have added to terrorist arsenals and their ability to coerce governments. The United States spends roughly five billion dollars a year combating terrorism.

Nations concentrate upon two areas in their fight against terrorism: *antiterrorism,* which is designed to prevent terrorist acts before they occur; and *counterterrorism,* which includes direct acts against terrorists to capture and then eliminate the threat they represent. Passenger screening at airports is an example of antiterrorism, while the takedown of a terrorist stronghold or the freeing of hostages is counterterrorism.

The first counterterrorism teams came into existence in the 1920s, when Colombia formed a team to free hijacked passenger planes. The modern form of CT (counterterrorism) got its start in 1968 after Palestinian terrorists hijacked an Israeli passenger jet. Still, most countries lacked any effective CT until after the 1972 Munich Olympics, when a group calling itself "Black September" machinegunned 11 Israel athletes.

The bomb-slaying of 247 U.S. Marines in Beirut in 1983 pointed out the need for the United States to employ both antiterrorism and CT methods. Since then, the United States has been the target of numerous terrorist attacks around the world, including attacks on American embassies, the 1993 World Trade Center bombing in New York City, and the bombing of the USS *Cole* in 2000. The worst attack of any sort on American soil occurred on the morning of September 11, 2001, when extremist Islamic terrorists hijacked four commercial airliners and slammed two of them into New York's World Trade Center and a third into the Pentagon. The fourth crashed into a field in Pennsylvania, killing all aboard, after passengers resisted the takeover. It was reportedly headed for Washington, D.C., to crash into the White House. More than 3,000 people were killed in the four incidents and the World Trade Center was demolished.

The terrorist action led to President George W. Bush's declaring a "war on terror" and the American attack on Osama bin Laden and his al-Qaeda terrorist network harbored by the ruling Taliban government in Afghanistan. Special operations forces, including Navy SEALs, are being used extensively in the war, which (as of this writing) President Bush has declared may last for years.

See also *ACHILLE LAURO*; MARCINKO, RICHARD; MOBILITY SIX (MOB SIX); NAVAL SPECIAL WARFARE DEVELOPMENT GROUP (DEVGRU); OPERATION EAGLE CLAW; OPERATION JUST CAUSE; OPERATION URGENT FURY; "RED CELL"; SEAL TEAM SIX.

Tesei, Teseo

Along with Lt. Elios Toschi, Italian submarine officer Teseo Tesei designed a manned torpedo, called "Maiale" (pig or pork), with which he intended to sink surreptitiously Allied shipping at the beginning of World War II.

See also MAIALE.

Tet Offensive

Tet, the lunar New Year, is a widely celebrated holiday throughout Vietnam. On January 30, 1968, over 84,000 Viet Cong (VC) and North Vietnamese army (NVA) troops launched the largest communist offensive of the entire Vietnam War. By February 1, Saigon and 36 provincial capitals and 64 district capitals were under attack. Three SEAL platoons in-country at the time handled themselves capably and professionally.

Two SEAL platoons, one in each of the towns of Vinh Long and My Tho, thwarted the Viet Cong attempt to take over the city, in heavy street fighting. A third SEAL platoon, the Eighth, actually liberated the capital of Chau Doc province. "The SEALs in vicious house-to-house fighting succeeded in breaking the hold that the Viet Cong had established in the city," read a commendation to the platoon. "The members of CORDS [Civil Operations and Revolutionary Development Support] staff in Chau Doc have the deepest admiration for and extend profound gratitude to each member of the platoon of Navy SEALs."

Although the Tet offensive was a resounding military defeat for the communists, it proved to be a political victory. Fed by the U.S. media, protests against the war intensified within the United States.

Thornton, Michael Edwin (b. 1949)

Petty Officer Second Class Michael Thornton was the first enlisted SEAL to be awarded the Congres-

sional Medal of Honor and one of three SEALs to win it during the Vietnam War. The other two SEALs were Lt. Thomas R. Norris and Lt. Joseph R. "Bob" Kerrey.

By the fall of 1972, the SEAL presence in Vietnam had dwindled to only three officers and nine enlisted men. To keep track of North Vietnamese forces along the Demilitarized Zone (DMZ), as well as to pinpoint targets for bombing attacks, small units of South Vietnamese frogmen known as Lien Doc Nguoi Nhai (LDNN) patrolled between the Cua Viet River and the DMZ. U.S. SEAL advisers often led the LDNN patrols. A typical patrol consisted of two American SEALs and three or four LDNN.

On October 31, 1972, SEAL lieutenant Thomas R. Norris and Engineman Second Class Michael Thornton accompanied three LDNN on a DMZ patrol. Ironically, Norris was already to receive the Medal of Honor himself for action in April 1972, six months earlier.

As usual with such a patrol, the team sailed north in a Vietnamese junk and made contact with a U.S. destroyer that would standby offshore to provide gunfire support if it should be needed. The junk then eased close to the beach and put the patrol ashore in rubber boats—but the SEALs were north of the Cua Viet River, when they thought they were south of it. It was 0400, still two hours or so before dawn. The team intended to patrol north to the Cua Viet and then return south for extraction.

By dawn, after threading their way through numerous NVA enemy encampments, Norris and Thornton had realized the error. The river was south of them; they were about to enter North Vietnam. The situation was made doubly hazardous due to the fact that the team could not count on air cover or helicopter support because of formidable NVA air defenses in the area. The only help they could depend on was the destroyer's five-inch guns. The destroyer, however, had to know their precise location in order to provide fire support; the SEALs didn't know where they were. They were virtually on their own, surrounded by the enemy.

Norris ordered the patrol toward the shoreline where he hoped to find a recognizable landmark. Instead, the five-man team encountered an NVA patrol of more than 40 soldiers. The firefight lasted for the better part of an hour. Enemy soldiers crept closer and closer, until some of them were at almost point-blank range in the dunes. Thornton suffered shrapnel wounds in both legs and his back. One of the LDNN was shot through the hip.

By this time, Norris had figured out where they were and had decided upon a desperate gamble. Gunners on the destroyer could not fire on the NVA without also hitting the patrol. Norris radioed the ship with instructions to give him five minutes and then open fire on his own position.

While he and one of the LDNN provided covering fire, Thornton and the two other Vietnamese sprinted 125 yards through a hail of bullets to the dune line nearest the sea. They sprawled behind cover and opened rapid fire to support the withdrawal of the other two. A bullet struck the left side of Norris's head and knocked him to the ground. The Vietnamese with him dashed to Thornton's position. He said Norris was dead.

A SEAL does not abandon a buddy, dead or not. With less than three minutes remaining before the destroyer would open up its devastating barrage, Thornton jumped from cover and raced back to his fallen comrade. Fortunately, he was a big man, and Norris was slightly built. He hoisted the officer across one shoulder and carried him at a run toward the sea. Five-inch shells began exploding in his wake.

Still in a precarious situation, the five-man patrol, three of whom were now wounded, one seriously, took to the sea. Thornton inflated Norris's life jacket and pushed the unconscious officer ahead of him while also helping the wounded LDNN. They managed to swim nearly 300 yards from the beach, hidden from the enemy ashore by four-foot surf, before they were picked up by a junk just before noon. All survived, including Norris.

Thornton's citation, signed by President Richard Nixon, read in part:

> Upon learning that the Senior Advisor [Norris] had been hit by enemy fire and was believed to be dead, PO Thornton returned through a hail of fire to the lieutenant's last position, quickly disposed of two enemy soldiers about to overrun the position, and succeeded in removing the seriously wounded and unconscious Senior Naval Advisor to the water's edge. He then inflated the lieutenant's lifejacket and towed him seaward for approximately two hours until picked up by support craft. By his extraordinary courage and perseverance, PO Thornton was directly responsible for saving the life of his superior officer and enabling the safe extraction of all patrol members.

See also NORRIS, THOMAS R.

Tilghman, Christopher (1959–1989)

Petty Officer Christopher Tilghman was killed in combat during Operation Just Cause against Panama in 1989. He and three of his teammates died during a fierce firefight in their assault against the Paitilla airfield in Panama City.

See also OPERATION JUST CAUSE.

time fuse

A time fuse for detonating a nonelectrical blasting cap burns at a predictable rate which allows a demolitioneer to calculate the time from ignition to explosion.

See also EXPLOSIVES.

TNT

Trinitrotoluene is a powerful explosive that largely replaced dynamite but that can be used in the same fashion.

See also EXPLOSIVES.

Toschi, Elios

Italian lieutenant Elios Toschi, along with Lt. Teseo Tesei, designed a manned torpedo, called a "maiale" (pig), with which he intended to sink Allied shipping at the beginning of World War II. So-called manned torpedoes led to experiments with other forms of small submersible craft to be used by underwater commandos.

See also MAIALE; TESEI, TESEO.

trident

The U.S. Navy designed special warfare insignia for both the underwater demolition teams and the U.S. Navy SEALs in 1970. Wearers of the insignia commonly referred to them as "tridents" or as "Budweisers."

Tunney, Gene (1897–1978)

Gene Tunney, professional boxer and heavyweight champion of 1926–28 after defeating Jack Dempsey twice, signed up as a U.S. Navy recruiter only weeks after Pearl Harbor brought the United States into World War II. One of the first men he recruited was Philip H. Bucklew, who became known as the "father of naval special warfare."

See also AMPHIBIOUS SCOUTS AND RAIDERS; BUCKLEW, PHILIP H.

Tuohy, Pat

Lt. Pat Tuohy was the on-site commander of the assault force at the ill-fated Paitilla airport in Panama during Operation Just Cause in 1989. He was also previously involved in Operation Urgent Fury in Grenada in 1983.

See also OPERATION JUST CAUSE; OPERATION URGENT FURY.

Turner, Richmond Kelly (1885–1961)

Rear Admiral Turner was ordered to the Pacific in July 1942, during World War II, to become the leading naval amphibious commander in the Pacific Ocean. The invasion of Tarawa on November 20, 1943, was the navy's first step in its plan to hop from island to island across the Pacific to attack Japan itself. It was launched with inadequate hydrographic information, resulting in more U.S. Marines dying in the treacherous coral shoals and tide pools trying to reach the atoll than were killed by the Japanese on the island.

Almost immediately after the battle, Turner became a primary advocate of the creation and use of units trained to scout out enemy beaches, remove natural and man-made obstacles, and guide invading forces ashore. Through his advocacy and support, the underwater demolition teams (UDTs), predecessors of the U.S. Navy SEALs, came into being.

Turner served as amphibious commander in most naval actions in the central and southern Pacific, including Guadalcanal, New Georgia, the Gilbert, Marshal, and Mariana Islands, Iwo Jima, and Okinawa. UDTs were always a part of his planning after Tarawa.

After the war, he served on the military staff committee of the United Nations Security Council. He retired in 1947.

See also NAVAL COMBAT DEMOLITION UNITS (NCDUS); TARAWA; UNDERWATER DEMOLITION TEAMS (UDTS).

"turtleback"

An operator swimming on his back while tactically maintaining a course in order to conserve energy and air is referred to by SEALs as a "turtleback," and the action itself as "turtlebacking."

U

UDT-16

Most SEALs and former UDT frogmen would just as soon forget about what happened to UDT-16 during the World War II battle of Okinawa, which began on March 30, 1945. Okinawa was by far the largest operation in the history of the underwater demolition teams. At one time or another during the Okinawa operation, more than 1,000 frogmen were put into the water, both on the real invasion beaches and on others where commanders wanted the Japanese to expect a landing. Involved in the operation were veteran UDTs-7, 12, 13, 14 and untested UDTs-11, 16, 17, and 19. UDT-16's inability to accomplish its mission is considered the most serious failure of any team in the history of naval special warfare.

The Japanese defenders of Okinawa had hammered an array of sharpened poles, each about six feet high and eight inches in diameter, some with explosives attached, into the reef about 40 yards out from the high-water mark. If these obstacles were not destroyed prior to the assault, the invasion force would be trapped at the reef line like setting ducks.

UDT commander Draper L. Kauffman sent in two teams—UDT-11 and UDT-16, some 160 men—to blast out the obstacles. Each swimmer carried from three to five Hagensen Packs of explosives. It was to be a long, dangerous mission.

Four landing craft, three destroyers, two aircraft carriers, and three battleships blasted away at the Japanese while the frogmen swam underwater from one obstacle to the next, surfacing only long enough to catch a breath before diving down to attach explosives and connect primacord to the next. When the swimmers finally swam back and the triggermen set off the charges, only half the beach, that part rigged by UDT-11, erupted in flame and smoke. Most of the posts remained on the part of the beach for which UDT-16 was responsible. Frogmen of UDT-11 claimed they had noticed UDT-16 men swimming away from the beach while they were still working on their half of it. Word was that UDT-16 had panicked after a sniper shot and killed one of them, and the rest had fled for their lives.

"It had been badly done," Kauffman later recalled. "The next day, I really made a group of enemies because I refused to send back the team that had botched the job to fix it. Naturally, they wanted very much to go in, but I didn't dare take a chance because this was almost our last opportunity. I sent my best team back in and they did a very fine job."

That "best" team was UDT-11, which spent its third straight day under Japanese fire. "On 31 March," the history of UDT-11 recorded, "the team received word that 'the job must be done.' Four boats with 89 officers and men moved toward the obstacle line. Landing craft sailed up and down, as close as they could come, hammering the shore with gunfire." UDT-11 cleared some 1,300 yards of beach, previously assigned to UDT-16, of nearly 1,400 obstacles. It suffered not a single casualty.

Petty Officer First Class John A. Devine of UDT-16 contested the stories of his team's cowardice. To begin with, he said, his team did not even know about the death of the one member, coxswain Frank Lynch, until the next morning. He suspected that the failure of UDT-16's explosives was due to wave action that cut the main trunk line.

"One fact that has not been mentioned," he said, "is that approximately fifteen men and a few officers from our team volunteered to swim back out in the afternoon, to wipe the remaining obstacles out. I was one of the men that swam back in, after the tide had receded and without any gunfire support. With the Japanese firing at us, we crawled on our bellies across the coral to get to the obstacles. We did blow some of them out, but again left some still standing—for whatever reason, only God knows."

Lt. Robert Fisher, the executive officer of UDT-16, supported Devine's version of events. "We put on the explosives, we put on the primacord, and then we pulled the fuse and nothing happened. That afternoon I asked for volunteers to go back in to finish the job. The ships that were providing us cover were pulling out and the tide was going out. I had to ask them to go in bare ass in a receding tide. Everyone except one man volunteered. I took fourteen guys. We went back in, hooked it up, and blew it. We got it cleared this time."

The true story of how exactly UDT-16 was disgraced may never be known. However, immediately following Okinawa, the team was sent to California for stateside duty for the rest of the war. The other UDTs began preparation for the invasion of Japan.

See also KAUFFMAN, DRAPER L.; OKINAWA.

UDT/SEAL Museum

Located at 3300 North A1A, North Hutchinson Island, Fort Pierce, Florida, the birthplace of the U.S. Navy frogmen, the UDT/SEAL Museum is the only museum in the world devoted exclusively to the elite fighting men of naval special warfare. Established in 1983, the museum contains the history of Amphibious Scouts and Raiders, naval combat demolition units, underwater demolition teams, and the SEAL teams. It preserves the weapons, equipment, vehicles, and artifacts of America's most extraordinary warriors.

Included among the museum's collection are diving gear, everything from early Lambertsen rebreather units to the mixed-gas rigs of today's SEALs; masks and other diving equipment; weapons; demolition gear; parachutes; uniforms; patrol boats; SEAL delivery vehicles; a space capsule; a Seawolf helicopter; a captured North Vietnamese gunboat; and photographs and other memorabilia from every era of the birth and growth of today's U.S. Navy SEALs.

The founding director and first curator of the museum was retired captain Norman H. Olson.

See also OLSON, NORMAN H.

UH-1 "Huey"

The "Huey" was the primary helicopter used in support of operations during the Vietnam War and afterward. It and the sound of its blades became the enduring symbol of the war. All U.S. forces used it, including Navy SEALs.

See also HELICOPTERS; SEAWOLVES.

Unconventional Activities Committee

In 1961, the Chief of Naval Operations established an Unconventional Activities Committee to study the formation of a naval commando unit. That unit, first referred to as a "special operations team," was commissioned on January 1, 1962, as the U.S. Navy SEALs.

See also SEALS.

underwater defense gun, Mark I Mod 0

A personal weapon that would fire underwater was developed, in part, at the Naval Surface Weapons Center, White Oak Laboratory, in Silver Spring, Maryland, and was first made available in late 1970. The "underwater defense gun" was used by both

The Huey was the primary helicopter used in support of operations during the Vietnam War and afterward into the 1980s. Here, a Huey participates in "helo casting" training for Special Operations troops. (Charles W. Sasser)

underwater demolition teams and SEALs throughout the 1970s and into the 1980s. The weapon, shaped like a bloated revolver and weighing 4.17 pounds, could be fired either in the open air or underwater. It fired a slender tungsten dart with fins to give it a stabilizing spin. It had an effective lethal range of about 30 feet at a depth of 60 feet and of about 90 feet in the open air.

The body of the gun was a steel cylinder consisting of the barrel, charge plug assembly, shear pin, and projectile pusher. It was fired by a percussion primer and a charge of smokeless-powder propellant, which drove the dart down the barrel. The large cylinder held six projectiles, each inside its own barrel, in a "pepperbox" design. The cylinder was completely enclosed within the mechanism of the gun. In general, it operated like any other double-

action pistol. Because the end of the barrel constricted upon firing, to retain all propellant gas, it was flashless, effectively soundless, and caused no underwater muzzle-blast shock waves. It had a rate of fire of about twelve rounds a minute and could be operated and reloaded underwater.

The frame, cylinder, door assembly, and action were constructed of aluminum, while all other operating parts, with the exception of the trigger, were made of stainless steel. The trigger was self-lubricating nylon and had no guard, to allow the weapon to be fired by a gloved hand.

In the open air, the loudest sound produced during firing was that of the action and the slapping sound of the projectile pusher and buffer system.

It was gradually replaced throughout the 1980s by the Heckler and Koch P11 ZUB underwater weapon.

See also HECKLER AND KOCH P11 ZUB UNDERWATER WEAPON.

underwater demolition teams (UDTs)

While the navy considers the Amphibious Scouts and Raiders to be the direct forerunner of the U.S. Navy SEALs, the underwater demolition teams (UDTs) were the earliest SEAL prototype and, in fact, eventually merged with the SEALs.

The Amphibious Scouts and Raiders trained its first class in May 1942 at Fort Pierce, Florida, and subsequently saw action during Operation Torch in North Africa and later in Europe, including on D-day. The Scouts were needed to reconnoiter landing beaches, mark the location of obstacles and defensive works, and guide assault waves ashore.

In 1943, the naval combat demolition units (NCDUs) were created and trained. A new skill was added to the repertoire. Not only would the NCDUs reconnoiter beaches, mark obstacles, and guide assault forces ashore, but they would use demolitions to clear obstacles from the assault lanes.

After "Terrible Tarawa" in November 1943, during which hundreds of Marines died in the surf while attempting to invade the atoll, Adm. Richmond Kelly Turner called for NCDUs to assist in Pacific operations. Thirty officers and 150 enlisted men, skimmed from the Scouts and Raiders and NCDUs, moved to Waimonalo Amphibious Training

The underwater demolition teams (UDTs) of World War II are looked upon as the direct ancestors of modern SEALs. Here, a UDT team conducts a beach clearance operation in the South Pacific. (National Archives)

Base, Hawaii, and were redesignated as underwater demolition teams. They formed the nucleus of the demolition training program and became UDT-1 and UDT-2. Each team would eventually be composed of 100 men and 13 officers.

UDTs first saw combat on January 31, 1944, during Operation Flintlock, in the Marshall Islands. Beginning at Kwajalein, where the UDTs were expected to do their jobs in full uniform and tethered to boats by lines, the teams gradually evolved until "naked warriors" wore only tan trunks, swim fins, and face masks, in order to swim to their targets and destroy them.

After Tarawa, Pacific UDTs participated in every major action until the end of the war in 1945. There were 34 separate teams working the Pacific by VJ Day. These were soon cut back to four teams, two

on a coast, each team consisting of seven officers and 45 men.

On June 25, 1950, North Korea invaded South Korea. The Korean War saw a rebirth and growth of the UDTs. Beginning with a detachment of 11 men from UDT-3, frogman participation in the war soon expanded to three teams with a combined strength of over 300 men. In addition to being tasked with the normal beach reconnaissance and clearing missions, UDTs in Korea began to change in subtle ways. As the concept of naval special warfare grew, UDT missions gradually expanded to include patrolling and sabotage missions; operations behind enemy lines; demolition of railroads, bridges, and tunnels; parachute jumps; and other guerrilla activities.

UDTs again saw combat in the Vietnam War, in support of amphibious ready groups. Attached to the riverine units, UDTs conducted operations with river patrol boats to destroy obstacles and bunkers. In many cases UDT frogmen patrolled the hinterlands.

On May 1, 1983, all UDTs were decommissioned and redesignated as either SEAL teams or swimmer (later SEAL) delivery vehicle teams (SDVTs). Rear Adm. Cathal L. "Irish" Flynn, himself a SEAL, was the leading advocate of this change. "The distinction between SEALs and UDTs had started to blur, and there was an overlap in capabilities," he says. "The amphibious force needed a force that could do both SEAL and UDT things, but there wasn't enough room on the ships for both. We saw that the UDT and SEAL portions of a mission tended to be sequential rather than concurrent. We saw that the same guys could do both things, provided we broke down the doctrinal barriers between them. We cross trained them. And then we thought, the hell with it, let's just call them all SEALs. That's what we did."

See also ACHESON, BILL; AMPHIBIOUS SCOUTS AND RAIDERS; ALAMO SCOUTS; DYNAMITING AND DEMOLITION SCHOOL; FLYNN, CATHAL L.; KAUFFMAN, DRAPER L.; KING, ERNEST J.; KOREAN WAR; KWAJALEIN; NAVAL COMBAT DEMOLITION UNIT (NCDU); NAVAL DEMOLITION UNITS (NDUS); OFFICE OF STRATEGIC SERVICES (OSS); OPERATION FLINTLOCK; OPERATION TORCH; RIVERINE WARFARE; SEALS; TARAWA; TURNER, RICHMOND KELLY; UDT-16.

underwater obstacles

Naval combat demolition units and underwater demolition teams were created specifically during World War II to reconnoiter, mark, and clear any underwater obstacles, either natural or man-made, that might hinder assault forces from reaching the beaches during amphibious landings.

See also ACHESON, BILL; BEACH CLEARANCE; BELGIAN GATES; CHINA BEACH; D-DAY; DYNAMITING AND DEMOLITION SCHOOL; EXPLOSIVES; HAGENSEN PACK; HYDROGRAPHIC SURVEY; IWO JIMA; KAUFFMAN, DRAPER L.; KING, ERNEST J.; KWAJALEIN; OMAHA BEACH; TARAWA.

U.S. Naval Special Warfare Command (SPECWARCOM)

The naval command responsible for preparing naval special warfare forces to carry out their assigned missions and for developing maritime special operations strategy, doctrine, and tactics is the U.S. Navy Special Warfare Command, headquartered at the Special Warfare Center, Coronado, California.

See also NAVAL SPECIAL WARFARE; ORGANIZATIONAL STRUCTURE, SPECIAL OPERATIONS.

U.S. Navy Special Operations Command (NAVSOC)

NAVSOC is the naval command that contributes assets to the U.S. Special Operations Command (USSOCOM). USSOCOM was created by the Goldwater-Nichols Act of 1986 to combine the special operations forces of all branches of the U.S. military under a single command.

See also NAVAL SPECIAL WARFARE; ORGANIZATIONAL STRUCTURE, SPECIAL OPERATIONS.

U.S. Space Command (SPACECOM)

The U.S. Space Command is vitally important to all special operations forces, including SEALs. Based at Peterson Air Force Base near Colorado Springs, Colorado, SPACECOM is the clearinghouse for all satellite-communication services (SATCOM). It also supplies weather and intelligence data, all vital to SEAL missions.

See also GLOBAL POSITIONING SYSTEM (GPS); INTELLIGENCE.

U.S. Special Operations Command (USSOCOM)

The Goldwater-Nichols Act of 1986 restructured the U.S. military and placed command of all special operations forces within all branches of the military under the U.S. Special Operations Command.

See also GOLDWATER-NICHOLS ACT OF 1986; ORGANIZATIONAL STRUCTURE, SPECIAL OPERATIONS.

"Utes"

Underwater demolition teams during the Korean War became known as "Utes."

VENTID

SEALs use an acronym to remember the symptoms of oxygen poisoning—VENTID.

V—Vision. Blurred or tunnel
E—Ears. Ringing
N—Nausea
T—Twitching. Usually facial muscles
I—Irritability
D—Dizziness.

See also OXYGEN POISONING.

Ventura, Jesse ("The Body") (b. 1951)

After leaving the Navy UDTs/SEALs, James Janos became a professional wrestler and actor, adopting the professional name of Jesse "The Body" Ventura. He later became governor of Minnesota.

See also JANOS, JAMES.

Viet Cong

The Vietnamese enemy existed in two primary organizations during the Vietnam War. The first was the North Vietnamese Army, which was recruited and trained in North Vietnam and sent south to engage in conventional battle with South Vietnamese and American forces. The other was the guerrilla element of South Vietnam, the People's Revolutionary Army, under control of the National Liberation Front (NLF). The guerrillas became known as Viet Cong, or VC. "Viet Cong" was a pejorative label invented by the South Vietnamese government to brand the rebels as communists.

Most VC were villagers or fieldhands, city dwellers being but a small minority of the force. The main-force units forming the true guerrilla army were overwhelmingly recruited in the villages, from men in their teens. They either volunteered or were forcibly conscripted. Each new recruit joined a three-man cell that included at least one veteran. Each three-man cell was part of a three-cell squad. Three squads formed a platoon, the basic operating unit of the VC.

American SEALs, who fought most of their combat actions in the Mekong Delta against VC, were astounded by the enemy's simple endurance and tenaciousness in battle. Most SEALs developed a great deal of respect for the VC as a foe.

See also NORTH VIETNAMESE ARMY (NVA); VIETNAM WAR.

Vietnam SEAL casualties

Forty-nine SEALs and underwater demolition team (UDT) commandos were killed in combat during the Vietnam War. They are broken down by units as follows:

> 34 KIA (killed in action) from SEAL Team One
> Nine KIA from SEAL Team Two
> Three KIA from UDT-13
> One KIA from UDT-12
> One KIA UDT assigned to MACV-SOG
> One SEAL from Special Warfare Group, Pacific, assigned to Detachment Golf.

Vietnam War

Hardly had the SEAL teams been formed in 1962 than they became enmeshed in the Vietnam War. SEALs found themselves involved in the very beginning of the war; they were to be involved to the very end.

Vietnam is a country on the South China Sea, about the size of California. Its population, north and south, in the 1960s was about 50 million. The United States began sending military supplies and advisers to French forces fighting the communist Viet Minh as early as 1950. When the French lost their war in 1954, the United States sent in army Special Forces advisers to assist the South Vietnamese government against the insurgency. In 1957, forces supported by communist North Vietnam began attacking in the South, and America found itself increasingly involved in the conflict.

Army Green Berets and SEALs were dispatched to Vietnam during the early 1960s. U.S. combat units arrived in 1965 after the Gulf of Tonkin incident; U.S. troops were to reach a peak number of more than 543,000 by 1969. The war continued until January 1973, when the United States, North and South Vietnam, and the Viet Cong signed a cease-fire agreement. Although the cease-fire ended U.S. involvement, fighting continued in Vietnam until the war ended decisively on April 30, 1975, when the North Vietnamese invaded Saigon and the South surrendered.

Underwater demolition teams (UDTs) had already been involved in the war before the SEALs were commissioned. In 1960, Lt. David Del Guidice led 10 members of UDT-12 in an epic voyage through Vietnam and into Cambodia and Laos, up

Communist guerrillas during the Vietnam War were known as Viet Cong, a pejorative label invented by the South Vietnamese government to brand the rebels as communists. Here, VC stand atop a captured U.S. armored personnel carrier.

the Mekong River, to deliver five 52-foot LCMs (Landing Craft, Mechanized) and five smaller LCVPs (Landing Craft, Vehicle and Personnel) to Laotian forces to strengthen them against the communist threat.

Del Guidice was made commander of SEAL Team One upon its commissioning in January 1962. That same month, he and another SEAL officer went to Vietnam to determine the specific requirements of the South Vietnamese armed forces and how SEALs could best satisfy these needs. On March 10, 1962, the first SEALs—two instructors from Team One— arrived in Vietnam for six-month tours of duty teaching the South Vietnamese how to conduct clandestine operations.

In April 1962, the first SEAL mobile training team (MTT) left for Vietnam. Under the command of Lt. (j.g.) Philip P. Holtz, MTT-10-62 consisted of nine enlisted men, seven from Team One and two from Team Two. A number of other SEAL MTTs went over in the early years, their numbers in-country gradually growing. Their mission was to train the South Vietnamese Coastal Force in reconnaissance, sabotage, and guerrilla warfare.

SEAL Team One deployed two platoons in 1965 and assigned them to the Rung Sat Special Zone, near the capital city, Saigon. Four additional platoons arrived shortly thereafter—two assigned to Nha Be, one at Binh Thuy, and another to My Tho. These teams operated only in an "advisory" capacity. It was not until February 1966 that Team One sent Detachment Golf, a pilot group of three officers and 15 enlisted men, for active combat duty.

Detachments Golf and Hotel, with the riverine patrols in the Mekong Delta, were the SEAL units that most frequently closed with the Viet Cong in the Delta. They were the source of many of the legends about SEALs in the Vietnam War. Although there were seldom more than 200 SEALs in-country at any one time, they became a constant presence in Southeast Asia and would remain there until the U.S. withdrawal in 1973.

See also AMBUSH; AREA OF OPERATIONS (AO); ARMY OF THE REPUBLIC OF VIETNAM (ARVN); BAILEY, LARRY W.; "BARNDANCE CARDS"; BOEHM, ROY; BOOBY TRAPS; "BRIGHT LIGHT"; BRUHMULLER, WILLIAM N, II; BUCKLEW, PHILIP H.; CHINA BEACH; COUNTERINSURGENCY; DETACHMENT BRAVO (DET BRAVO); FLYNN, CATHAL L. "IRISH"; GOLF DETACHMENT; GUERRILLA WARFARE; GULF OF TONKIN RESOLUTION; HO CHI MINH TRAIL; ILO ILO ISLAND; JUNK; JUNK FORCE; KERREY, JOSEPH R. "BOB"; LIEN DOC NGUOI NHAI (LDNN); LIGHT SEAL SUPPORT CRAFT (LSSC); MACHEN, BILLY W.; MACIONE, JACK; MACV-SOG; MEKONG DELTA; "MEN WITH GREEN FACES"; MOBILE TRAINING TEAM (MTT); NORRIS, THOMAS R.; OPERATION JACKSTAY; OPERATION THUNDERHEAD; PHOENIX PROGRAM; PROVINCIAL RECONNAISSANCE UNITS (PRUS); QUONG KHE NAVAL BASE; RIVERINE WARFARE; RUNG SAT SPECIAL ZONE; SCOUT

An unidentified SEAL prepares for combat in the Mekong Delta during the Vietnam War. SEALs "advised" South Vietnam forces. This SEAL wears his black beret and carries a CAR-15 rifle and a radio. (U.S. Navy)

DOGS; SEALORDS; SEAWOLVES; THORNTON, MICHAEL EDWIN; VIET CONG; ZUMWALT, ELMO R., JR.

visit, board, search, and seizure (VBSS)

"Visit, board, search, and seizure" describes operations in which the U.S. Navy, often assisted by SEALs, board foreign craft in war zones and search them for contraband. Such operations were extensively conducted by SEALs in the Persian Gulf prior to and during the 1991 Operation Desert Storm.

See also IRAN AJR.

Walker, Johnny

SEAL chief petty officer Johnny Walker helped pioneer the technique of jumping, safely opening a parachute canopy, and "flying" at extremely high altitudes. His experiments helped SEALs develop skills in flying long distances in parachute formation in order to make surreptitious landings. He also helped establish the free-fall parachute school at the Coronado Naval Special Warfare Center in 1985.

As a member of SEAL Team Two, Walker underwent his initial free-fall training in 1976. In 1980, as an original member of Richard Marcinko's SEAL Team Six, he and other SEALs of the team began experimenting with HAHO (high altitude, high opening) and HALO (high altitude, low opening) parachute jumps, with the objective of forming up in the air and "flying" together to a target.

He has since logged nearly 3,500 parachute jumps. His highest HAHO was at 33,000 feet, his highest HALO at 36,000. "One of the jumps we did," he recalls, "the outside temperature was minus 82 degrees. And you jump out into extreme cold and the goggles would shatter. . . . Then our eyes would freeze shut because of the water on your eyelashes. There'd be big gobs of ice.

"As you go through various cloud layers, it might be snowing in the cloud. . . . If you get in an ice storm, you start getting ice rammed into this parachute and it starts to settle back there in the tail section. And if you get enough ice in there. . . . the tail starts dropping from the weight and some of the canopies would start to stall."

In 1985, Chief Walker began teaching HAHO and HALO techniques at Coronado, the Naval Special Warfare Center. Eventually, a school for free-fall tactics was established.

See also AIRBORNE.

weight belt

A weight belt with an adjustable weight system, working in coordination with a buoyancy control device, helps a diver maintain neutral buoyancy while underwater.

See also BUOYANCY CONTROL DEVICE (BCD); DIVING, HISTORY OF.

wet suit

SEALs utilize both "wet suits" and "dry suits" in diving. A wet suit is a skin-tight body suit made of

SEALs wore skin-tight bodysuits made of a rubber material to preserve body heat during diving operations. (U.S. Navy)

a foam-rubber material that absorbs a layer of water. This layer of water is then warmed by body heat and acts as insulation against the colder surrounding water.

See also DRY SUIT.

"Willie Pete"

"Willie Pete" is a short form of the World War II–era slang term (properly "Willie Peter") for white phosphorus explosives.

See also EXPLOSIVES.

"woofus boat"

The "woofus boat" was an invention of the underwater demolition teams (UDTs) during World War II. It was simply a landing craft loaded with rockets aimed down at reefs for beach clearance. Its results were so unsatisfactory that the UDTs discarded the woofus boat after only a few trial attempts to use it. It was never used in combat.

X-Craft

During World War II, the British developed an experimental minisubmarine that they dubbed the X-Craft. Years later, the U.S. naval special warfare community built upon techniques and tactics of the X-Craft in the development of SEAL delivery vehicles.

Earlier, the British had built manned torpedoes, called Chariots, with the express aim of sinking the German battleship *Tirpitz*. These proved unreliable, and the British began building a much more sophisticated undersea craft, a true minisubmarine. The X-Craft was 52 feet long, had a beam of six feet, and was powered by a single electric motor capable of a speed of six knots. Its crew of four could go to war with a cargo of more than two tons of explosives and limpet mines.

The X-Craft extended the capability of the oceangoing submarine into areas otherwise denied it by its size, such as harbors, bays, and anchorages. Its first use was in a special operations capacity. An X-Craft put a man ashore to blow up a Turkish viaduct, illustrating the utility of such a small clan-destine craft. The primary aim of the X-Craft program, however, was to blow up the *Tirpitz*. "The whole strategy of the war turns at this point on this ship," Winston Churchill explained.

In September 1943, six British submarines, each piggybacking an X-Craft, set out from a secret naval base in Scotland on a mission to blow up the *Tirpitz*, anchored with other ships in a Norwegian fjord. Two X-Craft were lost to high seas on the ten-day journey. The other four, with crews, were launched on their mission on the evening of September 20. Two of them actually placed explosives underneath the monstrous battleship. It was damaged but not sunk. One X-Craft was disabled by collision with the *Tirpitz* and surfaced; its four-man crew surrendered to the Germans. The second was sunk by machine-gun fire. Two of its crew survived and were captured.

The design of the minisubmarine and its application in unconventional warfare were adapted more than 20 years later in SEAL operations.

See also CHARIOT.

Z

Zodiac

The Zodiac Company was the original primary manufacturer of the SEALs' combat rubber raiding craft. SEALs therefore often refer to the rubber boats as either "Zodiacs" or as "rubber ducks."

See also INFLATABLE BOATS.

Zumwalt, Elmo R., Jr. (1920–2000)

A great believer in the value of SEALs, Vice Adm. Elmo R. Zumwalt, Jr., became the commander of naval forces in Vietnam in September 1968. He immediately began asking for more SEALs. Francis Riley "Frank" Kaine, who was by then commander of the Special Warfare Group, Pacific, which included underwater demolition teams, SEALs, and Beach Jumpers, remembers frequent calls from Zumwalt: "I need fifteen more, twenty more, one hundred more SEALs."

SEALs were perfectly suited for Zumwalt's innovative, fast-moving strategy to disrupt the use by the enemy of the Mekong Delta's vast network of rivers and tributaries. He initiated the SEALORDS (Southeast Asia lake, ocean, river, and Delta strategy) program for cutting off supply lines in the Delta to prevent weapons, men, and material from reaching Viet Cong units farther north.

See also SEALORDS.

SELECTED BIBLIOGRAPHY

This bibliography cannot hope to provide the last word on the U.S. Navy SEALs. Special warfare is a relatively new field and is exploding rapidly. Therefore, this bibliography is not intended to be exhaustive; it is a *selected* bibliography. It includes books as well as an extensive listing of documents and periodicals. It is hoped that readers and researchers will find this bibliography helpful in selecting further reading.

Adkin, Mark. *Urgent Fury: The Battle for Grenada.* Lexington, Mass. Lexington Books, 1989.

"Airborne & Special Operations Museum." *Military,* November 2000.

Allen, Thomas B., F. Clifton Berry, and Norman Polmar. *War in the Gulf.* Atlanta: Turner Publishing, 1991.

"America's Secret Soldiers: The Buildup of U.S. Special Operations Forces." *Defense Monitor,* June 4, 1985.

Anderson, William. *Bat-21.* New York: Bantam Books, 1983.

Andrade, Dale. *Trial by Fire: The 1972 Easter Offensive, America's Last Vietnam Battle.* New York: Hippocrene Books, 1994.

————.*The War in Cambodia.* New York and Oxford, U.K.: Osprey Books, 1988.

————.*The War in Laos.* New York and Oxford, U.K.: Osprey Books, 1990.

"The Battle for Grenada." *Newsweek.* November 7, 1983.

Beckwith, Charlie A., and Donald Knox. *Delta Force.* New York: Harcourt Brace Jovanovich, 1983.

Bodard, Lucien. *The Quicksand War: Prelude to Vietnam.* Boston: Atlantic Brown, 1967.

Boehm, Roy, and Charles W. Sasser. *First SEAL.* New York: Pocket Books, 1997.

Bohrer, David. *America's Special Forces: Weapons, Missions, Training.* Osceola, Wisc.: MBI Publishing, 1998.

Bolger, Daniel P. *Americans at War: 1975–1986.* Novato, Calif.: Presidio Press, 1988.

Bowden, Mark. *Black Hawk Down: A Story of Modern War.* New York: Atlantic Monthly Press, 1999.

Burchett, Wilfred. *Vietnam: Inside Story of the Guerrilla War.* New York: International Publishers, 1965.

Burrs, Richard, and Milton Leitenburg. *The Wars in Vietnam, Cambodia and Laos, 1945–1982.* Santa Barbara, Calif.: ABC-Cleo, 1984.

"C-130 Hercules." *USAF Fact Sheet,* November 20, 2000.

"Cambodian Incursions." *Northwest Veterans Newsletter,* 2000.

Conroy, Ken. *Southeast Asian Special Forces.* New York and Oxford, U.K.: Osprey, 1991.

Crawley, James W. "SEAL Finds Parallel World as Astronaut." *Navy SEALs Win/Lose.* http://www.mi-vida-loca.com/sealswinlose.htm. Retrieved August 12, 1999.

Croizat, Victor. *Vietnam River Warfare 1945–75.* London: Blandford Press, 1986.

"Debacle in the Desert." *Time,* May 5, 1980.

Dockery, Kevin. *SEALs in Action.* New York: Avon, 1991.

————. *Special Warfare, Special Weapons: The Arms and Equipment of the UDT and SEALs.* Chicago: Emperor's Press, 1996.

Dockery, Kevin, and Bill Fawcett. *The Teams: An Oral History of the U.S. Navy SEALs.* New York: Avon, 1998.

Donald, Kenneth. "Oxygen and the Diver." http://dir-asia.com/oxygen and the diver.htm. Retrieved December 15, 2000.

Donnelly, Thomas, Margaret Roth, and Caleb Baker. *Just Cause: The Storming of Panama.* New York: Macmillan, 1991.

Drury, Richard. *My Secret War.* New York: St. Martin's Press, 1979.

Dwyer, John B. *Seaborne Deception: The History of U.S. Navy Beach Jumpers.* Praeger, 1992.

Fane, Francis Douglas. *The Naked Warriors.* Annapolis, Md.: Naval Institute Press, 1975.

Fawcett, Bill. *Hunters and Shooters: An Oral History of the U.S. Navy SEALs in Vietnam.* New York: Morrow, 1995.

Fulton, William. *Riverine Operations 1966–1969.* Washington, D.C.: U.S. Government Printing Office, 1973.

Gormly, Robert A. *Combat Swimmer.* New York: Onyx, 1999.

Goulden, Joseph C. *Truth is the First Casualty: The Gulf of Tonkin Affair—Illusion and Reality.* Chicago: Rand McNally, 1969.

Gregory, Barry. *United States Airborne Forces.* New York: Gallery Books, 1990.

Halberstadt, Hans. *U.S. Navy SEALs in Action.* Osceola, Wisc.: MBI Publishing, 1995.

Hall, Daniel. *A History of Southeast Asia.* New York: St. Martin's Press, 1995.

Herring, George C. *The Secret Diplomacy of the Vietnam War: The Negotiating Volumes of the Pentagon Papers.* Austin: University of Texas Press, 1983.

"History of Diving." *U.S. Navy Diving Manual,* NAVSEA 0994-lp-001-9110, Revision 2. December 15, 1988.

Hogg, Ian V. *The Illustrated Encyclopedia of Ammunition.* Secaucus, N.J.: Chartwell Books, 1985.

Hoyt, Edwin P. *SEALs at War.* New York: Dell, 1993.

"Intratheater Airlift: Information on the Air Force's C-130 Aircraft." Washington, D.C.: General Accounting Office, April 21, 1998.

Irvine, Reed. "Accuracy in Media." *Military,* July 2001.

"I Want to Be a SEAL." Official Recruiting Site, U.S. Navy SEALs. http:www.sealchallenge.navy.mil/Iwanttobea-seal.htm. Retrieved July 11, 2000.

Jonas, G. "Jacques Cousteau." *New York Times,* June 26, 1997.

Karnow, Stanley. *Vietnam: A History.* New York: Viking Press, 1983.

Kelly, Francis. *U.S. Army Special Forces 1961–1971.* Washington, D.C: U.S. Government Printing Office, 1973.

Kelly, Orr. *Brave Men, Dark Waters: The Untold Story of the Navy SEALs.* Novato, Calif.: Presidio Press, 1992.

———. *Never Fight Fair.* Novato, Calif.: Presidio Press, 1995.

Ladd, James. *SBS—The Invisible Raiders: The History of the Special Boat Squadron from World War Two to the Present.* London.: Davis and Charles, 1989.

Lambertsen, Christian J. "Current Status of Underwater Operations Program of U.S. Navy Underwater Demolition Teams." Letter to Chief of Naval Operations. June 17, 1949.

Landau, Alan M., and Frieda, Terry Griswold, D. M. Giangreco, and Hans Halberstadt. *U.S. Special Forces: Airborne Rangers, Delta & U.S. Navy SEALs.* Osceola, Wisc.: MBI Publishing, 1992.

LaRocque, Gene. "Animals in the Service of the Military." *America's Defense Monitor.* 1991.

Marcinko, Richard, and John Weisman. *Rogue Warrior.* New York: Pocket Books, 1992.

Markham, George. *Guns of the Elite.* Dorset, U.K.: Arms and Armour Press, 1987.

Marolda, Edward J., and Oscar P. Fitzgerald. *The United States Navy and the Vietnam Conflict: From Military Assistance to Combat, 1959–1965.* Washington, D.C.: U.S. Government Printing Office, 1986.

McConnell, Malcolm. "The Toughest School on Earth." *Reader's Digest.* August 1999.

McNamara, Robert S. *In Retrospect: The Tragedy and Lessons of Vietnam.* New York: Times Books, 1995.

Mobile Riverine Force Association. "Task Force 115." February 23, 1999.

"Navy SEALS Spend Christmas in Bosnia Dead-Cow River." Reuters. December 25, 1995.

Newman, Richard J. "Hunting War Criminals: The First Account of Secret U.S. Missions in Bosnia." *World Report,* July 6, 1998.

———. "Tougher than Hell." *U.S. News Online.* November 11, 1997.

Oberdorfer, Don. *Tet: The Turning Point of the Vietnam War.* New York: Dae Capo, 1983.

The Ocean World of Jacques Cousteau. New York: Danbury Press, 1975.

Page, Tim, and John Pimlott. *Nam: The Vietnam Experience, 1965–75.* London: Hamlyn Publishing Group, 1995.

Reske, F. *First Secrets of the Vietnam War.* MAC V-SOG Command History Annexes A, N. & M (1964–1966).

"Rivero, Horacio. Hispanos Famosos." *Puerto Rico Herald,* April 5, 2001.

Roat, John Carl. *The Making of U.S. Navy SEALs: Class-29.* New York: Ballantine Books, 1998.

Rosenberg, Howard L. "Six Brave Men." *Sealift,* July 1975.

Rosser-Owen, David. *Vietnam Weapons Handbook.* Wellingborough, U.K.: Patrick Stephens, 1986.

Sasser, Charles W. *Raider.* New York: St. Martin's Press, 2002.

———. "SEALs: U.S. Navy's Elite Sea Warriors." *Vietnam,* April 2001.

Schlemmer, Benjamin. *The Raid.* New York: Harper and Row, 1976.

Schraeder, Peter J. "The Horn of Africa: U.S. Foreign Policy in an Altered Cold War Environment." *Middle East Journal,* 46 no. 4, Autumn 1992.

"Scuba Diving Safety." *Undersea World,* November 20, 2000.

Shalom, Stephen R. "Gravy Train: Feeding the Pentagon by Feeding Somalia." *Z Magazine,* February 1993.

Sheppard, Don. *Riverine: A Brown-Water Sailor in the Delta, 1967.* New York: Pocket Books, 1992.

Silverstein, David. "Special Operations Forces: Finishing the Job of Reconstruction." *Backgrounder 828.* May 3, 1991.

Strahan, Jerry E. *Andrew Jackson Higgins and the Boats That Won World War II.* Baton Rooge: Louisiana State University Press, 1999.

Summers, Harry G., Jr. *Persian Gulf War Almanac.* New York: Facts On File, 1995.

Thomas, Brian. "Special Forces Soldiers Teach Waterborne Basics in Panama." Army News Release. May 6, 1998.

Time-Life Books. *Commando Operations.* Alexandria, Va.: Time-Life, 1991.

———. *Electronic Spies.* Alexandria, Va.: Time-Life, 1991.

———. *Island Fighting.* Morriston, N.J.: Time-Life, 1978.

———. *Special Forces and Missions.* Alexandria, Va.: Time-Life, 1991.

Tomajczyk, S. F. *U.S. Elite Counter-Terrorist Forces.* Osceola, Wisc.: MBI Publishing, 1995.

Tourison, Sedgwick. *Secret Army, Secret War.* Annapolis, Md.: Naval Institute Press, 1995.

Uhlig, Frank. *Vietnam: The Naval Story.* Annapolis, Md.: Naval Institute Press, 1986.

"U.S. Naval Special Operations Forces." *Special Operations Forces Reference Manual,* Washington, D.C.: Department of Defense, 2000.

"U.S. Navy Special Boat Units." *NEWS Articles,* March 8, 2001.

Veith, George J. *Code Name Bright Light: The Untold Story of U.S. POW Rescue Efforts during the Vietnam War.* New York: Free Press, 1998.

Villagran, Paul D. "Fulton Recovery System Ceases Operation." AFNS Feature Release. September 1996.

Walsh, Michael J. "Men with Green Faces." *Vietnam.* August 1996.

Walsh, Michael J., and Greg Walker. *SEAL!* New York: Pocket Books, 1994.

Walt, Lewis. *Strange War, Strange Strategy.* New York: Funk and Wagnall, 1976.

Watson, James, and Kevin Dockery. *Point Man: Inside the Toughest and Most Deadly Unit in Vietnam.* New York: Morrow, 1993.

Wellham, Michael. *Combat Frogmen: Military Diving from the Nineteenth Century to the Present Day.* London: Patrick Stephens, 1989.

Wyden, Peter. *Bay of Pigs.* New York: Touchstone Press, 1979.

Zedric, Lance Q. *Silent Warriors of World War II: The Alamo Scouts behind Japanese Lines.* Ventura, Calif.: Pathfinder, 1995.

INDEX

Boldface page numbers denote main entries in the encyclopedia. *Italic* page numbers denote illustrations.